Understanding Customers 1998–99

The Chartered Institute of Marketing/Butterworth-Heinemann Marketing Series is the most comprehensive, widely used and important collection of books in marketing and sales currently available worldwide.

As the CIM's official publisher, Butterworth-Heinemann develops, produces and publishes the complete series in association with the CIM. We aim to provide definitive marketing books for students and practitioners that promote excellence in marketing education and practice.

The series titles are written by CIM senior examiners and leading marketing educators for professionals, students and those studying the CIM's Certificate, Advanced Certificate and Postgraduate Diploma courses. Now firmly established, these titles provide practical study support to CIM and other marketing students and to practitioners at all levels.

The Chartered
Institute of Marketing

Formed in 1911, The Chartered Institute of Marketing is now the largest professional marketing management body in the world with over 60,000 members located worldwide. Its primary objectives are focused on the development of awareness and understanding of marketing throughout UK industry and commerce and in the raising of standards of professionalism in the education, training and practice of this key business discipline.

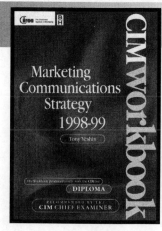

Understanding Customers 1998–99

Rosemary Phipps and Craig Simmons

Published on behalf of
The Chartered Institute of Marketing

OXFORD   BOSTON   JOHANNESBURG   MELBOURNE   NEW DELHI   SINGAPORE

Butterworth-Heinemann
Linacre House, Jordan Hill, Oxford OX2 8DP
225 Wildwood Avenue, Woburn, MA 01801-2041
A division of Reed Educational and Professional Publishing Ltd

Ⓡ A member of the Reed Elsevier plc group

First published 1998

British Library Cataloguing in Publication Data
A catalogue record for this book is available from the British Library

ISBN 0 7506 4037 5

Composition by Genesis Typesetting, Laser Quay, Rochester, Kent
Printed and bound in Great Britain

Contents

A quick word from the Chief Examiner

I am delighted to recommend to you the new series of CIM workbooks. All of these have been written by either the senior examiners responsible for marking and setting the papers or by experienced CIM lecturers.

Preparing for the CIM Exams is hard work. These workbooks are designed to make that work as interesting and illuminating as possible, as well as providing you with the knowledge you need to pass. I wish you success.

Trevor Watkins,
CIM Chief Examiner,
Deputy Vice Chancellor,
South Bank University

Acknowledgements

The authors would like to thank Andrew Gillespie for his substantial contribution to the section on economics; Jonathan Glasspool for some brilliant editing; Robin Harrison for helpful advice; Sophie and William for putting up with a bad diet for two months; Elise and Don for bearing up under the burden of increased household duties, and Elise for her proofing and chart work.

Thanks are also due to Elizabeth at UserData Limited for deflecting business over the period of writing and to all our students who have knowingly, or unknowingly, helped us develop and refine many of the ideas and examples presented in this book.

Rosemary Phipps
Craig Simmons

How to use your CIM workbook

The authors have been careful to structure your book with the exams in mind. Each unit, therefore, covers an essential part of the syllabus. You need to work through the complete workbook systematically to ensure that you have covered everything you need to know.

This workbook is divided into eighteen units each containing the following standard elements:

Objectives tell you what part of the syllabus you will be covering and what you will be expected to know having read the unit.

Study guides tell you how long the unit is and how long its activities take to do.

Questions are designed to give you practice – they will be similar to those you get in the exam.

Answers give you a suggested format for answering exam questions. *Remember* there is no such thing as a model answer – you should use these examples only as guidelines.

Activities give you the chance to put what you have learnt into practice.

Exam hints are tips from the senior examiner and authors which are designed to help you avoid common mistakes made by previous candidates.

Definitions are useful words you must know to pass the exam.

Extending activity sections are designed to help you use your time most effectively. It is not possible for the workbook to cover *everything* you need to know to pass. What you read here needs to be supplemented by your classes, practical experience at work and day-to-day reading.

Summaries cover what you should have picked up from reading the unit.

A glossary is provided at the back of the book to help define and underpin understanding of the key terms used in each unit.

Who is the customer?

In this unit you will:

- Understand the way in which consumer goods and industrial goods are classified.
- Examine the use of the word 'customer' and the decision making unit (DMU).
- Consider the decision making process (DMP).
- Look at the similarities and differences between the individual and industrial buying situations.

By the end of this unit you will:

- Understand the decision making unit (DMU).
- Understand the decision making process (DMP).
- Relate your understanding of the decision making process to individual and industrial buying situations.
- Be able to analyse and understand the various factors that influence the customer and industrial decision making process.

Traditionally the word 'customer' was used to define people whom the organization dealt with externally. Today it is used more broadly to include people working within the organization as well.

This Unit covers the decision making process and how it is applied to consumer and industrial situations as outlined in the syllabus and the different levels of complexity of buying decisions, the decision making unit and the associated roles in the buying process.

Organize your study materials from the beginning of your course:

- Use file dividers to keep broad topic areas indexed and relevant materials and articles with the relevant notes.
- Look out for relevant articles and current examples, you fill find these useful to illustrate examination answers.

This unit will take you about two to three hours to read through and think about. The activities you have been asked to carry out will take you about four or five hours.

The decision making unit (DMU)

What is a customer?

Although it is useful to use the word 'customer' as a single unit, it is important from the start to understand that purchases are made both by individuals and groups of people involved in the decision making process.

> The term customer refers to the purchaser of a product or service. They may or may not be the consumer. The term consumer refers to the end user of a product or service. They may or may not be the customer. The term DMU refers to the decision making unit, that is the group of people who decide whether to buy a product/service.

Internal customers

People working within the same organization are also referred to as customers. This is not strictly correct, internal customers are actually users.

The DMU ensures that the marketer makes a distinction between the people who are actually buying the product/service from the people who are using the it – the users – and not to confuse the two (although in some cases the user, decider and buyer are the same person). These terms are discussed in detail later on in this unit.

Autonomous purchase
Example: individual purchase – face cream
User: the woman
Decider: the woman
Buyer: the woman
Influencer: a friend

Family purchase
Example: a child's purchase – toy
User: child
Influencer: child's friends
Decider: parents
Buyer: one or both parents

Organizational purchase
Example: a photocopier
Initiator: typist
User: typist, general office staff
Influencer: department head
Decider: purchasing committee
Buyer: buying department
Gatekeeper: receptionist
Financier: finance department

As the examples show a decision making unit identifies the number of people who are involved in the decision making process and ascribes a role to them. Each person will have their own concerns, motivations and interests in determining the outcome. Organizational roles in industrial purchasing are considered in more detail below.

1 What do the terms customer and consumer mean?
2 In what ways can the term DMU be applied. Give examples.

The buyer decision process

The buyer decision process, and hence marketing strategies and techniques are influenced by the following:

1 Product characteristics.
2 The type of market and its characteristics.
3 The product's stage in the life cycle (*see Fundamentals of Marketing*, Butterworth-Heinemann, 1994, p. 32).
4 The degree of market segmentation.
5 The number of competitors.
6 The number of customers and their geographic spread.
7 The condition of the economy and other environmental factors.
8 Individual psychological factors such as motives, approach to risk, attitudes, personality, unique ability, knowledge, demographic and situational factors.
9 Social factors such as roles and family influences, reference groups, social classes, culture and subculture.
10 The decision making process (DMP) and the extent of the decision making involved – extended and limited problem solving, routine response buying, impulse buying and the degree of involvement in the purchase.
11 The decision making process within the decision making unit.

Some of these topics are considered in this Unit, others are examined elsewhere.

> What factors influence the decision making process?

QUESTION 1.2

Product/service classification

To establish marketing strategies for individual products, marketers have developed different classification schemes based on the characteristics of the products.

Products can be classified into three groups depending on how long they last – that is their durability and their tangibility.

1 Non-durable goods – these are tangible and consumed quickly (cold drinks, washing powder, etc.).
2 Durable goods – these are tangible and last a long time (washing machines, clothes, etc).
3 Services – these are intangible and can last a long or a short time (accountancy, education, etc.).

A mix of tangibility and service

It is useful to view products and services as a mix of tangibility and intangibility:

- a pure tangible good which has no service attached to it
- a tangible good with accompanying services to enhance its consumer appeal
- a service with accompanying goods and services
- a pure service

> Distinguish between the terms durable goods, non-durable goods and services.

QUESTION 1.3

The classification is further developed by a distinction being made between consumer and industrial goods. Industrial goods are bought by organizations for use in their business or for processing. Consumer goods are bought for their own use.

It is on this basis that the following classification is made for consumer goods; industrial goods are considered later on.

Consumer goods

Consumer goods can be divided into convenience goods, shopping goods, speciality goods and unsought goods.

Convenience goods

Items that are purchased regularly with a minimum of comparison and buying effort (matches, bread, soap, etc.). Manufacturers attempt to predetermine the purchasing decisions by promoting them as branded products, so the consumer looks for a certain brand rather than a generic (non-branded product). Convenience goods are also further classified into staple, impulse and emergency purchases.

- Staple goods are consumed on a regular basis (fruit and vegetables, tomato sauce, baked beans) and product differentiation tends to be minimal.
- Impulse purchases are not pre-planned (magazines and sweets at a supermarket check-out counter).
- Emergency goods are needed at short notice (shovels in a snow storm, umbrellas at an open air concert, etc.)

Shopping goods

These include major durable or semi-durable items which are bought less frequently. The consumer compares price, quality, style, suitability (hi-fi, clothes, washing machines, etc). Much pre-planning goes into the purchase. Branding strategies aim to simplify the decision process for consumers. Shopping goods can be further classified as homogeneous or heterogeneous.

- Homogeneous goods are broadly similar to each other in technical performance and price, examples are refrigerators and washing machines. Certain brands attempt to differentiate themselves through image or technical or design superiority. Generally price is a major influence on the purchasing decision.
- Heterogeneous goods tend to be non-standard, and price is often of secondary importance. Behavioural factors play an important role in the purchasing decision. A wide range to satisfy individual tastes is important.

Speciality goods

Items which have a unique character (branded clothing, a Porsche). Their purchase is characterized by an extensive search and a reluctance to accept substitutes. Consumers are usually prepared to pay a premium price and it is important to create and preserve the correct image. Customers rarely compare speciality goods.

Unsought goods

Those goods the customer has not considered buying before being made aware of them such as smoke detectors and compact discs, insurance, double glazing. Unsought goods often satisfy a genuine need that the consumer did not recognize existed.

As you have seen a product's characteristics will have a major effect on the decision making process and the marketing strategy and techniques used to sell it.

QUESTION 1.4

Consumer goods can be divided into convenience goods, shopping goods, specialty goods and unsought goods. How would this distinction help you to decide on the decision making process and the use of the appropriate marketing mix? Give examples.

The decision making process (DMP)

Customer behaviour involves a very wide variety of personal and situational variables. There are various ways of making a decision but in general terms the ways in which customers make decisions are outlined below in a number of models. These are also covered in more detail in Unit 13.

Models

> A model is an attempt to translate relationships into diagrams that represent a number of factors and put them into a system in which they are all interrelated. Models can help with providing a frame of reference and suggest lines of inquiry which can be pursued, or point to marketing variables which might not be immediately apparent. They can also show you what information is missing.

The model described below has three major components – input, process and output.

The input component

This draws on external influences that serve as sources of information about a product that influence the consumer's attitude and behaviour towards the product. It includes marketing mix activities and sociocultural influences (see Unit 11).

The process

This is concerned with how consumers make decisions. These psychological concepts are covered in Unit 12 and represent the internal influences such as motivation, perception, learning, personality and attitudes that affect the decision making process.

The output

This covers the post-decision behaviour – purchase, trial, repeat purchase and post purchase evaluation.

The six-stage model

The model of the customer decision making process associated with new products is the six stage model, as shown in Figure 1.1.

Awareness

The consumer becomes aware of the new product/service by word of mouth or marketing efforts.

Interest

The consumer is stimulated to look for information.

```
Awareness
   ↓
Interest
   ↓
Evaluation
   ↓
Trial
   ↓
Adoption
   ↓
Post-adoption confirmation
```

Figure 1.1 The six-stage model

Evaluation

The consumer weighs the relative advantages of the new product against those of other products and decides whether to try it.

Trial

The consumer then decides to try the product.

Adoption

The consumer decides whether or not to begin to buy and use the product.

The post-adoption confirmation

This stage comes when the product has been adopted and the consumer is seeking assurance that they made a sensible decision.

Five-stage model

The model of the customer decision making process for existing products is the five stage model (Newell and Simon), see Figure 1.2.

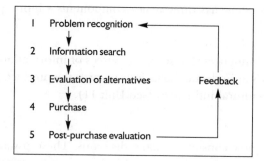

Figure 1.2 The five-stage model

Problem recognition

The customer recognizes they would like to change the current situation, they have a need. The stimulus could be internal or external (for example, feels in need of a break and/or sees a holiday brochure).

Search for information

The customer looks for information either from external sources or from memory. The more complex the area the more information will be required. The marketer must be able to get the product/service into the consumer's awareness and choice set (Figure 1.3).

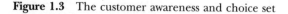

Figure 1.3 The customer awareness and choice set

Alternative evaluation

The customer looks at alternatives from a need-satisfying perspective – they look for benefits.

Purchase

After evaluation the customer buys the preferred alternative or a substitute. The decision to modify or postpone purchase is influenced by the risk they perceive and any anxiety they feel.

Evaluation

The purchase is then evaluated against the original criteria.

Risk

When consumers make decisions the outcome may be uncertain purchasing involves risk and anxiety. However, risk is personal and related to the consumer's perception of what they consider to be risky – functional risk (will the product perform?), physical risk (will I be harmed?), financial risk (is it worth the money?), social risk (will the deodorant work?), psychological risk (will it affect my self-image?), time risk (am I wasting my time?).

Managing risk

Consumers may minimize risk by staying with the same brand, buying a well-known brand, purchasing from a reputable dealer, buying a more expensive brand, looking for reassurance (such as money-back guarantees, laboratory test results, prepurchase trial, warranties) and looking for information (such as from family, friends, opinion leaders, consumer reports, testimonials and information found in the media).

Post-purchase dissonance

Often after an important purchase has been made, a phenomenon called 'post-purchase dissonance' is present; this is a feeling of unease that the goods may not represent good value. Consumers frequently rationalize and reinforce their purchase decisions by looking for messages that confirm their past beliefs, or by ignoring the dissonant information by refusing to discuss it or rejecting it. Marketers should therefore reduce post-purchase dissonance by providing reassuring messages, providing after-sales service and general customer care. Cognitive reinforcement and cognitive dissonance are discussed in more detail in Unit 15.

Levels of consumer decision making

Extended problem solving and limited problem solving

Not all consumer decision making requires the same degree of information search. The actions at each stage vary and depend on the extent to which customers are engaged in extended problem solving (EPS) or limited problem solving (LPS).

When customers purchase, two factors are particularly useful in explaining how they come to a decision.

1   How involved they are in purchasing the product/service.
2   The difference in their perception between competing brands.

Involvement

The extent to which the customer gets involved in a purchase depends on the individual. Involvement can be transient or enduring especially where the choice is repetitive and past experience produces a brand preference (for example: perfume, cigarettes, magazines and newspapers) (see Figure 1.4).

Extended problem solving (EPS)

When customers are highly involved in the purchase and they can see that the differences between brands are significant. High involvement purchases involve a degree of risk, for example:

- They are highly priced (financial risk), e.g. cars.
- Very complex (psychological risk) the wrong decision will cause stress, e.g. computers.
- They reflect self-image (social risk) and peer group approval is important, e.g. clothing, jewellery.

   The stages are as follows:
1   *Problem recognition*
2   *Information search*
   Customers will look for information from a wide variety of media sources and personal selling will influence their choice. The decision making may be carried out over an extended period of time.

For each of the 10 statements, circle the extent to which you agree or disagree. The scale ranges from (1) strongly agree to (6) strongly disagree.

1	I would be interested in reading about this product.	1	2	3	4	5	6
2	I would read a *Consumer Reports* article about this product.	1	2	3	4	5	6
3	I have compared product characteristics among brands.	1	2	3	4	5	6
4	I think there are a great deal of differences among brands.	1	2	3	4	5	6
5	I have a most preferred brand of this product.	1	2	3	4	5	6
6	I usually pay attention to ads for this product.	1	2	3	4	5	6
7	I usually talk about this product with other people.	1	2	3	4	5	6
8	I usually seek advice from other people prior to purchasing this product.	1	2	3	4	5	6
9	I usually take many factors into account before purchasing this product.	1	2	3	4	5	6
10	I usually spend a lot of time choosing what kind to buy.	1	2	3	4	5	6

Figure 1.4 A personal involvement checklist. *Source:* Engel, Warshaw, Kinnear, Richard D Irwin, Inc 1994. Adapted from Edward F. McQuarrie and J Michael Munson, A revised product involvement inventory: improved usability and validity, in *Advances in Consumer Research*, vol. 19, eds John F. Sherry, Jr., and Brian Sternthal (Provo, Utah: Association for Consumer Research, 1992), p. 111. Used by special permission.

3 *Alternative evaluation*

Multiple criteria will be used to evaluate the brand and each brand will be seen as significantly different from each other.

4 *Purchase*

Customers will travel and visit a lot of shops. Personal selling will influence their choice.

5 *Post-purchase evaluation*

Satisfaction will increase their loyalty to the brand.

Limited problem solving (LPS)

Customers are not very involved in the purchase, there are minor perceived differences and the problem that needs to be solved is not large. The stages are as follows:

1 *Problem recognition*
2 *Information search*

The customer is unlikely to look extensively for information.

3 *Evaluation of alternatives*

When involvement and interest in a brand is low, brand switching is likely to take place. The brand decision is not considered important enough to warrant pre-planning and will often take place in the shop.

4 *Purchase*

Customers are likely to try the brand out when they come across a purchase trigger like an in-store display, a coupon, a free trial. Point-of-sale display, price and packaging are important aspects of the marketing mix as buying action is also influenced by brand recognition. Customers may switch brands out of boredom, others may buy the same brand again out of 'inertia' because it is just not important enough to give it any thought.

It may also be better to position these products functionally (see positioning Unit 3).

5 *Post-purchase evaluation*

Beliefs about the brand may be formed by learning passively about the brand and recalled from memory or the brand may be evaluated after use and beliefs about it formed by experience.

How much information do customers need?

It is generally believed that customers make decisions to purchase on a small number of selectively chosen pieces of information.

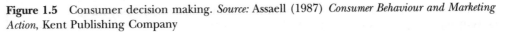

	High-involvement purchase decision	Low-involvement purchase decision
Decision making (information search, consideration of brand alternatives)	Complex decision-making (autos, major appliances)	Variety seeking (cereals)
Habit (little or no information search, consideration of only one brand)	Brand loyalty (cigarettes, perfume)	Inertia (canned vegetables, paper towels)

Figure 1.5 Consumer decision making. *Source:* Assaell (1987) *Consumer Behaviour and Marketing Action*, Kent Publishing Company

It therefore follows that it is extremely important to understand what information the customer feels will help them to be able to evaluate goods and services. In group decision making it is likely that each member of the group may have different needs for information.

This process is now considered in more detail and the following activity will enable you to get some hands-on experience of customer decision making. Working with a partner take a recent or planned purchase and work through the five stages answering the following questions.

1 Need recognition
The customer recognizes they would like to change the current situation.

- What is motivating the person? (think about basic psychological needs and benefits, these can be driven internally or externally by the environment).
- Are the needs dormant or can the customer express them?
- How involved with the product are they? Think about the situation, is it one of extended problem solving or limited problem solving?

2 Search for information
The customer looks for information either from external sources or from memory to solve the problem. The amount of information that is found will be influenced by a number of factors such as time available, past experience involving ways in which attitudes have been formed and patterns of learned behaviour, and other influences such as social factors which include reference group influence, personal contacts, etc.

- Do you understand what information they need to proceed to the next stage of evaluation?
- Do you know where information about the product/service comes from?
- Do you know what information they have?
- Do you know if the customer is motivated enough to look for alternative information?
- What criteria (features, benefits) do they use to assess the information?

3 Alternative evaluation – the customer looks at alternatives from the perspective of need-satisfying benefits.

- What else is being evaluated at the same time?
- What criteria (features, benefits) are the competition using?
- Are there existing customer–supplier relationships?
- Are the criteria used perceived by the customer as being different or essentially the same?

- How important are the differences?

4 Purchase
   After the evaluation has been made the customer then buys the preferred alternative or a substitute.

   - Do they have the money?
   - Will the offer have to be adapted in order to clinch the deal?
   - Will the customer go on looking until they find exactly what they want?
   - Will they accept a substitute?
   - Where do they expect to make the purchase?

5 Post purchase evaluation
   The purchase is then evaluated against the original criteria. Does it meet the needs and expectations of the customer?

   - How satisfied are they and what reasons do they give for their satisfaction/dissatisfaction?
   - How does this experience compare with previous experiences with other products/services?
   - Have they told anybody else about their satisfaction/dissatisfaction?
   - Have they tried to complain? What reaction did they get?
   - Will they purchase again or will they use an alternative?

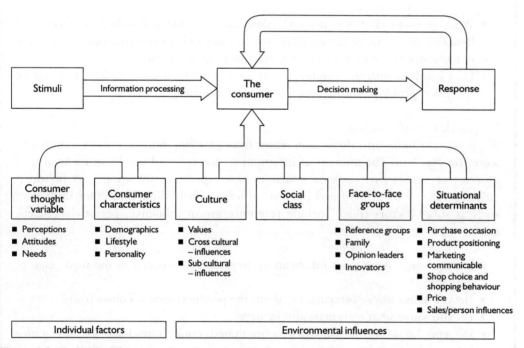

Figure 1.6 Individual factors and environmental influences on the purchase decision. *Source:* Assaell (1987) *Consumer Behaviour and Marketing Action*, Kent Publishing Company

Family purchasing

The most comprehensive marketing model on family purchasing and decision making assumes that children are growing up in a two parent family structure (Sheth 1974). In reality family structures today include not only married couples with children but also a variety of alternative family structures, including female and male-headed single parent families.

With family purchasing decisions can be be made autonomously or jointly: on one's own behalf, on behalf of one or more other family members, or for the family as a unit.

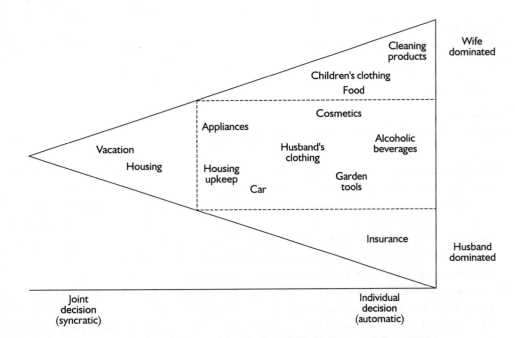

Figure 1.7 Purchasing decisions. *Source:* Adcock, Bradfield, Halberg and Ross (1994)

Purchasing services

A distinction was drawn at the beginning of this unit between goods and services. A number of factors need to be taken into consideration when marketing a service.

Services are different from goods in that they are sold before production and consumption take place. Goods are produced first, then sold and then consumed.

They also have particular characteristics such as their intangibility and variability in that they are difficult to standardize which make it is more difficult for customers to evaluate them (especially when they have no understanding of the service being provided and are relying on professional competence).

What effect do EPS and LPS have on the promotional mix?

QUESTION 1.5

The organizational buying process

- the type of buying situation will be different but the categorization in terms of low involvement and high involvement purchases made by individuals is similar:

    - routine behaviour or **straight rebuy** where the buyer reorders something without any changes being made. History is a significant factor here and there is an inertia which tends to make it difficult for a new supplier to enter the market – very often price cutting is a way in
    - limited problem solving or **modified rebuy** is where the buyer wants to modify the specification, prices, terms or suppliers
    - extended problem solving or **new buy** is where the buyer is buying something for the first time; these tend to be lengthy as the buying criteria will have to be established and developed from scratch

See Figure 1.8 for some examples

Industrial goods

Industrial goods are divided into capital items, materials and parts and supplies and services:

Capital items

These include installations and accessory equipment.

- Installations consist of buildings (factories, offices) and fixed equipment. They are expensive and critical to the long-term success of a company. Purchase is often the result of a very extensive search. Price factors must be viewed as important in such a decision, however it is rarely the single deciding factor. Much emphasis is placed on the quality of sales support and advice, and subsequent technical support and after-sales service. The producers have to be willing to design to specification. They use advertising, but much less so than personal selling.Personal selling is more important than advertising.
- Accessories include portable factory equipment (ancillary plant and machinery, office equipment and office furniture) and are usually less expensive than installations. They have a shorter life than installations, but a longer life than operating supplies. Quality, features, price and service determine how suppliers are selected. Middlemen are used as the market tends to be geographically spread. Buyers are numerous and orders are quite small.

Materials and parts

These include raw materials and manufactured materials and parts.

- Raw materials (farm products such as wheat, cotton, livestock, etc., and natural products such as fish, lumber, crude petroleum, iron ore, etc.). Farm products are supplied by many different producers to marketing intermediaries who process and sell them. Quality, consistency of supply, service, price and delivery are important. The uniformity of natural materials limits demand creation. They are rarely advertised and promoted. Grower groups promote their products in campaigns (e.g. potatoes, oranges, milk, eggs). Some brand their goods (e.g. Outspan oranges).
- Manufactured materials and parts include component materials (iron, cement, etc.) which are usually processed further, and component parts (small motors, adhesives, etc.), replacement and maintenance items for manufacturing which enter the finished product with no further changes in form. Most manufactured materials and parts are sold directly to the industrial users. Price and service are the major marketing factors and advertising is less important.

Supplies and services

These are industrial goods that do not enter the finished product at all.

- Supplies are sometimes called the convenience goods of industrial requirements as they are bought without much effort or comparison, their purchase is routine and undertaken by less senior employees. They include operating supplies (lubricants, stationery, etc.) and maintenance and repair items (paint, nails, brooms). They have a low unit value and are marketed through resellers, there are a large number of customers who are spread geographically. Price and service are important because of the similarity between suppliers and brand preference is not high.
- Business services (also called industrial services) include business advisory services (advertising, legal, professional, consulting) and maintenance and repair services (window cleaning, office equipment repair). Generally these services are carried out under contract although some original equipment suppliers include maintenance and repair as an ongoing aspect of their services. Business advisory services are often new-task buying situations.

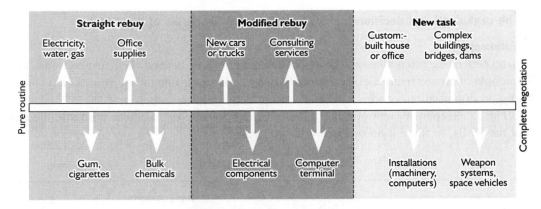

Figure 1.8 Three types of industrial buying situation. *Source:* Enis, Ben, M. (1980) *Marketing Principles,* Copyright 1980, Scott, Foresman and Company. Reprinted by permission

Differences between consumer and industrial buying

- many buyers prefer to deal with suppliers who can offer complete systems
- there are fewer customers than the consumer marketer
- the market is clearly segmented – a supplier may know all potential customers and a potential buyer may know all potential suppliers
- some large organizations have enormous purchasing power
- the practice of reciprocal buying may exist
- the external environment will influence the organization in different ways. For example: the level of primary demand, the cost of money
- many organizational markets have inelastic demand (see Unit 8)
- decisions are made through a group buying process
- buying is often carried out by purchasing professionals
- an unsuccessful decision carries much greater risks than the average customer purchase, a bad decision will affect both the individuals, the groups involved in the purchase and the organization itself
- the buying process is more formal – with written reports, detailed product specifications, and purchase orders
- there is an interlinking customer–supplier chain of dependency and counter dependency
- the demand fluctuates quite widely, a small increase in consumer demand will create a large increase in industrial demand
- much of the purchasing is done on the basis of history and ongoing relationships are of crucial importance. Organizational marketers very often work closely with their customers – they help them to define their needs, customize the offer and deal with the after-sales service
- the organizational culture and structure will influence the buying process and the way decisions are made
- because organizations consists of many people, individual needs will be more varied and need to be taken into account
- no two organizations are the same. Although the standard promotional material may be the same the people who are in direct contact with the customer need to be aware of the differences
- the buying criteria that will be used to judge 'good value' will be much wider. These criteria could include: price/discounts, technical quality, advantage and advancement, after-sales service, reliability and continuity of supply, back-up advisory service, credit facilities.

In what way does an industrial buying situation differ from the consumer market? Use an example of your choice.

QUESTION 1.6

The organizational decision making unit: internal processes of the DMU

Gatekeepers

Gatekeepers are often able to acquire power that goes well beyond their formal status. For example, many secretaries exert a special influence by controlling what information comes into an organization, or who is allowed into the organization.

The gatekeeper can very often be a specialist who feeds relevant information into the rest of the DMU, so there is an overlap with other roles.

	Buying situations		
Stages of the buying process	New task	Modified rebuy	Straight rebuy
1 Problem recognition	Yes	Maybe	No
2 General need description	Yes	Maybe	No
3 Product specification	Yes	Yes	Yes
4 Supplier search	Yes	Maybe	No
5 Proposal solicitation	Yes	Maybe	No
6 Supplier selection	Yes	Maybe	No
7 Order routine specification	Yes	Maybe	No
8 Performance review	Yes	Yes	Yess

Figure 1.9 Major stages of the industrial buying process in relation to major buying situations.
Source: Kotler (1980), *Principles of Marketing*, Prentice-Hall International, Inc., adapted from Patrick J. Robinson, Charles W. Faris, and Yoram Wind, Industrial Buying and Creative Marketing (Boston: Allyn and Bacon, 1967), p. 14.

Initiators

The initiator (the person who triggers off an idea or identifies a problem) may have great ideas but may not have the power within the organization to carry out ideas. It is always important to find the decider in the DMU and to involve them as soon as possible.

Influencers

Influencers are people who influence decision making. They perform the role of informing, persuading or stimulating the decision making process. They can be inside the organization, for example technical people in research and development. They could be outside the organization, for example, stakeholders, pressure groups.

Deciders

Deciders actually make the decision to buy and have the power to decide on what is required and who will provide it.

Buyers

Buyers do not necessarily make the decision to buy, they do, however, make the purchase. They have formal authority from within the organization to select a supplier and negotiate the terms of purchase. In some cases their role is purely administrative.

Users

Users are the people who actually use the product or experience the service. In many cases, they initiate the buying proposal and help define the product specifications and have a high level of technical expertise. They may or may not be the deciders or the buyers.

Financiers

Financiers are the people who determine and control the budget.

What roles do people take up within the industrial DMU and what part do each play within the DMP? Relate your understanding to an organizational situation you have some experience of.

Forces influencing organizational behaviour

Choose an organization with which your company has a commercial relationship and see how much of the following information you can find out: (if your work does not provide you with the opportunity to carry out this task, work with another colleague). Remember to look at the whole system, not only one aspect of it.

Past history with your organization

- records on: sales visits, purchases made, frequency of purchase, time of purchase, credit arrangements, complaints, etc.
- information on previous relationships they have had with members from your own organization
- information on the current supplier chain within your own organization – who else in your business has contacts with this customer and are these relationships satisfactory and how has history affected them (misbilling, personal friction, late delivery etc.)?

Information on the organization

1   Organizational environment

- how does the macro-environment (PEST) influence their business?

  - Economic, commercial and competitive factors such as interest rates, exchange rates, industrial optimism/pessimism
  - Also the political, legal and social environment such as the green movement, equal opportunities policies, BS5750 or BS7750
  - Technological change
  - Supplier size and flexibility, financial reputation
  - Co-operative buying.

You will also need to find out about:

- Their customers – information on their customers and how their needs will have an influence on what your organization produces.
- Other competitors – information on any other organizations competing for their business.

2 The organization as a whole

- how does the organization stand commercially?
- can you describe the overall size and culture of the organization? (Don't forget different sub cultures you need to be aware of.) This will effect the structure of the organization, the reporting relationships, the buying policies, the level of autonomous decision making.

3 The group DMU

- What is the type of purchase (straight rebuy, modified rebuy or new buy)?
- How do they get information?
- What other sources of information are available to them (any other external influences on their purchasing behaviour like other businesses, journals, co-operative buying, etc.)?
- How active are they in the search for alternative information?
- How is the decision making unit structured and how does it fit into the organizational structure?
  - Is the DMU centralized?
  - Is the decision making process (DMP) formalized to the extent that rules and procedures are stated and adhered to by members of that organization? Are there any meta rules (unseen rules that govern the rules)?
  - Is the DMU specialized to the degree in which different departments take on different aspects of the decision making process?
  - How does the DMU function?
  Initiators
  Influencers
  Gatekeepers
  Users
  Deciders
  Buyers
  Financiers
- Is there information on the buying criteria?

Are there any group attitudes to:

- Time pressure?
- Price–cost factors?
- Supply and continuity?
- Risk and their methods of avoiding risk?
- Quality?
- Seeing problems?

What are the relationships between groups?

- Any record of conflict in the DMU between people or departments?
- Any record of functional interests in defining the problem?
- How is conflict resolved (joint problem solving, persuasion, bargaining or politicking)?

4 The individuals

- The names and roles of the people involved in the decision making unit
- How do they see their problems? Different backgrounds and training will influence the way problems are perceived
- How satisfied are they with previous purchases and why?

- The needs of the individuals in the DMU, how they perceive themselves and the quality of relationship they like to have with suppliers. For example:

  - What is their background (class, age, education and lifestyle)?
  - How much time do they want spent with them?
  - How frequently do they want suppliers to contact them?
  - Do they treat suppliers as peers?
  - What level of intimacy do they want?
  - Will they want to dominate the relationship
  - Will they want to become dependent on suppliers?
  - Will they be aggressive?
  - What attitudes do they have towards risk? And how does this show in the way they procrastinate and throw up objections?
  - how will sex, race and other forms of difference influence the relationship?
  - how will they play their professional role and what sort of relationship will their professional role allow the supplier to play – how is the supplier expected to behave? Remember you have to create an ongoing relationship with them!

Unforeseen factors

These could relate to the internal and external environment. Is there any thing outside the control of the DMU that could affect the decision making (industrial relations problems, cash flow, tax changes, etc.)?

QUESTION 1.8

What factors would you need to bear in mind when considering the overall position of your business in relation to an organizational customer?

SUMMARY

When you approach an organization it is important to look at the whole system and not only at one aspect of it. You start with what has gone before, past history. You then go on to look at the organization from the outside – external factors affecting it within the macro and micro environment (see Unit 4), then the inside of the organization – first as a whole, then the DMU groups within it and lastly the individuals. In any situation possible unforeseen circumstances should be taken into account.

Forces influencing organizational behaviour

1 The selling organization

- Past history

2 The buying organization

External factors

- macro environmental factors (PEST)
- micro environmental factors (competitors, suppliers, distributors, customers)

Internal factors

- The organization
- The group
  - what happens in the DMU group as a whole (intragroup)
  - what happens between groups (intergroup)
- The individuals
  - what happens between individuals in the group (interpersonal)
  - what happens in the individuals' minds (intrapersonal)

3   Unforeseen circumstances

Customer care

Perfect Customer Care, Ted Johns, Century Business, 1994.

QUESTION 1.9

What role do sales people play in helping customers to make decisions? Use the decision making process as a structure on which to base your discussion. Consider both a retail situation and an industrial situation.

Revision summary

In this unit we have seen:

- There are similarities and differences between buyer behaviour towards consumer and industrial goods and services.
- Buyer behaviour is influenced in many different ways – products characteristics, the type of market and its characteristics, the product's stage in the life cycle, the degree of market segmentation, the number of competitors, the number of customers and their geographic spread, the condition of the economy and other environmental factors, the psychological factors operating within individuals such as their motives, approach to risk, attitudes and personality and other personal factors that are unique to a person such as their ability and knowledge, demographic factors and situational factors, social factors influencing the buyer decision process such as roles and family influences, reference groups, social classes and culture and subculture.
- Different models can be used to explain the consumer decision making process.
- The decision making process (DMP) and the extent of the decision making involved – extended and limited problem solving, routine response buying, impulse buying and the degree of involvement in the purchase and the decision making process within the decision making unit.
- The following factors play an important part:
  - Perceived risk
  - Dissonance.
- Family purchasing behaviour can also be looked at as a DMU and has the following roles:
  - initiator
  - gatekeeper

- decider
- buyer
- preparer
- user
- maintainer
- disposer.
- The decision making unit (DMU) consists of the following roles:
  - initiators
  - gatekeepers
  - influencers
  - deciders
  - buyers
  - users
  - financiers.
- Industrial decision making process has special features.

In addition to this you will have checked your learning by answering questions and carried out various activities that will help you to apply what you have learned.

What do customers want?

In this unit you will:

- Study the meaning of Total Quality Management.
- Explore some aspects of organizational behaviour.
- Understand why interfunctional conflict exists between marketing and other departments.

By the end of this you will be able to:

- Relate the idea of the marketing concept, internal marketing, relationship marketing and customer care to Total Quality Management (TQM).
- Understand some key aspects of organizational behaviour.

STUDY GUIDE

The central factor in Japanese business success has been their ability to produce high quality products that are closely tuned to the requirements of the market. In a study carried out by The Profit Impact of Market Strategy (PIMS) programme it was concluded that the single most important factor affecting the performance of a business was the quality of its goods and services relative to those of its competitors.

In an increasingly competitive world, the distinguishing factor between organizations is often the service organizations provide for their customers or clients. This not only affects retail and sales outlets, but every aspect of industry and institutional life. All members of an organization, not only staff in direct contact with customers, have a part to play in improving standards of quality.

The importance of quality has been reflected in the growth of TQM.

Internal marketing and relationship marketing are implicit in TQM programmes and customer care programmes and need not stand alone.

Traditionally the word 'customer' was used to define people with whom the organization dealt externally. Today it is used more broadly in TQM to define customer–supplier relationships and includes people working within the organization.

Although the way in which an organization (such as a factory) develops is mainly determined by the product it produces and the technology it uses, from a psychological viewpoint the culture and structure are determined by the psychological needs of its members.

It can be very difficult for people to see things from another point of view and to appreciate the needs of external or internal customers. An insight into organizational behaviour will enable you to understand why this is so.

It should take you approximately two to three hours to work through this unit and a further four or five hours to undertake the various activities that have been suggested.

STUDY TIPS

Organize your study material from the beginning of your course:

- Use file dividers to keep broad topic areas indexed and relevant materials and articles with the relevant notes.
- Look out for relevant articles and current examples, you will find these useful to illustrate exam answers.

The marketing concept, internal marketing and relationship marketing

The marketing concept, internal marketing and relationship marketing have much in common with quality ideas.

According to the Chartered Institute of Marketing, *marketing* is 'the management process which identifies, anticipates and satisfies customer requirements efficiently and profitably'.

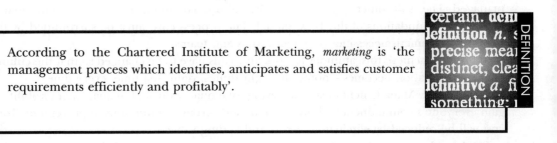

Christian Groonroos defines *internal marketing* as 'the creation of an internal environment which supports customer-consciousness and sales-mindedness amongst all personnel within an organization'.

Relationship marketing addresses two concerns – getting and keeping customers. It redefines marketing as being concerned with the establishment of enduring and mutually profitable relationships between the firm and its customers. Relationship marketing emphasizes three issues:

1 Concern for the broader scope of 'external' market relationships which include suppliers, business referral and 'influence' sources.

2 Focusing on internal (staff) relationships critical to the success of (external) marketing plans. 'Internal marketing' aims to achieve continuous improvement in marketing performance.

3 Improving marketing performance ultimately requires a resolution (or realignment) of the competing interests of customers, staff and shareholders, by changing the way managers 'manage' the activities of a business.

Christopher, M., Payne, A., Ballantyne, D. (1994)
Relationship Marketing, Butterworth-Heinemann

Customer care

A fundamental approach to the standards of service quality. It covers every aspect of a company's operations, from the design of a product or service to how it is packaged, delivered and serviced.

Clutterbuck

Total quality management

The word quality is now used in relation to total quality management (TQM).

The core of TQM is the customer–supplier relationship, where the processes must be managed. The 'soft' outcomes of TQM – the culture, communications and commitment – provide the foundations of the TQM model. The process core must be surrounded by the 'hard' management necessities of systems, tools and teams.

In order to achieve this, attitudes to work and skills have to be changed so that the culture of the organization becomes – doing the right things, right first time, every time.

Total Quality Management means achieving total quality through management's ability to gain everyone's commitment and involvement and through continuous improvement. Total cost will be reduced by eliminating errors and adding value.

TQM involves training people to understand customer–supplier relationships, not buying on price alone, managing systems improvement, modern supervision and training, managing processes through teamwork and improved communication, elimination of barriers and fear, constant education and development.

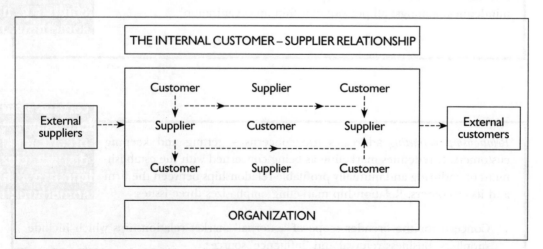

Figure 2.1 TQM involves looking at all the customer–supplier relationships in the whole system

Marketing quality assurance (MQA)

MQA is a third-party certifying organization specializing in providing assessment services to organizations wishing to develop quality systems for their marketing, sales and customer-service activities; in assessing companies in the service sector to the ISO 9000 series of Quality System Standards; and in developing third-party certification guidelines for specific areas, such as public relations (see Figure 2.2).

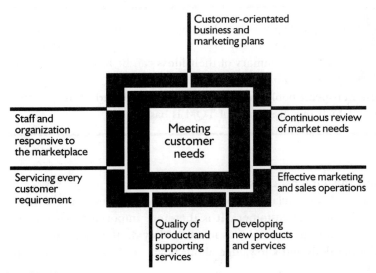

Figure 2.2 MQA objectives

Internal marketing, relationship marketing and customer care

Internal marketing and relationship marketing are implicit in TQM programmes and customer care programmes and need not stand alone.

Internal marketing and relationship marketing focus on:

1 Removing barriers to organizational effectiveness.
2 Developing an awareness of customers both internal and external to the organization.
3 Encouraging all employees to take an active role in looking after customers.

TQM and the marketing concept have much in common, discuss.

QUESTION 2.1

- What does quality mean to you and your organization? (Include customers, suppliers, employees and shareholders.) Is this your point of view or theirs?
- Has your organization MQA started a Total Quality initiative? If not, why not?
- If your organization has already started a Total Quality initiative, where did the pressure to improve quality come from?

ACTIVITY 2.1

- If TQM is part of your business strategy have costs been reduced in key areas and have service response times been improved?
- Has your organization managed to communicate this to their customers, suppliers, employees and shareholders?
- How involved was marketing in this initiative?
- Do your competitors have a Total Quality initiative?

EXTENDING READING

The quality gurus are Deming, Juran and Crosby, you may want to read what they have to say.

A useful summary of their ideas can be found in Bendall *et al.* (1993), *Quality, Measuring and Monitoring*.

The best European book on TQM is by John Oakland (Butterworth-Heinemann, 1995), upon which this discussion of TQM is based.

Working with the 'internal customer'

TQM, internal marketing, relationship marketing and customer care all involve marketing in dealing with the 'internal customer'. It is therefore important that marketers are able to understand their internal customers as much as they do their external customers. This will require additional skills and knowledge about how people within organizations behave.

Management of subcultures and sentient systems

Many different cultures often co-exist in an organization. Some examples of subcultures would include:

- managerial cultures
- occupationally based cultures
- group cultures based on geographical proximity
- worker cultures based on shared hierarchical experiences.
- unions

These subgroups very often have different objectives, different concepts about time, different ideas about what is important to them, different values, attitudes and beliefs about themselves. They often share secrets, and share cared-for rooms and possessions.

Leadership or management of any organization entails identifying its constituent task and sentient systems and understanding the relations between them. When a sentient system is threatened by change its defences will increase. Sometimes there is a conflict between a subculture and the objectives of the organization. For example, loyalty to a union can often outweigh loyalty to the organization itself.

These sentient groups exist within the organization and also extend outside the organization. For example, an organization may find an unexpected resistance to change coming from other stakeholders. Management has to manage the individual sentient groups and the relationship between them.

Intergroup behaviour

Individuals tend to idealize the groups that are important to them. Very often this means suppressing the less satisfactory aspect. Groups feel and believe that they have a relationship with each other. Some groups may be treated with suspicion, others are treated neutrally. Individuals in the group build up pictures of other groups from hearsay, guesswork and projected aspects of their own minds. When the task systems of different groups have different priorities, groups may find that they are at odds with each other.

The effective group is one that is in contact with reality and knows the boundary between what is inside the group and what is outside it.

Marketing and the internal customer

The marketing concept tries to focus everything in the organization towards meeting customers' needs. However, other departments can sometimes put more importance on their own tasks. An understanding of their priorities will help marketing go some way to understanding their internal customers a little more.

Interdepartmental conflicts

Research and development want:

- product quality
- research for its own sake
- plenty of time in which to develop their ideas

Marketing want:

- customer perceptions to lead the definition of quality
- ideas that can be applied
- products that have features that add value to them and differentiate them from their competitors

Manufacturing want:

- plenty of time
- long runs
- only a few models
- orders that are standard
- average quality control
- few changes

Marketing want:

- short lead times
- short runs
- a variety of models
- custom-made orders
- changes made when they need them
- tight quality control

Finance, accounting and credit want:

- standard transactions
- few standard reports
- fixed budgets
- pricing to cover costs
- strict reasons for spending
- full financial disclosure by customers
- low credit risks
- controlled and tough credit terms
- strict procedure for collecting money

Marketing want:

- special terms and discounts to suit different customers' needs
- many reports tailored for specific information needs
- flexible budgets so plans can be changed to suit developments in the marketplace
- prices that will help them to develop the market
- methods of examining credit that will not upset customers
- easy terms of credit
- procedures for collecting money that will not upset customers

Purchasing and inventory want:

- narrow product lines
- standard parts
- material that is bought on price not necessarily quality
- lot sizes that are economical
- infrequent intervals in which purchases are made

Marketing want:

- broad product lines so that customers can have variety and products can be delivered that will suit each customer's needs
- non-standard parts
- material that will meet customers' perceptions of quality and add value to the product
- large lot sizes and a high level of stock so that nothing runs out
- purchasing that can be carried out in relation to customers' needs

Adapted from: Kotler (1980), *Principles of Marketing*, Prentice Hall International, Inc., 1980.

ACTIVITY 2.2

1   What interdepartmental barriers, or conflicts, exist in your own organization?
2   Which of these impact specifically on the marketing department?
3   How do they affect your ability to satisfy your external customers' needs?
4   What do you do to help other departments to understand customer needs in order to help things go more smoothly?

QUESTION 2.2

1   What interfunctional conflicts do marketers come across in the course of carrying out their work?
2   What would you do to overcome them?

Assessing internal customer needs

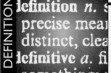

DEFINITION

certain. dem
definition *n.*
precise mea
distinct, clea
definitive *a.* fi
something:

Departmental process analysis (DPA)
This process tries to find answers to the following questions:

- What purpose do we serve?
- Has our purpose changed?
- How do our internal customers want things done?
- Is there a better way to do this?
- Does our work satisfy any external customers' needs?
- Do our suppliers understand our needs, time and resource constraints?

Quality gap analysis
Customer satisfaction is a result of a match between what they expect and what they get. A key element of marketing research is finding out what customers think and what they really want. The objectives are to find out and measure what people are satisfied or dissatisfied with and make any necessary changes.

Useful addresses

BSI
BSI Quality Assurance
PO Box 375
Milton Keynes
MK14 6LL
Tel: 01908 220908

DTI
Department of Trade and Industry
Management and Technology Services
Room 4.18
151 Buckingham Palace Road
London SW1W 9SS
Tel: 0171 215 8142

Lloyds
Quality Assurance Dept
Engineering Services Group
Lloyds Register House
29 Wellesley Road
Croydon CR0 2AJ
Tel: 0181 681 4040

EFQM
European Foundation for Quality Management
Avenue des Pleiades 19c
B1200 Bruxelles, Belgium
Tel: +32 2 775 3511

BQF
British Quality Foundation
215 Vauxhall Bridge Road
London SW1V 1EN
Tel: 0171 931 0607

Best Practice Club
IFS International Ltd
Freepost BF112
Wolseley Business Park
Kempston
Bedford MK42 7BR
Tel: 01234 853605

Benchmarking
The Benchmarking Centre
c/o Dexion Ltd
Maylands Avenue
Hemel Hempstead
Herts HP2 7EW
Tel: 01442 250040

SUMMARY

In this unit you have seen:
- The principles of customer focus in TQM are not dissimilar from the marketing concept, internal marketing, relationship marketing and customer care.
- As TQM programmes are increasingly being introduced into the workplace it is important for the marketer to understand what they involve and the place marketing has within a TQM programme.
- Marketers should be able to understand and apply the principles of Total Quality Management as a method of addressing these problems and to extend their thinking to people working within the organization as well as their suppliers and marketing intermediaries.

Market segmentation – how can we tell one customer from another?

In this unit you will:

- Examine the process of segmentation.
- Examine segmentation systems and understand their purpose.
- Consider the uses and tools of segmentation.
- Assess the relative value of traditional versus contemporary segmentation methods.
- Distinguish between consumer and industrial segmentation.

By the end of this unit you will:

- Understand the following systems of segmentation:
    Geographic
    Geo-demographics
    Demographics
    Behavioural
    Psychographic.
- Understand the concept of positioning.
- Understand an industrial segmentation system.
- Be able to apply your understanding.

This unit introduces the concept of target marketing. Target marketing involves three major steps: segmentation, targeting and positioning. This process covers one of the main cornerstones of marketing.

Although there is a trend toward targeted marketing, unless we only have very few customers, in most cases it is not generally feasible to tailor a complete marketing mix to each and every individual. The whole objective of segmentation is to identify groups of people within the broader market who have needs which are broadly similar to each other and who respond in a similar way to the marketing mix.

Organize your study material from the beginning of your course:

- Use file dividers to keep broad topic areas indexed and relevant materials and articles with the relevant notes.
- Look out for relevant articles and current examples, you will find these useful to illustrate examination answers.

It should take you about two hours to work through this unit and you should allow two to three hours to undertake the various activities. The practical exercises will reinforce your learning and provide you with examples that you will find useful in the examination.

Market segmentation

You will find a number of ways in which market segmentation is defined:

The process of dividing large heterogeneous markets into smaller, homogeneous subsets of people or businesses with similar needs and/or responsiveness to marketing mix offerings.

> Kinnear, Thomas C. and Bernhardt, Kenneth L. (1990)
> *Principles of Marketing.* 3rd edn, Scott Foresman/Little Brown

To segment is to divide into parts. In the marketing context these parts may be groups of consumers with like requirements or groups of products/services with like attributes.

> Crimp, Margaret (1990) *The Marketing Research Process,* Prentice Hall

Market research

A market researcher is likely to approach the design of a segmentation study from one or two angles:

1 *Consumer typology* – clustering consumers
   Data will be collected and analysed to sort consumers and group them homogeneously according to geographic, geodemographic, demographic, psychographic and buyer behaviour factors.
2 *Product differentiation* – clustering products
   Data relating to the products/services/brands is collected and analysed with a view to sorting products into groups which in the eyes of the consumer have similar attributes.

The examiners may well use the terms 'target marketing' and 'market segmentation' interchangeably. In this unit we have seen that in fact market segmentation is only one step in the target marketing process. The terms product or market positioning are also used interchangeably.

Although many marketers can see the rationale of segmentation, many are dissatisfied with it as a concept. They often find it difficult to apply to certain markets. It is therefore important to remember that:

- it is a creative tool
- it is different for every situation
- the majority of markets can be segmented in a variety of different ways
- there is no one right way to segment a market
- it is not a one-off exercise and needs constant monitoring to maintain its usefulness.

The marketer has to try different segmentation variables to find the best market view.

Value of segmentation

For the customer
- provides greater choice of products/services
- products/services should more closely match the needs of consumers

For the organization
- better marketing planning as reactions to marketing activities can be predicted.
- it helps organizations to identify prospects who are most likely to buy
- marketers will get to know their customers better so that they can provide a better service
- budgets can be more closely allocated on the basis of the investment and return needed from different segments
- smaller segments may be easier to dominate
- marketing and sales activity will be closely focused, leading to more sales, lower costs and higher profitability.

QUESTION 3.1

What is the value of segmentation to the marketer?

Uses of market segmentation
1 To spot a gap in the market that is either empty or partly filled.
2 To position a brand in relation to competitor brands within its product field.

The five major bases for segmenting consumer markets are shown below:

1 Geographic techniques.
2 Geodemographic techniques.
3 Demographic techniques.
4 Behaviour in the product field.
5 Psychographic.

These will now be considered in more detail.

EXAM HINT

You should be able to memorize this classification and reproduce it if asked in the exam. You should also be able to criticize the limitations of each system.

What market segmentation systems are commonly used by marketers?

Geographic techniques

This is the simplest technique and simply involves dividing markets into different geographical units such as nations, states, regions, counties, cities. The marketer then chooses to operate in a few or all of the areas. The marketing mix will change to take into account any regional differences.

Culture

Culture refers to a complex set of values, beliefs and attitudes that help individuals to communicate, interpret and evaluate members of a given society. It has three important features:

1   It includes both abstract (values, beliefs, attitudes, symbols, rituals) and material elements (art, music, literature, buildings).
2   It is socially transmitted and learned.
3   It influences human behaviour.

Since consumption involves behaviour, culture is an important influence. You will need to refer to cultural affinity zones and cultural affinity classes, which are covered in Unit 16. Culture is also discussed in Unit 11.

Geodemographic techniques

Geodemographics is an extension of geographic techniques in which recognition is given to the fact that, broadly speaking, people with similar economic, social and lifestyle characteristics tend to congregate in particular neighbourhoods and can be considered as micro-cultures.

This technique is useful in identifying new retail sites and the stock they should carry, selecting sales territories, allocating marketing resources, leaflet distribution and direct marketing.

However, in market research, geodemographic systems can only tell the marketer:

• what type of area a brand is doing well or badly in
• where further research can be carried out once the target has been defined

Unless the geodemographic technique is linked to attitudinal, behavioural or motivation studies, they do not tell the marketer:

• how to define the target segment in terms of consumer behaviour
• the consumer attitudes which help to explain that behaviour

Residential neighbourhood classifications

Every one of the postcodes in the country has been analysed according to the type of housing it represents and classified into a neighbourhood group. Each of these neighbourhood groups now has its own detailed lifestyle profile which lists every type of behaviour from typical marriage and employment patterns, to car ownership and holidays abroad.

One of the best known classifications is ACORN, standing for A Classification of Residential Neighbourhoods (Figure 3.1). This was developed by Richard Weber in 1973, who applied techniques of cluster analysis to 38 separate neighbourhood types, each of which was different in terms of its housing, population and socio-economic characteristics. Kenneth Baker (1982) of the British Market Research Bureau saw how useful it could be and it was used for supervising the field work of the bureau's Target Group Index. Later Richard Weber joined Consolidated Analysis Centres Inc. (CACI) and developed his ideas. See Figure 3.1 for the ACORN classification.

More sophisticated approaches have been developed including CCNs MOSAIC, CDMSs SUPERPROFILES, Infolink's DEFINE and PINPOINT Analysis's PiN and FiNPiN.

The common element in all geodemographic systems is their use of census enumeration district (ED) data. Other systems are broadly similar although each uses a variety of other variables. MOSAIC for example includes housing data similar to the Acorn system but also includes:

- financial data (county court judgments, finance house/credit card searches
- socio-economic census data (occupations and car ownership)
- census data (ownership, facilities and size of household, number and ages of residents)
- demographics (people who have moved house)

You have been given the task of arranging a direct mail shot to potential customers. Write to ACORN and CCNs MOSAIC, CDMSs SUPER-PROFILES, Infolink's DEFINE, and PINPOINT Analysis's PiN and FiNPiN and get some more information about them.

Geographic modelling

GMAP University of Leeds

Geographic modelling is different from residential neighbourhood classification systems because it is based on using catchment areas, demographic data within those areas, with information from market research on patterns of behaviour and competitor information. Geographical models then simulate the interaction between supply and demand.

Find out more about GMAP from the University of Leeds.

Demographic techniques

Demography studies the measurable aspects of society such as: age, gender, education, occupation, social grade, religion, race, culture, nationality, family size and family life cycle. Most secondary data (see Unit 5) is expressed in demographic terms and the information helps marketers to:

- provide an understanding of market structure and potential customer segments
- identify potential for sales
- identify trends in population
- locate a target market.

Data is easy to get hold of, and compared to other segmentation methods it isn't too expensive.

CACI ACORN PROFILE OF GREAT BRITAIN

The ACORN© consumer targeting classification was developed by CACI Information Services. The table below shows the ACORN clasification's 6 Categories, 17 Groups and 54 Types (plus 1 'unclassified' in each case), and their share of the GB population in 1991. The ACORN classification is derived from the Government's 1991 Census of Great Britain.

ACORN Types		% of 1991 population	ACORN Groups		
	ACORN Category A: THRIVING	**19.8**			
1.1	Wealthy suburbs, large detached houses	2.6	15.1	Wealthy achievers, suburban areas	1
1.2	Villages with wealthy commuters	3.2			
1.3	Mature affluent home-owning areas	2.7			
1.4	Affluent suburbs, older families	3.7			
1.5	Mature, well-off suburbs	3.0			
2.6	Agricultural villages, home-based workers	1.6	2.3	Affluent greys, rural communities	2
2.7	Holiday retreats, older people, home-based workers	0.7			
3.8	Home-owning areas, well-off older residents	1.4	2.3	Prosperous pensioners, retirement areas	3
3.9	Private flats, elderly people	0.9			
	ACORN Category B: EXPANDING	**11.6**			
4.10	Affluent working families with mortgages	2.1	3.7	Affluent executives, family areas	4
4.11	Affluent working couples with mortgages, new homes	1.3			
4.12	Transient workforces, living at their place of work	0.3			
5.13	Home-owning family areas	2.6	7.8	Well-off workers, family areas	5
5.14	Home-owning family areas, older children	3.0			
5.15	Families with mortgages, younger children	2.2			
	ACORN Category C: RISING	**7.5**			
6.16	Well-off town & city areas	1.1	2.2	Affluent urbanities, town & city areas	6
6.17	Flats and mortgages, singles & young working couples	0.8			
6.18	Furnished flats & bedsits, younger single people	0.4			
7.19	Apartments, young professional singles & couples	1.1	2.1	Prosperous professionals, metropolitan areas	7
7.20	Gentrified multi-ethnic areas	1.0			
8.21	Prosperous enclaves, highly qualified executives	0.7	3.2	Better-off executives, inner city areas	8
8.22	Academic centres, students & young professionals	0.5			
8.23	Affluent city areas, tenements & flats	0.4			
8.24	Partially gentrified multi-ethnic areas	0.7			
8.25	Converted flats & bedsits, single people	0.9			
	ACORN Category D: SETTLING	**24.1**			
9.26	Mature established home-owning areas	3.3	13.4	Comfortable middle agers, mature home-owning areas	9
9.27	Rural areas, mixed occupations	3.4			
9.28	Established home-owning areas	4.0			
9.29	Home-owning areas, council tenants, retired people	2.6			
10.30	Established home-owning areas, skilled workers	4.5	10.7	Skilled workers, home-owning areas	10
10.31	Home owners in older properties, younger workers	3.1			
10.32	Home-owning areas with skilled workers	3.1			
	ACORN Category E: ASPIRING	**13.7**			
11.33	Council areas, some new home owners	3.8	9.8	New home owners, mature communities	11
11.34	Mature home-owning areas, skilled workers	3.1			
11.35	Low rise estates, older workers, new home owners	2.9			
12.36	Home-owning multi-ethnic areas, young families	1.1	4.0	White collar workers, better-off multi-ethnic areas	12
12.37	Multi-occupied town centres, mixed occupations	1.8			
12.38	Multi-ethnic areas, white collar workers	1.1			
	ACORN Category F: STRIVING	**22.8**			
13.39	Home owners, small council flats, single pensioners	1.9	3.6	Older people, less prosperous areas	13
13.40	Council areas, older people, health problems	1.7			
14.41	Better-off council areas, new home owners	2.4	11.6	Council estate residents, better-off homes	14
14.42	Council areas, young families, some new home owners	3.0			
14.43	Council areas, young families, many lone parents	1.6			
14.44	Multi-occupied terraces, multi-ethnic areas	0.8			
14.45	Low rise council housing, less well-off families	1.8			
14.46	Council areas, residents with health problems	2.0			
15.47	Estates with high unemployment	1.1	2.7	Council estate residents, high uemployment	15
15.48	Council flats, elderly people, health problems	0.7			
15.49	Council flats, very high unemployment, singles	0.9			
16.50	Council areas, high unemployment, lone parents	1.9	2.8	Council estate residents, greatest hardship	16
16.51	Council flats, greatest hardship, many lone parents	0.9			
17.52	Multi-ethnic areas, large families, overcrowding	0.6	2.1	People in multi-ethnic, low-income areas	17
17.53	Multi-ethnic estates, severe unemployment, lone parents	1.0			
17.54	Multi-ethnic estates, high unemployment, overcrowding	0.5			
	Unclassified	**0.5**			

Source: CACI Information Services: 0171 602 6000 (London)/0131 557 0123 (Edinburgh). © CACI Limited, 1993 (Source: OPCS and GRO(S) © Crown Copyright 1991) All rights reserved. ACORN is a registered servicemark of CACI Limited.

Figure 3.1 CACI ACORN profile of Great Britian

Social class and status

Two of the most commonly used terms in segmentation are class and status.

Social class is the most heavily used segmentation technique used in the UK because it relies on an existing class system and provides an objective measure for classifying people.

For example:

Social grade indices of using (national Av = 100)

	Toothpaste		Tea		Baked Beans
AB	140		78		89
C1	119		90		95
C2	123		108		128
D	75	DE	103	DE	40
E	29				

(MRS 1981)

Social class gives a hierarchical classification in which each group is stratified into strata or classes. The technique relies heavily on a combination of:

- occupation
- income
- educational attainment.

The idea of class is complex but some of the key ideas are as follows:

1. The notion of hierarchical distinction which is also expressed in ideas such as social stratification – upper class, middle class, lower class, working class.
2. The use of census data to provide descriptive categories such as those used by the Registrar General in dividing the population of the United Kingdom.
3. The use of occupations to identify socio-economic status groups such as manual and non-manual, or white collar and blue collar.
4. The description of a society in terms of the degree of social mobility. This leads directly to classifications such as open societies (social mobility and movement from one class to another being possible) and closed societies (social class being defined and fixed at (and by) birth as in a caste system).
5. The ideas of Marx which centre on ownership and non-ownership of property and resources and which give rise to the classification of bourgeoisie and proletariat as the dominant classes in capitalistic societies.
6. Weber's use of similar analysis focused on the subdivisions of property, including ideas such as knowledge or education.

Source: Rice, C. (1993) *Consumer Behaviour,* Butterworth-Heinnemann.

Social grade	Social status	Occupation
A	Upper middle class	Higher managerial, administrative or professional
B	Middle class	Intermediate managerial, administrative or professional
CI	Lower middle class	Supervisory or clerical, and junior managerial, administrative or professional
C2	Skilled working class	Skilled manual workers
D	Working class	Semi and unskilled manual workers
E	Those at lowest level of subsistence	State pensioners or widows (no other earner), casual or lowest-grade workers

These are the standard social grade classifications using definitions agreed between Research Services Ltd., and NRS. A JICNARS publication *Social Grading on the National Readership Survey* and National Readership Survey Appendix E describe the definitions and methodology used.

Sources: National Readership Survey.

Figure 3.2 NRS Social Grade definitions

Distribution of the population by social grade

Social grade	All adults 15+ '000s	All adults 15+ %	Men '000s	Men %	Women '000s	Women %	Main shoppers* (female) '000s	Main shoppers* (female) %
A	1391	3.1	714	3.3	677	2.9	554	2.8
B	7106	15.7	3617	16.5	3489	14.9	2949	14.9
C1	11,654	25.7	5316	24.3	6338	27.0	5280	26.7
C2	11,756	26.0	6192	28.3	5564	23.7	4656	23.5
D	7689	17.0	3775	17.3	3913	16.7	3305	16.7
E	5705	12.6	2248	10.3	3456	14.7	3047	15.4
Total	45,300	100.0	21,863	100.0	23,437	100.0	19,791	100.0

Note: These social grades are based on grades of the chief income earner.
*Main shoppers are identified as those who personally select half or more of the items bought for their household from supermarkets and food shops. This member may be male or female:

	'000s	%
Female main shopper	19,791	70.6
Male main shopper	8,229	29.4
All main shoppers	**28,020**	**100.0**

Source: National Readership Survey (NRS Ltd.) July 1992 – June 1993.

Figure 3.3 Distribution of the population by social grade

> Class is used by the marketer to identify groups of people of similar status to share beliefs, aspirations and values. It is an objective way of classifying people according to such criteria as occupation, education, lifestyle, place of residence and income. It implies an awareness of class consciousness within the group, a degree of uniformity of lifestyle, and social interaction.
>
> Rice, C. (1993) *Consumer Behaviour*, Butterworth-Heinnemann

DEFINITION

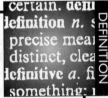

ACTIVITY 3.1

1 What class are you? On what basis do you make that judgement?
2 Do your colleagues agree with you?
3 What class are the other people living in your neighbourhood?

Allocation to social class categories

Allocating people to a particular category usually involves one of three approaches:

1 The *subjective* approach where participants are asked to decide their own social class.
2 The *reputational* approach where individuals are asked to determine the social class of others in the community.
3 The *objective* approach where non-participants allocate individuals on the basis of pre-determined factors (e.g. occupation, education, income and wealth, lifestyle).

In 1990, the Market Research Society published an up-to-date guide to socio-economic status. The guide defines the pecking order of 1500 jobs and is based not on earnings, but on qualifications and responsibilities.

ACTIVITY 3.2

Look at Figure 3.4. Do you agree with the classifications?

Status

Status is a subjective phenomenon which is a result of the judgement of the social position the person occupies. Here the distinction from class becomes somewhat blurred as the judgement is usually also based on factors such as power, wealth and occupation.

It is possible to identify three forms of status:

1 *Ascribed status* – this is similar to the ideas of ascribed groups (see Unit 11). Individuals have little control over this as it covers the status accorded by society to classifications such as gender (male/female) and race/colour.
2 *Achieved status* – in contrast, is that which has been acquired by individuals through occupation, place of residence and lifestyle.
3 *Desired status* – this is the social status an individual wishes to attain. Here the analogy is with the aspirational group (see Unit 11).

Social grade/class

The social grades, class, occupation and percentage of the UK population has already been outlined in Figure 3.2 and Figure 3.3.

Criticisms of social class

The major criticism of class being used is that it is too restrictive and may not reflect the changing nature of UK society. It is also too narrow – six categories cannot possibly provide an accurate reflection of 55 million people. In addition, nearly a third of those earning over £21,000 are C2DE and half those earning £15,000–£21,000 are C2DE. The correlation between social grade and income no longer exists.

People find it difficult to define themselves and most people believe themselves to be a different class. Some people like and cling to the idea of being working class, even though objective data proves this belief to be incorrect.

Head of the household categories don't take into consideration what is happening in society. Women now return to work, and many households have two earners.

Access to education has removed many class barriers.

Although values, attitudes, beliefs and purchasing habits don't change overnight, unemployment has reduced the spending power of many middle class managers. However, class is still reflected in certain types of behaviour, for example eating habits reflect class structure. In a recent survey of 7000 British households, it was convincingly shown that our eating habits are affected not just by our income, but also by class, gender and age ('social class and change in eating habits', *British Food Journal*, **95**(1), 1993).

QUESTION 3.3

1 What are the differences between social class and status? Of what value are these concepts to the marketer?
2 What criticisms have been made about using social class as a segmentation variable?

A: admiral, advocate, air marshal, ambassador, archbishop, attorney, bank manager, bishop, brigadier, chemist shop manager (more than 25 staff); chief constable, chief engineer, chief fire officer, chief rabbi, chiropodist (more than five staff); national orchestra conductor, coroner, university dean, dental surgeon with own practice, chartered estate agent, self-employed farmer (more than 10 staff), financier, general practitioner (own practice/partner), school head-teacher (more than 750 pupils), homoeopath, insurance underwriter, magistrate, hospital matron, judge, MP, professor and town clerk.

B: advertising account director, archdeacon, area sales manager, ballistics expert, qualified brewer, bursar, church canon, chef (more than 25 staff), police chief inspector, computer programmer, stock exchange dealer, deputy power station manager, drawing office manager, fund manager, master mariner, orchestra leader, parish priest, parson, prison governor, probation officer, rabbi, senior buyer, senior engineer, qualified social worker, secondary-school teacher, television newscaster, lecturer and nursing sister.

C1: advertising account executive, accounts clerk, announcer (television, radio or station platform), art buyer, articled clerk, athlete, band master, bank cashier, boxer, bus inspector, calligrapher, campanologist, telephone canvasser, cardiographer, cartographer, chef (five to 24 staff), chemist dispenser, chorister, chorus girl, clown, sports coach, coastguard, computer operator, skilled cook, police constable, advertising copywriter, travel courier, curate, cricketer, dancer, dental hygienist, private detective, dietician, driving examiner/instructor, estate agent (not chartered), fashion model, film projectionist, golfer, hospital houseman, book illustrator, disc jockey, juggler, domestic loss adjuster, magician, maitre d'hotel, masseur/masseuse, midwife, monk, nun, staff nurse, non-manual office worker, pawn-broker, plant breeder, RSPCA inspector, receptionist, secretary, telephone operator, sports umpire, youth worker.

C2: AA patrolman, self-employed antique dealer, boat builder, bus driver, shoemaker, bricklayer, carpenter, chimney sweep, bespoke tailoring cutter, deep-sea diver, dog handler, hairdresser, skilled electrician, fireman, thatcher, train driver, Rolls-Royce trained chauffeur, skilled miner.

D: au pair, bingo caller, dustman, bodyguard, bus conductor, chauffeur, croupier, dog breeder, lumberjack, unskilled miner, nursemaid and ratcatcher,

E: anyone brave enough to admit it.

Figure 3.4 Some examples from the Market Research Society's occupation groupings. *Source:* MRS (1990)

Sex

Changes in society brought about by the change in women's role has resulted in a number of marketing campaigns being directed at women (cigarettes, cars, hotels).

Income

Generally income provides a useful guide to the capacity to purchase goods, but other factors such as lifestyle, life cycle, cultural values will determine how it is spent.

Age

Age is a useful discriminator in many consumer markets.

Family life cycle

The idea of family life cycle is that as people progress through their lives their membership of the family and lifestyle will change. These changes will then have an effect on the economic character of the household as well as income and household expenditure. There are various models used (see Figure 3.5 and Figure 3.6).

The family life cycle (FLC) has been criticized because the changes taking place in society are not reflected in the basic FLC models. Women's roles have changed, there is also a high divorce rate and a large number of single parent families, many couples are childless and remain so, many marriages take place much later, if at all. The labour market has changed and many families have dual income earners, some are out of work, or retire early.

There is however a distinctive life time pattern to saving and spending. When we are in our twenties and thirties – getting married, buying houses, having children – we borrow and spend. When we are old and retired, we 'dissave' and spend. In middle age, therefore, we have to save to repay debts and build up capital for our old age.

Reading (1988)

Stages in the family life cycle	Buying patterns
1 Bachelor stage: young, single people living at home	Few financial commitments. Recreation and fashion orientated. Buy: cars, entertainment items, holidays
2 Newly married couples: young, no children	Better off financially than they are likely to be in the near future. High purchase rate of consumer desirables. Buy: cars, white goods, furniture
3 Full nest 1: youngest child under six	House buying is at a peak. Liquid assets are low. Dissatisfied with level of savings and financial position generally. Buy: medicines, toys, baby food, white goods
4 Full nest 2: youngest child six or over	Financial position is improving. A higher proportion of wives are working. Buy: wider variety of foods, bicycles, pianos
5 Full nest 3: older married couples with dependent children	Financial position is improving yet further. A greater proportion of wives work and some children get jobs. Increasing purchase of desirables. Buy: better furniture, unnecessary appliances and more luxury goods
6 Empty nest 1: older married couples, no children at home, head of household still in the workforce	Home ownership is at a peak. The financial situation has improved and savings have increased. Interested in travel, recreation and self-education. Not interested in new products. Buy: holidays, luxuries and home improvements
7 Empty nest 2: older married, no children living at home, head of household retired	Substantial reduction in income. Buy: medical products and appliances that aid health, sleep and digestion
8 Solitary survivor in the workforce	Income still high but may sell home.
9 Solitary survivor, retired	Same medical and product needs as group 7. Substantial cut in income. Need for attention and security.

Figure 3.5 The family life cycle and its implications for buying behaviour. *Source:* Adapted from Wells and Gubar (1966); Wilson and Gilligan with Pearson (1993), *Strategic Marketing Management,* Butterworth-Heinemann

The basic thesis of the SAGACITY grouping is that people have different aspirations and behaviour patterns as they go through their life cycle. Four main stages of life cycle are defined which are sub-divided by income and occupation groups:

1 Life cycle	Dependent		Pre-family		Family				Late			
2 Income					Better off		Worse off		Better off		Worse off	
3 Occupation	White	Blue	White	Blue	White	Blue	White	Blue	White	Blue	White	Blue
% of adults 1993[1]	7.1	6.2	5.6	5.0	11.7	10.1	2.3	7.3	10.2	7.3	9.5	17.6
% of adults 1994[1]	6.9	5.8	6.3	5.1	11.8	9.3	2.4	6.5	11.1	7.3	10.1	17.3

Definitions of life cycle stages

Dependent   –   Mainly under 24s, living at home or full-time student.
Pre-family   –   Under 35s, who have establshed their own household but have no children.
Family   –   Housewives and heads of household, under 65, with one or more children in the household.
Late   –   Includes all adults whose children have left home or who are over 35 and childless.

Definitions of occupation groups

White   –   Head of household is in the ABC1 occupation group.
Blue   –   Head of household is in the C2DE occupation group.

Notes: [1] Year January to December.
[2] Head of Household definition changed to Chief Income Earner in 1992.

Figure 3.6 The SAGACITY life cycle groupings. *Source:* RSL (Research Services Ltd) and NRS Ltd

You have now read through the section on life cycle. Which markets do you think you could usefully apply it to?

In what way could a portfolio of products for an insurance company be designed for consumers using life cycle segmentation as an approach?

Behaviour in the product field
This method is based on a series of behavioural measures including:

- Attitudes to the product/service – positive, indifferent, negative etc
- Knowledge – aware, unaware, interested, intending to buy
- Benefits sought – apply to product/service
- User status – non-user, ex-user, potential user, first time user, regular user
- Usage rate – light, medium, heavy
- Loyalty status – none, medium, strong, absolute,
- Purchase occasion – regular, special occasion, critical event
- Adoption process

A few of these are discussed in more detail, others are fairly self-evident.

Benefit segmentation
Marketers focus on selecting the major benefit on which the unique selling proposition (USP) can be based.

Marketers can however use more than one benefit to position a product/service (see positioning further down).

How would you segment the soft drinks market? Fill in the space below with some well-known brand names.

Sport drink/ice tea/nutrition drinks/functional drinks/fruit juices

- User status – non-users, ex-users, potential users, first-time users and regular users. First-time users and regular users can also be considered in terms of the rate of usage – heavy, medium, light. This segmentation variable can be used in formulating strategy. For example: a company with a high market share will focus on converting potential users into actual users. A company with a smaller or lower market share will often concentrate on persuading users of competitive brands to switch brands.
- Loyalty status can also be used to segment a market – hard-core loyals, soft-core loyals, shifting loyals and switchers. If consumers are very loyal to a product it is unlikely that they will switch.
- The adoption process could also be used to segment a market–innovators, early adopters, early majority, late majority, laggards (see Unit 14 for a detailed explanation).

The US fitness market can be broken into three market segments, comprising 50 per cent of US families:

Winners who recognize the need to get fit and equate it with their desire to achieve generally; **Dieters** who perceive fitness as a way of controlling their weight; and **Self-improvers** who perceive fitness as a necessary part of their sense of well-being.

These three segments can be easily targeted by marketers working in health services marketing, such as hospital marketing managers.

Source: 'Benefit segmentation of the fitness market, *Health Marketing Quarterly*, **9**, 1992.

Psychographic

What is psychographics?

Psychographics is not the same as demographic analysis as it tends to include qualitative data on motives, attitudes and values.

Although psychographics includes qualitative factors, like motivation, its findings are presented as quantified, statistical data in tabular format. It is different from motivation research as it relies on less intensive techniques like self-administered questionnaires and inventories (ordered listing or catalogue of items that assesses traits, opinions, beliefs, behaviours, etc.).

The technique of measuring lifestyles is known as psychographics. In the classification shown below the word psychographic has come to cover personality, lifestyle and various other systems of classification.

The term psychographic segmentation is given to the main way in which lifestyle analysis is carried out. It is commonly called AIO analysis and it focuses primarily on developing personality inventories based on attitudes when discussing:

- The relevant activities which are usually observable, measurable and objective and relate to how people spend their time: work, hobbies, social events, shopping habits, sports, entertainment, reading, holidays, club membership.
- Interests which imply all or some of the following: attention, curiosity, motivation, focus, concern, goal-directedness, awareness, worthiness and desire related to – topics, events, subjects, family, home, achievements, food, media, recreation, fashion, community.
- Opinions – where people stand on product related issues. It is a term used to describe something that is intellectually held and based on expectations, evaluations and interpretations about objects, events, people, social issues, or topics such as politics, business, education.

Activities, interests and opinions are different from beliefs where there is an emotional component, and from attitudes which can also be thought of as something internal.

Lifestyle

Lifestyle is the way in which a person tries to achieve their desired self-concept.

The term lifestyle was introduced to marketing in 1963 by William Lazer with the idea that a systematic relationship exists between consumption and lifestyles of a social group. It is important to remember that people in the same demographic group can have very different psychographic profiles.

Max Weber thought of lifestyle as a mark of status which enabled the person to be recognized as belonging to a group and helps them to become socially integrated.

Alfred Adler used the same term but thought of lifestyle as the way in which the individual adapts psychologically to society.

---

1   The uninvolved
Very low interest or involvement with car or with motoring. This group seldom tinkers with the car and does very few repairs; does a low mileage, has little technical ability, and gets little satisfaction from maintaining the car.

Likely to be older white collar; this group includes most women motorists. This group relies heavily on the garage and will follow the dealer's advice in the choice of motor oil.

2   The enthusiast
A high degree of interest and involvement with the car and with driving and working on it. This is almost the reverse of the uninvolved group. These people do many repairs, have high technical ability and obtain much satisfaction from maintenance. They have many accessories on their cars, enjoy talking about cars, and are interested in motor sport. Nearly all are male and an above-average proportion, about half, are working class. They have a high level of driving experience, and likely to own an older second-hand car.

Nearly all change and top up the oil themselves and have strong opinions about brands. Have a strong tendency to buy from non-garage outlets, especially motorist accessory shops.

3   The professionals
These are highly involved with driving and with the car, but only as a necessary part of the working life. Mainly use the car for business, do high mileage, but do little of the servicing or repairs themselves.

Likely to be male and white collar, driving relatively new car – often a company car.

4   The tinkerer
Through a combination of economic necessity and enthusiasm, are more involved in working on the car than in driving it. Much the reverse of the professional group, they get much satisfaction from maintenance work and tinkering, but although they do many repairs they have low mileage.

Tend to be male and working class, very often skilled. Car likely to be old, second-hand, used mainly for pleasure and driving to work.

They do most of the minor work on the car but may leave bigger jobs to the garage. Tend to top up and change oil themselves, but are brand-conscious.

5   The collector
An enthusiasm for collecting trading stamps is the distinguishing characteristic of this group, which tends to be normal in most other respects. They tend to be young and inexperienced.

Figure 3.7   The five types of motorist. *Source:* England, Grosse and Associates (1969). Margaret Crimp (1990), *The Marketing Research Process,* Prentice Hall

Lifestyle can therefore be looked at in two ways, either as a reflection of personality and motivation (inwardly driven), or a sign of social stereotyping (externally driven).

Lifestyle analysis starts with individual motivation using techniques of group discussion and depth interview, and then links it to groups of people. Once the groups have been defined the marketer is then able to decide on the group and create a stereotype at which the advertising message is to be targeted.

Social value groups
Social value groups are founded on shared values and beliefs but the members of each group also share distinct patterns of behaviour.

Examples of social value groups
The VALS System (SRI International)   The VALS system was developed in the USA by Arnold Mitchell of the Stanford Research Institute.

The VALS framework used the answers of 2713 respondents to 800 questions to classify the American public into nine value lifestyle groups. This framework shows that individuals pass through various stages of development, each of which influences attitudes, behaviour and psychological needs. They move from being driven by needs (survivors and sustainers) to an outwardly directed hierarchy (belongers, emulators and achievers) to an inner directed hierarchy (I-am-me, experientials, societally conscious).

These nine groups, together with estimates of the percentage of the US population within each group are:

1 Survivors who are generally disadvantaged and who tend to be depressed, withdrawn and despairing (4%).
2 Sustainers who are again disadvantaged but who are fighting hard to escape poverty (7%).
3 Belongers who tend to be conventional, nostalgic, conservative and generally reluctant to experiment with new products or ideas (33%).
4 Emulators who are status conscious, ambitious and upwardly mobile (10%).
5 Achievers who make things happen, and enjoy life (23%).
6 I-am-me who are self-engrossed, respond to whims and generally young (5%).
7 Experientials who want to experience a wide variety of what life can offer (7%).
8 Societally conscious people with a marked sense of social responsibility and who want to improve the condition of society (9%).
9 Integrateds who are psychologically fully mature and who combine the best elements of inner and outer directedness (2%).

The bottom group do not represent much of a market, and neither do the top group. The top group is important for setting trends and is growing. The needs-driven group is getting smaller. The middle group remain the main market for consumption and are staying the same.

Other models have been developed over the years from the insights offered by lifestyle analysis such as Young and Rubicam's 4Cs and Taylor Nelson's Monitor and Stanford Research Institute's life ways.

Monitor (Taylor Nelson) This typology has the following framework and is rather similar to VALS.

1 Sustenance-driven. Motivated by material security, they are sub-divided into:
   (a) aimless, who include young unemployed and elderly drifters and comprise 5% of the population;
   (b) survivors, traditionally-minded working class people who comprise 16% of the population;
   (c) belongers, these conservative family-oriented people form 18% of the population, but only half of them are sustenance driven.
2 Outer-directed. Those who are mainly motivated by the desire for status, they are divided into:
   (a) belongers
   (b) conspicuous consumers (19%)
3 Inner-directed. These are subdivided into:
   (a) social resisters who are caring and often doctrinaire (11%)
   (b) experimentalist, who are hedonistic and individualistic (14%)
   (c) self explorers, who are less doctrinaire than social resisters and less materialistic than experimentalist.

Young and Rubicam 4Cs
This is a Cross-Cultural Consumer Characterization based on the following framework:

1 the constrained:
   (a) the resigned poor
   (b) the struggling poor
2 the middle majority:
   (a) mainstreamers
   (b) aspirers
   (c) succeeders

3 the innovators:
  (a) the transitionals
  (b) reformers

The 4Cs define the individual and group motivations and needs. Young and Rubicam have used this to develop marketing and advertising campaigns both domestically and internationally. The British Gas 'Tell Sid' shares campaign and Legal and General's 'Umbrella Campaign' were based on this analysis.

The terms Yuppie (young upwardly mobile professional) and Bumps (borrowed-to-the-hilt, upwardly mobile professional show-off) have been used to illustrate a particular style of life.

The Stanford Research Institute's life ways cover the relationship between people and society and suggest that people fall into one of six groups. Kotler (1988) summarized them as follows:

- *Makers* Makers are those who make the system work. They are the leaders and up-and-comers. They are involved in worldly affairs, generally prosperous and ambitious. They are found in the professions and include the managers and proprietors of business.
- *Preservers* Preservers are people who are at ease with the familiar and are proud of tradition.
- *Takers* Takers take what they can from the system. They are attracted to bureaucracies and tenured posts.
- *Changers* Changers tend to be answer-havers; they commonly wish to change things to conform with their views. They are critics, protestors, radicals, advocates and complainers.
- *Seekers* Seekers are the ones who search for a better grasp, a deeper understanding, a richer experience, a universal view. They often originate and promulgate new ideas.
- *Escapers* Escapers have a drive to escape, to get away from it all. Escape takes many forms from dropping out, to addiction, to mental illness, to mysticism.

These life groups differ in many ways and need to be seen as market segments with specific material and symbolic needs.

Practical application of market research

You will remember that the market researcher is likely to approach the design of a segmentation study from one of two angles:

1 Consumer typology – clustering consumers.
2 Product differentiation – clustering products.

However, in practice many marketers face a situation where they do not have the information to do this in any depth and a general 'thumb nail' approach is shown to you below under method one. The second approach, where the objective is to cluster products, is shown to you under method two.

Method one – a thumb nail sketch clustering consumers

Sometimes students get the target marketing process confused with the marketing mix. So, in order to get these out of the way, first think about the product/service, the place (channels of distribution) and the price. Then think about the target marketing process and follow these steps:

Target marketing process

1 Market segmentation
  Using the segmentation systems explained to you above – geographic, geodemographic, demographic, behavioural and psychographic – think about dividing the market into distinct groups of buyers who might call for separate products or marketing mixes.
  Then see if any natural segments already exist. The most important ones will show you the basic structure of the market.

2 Market targeting

After the different ways in which a market can be segmented are identified the marketer develops different profiles of the market segments. These are then evaluated and a decision is made on which market segment/s to enter.

3 Market positioning

The third step is market positioning which involves deciding on the competitive position for the product/service.

4 Designing the marketing mix

After this has been carried out the marketing mix is designed – product, price, place and promotion.

Example:

Historic site publications

Product features: photography, illustration, map, postcards, writing style and design, quantity of information, size of publication, language

Price: a range – low, medium and high price

Place of purchase: on-site shop, off-site shops

Target marketing process

1 Market segmentation

Geographical: UK, Europe, USA, historic site

Demographic: family life cycle (child, adult, family), income, language group (home or visitor from abroad), school, class

Behavioural: purchase occasion – one-off purchase, could be a collector of a series

benefits sought – memento, record of history, entertainment, curriculum related activities

Psychographic: ? no information available

The main segmentation variable here in the UK would be for overseas or home visitor use. Segmentation on home visitor use would be life cycle and schools use. There would therefore be three primary segments – overseas visitors, home visitors and schools.

2 Market target

These will need to be assessed using the criteria explained to you above in market targeting – how to choose (a) usable market segment/s.

For example: this information could then be related to other information such as the number of visitors (with or without children), foreign language visitors, schools coming to a site and an estimate of the potential market and market segments made on the basis of an analysis of these figures and the target market/s chosen.

3 Product positioning (this is discussed in more detail below)

The product would be positioned on:

• price
• quality
• product features

4 Marketing mix

Once you have decided on your segments you will need to develop the appropriate marketing mix. You may decide to use:

• one marketing mix for the whole market (undifferentiated marketing strategy)

- a number of marketing mixes designed to meet the needs of each market segment (differentiated marketing strategy)
- choose a market segment that is your major market segment and allow the mix to filter through to the rest (concentrated marketing strategy)

To help you decide which method to use it is often helpful to lay out the following grid:

Home market – family life cycle

	Segment one Child	*Segment two* Adult	*Segment three* Family
Product	Illustration Stickers Postcards Poster	Photography Map	Illustration and photography Map Postcards Poster
Number of pages (rough guide)	12	30/100/200 (3 products)	30
Price	£1	£3/£10/£20	£2

Promotion

Sales promotion	possible trade deals
Public relations	press release only
Selling	sales visits to outlets

Place	on-site and immediate surrounds of site

Schools and foreign language publications developed separately.

Method two – product differentiation – clustering products

Here the focus would be on consumer use and perception of types of product or service and, more especially, brands.

In this method the marketer works backwards from the position the product occupies in the marketplace in relation to the competition. They would think about the sequence of variables which consumers may consider when they make a purchase. This information is then related to other geographic, geodemographic, demographic, behavioural and psychographic information.

This could be done by: creating a perceptual map on two (or more) dimensions; or creating a brand map by using attributes.

Creating a perceptual map on two dimensions

The thread that runs through all this is the need for the marketer to understand the structure of the market. This is most commonly done by focusing on three areas:

1 Develop a spatial map of consumers' perceptions of brands within a given market sector.
2 Identify how consumers see existing products/services in relation to this map and put the names of competitors' brands onto this map. You will then be able to use the map either to spot a gap or develop an ideal position for your brand.
3 From this map you will then be able to develop a model which will help you to predict consumer responses to new and modified products/services.

Example:

Here the wine market is positioned on two dimensions – type of drinker, and usage occasion.

                                Formal occasion

Harvey's Claret   Blue Nun
Mouton Cadet   Black Tower
Quality generics   Mateus
                                                       Lutomer

More experienced ─ ─ ─ ─ ─ ─ ─ ─ ─ ─ ─ ┼ ─ ─ ─ ─ ─ ─ ─ ─ ─ Less experienced
heavy drinkers   heavy drinkers

Own-label   Hirondelle
Cheap (Vin de Table)   Nicolas
generics   Don Cortez

                                Informal occasion

From this map the advertising agency, Abbott Mead Vickers, was able to examine the duplication of brand usage among wine drinkers and establish the degree of overlap between the different brands. By doing this, clusters of brands emerged according to usage and provided the agency strategist with an understanding of the market's structure, the existence of any gaps, the nature and intensity of the competition, and the type of marketing mix needed to establish or support a brand.

This sort of picture of the market can then be taken a step further by superimposing a second map illustrating in greater detail consumer profiles. This might typically include sex (male versus female), age (young/middle-aged, old), income group (high earners versus low earners), and marital status (married versus single).

Source: Wilson and Gilligan with Pearson (1993), *Strategic Marketing Management*,
        Butterworth-Heinemann

ACTIVITY 3.5

Think about the textbooks that you're using on this course and fill in the names of the publisher and titles of the books.

                        Academic approach
                          (facts only)

Low price ─ ─ ─ ─ ─ ─ ─ ─ ─ ─ ─ ─ ─ ┼ ─ ─ ─ ─ ─ ─ ─ ─ ─ ─ ─ High price

                        Practical approach
                   (facts and how to apply the facts)

Ask yourself: Are your needs being met? Is there a gap in the market?

Creating a brand map by using attributes

Another way of doing it is to list the attributes and put them into a hierarchy.

Example:

Initial perceptions of instant coffee brands

Expensive .... Cheap

Gold Blend	Nescafe	Red Mountain	Own label
Blend 37	Maxwell House		
The best instants	Popular	Cheaper	Cheap and nasty
Special	Everyday	Not as classy	Weak
Expensive	Reliable	Middle of the road	Bitter
When one has	The standard	Cheap and cheerful	Lack flavour
people around	Frequent use		
Christmas	Old favorites		
	Ordinary		

Source: Feldwick, (1990) p. 210

These perceptions led to qualitative research in which the perceptions of Red Mountain elicited the image and personality as being:

Outdoor, rugged, working class, eccentric, ordinary, scruffy, lumberjack, macho, farmer, normal, dull, boring, rough and ready, strange, untidy, basic.

From these findings the product was repositioned not to compete directly with Gold Blend but at the market occupied by Nescafe and Maxwell House. The brand proposition that was decided on was 'Ground coffee taste without the grind'.

Source: Advertising Works 5, Holt, Rinehart Winston, 1990.

Perceptual maps can be used to:

1 Establish the bases for segmentation.
2 Identify gaps in the market.
3 Identify which brands are perceived to be similar to your own brands.
4 Assess your strengths and weaknesses.
5 Reposition yourself in the marketplace.

Although these methods show the underlying process, the marketer will also have to decide between 'a priori' and 'post hoc' methods. Both methods have their place.

A priori methods   Segmenting in advance – for example where you know who is purchasing from you, it is then possible to tailor the marketing strategy to the needs and expectations of each group.

The examples of historic site publications, wine and coffee are a priori methods. Other a priori examples, using method one, are given to you in the worked answers.

Post hoc methods   Segmenting the market on the basis of research findings. Where the market is new, the marketer has no experience of it, or the market is changing or there are no natural segments, a more formal procedure is needed. Segmentation, targeting and positioning are based on information from the analysis.

The method is shown to you overleaf.

Seven steps in market segmentation, targeting and positioning

Market segmentation   1   At an individual level identify what the needs are through informal interviews and focus groups.

      2   Based on their needs profile, group the customers into homogeneous subgroups or segments.

      3   Based on these findings prepare a formal questionnaire that is administered to a sample of consumers to collect data on:

- attributes, and their rating
- brand awareness and brand ratings
- product usage patterns
- attitudes towards the product
- demographics, psychographics and mediagraphics

The needs-based subgroups will then be identified with *other characteristics* that will enable you to reach the segment with your promotional mix.

Market targeting   4   Cluster analysis (see Unit 6) will then allow you to create a number of different segments (internally homogeneous and externally different). The potential of each segment can be evaluated and the segment selected that will give you the greatest opportunity – this is your target market (see below how to choose a usable market segment).

      5   Choose which segment/s you will target.

Market positioning   6   The product/service will then need to be positioned within the selected segment/s.

      7   Develop the right marketing mix for each target segment.

Market targeting: how to choose a usable market segment/s

Ideally segmentation bases should allow us to reveal segments that have the following characteristics:

- *Measurable*   The segments should be measurable. In many markets it can be more difficult to do if there is a lack of specific published data.
- *Accessible*   The marketers should be able to reach the segments with promotion.
- *Substantial*   The segments revealed should be large enough to serve profitably. This decision is relative because what one organization may consider as being appropriate for them, another may not. Ford may not be interested in custom-built cars whereas a smaller company may be able to target this segment.
- *Stable*   Ideally it should be possible to predict how the segment will behave in the future and that it will exist long enough to warrant the time and cost of development.
- *Appropriate*   The segment should be chosen so that there is a fit between it and the organization's objectives and resources.
- *Unique*   The segment should be distinguishable from other market segments and show clear variations in market behaviour in comparison with other segments.

On what basis would you choose a market segment?

Positioning

- positioning refers to the way in which a product/service is defined by the consumer in their minds relative to that of the competition.
- positioning is carried out after market segmentation.
- the message should be distinctive and the customer should understand it as the basis for their buying decisions.
- positioning should take into account the position of a market leader, follower or challenger – followers should not position themselves too close to or directly against the market leader.

A smaller firm should be able to find its own customers and position in the marketplace.

Positioning strategies can be related to:

- the product attributes
- the benefits they offer
- the price
- the quality
- the application – extending cornflakes from a breakfast cereal to something that can be eaten all day
- the users – extending the eating of cornflakes to adults
- by product class – against another product class (margarine tastes like butter) or with another product class (soap that acts like a moisturizer)
- by competitor – against a competitor (products are compared with a competitor), or away from a competitor (we are not the same we are different)

Very often there is an overlap between the original market segmentation and the positioning, this can cause some confusion as the same ideas are repeated and one gets lost between thinking – is it segmentation I am doing or is it positioning?

Worked examples

Try doing these examples without looking at the answers below. You may or may not agree with the worked examples as they have not been done with any of the added benefits of research. Think about how you would extend or change what has been suggested to you. A question mark has been put in where there is not enough information available.

Remember

It is not always possible to fill all the information into the segmentation systems, either because not enough is known about the market, or the category does not apply.

- look for natural segments
- most marketers will segment a market in more than one way and use two or more demographic variables
- try and think of which method will be most suited to the particular product/service
- not all the ways in which a market can be segmented are covered in the classifications shown to you above, so use them as a guide
- segmentation is a creative exercise and must be related to the market with which you are dealing.

1 Clothes washing market.
2 Analgesic market.
3 Vitamin market.
4 Air travel.
5 Greeting cards.

First think about the product/service, the place (channels of distribution) and the price in order to get them out of the way so you do not get them confused with market segmentation. They can also be helpful when you consider market positioning and the marketing mix.

Target marketing process

1 Market segmentation
   Using the segmentation systems explained to you above (geographic, geodemographic, demographic, behavioural and psychographic) think about dividing the market into distinct groups of buyers who might call for separate products or marketing mixes.

2 Market target
   These will need to be assessed using the criteria explained to you above in market targeting – how to choose a usable market segment/s.

3 Market positioning
   Now think about the sequence of variables which consumers may consider when they make a purchase, how you think the product would be positioned within that market segment in relation to the competition.

4 Marketing mix
   The marketing mix would be designed on the basis of the above information.

Answers

Clothes washing market

Target marketing process

1 Market segmentation

Geographic:	US
Demographic:	age, male, female
Behavioural:	benefits and different mixes of benefits – extra action, hot, warm, cold water, enzyme, non-enzyme, concentrated, less suds, fabric softener, mild and gentle, with bleach, with special ingredients (proteins, borax, detergent to get out stains), scented, unscented, extra-scented, liquid/powder, concentrated/unconcentrated (based on Kotler) – can you think of any more?
Psychographic:	? no information available

2 Market positioning
   Market positioning would take place on one of these benefits.

Analgesic market

Product ingredients:	aspirin, paracetamol, codeine, etc.
Product features:	size of tablet, shape of tablet, colour of tablet, container size
Place of purchase:	chemist or general distribution
Price:	a range

Target marketing process

1 Market segmentation

Geographic:	UK
Demographic:	age of user, male, female
Behavioural:	purchase occasion: regular, special
	benefits sought: speed of treatment, safety, ease of swallow, frequency of dosage
	user status: non-user, ex-user, potential user, first-time user, regular
	loyalty status: none, medium, strong, absolute
	the usage: type of ailment (head, period, arthritis, cold, flu, hangover, migraine)
	the usage rate: light, medium, heavy
	usage time: morning, day, evening
Psychographic:	? no information available

The main segmentation variables would be the usage (type of ailment), benefits sought. Other demographic information related to this would be age of user and sex. This information should reveal the basic market structure.

2   Market positioning
    Market positioning would be done on using a selection/combination of these points:

    Product features
    Product ingredients
    Benefits sought
    Price
    Against a competitor

Vitamin market

Product ingredients: ?
Place of purchase: chemist, general distribution
Price: ?

Target marketing process

1   Market segmentation
    Geographic: UK
    Demographic: age
    Behavioural: needs/benefits related to each age group
    Psychographic: ? no information available

The main segmentation variables would be the needs/benefits related to each age group.

2   Market positioning
    Market positioning would be done on using a selection/combination of these points:

    Product features
    Benefits
    Price
    Quality

Air travel – air passenger market

Target marketing process

1   Market segmentation
    Geographic: international
    Demographic: age, occupation, male, female, cultural differences
    Behavioural: purchase occasion – journey purpose: business – corporate, independent, conference and incentive travel
      leisure – holiday, visiting friends and relatives
      length of journey – long haul, short haul
      benefits sought – excess baggage, schedule convenience, in-flight amenities, status recognition, safety, status of airline, type of aircraft, punctuality, flexibility
      usage rate – light, medium, heavy (frequent flyer)
      loyalty status – none, medium, strong, absolute (also relate this to country of origin loyalty)
      critical event – sudden illness, or emergency back home
    Psychographic: ? no information available

The main segmentation variable would be business or leisure. Further development of this would involve looking at all the other variables shown above. This should reveal distinct groups of buyers who might call for separate products or marketing mixes.

2   Market positioning
    The product would be positioned within those segments using a combination of these points.

> Product features
> Benefits
> Price
> Quality
> Against a competitor (better than)
> Against a product class (train, road, ship)

Greeting cards
Product features: humour, romantic, cartoon, classic artwork, photography, stickers, badges, electronic music and so on
Place of purchase: corner shop, greeting shop, garage, giftshop, etc.
Price: under £1, over £1 etc.

Target marketing process

1   Market segmentation
    Geographic: UK
    Demographic: age, class, sex
    Behavioural: type of occasion – Christmas, Easter, birth, birthday, Valentine, Mother's Day, bereavement, thank you, just to say hello, remember me, miss you, love you, and so on.
    Psychographic: ? no information available

    The major segmentation variables would be on the type of occasion and benefits sought. This would be related to other segmentation variables such as social class, age, sex, race.

2   Market positioning
    The product would be positioned within those segments using a combination of:

> Product attributes
> Price
> Quality

Now carry out the same exercise on your own organization.
Are there any gaps in the information available to you?
What can you do to acquire the information that you need?

1   You must be able to tell the difference between the overall process – target marketing – and the steps involved in carrying this out, which are – market segmentation, market targeting and market positioning.
2   The marketing mix (product, price, promotion, place, and in the case of services, people, process and physical evidence) is designed after this process has been carried out. Not before.

Segmenting industrial markets

Much of the work done on consumer market segmentation can be applied to industrial markets – such as usage rates, benefits sought, geographical location, etc. Other factors which would affect the buying situation would be: (some of these have been discussed in Unit 1).

1   Buying situation – new buy, modified rebuy or new task.
2   Type of product and the degree of standardization.
3   Significance of the purchase to the buying organization.
4   Degree of risk and uncertainty involved for the buying organization.
5   Source loyalty.

Another approach is to look at the major industrial market segmentation variables. A summary of these questions in declining order of importance is shown below.

Demographic

- *Industry* – on which industries that use this product should we concentrate?
- *Company* – on which size of company should we concentrate?
- *Location* – in which geographical areas should we concentrate our efforts?

Operating variables

- *Technology* – which customers' technologies are of greatest interest to us?
- *User status* – on which types of user (heavy, medium, light, non-user) should we concentrate?
- *Customer capabilities* – should we concentrate on customers with a broad or a narrow range of needs?

Purchasing approaches

- *Buying criteria* – should we concentrate on customers seeking quality, service or price?
- *Buying policies* – should we concentrate on companies that prefer leasing systems, systems purchases, or sealed bids?
- *Current relationships* – should we concentrate on existing or new customers?

Situational factors

- *Urgency* – should we concentrate on customers with sudden delivery needs?
- *Size of order* – should we concentrate on large or small orders?
- *Applications* – should we concentrate on general or specific applications of our product?

Personal characteristics

- *Loyalty* – should we concentrate on customers who exhibit high or low levels of loyalty?
- *Attitudes to risk* – should we concentrate on risk taking or risk avoiding customers?

From Bonoma and Shapiro (1983); Wilson and Gilligan with Pearson (1993), *Strategic Marketing Management*, Butterworth-Heinemann

Example

Market segmentation for Academic and Professional Library Supply

	Region					
	Europe	*UK*	*USA*	*Middle East*	*Asia*	*Aust/NZ*
Library Market						
State						
University Main						
University Faculty						
Commerce						
Public						
Science/Tech/ Medical						
Trade						
School						

SUMMARY

In this unit you have seen:

- How the whole objective of segmentation is to identify groups of people within the broader market who have needs which are broadly similar to each other and who respond in a similar way to the promotion methods and the rest of the marketing mix.
- How the concept of segmentation is related to consumer and industrial markets and is one of the main cornerstones of marketing.
- That the market researcher is likely to approach the design of a segmentation study in two ways – by collecting data in order to cluster consumers or by collecting data to cluster products.
- That the process of target marketing calls for four different steps:
  1 *Market segmentation* The first is market segmentation which calls for dividing a market into distinct groups of buyers who might call for separate products or marketing mixes.
  2 *Market targeting* After the different ways in which a market can be segmented are identified, the marketer develops different profiles of the market segments. These are then evaluated and a decision is made on which market segment/s to enter.
  3 *Market positioning* The third step is market positioning which involves deciding on the competitive position for the product/service.
  4 *Designing the marketing mix.*
- You have also considered the limitations of some of the methods that can be used.

Investigating customers

In this unit you will:

- Appreciate the role of marketing research in investigating customers' needs.
- Identify the different kinds of information an organization might use in identifying customers' needs.
- Gain an understanding of sources of data and the techniques used to get data.

By the end of this unit you will:

- Be able to appreciate the role of marketing research and its importance in decision making.
- Be able to identify what sort of information is needed.
- Know which research technique to use.
- Know where to go for information.

In this unit we consider the important role that marketing research plays in understanding customers' needs and their behaviour.

Organizations and their customers live within two environments, the macro environment and the micro environment. Both environments affect consumer behaviour and influence strategic decision making within an organization itself.

The marketer therefore needs to be able to:

- Identify the different kinds of information an organization might use in identifying customers' needs and behaviour.
- Understand the techniques that are available to them in order for them to get the necessary data.
- Know where to go for information.
- Apply similar techniques within the organization itself.

Unit 4 introduces you to the concept of marketing research, the use of secondary and primary data. Secondary data is covered in detail in Unit 5, primary data in Unit 6.

It should take you about two hours to work through this unit and you should allow two to three hours to undertake the various activities. The practical exercises will reinforce your learning and provide you with the necessary experience.

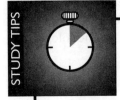

Organize your study material from the beginning of your course:

- Use file dividers to keep broad topic areas indexed and relevant materials and articles with the relevant notes.
- Look out for relevant articles and current examples, you will find these useful to illustrate examination answers.

The value of market research

The marketing concept is based on the notion that an organization can only be successful if there is a constant attempt to match its own capabilities to the needs of the customers. Market research provides information which can be used in making marketing decisions and should help to reduce the risk in decision making.

Market research is therefore an integral part of the marketing task. It provides the marketer with:

- information on what is happening in the marketplace
- the means of identifying marketing opportunities
- some understanding of the marketing processes
- data for the control of marketing programmes.

1 Think about your experience as a customer. Have you ever filled in a survey form, been asked for your opinions or talked directly to a producer? Give examples.
2 What complaints have you made about products/services you have bought or used? Give two examples. How could these have been avoided?

DEFINITION

Marketing research is the collection and analysis of data from a sample of individuals or organizations related to their characteristics, behaviour, attitudes, opinions or possessions. It includes all forms of research such as consumer and industrial survey, psychological investigations, observational and panel studies.

Market Research Society 1995.

The information that marketers need to make decisions comes from a variety of sources. It forms the basis of a marketing information system. A good marketing information system balances the information that managers would like to have against what they really need and what is feasible to offer.

Information always has a cost and generally the more accurate the information, the higher the cost. Most marketing research involves some form of trade-off between accuracy and cost.

Figure 4.1

Hint

Sometimes a distinction is drawn between marketing research and market research. Marketing research tends to cover the gathering, recording and analysing of all facts relating to the marketing process. It includes the use of secondary and primary data. Market research tends to refer specifically to primary research. Both terms are used interchangeably.

To avoid confusion the term market research will be used, and the difference between secondary and primary data will be used to distinguish between the two methodologies where appropriate.

The macro environment

Customers live within a 'macro environment' which the marketer is unable to control. The macro environment has an impact on the way customers behave and therefore needs to be monitored.

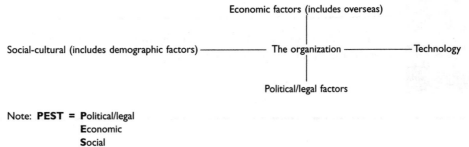

Note: **PEST** = Political/legal
Economic
Social
Technological

Figure 4.2

The PEST analysis forms the basis for understanding the opportunities and threats that an organization faces.

Political factors
These might include: political instability in eastern Europe, a decrease in the relative power of trade unions, the way in which government behaves towards business such as initiatives, restrictions, privatization and regulation, taxation, attitudes to import and export, relationships with the European Union.

Legal factors
These might include data protection, Sales of Goods Act, Law of Contract, Trade Descriptions Act, Consumer Credit Act, product liability legislation, Law of Agency, Environmental Protection Act, health and safety legislation, etc.

Economic
These might include general economic depression in the west, protectionism, lowering of trade barriers, etc. More of these factors are dealt with in detail in Unit 16.

Social-cultural and demographic factors
These might include growth in higher education, consumer rights, green issues, mobility of labour, unemployment, part-time working, the changing role of women. More of these factors are dealt with in Unit 16.

Technology
These might include robotechnology, biotechnology, computerization and the growth in home and business computing.

> Try to think of ways in which changes in the political/legal, economic, social and technological environment have affected the organization in which you work.

The micro environment
Marketers should not restrict their analysis to the macro environment, the micro environment needs to be studied as well.

```
                        Competitors
                            |
Suppliers ————— The organization ————— Marketing intermediaries ————— Customers
                            |
                         Publics
```

Figure 4.3

Try to think of ways in which changes in the micro environment have affected the organization in which you work.

Types of marketing decisions

The types of marketing questions which market research can help with answering include:

- What is the size of the market?
- What are the trends in the market?
- What is our market share?
- Who are our competitors?
  - their number, size, strengths, weaknesses, performance, future plans, products/ services, image, price, promotion, channels of distribution, etc.
- Who are our customers?
  - their number, characteristics, needs, wants, buying motives, buyers, users, influencers, time of purchase, purchasing behaviour, attitudes, socio-economic background.
- Are our customers satisfied with our product/service?
- What is happening in the distribution channel?
  - channel selection, distribution cost analysis, wholesaler/retail margins, incentive policy, dealer sales levels, distribution achievement, penetration levels, stock checks, inventory policy.
- How do we plan our selling?
  - sales areas, testing alternative selling techniques and messages, setting sales targets, evaluating sales performance, evaluating sales compensation systems, making selling operations more productive.
- Are we using the right promotional methods?
- What about our corporate identity and image?
- Are the people in our organization behaving in a way our customers expect them to behave?

Other studies include:

- Plant and warehouse location studies
- Acquisition studies: leads for mergers, joint ventures and acquisition
- Export and international
- Ecological impact
- Social values
- Suppliers and raw materials and so on.

Forms of marketing research

Marketing research falls into two main categories – continuous and ad hoc.

Ad hoc research

A specific problem has led to the need to acquire specific information.

Continuous research

Ongoing monitoring and basic data about the marketplace, the performance of the organization or products/services within it.

Both approaches are commonly used since they serve different corporate information needs.

Data

There are two types of data: secondary data and primary data.

Secondary data

Secondary data is any data originally collected for any purpose other than the current research objectives. It is called secondary research or desk research.

Secondary research

Secondary research is based on data that has been collected for some other purpose and for this reason it may not precisely meet the needs of the secondary user. However, it provides a good starting point and very often can help the marketer to formulate and generate ideas which can later be refined further by carrying out primary research. Secondary research should always be carried out first.

There are two types of secondary research: internal and external.

Internal research   Some information will already exist within the organization and forms the basis of an internal information system. The information is quick and relatively cheap to obtain. There are three approaches:

- data collected in the normal course of running an organization such as sales records, production records, distribution statistics, data on costs, etc.
- data acquired through personal contacts made by members of the staff at conferences, meetings, customer complaints and sales calls
- data acquired through past research projects and experience

What secondary internal data does your organization collect?

ACTIVITY 4.2

External research   Other information needs to be collected from outside the organization and simply needs tracking down. The use of external data is discussed in Unit 5 and covers the official sources of economic and business data.

What secondary external data does your organization collect?

ACTIVITY 4.3

Primary data

Primary data is information collected directly by an organization for a specific purpose. The process of collection is called primary research. The design of primary data collection is discussed in Unit 6.

What primary data does your organization collect?

ACTIVITY 4.4

Primary research

There are two kinds of primary research: 'off-the-peg' and 'made-to-measure' research.

'Off-the-peg' There are two types of 'off-the-peg' research:

1 *Syndicated research* – information that is collected for a number of organizations. The research is too expensive to carry out individually and is therefore collected by a research agency and shared.
2 *Omnibus* – the term omnibus research refers to research that is carried out on a defined population through a regular survey.

'Made-to-measure' The term made-to-measure refers to research that has been specially formulated and designed for a specific purpose and involves using some of the techniques outlined in Unit 6.

Primary research is sometimes called field research because it is concerned with getting information from the existing or intended operational field.

Academics tend to use the terms secondary and primary research. In practice however the organizations carrying out the research tend to be defined by the research techniques in which they specialize.

Types of primary data

Primary research is often categorized as being either 'qualitative' or 'quantitative'.

Qualitative data Information that gives the marketer insight and understanding of the consumer. The information cannot be manipulated to any great extent by statistical methods.

Quantitative data Research that produces statistics. In consumer research surveys this usually means several hundred respondents, and for very large surveys several thousand. This is covered in detail see Units 6 and 7.

Deciding the research method

The type of data that is produced depends not only on the research approach, but also on the method of collecting the data. Different methods produce different types of data. There are many ways of collecting data. The terms ad hoc, continuous, primary, secondary, qualitative and quantitative have already been used.

- What proportion of your marketing budget is spent on research? Find out how effective it is.
- How was the proportion determined? Is this the best way to go about it?
- What balance do you have between qualitative and quantitative studies?
- What balance do you have between ad hoc and continuous marketing research?

1 What is the difference between qualitative and quantitative research? Give examples.
2 Outline what is meant by the following terms: continuous and ad hoc research, secondary research and primary research. Give examples of each.

Understanding the market research process

The research brief is the most important part of marketing research.

Defining the problem correctly, asking the right questions and choosing the correct method is fundamental to any marketing research. The marketer needs to be able to turn a general problem into a specific question.

Example

Why are sales of product x declining fast?

The question why are sales of product x declining fast needs to be to be turned into:

- What is happening to the economy?
- What is happening in the market?
- What are the competition doing?
- What has happened to the distribution?
- How do housewives react to it as a product?
- How do they rate its effectiveness compared with competitors' products?
- How do the sales force see their selling aids?
- What is the affect of the coupons?
- Is the advertising effective?

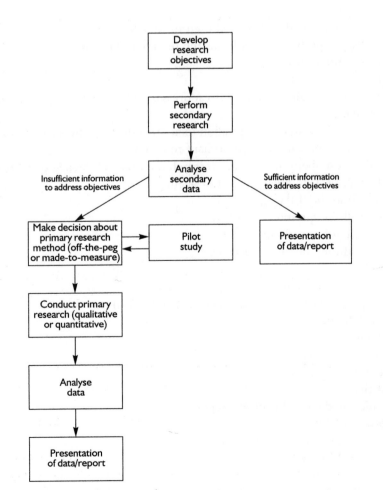

Figure 4.4 Primary and secondary research processs

These can be extended and refined even further.

A marketer may well have a feel for their market and may want to test this feel and go for a particular area, e.g. how do housewives react to it as a product? On the other hand they may feel that something is happening in the overall market that needs to be looked at in detail, e.g. has the fall in employment effected sales? Has a competitor entered the market? Does a 5p coupon really stimulate sales? etc.

The marketing research process follows the following steps.

1   Define the research objectives

What is the problem? Asking the right questions is fundamental to any marketing research. The marketer needs to be able to turn a general problem into a specific question.

Example

Why are sales of product x declining fast?

The question why are sales of product x declining fast needs to be to be turned into a specific question.

This can be done by:

1   Turning the problem into a specific question in order to decide which data are needed to solve it.
   - What effect is the economy having on consumer behaviour?
   - What is happening in the market?
   - What are the competition doing?
   - What has happened to the distribution?
   - How do housewives react to it as a product?
   - How do they rate its effectiveness compared with competitors' products?
   - How do the sales force see their selling aids?
   - What is the effect of the coupons?
   - Is the advertising effective?

   These can be extended and refined even further by:
2   Setting up an hypothesis which forms the research objectives.
3   Perform secondary research.
4   Analysing secondary data.
   - If there is enough information to address the objectives, write a report and present the data.
   - If there is not enough information to address the objectives a decision will need to be made about carrying out primary research.
5   Make a decision about the primary research method: off-the-peg or made-to-measure?
   - Who will provide the data? Self or agency?
   - How do we brief the agency?
   - How will the questions be asked?
   - Who will ask the questions?
   - How will the sample be specified?
6   Pilot study

   Carry out a pilot study.
7   Conduct primary research (qualitative or quantitative)
8   Collecting the data

   See Unit 7.
9   Analysing and interpreting the data

   What are the results?

   See Unit 7.
10   Presenting the data and writing a report

   Who will read it?

   What will happen to the answers?

   How should the report be written?
11   Using the research

   What will happen to the answers?

12 Feedback

    What can we learn from the exercise?

13 Time

    When is the research required?

14 Cost

    How much money can we spend? Executive time, fieldwork costs, analysis, tabulating and computing, phone, questionnaire printing, etc.

15 Accuracy

    How accurate does the information need to be?

Outline the process you would use in researching an organization that is in direct competition with your organization.

QUESTION 4.2

Criticism of marketing research

There are various criticisms of marketing research. These relate to the following:

- the limits of the methodologies used
- bad hypothesis formulation
- misuse of the results
- bad execution of the research itself
- consumers providing bad feedback.

The examiners expect you to be able to criticize market research methods and understand its limitations. These criticisms are developed in Units 5, 6, and 7.

EXAM HINT

1 Market research has been criticized for a number of reasons. Discuss.
2 What factors prevent the marketer from understanding customer needs so well that the product/service sells itself?

QUESTION 4.3

Speak to colleagues in class and at work to find out their experiences of market research. Were they positive or negative?

ACTIVITY 4.6

The Sunny Crouch research users' guide

The purpose of this guide is to provide an introduction to the various problems that marketers face. Each approach and data source is mentioned further on in the book.

Using research for market analysis

Problem 1
Where do our products/services stand in the market?
Should we enter a market?
Should we withdraw from a market?

Data requirements (market size and structure)

- How big is the market?
- How profitable is the market?
- Is the market growing or declining?
- What are the main products in the market?
- Who are the main producers in the market?
- Who are the major competing firms in the market?
- What is the distribution pattern?
- What marketing strategies are used in the market?

Data sources

- Secondary desk research: government and other published statistics, information services.
- Syndicated research services: if available for this market.
- Omnibus survey: to collect basic market data. Only possible for markets in which this service operates.

Problem 2
What different market segments exist and how do they differ?

Data requirements
Market characteristics

Data sources

- Secondary desk research.
- Syndicated research services.
- Omnibus survey: for basic data on market characteristics related to product attributes. Only possible if this service operates in the market.

Problem 3
What differing needs, motives, satisfactions could my product/service satisfy?

Data requirements
Characteristics and attitudes of users and potential users.

Data source
Made-to-measure: market segmentation study and psychographic market analysis.

Using research to develop new products and services

Problem 4
Generating ideas for possible new products or services.

Data requirements
New and creative ideas and suggestions.
Identify areas of unfilled customer need.
Brand mapping to identify possible market gaps (gap analysis).

Data sources

- Brain storming.
- Group discussions.
- Depth interviews.
- 'Made-to-measure' market survey: usage and attitude study.

Problem 5
Selecting the most promising ideas for further development.

Data requirements
Need to identify big, growing, profitable, not too competitive, relatively easy to enter markets, i.e., market size, structure, characteristics, trends, profitability, competitors, basic market facts.

Data sources

- *See* Using research for market analysis.
- Secondary desk research.
- Syndicated research services.
- Omnibus survey.

Problem 6
Identifying target market segments and appropriate appeals.

Data requirements
Reaction of different consumer groups to product appeals.
General consumer response and characteristics.
Identification of market segments.

Data sources

- Made-to-measure research surveys.
- Concept tests.
- Group discussions.
- Quantitative attitude survey using factor and cluster analysis.

Problem 7
Developing product attributes, design and formulation.

Data requirement
Consumer response to product attributes.
Data on product quality and attributes in use.
Product performance tests.
Comparative product performance.

Data sources

- Specialist research services for product testing.
- Made-to-measure research surveys for product testing
    - Test centres, hall tests, mobile vans, using monadic tests, or paired comparisons, blind testing.
    - In-home placement tests.
    - Test panels.

Problem 8
To test marketing plan.
To test different marketing strategies.
To predict market sales.

Data requirement
Consumer reactions to elements of marketing mix: product, price, promotion, people, process, physical evidence.
Rate of purchase of product (penetration level).
Pattern of repurchase of product.
Pattern of retail sales.
Consumer reactions to different marketing strategies.

Data sources
Research experiments using:

- Specialist research services for market testing.
- Consumer panels.
- Mobile shop/van purchasing panels.
- Matched area/town tests.
- Retail outlet test stores.
- Made-to-measure research surveys with users, buyers.

Using research to select brand names and pack designs

Problem 9
Which name to choose for a new product or service?

Data requirement
Is the name easy to pronounce?
Does the name carry any associations or expectations?
Does the name carry any, and/or appropriate, imagery?
Is the name easily recognized?
Is the name easily recalled?

Data sources

- Specialist research services.
- Made-to-measure research surveys, usually small scale, using pronunciation, name association, name imagery, recognition and recall tests.

Problem 10
Which pack and pack design to use for a product?

Data requirement
Does the pack 'stand out' in a display?
Is the pack easily recognized?
Is the pack easy to open, use and close if necessary?
Does the pack design communicate positive messages?

Data sources

- Specialist research services.
- Consumer surveys to measure: Attention value.
  Identification score.
- Test centres, hall tests or mobile van tests: for functional performance, e.g. ease of opening, understanding of pack instructions.

- In-home placement tests: for performance in normal use.
- Group discussions, depth interviews: for package concept association tests.
- Consumer survey using attitude rating scales for pack designs.
- Pseudo product-test: to uncover pack communication value.

Using research for pricing decisions

Problem 11
What price to charge for a new product or service?

Data requirement
What prices are competing products selling for?
What price would consumers expect to pay?
What price would consumers be prepared to pay?
What quantities are likely to be sold at different price levels?

Data sources

- Secondary desk research: recent market reports, or trade sources may provide information on the price structure.
- Observation research: a simple DIY exercise on price range and 'ruling prices'.
- Syndicated research services: retail audits provide price and quantity of sales in the markets they cover.
- Specialist research services: pricing is offered as a research specialism by some agencies.
- Made-to-measure research surveys: using 'buy-response' method, and/or 'propensity to purchase'.

Problem 12
What is the actual selling price for our products in retail outlets?
What is the actual selling price for competitive products in retail outlets?

Data requirement
Prices charged for our product in different retail outlets.
Prices charged for competitive products in different retail outlets.

Data sources

- Observation research: a simple but limited DIY exercise in local retail outlets.
- Syndicated research services: retail audit data for markets covered by this service.

Using research for decisions about advertising

Problem 13
Who should the advertising be aimed at?
What should the advertising be saying?
How much should we spend on advertising?

Data requirement
How big is the market/potential market?
What are the demographic characteristics of users/potential users?
What are the demographic profiles of different market segments?
What are the behaviour and attitudes of different market segments?
What language do consumers use in talking about the product field?
Are we underrepresented in particular market segments or geographic areas compared to our competitors?

Data sources

- Secondary desk research: especially market reports and trade press data
- Syndicated research services: e.g. MEAL.
- Omnibus research: for basic market data.
- Made-to-measure research surveys: group discussions, quantitative 'usage and attitude' surveys.

Problem 14

Which media should the advertisements go in?
How much space should be bought?
How much should we spend in the media?

Data requirement

How big are the media audiences?
What are the demographic characteristics of the media audiences?
Which media do our targets use?
How much do advertisements cost to place?
Which media do our competitors use?
How much are our competitors spending?

Data sources

- Secondary desk research: BRAD (British Rate and Data) or its international equivalent.
- Syndicated research services: BARB, JICMARS, JICRAR, TCA, Business Readership Survey.
- MEAL (Media Expenditure Analysis Ltd).

Problem 15

Which advertisement to use?

Data requirement

Consumer response to advertisement ideas/rough.
Do they understand the advertisement correctly?
Can they recognize it easily?
Can they remember it easily?
Do they like the advertisement?
Does it give positive associations and imagery to the product?
Does it make them want to buy the product?

Data sources

- Specialist research services: some advertisements specialize in advertisement testing.
- Made-to-measure research surveys: usually small scale qualititative research using recall tests, recognition tests, group discussions or depth interviews for comprehension, liking, positive associations and imagery.
- 'Hardware' techniques occasionally used for advertisement testing are eye-camera, tachiscope, psychogalvanometer area testing using quantitative techniques.

Problem 16

Were our advertisements seen?

Has the advertising worked?

Data requirement

Did the media chosen reach the target audience?

Did we get good value for our media expenditure?

Are more of our target audience aware of the brand name?

Can more of our target audience remember the brand name?

Does the target audience have more favorable attitudes toward the brand?

Do more of the target audience intend to buy the product?

Have more of the target audience used the product?

Data sources

- Syndicated research services: advertising measurement services; media measurement services.
- Omnibus research surveys: for advertising 'tracking' studies, repeated measurement of brand recognition and brand recall.
- Specialist research services: for measuring advertising effectiveness.
- Made-to-measure research surveys: measuring recall, recognition, attitude, pre- and post-advertising to detect shifts, coupon enquiry counts from keyed advertisements, sales enquiry counts post-advertising, point-of-purchase research to measure intent-to-buy, area testing.

The research users' guide. Sunny Crouch,
Market Research for Managers, Butterworth-Heinemann

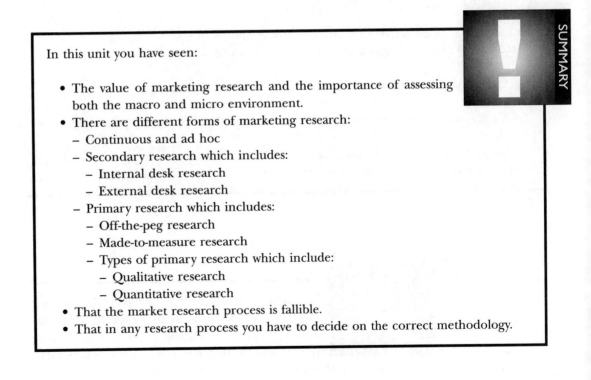

SUMMARY

In this unit you have seen:

- The value of marketing research and the importance of assessing both the macro and micro environment.
- There are different forms of marketing research:
  - Continuous and ad hoc
  - Secondary research which includes:
    - Internal desk research
    - External desk research
  - Primary research which includes:
    - Off-the-peg research
    - Made-to-measure research
    - Types of primary research which include:
      - Qualitative research
      - Quantitative research
- That the market research process is fallible.
- That in any research process you have to decide on the correct methodology.

Secondary data – official sources of economic and business data

This unit describes the different types of secondary research and the sources from which data is available. In this unit you will:

- Be introduced to the different sources of secondary data.
- Consider the advantages and disadvantages of using these sources.

By the end of this unit you will be able to:

- Understand the circumstances under which it would be appropriate to use the various sources of secondary data.
- Know where to go for certain data.
- Understand how to interpret secondary data.

Secondary research is the first stage of data gathering in any study. Finding a good, appropriate source of data can save much time and resources. There is nothing worse than embarking on a major research project only to find out – too late – that the data you have expended much effort collecting already exist elsewhere or could have been obtained less expensively from a third-party supplier

This unit examines secondary research and secondary data sources in detail. In conjunction with the previous unit and subsequent sections on Collecting Primary Data (Unit 6), Analysing Data and Presenting Data (Unit 7) this Unit will enable you to conduct high quality market research.

Organize your study materials from the beginning of your course:

- Use file dividers to keep broad topic areas indexed and relevant materials and articles with the relevant notes.
- Look out for relevant articles and current examples, you will find these useful to illustrate examination answers.

This unit will take you about one to two hours to read through and think about. The activities you have been asked to carry out will take you about two to three hours.

Secondary data is any data originally collected for any purpose other than the current research objectives. The process of collecting secondary data is termed secondary research or desk research simply because the person carrying it out can usually gather such data without leaving their desk!

The acquisition of secondary data is said to provide market intelligence, that is detailed information about the specific sector of the market under investigation.

Desk research

There are two forms of desk research: internal desk research, where data are gathered from your organization's own internal information systems, and external desk research, where data are gathered from elsewhere.

Internal desk research was covered in the previous unit. This unit explores those sources of data more generally available to organizations and individuals undertaking market research.

External desk research

Sources of secondary data can be placed into one of six categories:

- Government statistics.
- Popular media.
- Technical or specialist publications.
- On-line and electronic databases.
- Third party data.
- Casual research.

These are explained below.

Government statistics

In the UK most official statistics are provided by the Government Statistical Service (GSS). The two main organizations within the GSS, the Central Statistical Office (CSO) and the Office of Population Censuses and Surveys (OPCS), merged in 1996 to form the Office of National Statistics (ONS).

Although the GSS existed originally to serve the needs of government, it makes much of the data it collects widely available to businesses and the general public through the ONS. This data, and the analyses provided, are extremely useful sources for marketers.

The GSS publishes the *Guide to Official Statistics* listing all government sources of statistics. It is more than 500 pages long! The main publications are listed in the pamphlets *A Brief Guide to Sources* and the *ONS Publications Catalogue*.

Those interested in statistics for Northern Ireland should go to the Northern Ireland Statistics and Research Agency (NISRA) rather than the GSS.

Government statistical publications can be broadly divided into eight categories:

- Digests – that is collections of UK and regional statistics.
- The economy – statistics relating to the general economic indicators, financial and companies data, public sector, production industries, housing, construction and property industries and agriculture and fisheries.
- Defence – statistics covering forces personnel and defence expenditure.
- External trade – statistics covering overseas trade within Europe and outside Europe.
- Transport – statistics covering transport trends, road expenditure, road traffic figures, accidents and casualties, shipping passenger and freight information, and details of air traffic.
- Society – a large category covering the labour market, earnings, retail prices, taxation, standard of living, population and household statistics, family spending, education, home affairs, justice and law, health and safety and social security.
- Environment – statistics covering countryside, land use and planning decisions.
- Distribution and other services – statistics covering retailing, wholesaling, motor trade, catering and allied, and service trades.
- Overseas – statistics covering overseas aid and comparisons of European regions.

Altogether, the Government regularly publishes over 300 statistical sources in these areas. All are available from either The Stationery Office or direct from the ONS. Included among these are many regular surveys. Those of particular interest to marketers include:

- Social Trends – brings together key social and demographic series.
- UK Markets – Manufacturers' product sales data together with corresponding trade data, and derived net supply to UK market. Includes price and volume of sales.
- New Earnings Survey – earnings of employees by industry, occupation, region, etc.
- Retail Prices Index (Business Monitor MM23) – measures the average change from month to month in the prices of selected goods and services. Gives historical data from 1963.
- Population Trends – includes a broad range of family statistics (births, marriage, divorce), mortality and morbidity (deaths from various illnesses), electoral statistics and other population data.
- Family Expenditure Survey – income and expenditure by type of household.
- General Household Survey – covers five core topics: education, employment, health, housing and population/family information. Periodically covers other areas such as leisure, smoking and drinking habits.

Many Government statistics are also in electronic format, some of which are described later in this Unit.

Using government statistics

The chief advantage of government statistics is that they cover the complete United Kingdom. The disadvantage is that they cannot give tailor-made answers to a specific problem. The following list indicates some example marketing uses for these statistics:

- Using the UK market reports you can compare your own performance against general trends.
- Those involved in consumer products can gain valuable information on trends in expenditure from the Family Expenditure Survey.
- For test marketing, information from the Population Trends and General Household Survey can provide regional data on consumers.
- General trends in retail prices can be obtained from monitoring the Retail Price Index.

It would take a book a least the size of this to explain all of the published government statistics and their uses. However, it is useful to understand the derivation of some of the more commonly used statistics. Perhaps the most quoted single statistic of use to marketers is the Retail Price Index (or RPI).

The Retail Price Index (RPI)

The RPI is a single figure which tries to measure the change in prices of a 'basket' of products and services over a period of time. What constitutes this RPI 'basket' of goods and services is under constant review. A substantial, and controversial, change in content happended in 1996. It is presented as a percentage and is compared with a base year which is periodically revised. The current base year is January 1987. The current RPI therefore measures prices as a percentage of the prices that one would have paid in January 1987.

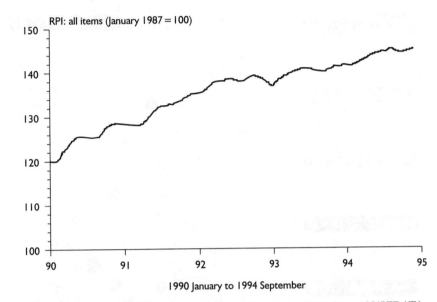

Figure 5.1 Retail Price Index (RPI) January 1990 to September 1994. *Source:* NAVIDATA sample dataset C1: Retail price index and Tax and price index

Popular media

Much information can be gained from keeping an eye on the popular media. Much of this information is not going to be numerical, but may provide leads to previously undiscovered sources of data. The main sources are:

- *Newspapers* – The broadsheet newspapers can provide much useful information. Occasionally, these papers contain regional or national supplements which are especially useful for marketers operating in these specific areas. For financial and business information, try the *Financial Times* or *Wall Street Journal*. For social information, try the *Guardian*. For information on Europe, try the *European*. Local papers can also be a good source of regional business information.
- *Magazines* – There are popular magazines on most subjects covering most business and leisure interests. If you are interested in learning about developments in yachting, for instance, you have a choice in the UK of *Practical Boat Owner, Yachting Monthly* and *Yachting World* plus several others. Business interests are perhaps most comprehensively covered by *The Economist*, and US titles such as *Business Week, Forbes* and *Fortune*.
- *Radio and television* – Current affairs, consumer programmes and news broadcasts are all potentially good sources of information.

Figure 5.2 shows some information gleaned from the *Financial Times* concerning regional house prices. This information might be extremely useful for anyone involved in the construction or allied trades and is of general use to marketers as an economic indicator. Note that the source is shown as the Halifax Building Society. It might be possible to get further information by contacting them.

Technical or specialist publications

For in-depth information about a particular field, a visit to a library or bookshop can provide technical and specialist data. The main sources are:

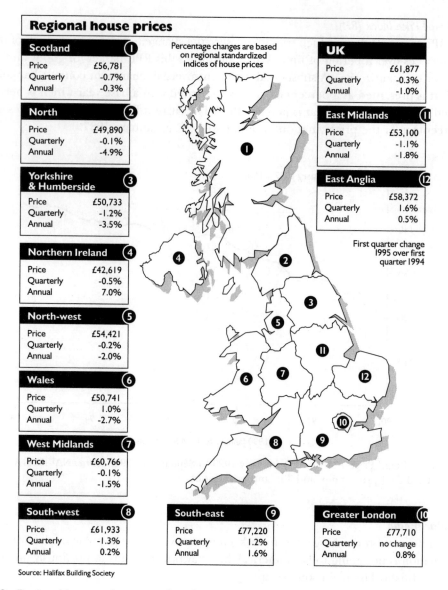

Regional house prices

Scotland	①
Price	£56,781
Quarterly	-0.7%
Annual	-0.3%

North	②
Price	£49,890
Quarterly	-0.1%
Annual	-4.9%

Yorkshire & Humberside	③
Price	£50,733
Quarterly	-1.2%
Annual	-3.5%

Northern Ireland	④
Price	£42,619
Quarterly	-0.5%
Annual	7.0%

North-west	⑤
Price	£54,421
Quarterly	-0.2%
Annual	-2.0%

Wales	⑥
Price	£50,741
Quarterly	1.0%
Annual	-2.7%

West Midlands	⑦
Price	£60,766
Quarterly	-0.1%
Annual	-1.5%

South-west	⑧
Price	£61,933
Quarterly	-1.3%
Annual	0.2%

South-east	⑨
Price	£77,220
Quarterly	1.2%
Annual	1.6%

Greater London	⑩
Price	£77,710
Quarterly	no change
Annual	0.8%

Percentage changes are based on regional standardized indices of house prices

UK	
Price	£61,877
Quarterly	-0.3%
Annual	-1.0%

East Midlands	⑪
Price	£53,100
Quarterly	-1.1%
Annual	-1.8%

East Anglia	⑫
Price	£58,372
Quarterly	1.6%
Annual	0.5%

First quarter change 1995 over first quarter 1994

Source: Halifax Building Society

Figure 5.2 Regional house prices: secondary data from the *Financial Times*

- Market research and academic periodicals – such as the *Harvard Business Review, Journal of the Market Research Society,* the *Journal of Marketing* and *Journal of Consumer Research.*
- Trade journals – such as *Campaign, Computer Weekly, The Grocer* and so on.
- Specialist books.

The disadvantage of such publications is that they may be out of date by the time they get printed.

Obtain a copy of one of the research journals mentioned above. What useful information does it contain? How might this information be used by marketers in certain market sectors?

Third party data services

Many market research companies sell data as a major part of the services they offer. Typically, such data comes from consumer panels. Panels exist which monitor a wide variety of purchases, opinions and activities by gathering data from a group of representative consumers. Such data is collected either continuously or at fixed, regular intervals so that trends can be determined and/or special analyses performed at the request of the data purchaser.

Data is collected either by personal visit, postal questionnaire, telephone or, increasingly, electronic means. One example of a particularly hi-tech consumer panel is 'Superpanel' run by Taylor Nelson AGB, the largest UK consumer panel. Superpanel monitors consumer purchases in 8,500 homes. Each house is equipped with a hand-held barcode reader which provides full details of items purchased and brought into the home. Details of the items purchased are retrieved over the telephone system each night making the information available to the data purchaser the next day. This rapid turn-around of data is essential for those monitoring the effects of special offers, targeted advertising and general economic factors.

A competitor to Superpanel is 'Homescan', run by Nielsen, which works in a similar fashion. Figure 5.3 is an excerpt from a typical Homescan analysis that might be provided to a data purchaser interested in the performance of their brand (in this case Brand B).

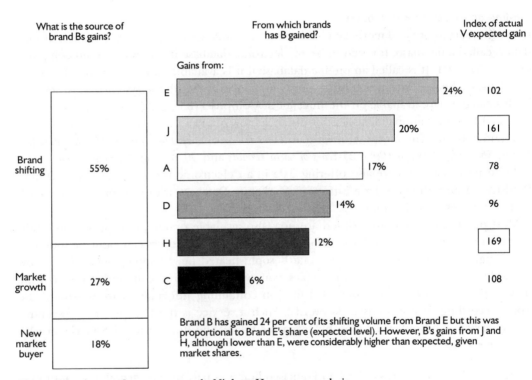

Figure 5.3   A page from an example Nielsen Homescan analysis

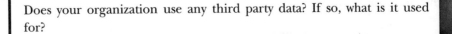

Does your organization use any third party data? If so, what is it used for?

Casual research

Much information can be gained by casual research. As its name suggests, this is not formal research nor strictly primary data collection, but occurs 'naturally' in the course of carrying out one's work as a marketer. There are numerous sources of information available to the 'casual researcher', some of these are listed below:

- *Conferences and fairs* – these will often highlight previously unknown sources of data and may provide valuable information on competitive products and services via literature or direct contact.
- *Contacts* – friends and associates in the marketing business and other business sectors of interest can provide valuable information.
- *Special interest groups* – most societies and associations, such as the Market Research Society, have special interest groups (or SIGs) which can provide a valuable source of information.

ACTIVITY 5.3

How did you first find out about the marketing course you are now enlisted on? What research did you carry out and how would you classify it?

On-line and electronic databases

In recent years, more and more data has become available via computer. A collection of such data is called a database. It is said to be an electronic database if it is available on computer disk or CD-ROM. It is called an on-line database if it is available 'live', usually via a modem (a relatively cheap device which links your computer into the phone system). Most services in this category are available on the Internet or Compuserve.

The Office for National Statistics, for instance, now offers a range of publications on CD-rom and diskette. The most useful for marketers are probably *The Guide to Official Statistics*, *Family Spending (1989 to 1995)*, *25 Years of Social Trends* and *30 Years of Regional Trends*.

Third party suppliers are also offering data in an electronic form. For example, Dun & Bradstreet International offer a European Marketing Database with information on over 3 million businesses in 17 countries!

Most publications that are printed are now also available on-line: newspapers, journals, magazines and so on. In this form, information about specific topics can easily be found by searching for 'keywords'. For instance, fairly sophisticated news clipping services are now available whereby you choose the topics you want to read about and an electronic 'newspaper' is automatically assembled for you containing information from around the world according to your chosen 'keywords'. Such a service is the CompuServe 'Executive News Service'. CompuServe's monthly magazine relates the story of one US marketer who uses the service:

Steven Zahm, who works in his San Francisco home as part of the 'virtual' corporation Prophet Market Research, doesn't own a television. Instead he reads two national newspapers and on-line business and news-wire articles to create what he calls a 'macro and micro news filter'. Without TV, he happily misses 'fluff stories' such as traffic reports and tallies of metropolitan crime. 'I get news of the macro – international crises, national policy changes, social trends' he says 'and the micro – what's the coffee of the week in the shop down the street, or which new movie is in my neighbourhood.'

(*CompuServe Magazine*, November 1994).

For those with access to a suitable computer, the advantages of on-line and electronic data outweigh all other secondary sources:

- *On-line data is immediate and therefore up to date* – financial prices, for instance, are often transmitted instantaneously.
- *Information is global* – data is available from much of the world in many languages.

- *Open all hours* – on-line services never close at night or for lunch.
- *Data can be used directly* – many statistical and spreadsheet computer packages are capable of loading on-line and electronic data for further analysis or presentation.
- *Searching on-line and electronic data is quick and easy* – within a matter of seconds it is possible to search the equivalent of more than 1,000 conventional publications. This is sometimes cited as a disadvantage. A search on an ambiguous keyword, 'culture' for instance, may return articles covering everything from 'bacterial culture' to the 1980s pop group 'Culture Club'.
- *Convenience* – most places of work now have a computer capable of reading electronic data or obtaining data on-line. With such a facility, trips to the library and other data suppliers are greatly reduced, saving time and resources.

Most libraries now have some form of electronic database – usually for finding books or technical papers on certain subjects. Next time you visit a library, or if you are lucky enough to have access to an on-line system, try a search on the database using the keyword 'marketing'.

Does this provide you with useful information?

Is there any information which is found that is irrelevant?

ACTIVITY 5.4

Competitive market intelligence

This is the general name given to data collected about your competitors. The information can be obtained in any one of the ways described above. Additional sources can include:

- *Competitive bench-marking* – where your product or service is compared with that of your competitors.
- *Company accounts* – these are lodged annually in Companies House in London and can provide information on the financial performance of your rivals.
- *Patent applications* – these can provide a useful source of information about corporate technology developments.
- *Job advertisements* – these can provide useful information on the skills required by a competitor organization and their growth rate. However, it is not unknown for fake ads to be placed to allay fears about a struggling company!

It is most important to keep a 'watching brief' on the activities of your competitors so that you can spot opportunities, learn from their mistakes and not get caught out by new developments in the marketplace.

What market intelligence does your company have about its competitors? Do you think it has enough information? How might you find out more?

ACTIVITY 5.5

General guidelines for gathering secondary data (adapted from **ONS** publication *Statistics for Students*)

1 Don't rush – allow yourself ample time for your research. Remember that some sources may have to be ordered.
2 Choose carefully – try to gather only data which is relevant. Having too much data is as bad as having too little.
3 Look before you leap – do not assume that data is available on everything. Data may be classified, otherwise unobtainable or simply does not exist.

4 Limit your time – is is easy to get bogged-down and side-tracked when researching data. Plan your project carefully and stick to a timetable.
5 Don't panic – if you get stuck help is usually available from either your lecturer or the publishers and suppliers of the data sources.

Limitations of secondary data

There are a number of general points to be aware of when using secondary data:

- *Age of data* – some secondary data is offered for general sale only when it is of no more use to the leaders in the field. Historical data can be of use but only for certain types of research.
- *Survey method used* – not all surveys are well designed or administered. You should be aware of the survey details (for instance number of respondees, geographical sampling and so on) so that you can be confident that the data is reliable and representative for your purposes.
- *Original purpose of data* – the data may well have been collected by an organization with a particular viewpoint which may have led to bias in the collection method used. For example, surveys by the pro-smoking lobby always seem to find no link between smoking and disease!

Despite these limitations, secondary research is still a vital and valuable first step in any research activity. In many cases, it may be all the research that is needed.

Useful contacts

The Stationery Office: book sales, 0171 873 9090; electronic sales, 0171 873 8732; book enquiries, 0171 873 0011; electronic enquiries, 01603 695766; free catalogues and leaflets (electronic and book titles), 01603 695907. Internet address: http://www.the-stationery-office.co.uk/

Office for National Statistics: Sales 0171 533 5678; enquiries, 0171 533 6363. Internet address: http://www.ons.gov.uk/

Cut out and keep any graphs or data tables you find in magazines or newspapers. Look at the 'source' quoted for the data. Make a note of the type of data presented (social, financial, political and so on) and relate this to the source. Is the source private or government? Are the source specialists in this sort of data gathering, or not? If you wanted to find out details about the data not contained in the article concerned, how would you contact the source?

In this unit you have learned about:

- The various sources of secondary data.
- The range of government statistics available and what they can be used for.
- The Retail Prices Index (RPI).
- The use of popular media, technical or specialist publications, third party data services, casual research and on-line and electronic databases.
- Market intelligence and the various sources of competitor information.
- The limitations of secondary data.

Primary data – methods of collection, sampling methods, survey methods and questionnaire design

This unit describes the different methods of primary data collection introduced in Unit 4. In this unit you will:

- Be introduced to the different methodologies and tools used in the collection of primary data.
- Consider the advantages and disadvantages of these methods.

By the end of this unit you will be able to:

- Understand the circumstances under which it would be appropriate to use the various methods and tools for primary data collection.
- Design your own market research.
- Appraise the way in which data has been collected by others.

Collecting data is time-consuming and costly. It should not be embarked upon unless:

1 You have a clear idea of what issues or questions you are addressing.
2 You are confident that the research method you are using is unbiased and experimentally sound.
3 The data gathering tools you are using are both reliable and valid.
4 The data you collect will be sufficient to draw conclusions and make recommendations.

This unit addresses these issues in detail. In conjunction with Units 5 and 7, the material in this unit will enable you to design and interpret your own basic market research.

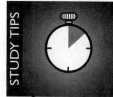

Qualitative and quantitative research

As has been discussed in Unit 4, primary research is either quantitative (it deals mostly with numerical information) or qualitative (dealing with less tangible data such as interview responses, individual opinions and the outcome of group discussions).

Of course, rarely is a particular piece of research either entirely qualitative or quantitative. It may be, for instance, that you conclude a quantitative questionnaire with an open-ended question seeking further comment. The responses to this would be qualitative in nature.

Also it is possible to 'code' qualitative responses to make them appear quantitative. For example, if you were interviewing a person about a product and, in the course of the interview, they said that they very much liked the packaging you might later rate their opinion by giving it a coding of '3'. If other people were interviewed who said that they disliked the packaging you might give them a coding of '1'. People who were undecided about the packaging might receive a coding of '2'. Thus a crude quantitative scale can be built up from qualitative data.

Qualitative research

There are three basic ways of collecting primary data in qualitative research:

- Depth interviews.
- Focus/discussion groups.
- Projective techniques.

These will now be discussed.

Depth interviews

A depth interview is an unstructured discussion between interviewer and respondent. They are generally lengthy (anything up to one hour) and are best carried out by trained, experienced interviewers.

The the aim is to secure the maximum amount of useful information from the respondent on a particular topic with minimum intervention from the interviewer. The role of the interviewer is therefore to:

- obtain detailed information on the topic(s) needed within the time available
- balance the need for open-ended discussion with the need to address certain topics
- avoid biasing the respondent by appearing to favour certain responses or asking leading questions

The interview is best recorded on audio tape. Transcripts are prepared from the tape, studied for ideas, useful comments and subjective opinions on the topic under investigation.

The respondents need to be chosen with care. Some people are not as good at expressing themselves verbally as others. It may be that respondents are chosen from those taking part in a larger study as a result of their 'extreme' opinions, particular knowledge or responsibilities within an organization.

Depth interviews are particularly useful during the early stages of a product/brand development when little has been decided and/or new ideas are required.

Focus groups

Focus groups are similar to depth interviews, the main difference being that the discussion is not one-on-one but involves a group of seven to ten respondents. The main effect of this is that the group forms it's own identity, much of the discussion is amongst its members. Under these circumstances the researcher facilitates the working of the group rather than actually interviewing its individual members. These groups are sometimes called discussion groups and the researcher leading the group the facilitator or moderator.

As with depth interviews, the role of the facilitator is to focus discussion on the research topic, directing the group where required but limiting their involvement as much as possible. Certain management of the group is also required:

- the discussion needs to be set in motion
- track must be kept of the progress of the discussion (time-keeping etc.)
- the involvement of all members must be ensured (some people are shy in groups, yet their knowledge or opinions may be just as valuable)
- the discussion needs to be brought to a close in a tidy manner.
- names and other details of the group members need to be gathered (this may be achieved with a small questionnaire which, of course, must be designed and produced)
- arrangements for follow-up discussion may also need to be arranged and communicated
- the practicalities of recording the discussion must be handled (this may involve the use of a flipchart, tape recorder or video tape)

Focus group members are often chosen to reflect a cross-section of the intended target customers for the product/brand under discussion. In this way, more debate is assured.

Focus groups are popular amongst marketers because:

- they allow qualitative information from many individuals to be collected in a short period of time
- they provide a good forum for 'testing the water' with new products/brands
- the group setting is 'emotionally-charged' in a way that a one-to-one interview can never be
- they are useful for generating new ideas and, under certain circumstances, problem-solving (suitable techniques are 'brainstorming' and 'synectics').

An advertising executive named Alex Osborn was the first to advocate brainstorming as a technique to devise new or creative solutions to difficult problems. His rules for brainstorming are reproduced below:

1 Given a problem to solve, all group members are encouraged to express whatever solutions and ideas come to mind, regardless of how preposterous or impractical they may seem.
2 All reactions are recorded.
3 No suggestion or solution can be evaluated until all ideas have been expressed. Ideally participants should be led to believe that no suggestions will be evaluated at the brainstorming sessions.
4 The elaboration of one person's ideas by another is encouraged.

Osborn, A. F. (1957) *Applied Imagination*, New York: Scribner

With synectics the aim is to focus on producing creative solutions and, to enhance the creative potential of the group, members are usually pre-selected on the basis of their creative abilities and may be recruited from a wide range of disciplines unrelated to the topic under discussion. The problems set before synectics groups are usually of a more complex or technical nature.

ACTIVITY 6.1

The year is 1995. You are tasked with finding a new name for a special brew of beer. The beer is to be produced in limited edition to celebrate the 80th birthday of the brewery owner, fondly known as 'The Colonel'. The following information is available about him:

- He is well-known and respected in the brewing industry.
- He has a 'handle-bar' moustache.
- He likes horses (his hobby).
- He was a military man and served in a mounted division.

The following is known about the brewery:

- The popular brews it produces are named with an 'academic' theme.
- The company is well-known nationally but with a strong local image.

Working in a group, set aside 15–20 minutes to try and brainstorm a name for the limited edition brew. Appoint a facilitator who writes down suggestions on a blackboard or flipchart. At the end of the allotted time, take your best three suggestions then, as a group, spend 5–10 minutes deciding on your preferred, final, name. For each of the three alternatives, give their advantages and disadvantages.

Projective techniques

This set of techniques is based on those used by clinical psychologists to understand a person's 'hidden' attitudes, motivations and feelings. In a marketing context, these techniques are used to elicit associations with a particular product or brand. Many psychological techniques have been successfully used for this purpose. They include:

- *Word association* – respondents are presented with a series of words or phrases and asked to say the first word that comes into their head. This is often used to check whether proposed product names have undesirable associations, particularly in different cultures and languages. You might not wish, for instance, to call a new life insurance policy 'Wish' if it turned out to be associated in many people's minds with 'death' (death wish), although you might if it brought to mind a 'wishing well'.

ACTIVITY 6.2

Word association

What is the first word or phrase you associate with each of the following:

Insurance . . . .

Ice cream . . . .

Computer . . . .

Mineral water . . . .

Psychology . . . .

Compare your responses with those of your classmates. Are any of your responses the same? Why do you think that is?

- *Sentence completion* – the beginning of a sentence is read out and the respondent asked to complete it with the first words that come to mind. To probe the ideas which are important to people in selecting an insurance policy you might provide the sentence: 'The kind of people that do without holiday insurance are . . .'

ACTIVITY 6.3

Sentence completion

Working on your own, complete the following sentences:

People who don't own cars are . . . .

Women who dye their hair are . . . .

Couples who go on holiday to Spain are . . . .

Now compare your answers with those of your classmates. Are your answers similar or different? What information does this technique provide?

- *Third-person technique* – Respondents are asked to describe a third person about whom they have little information. This technique was used by Mason Haire when instant coffee was first introduced in 1950. Two groups of housewives were given a shopping list to examine. The list given to each group was identical except that one contained instant coffee, the other ground coffee. The housewives perceived the writer of the list that contained instant coffee as 'lazy' and 'poor' whereas they perceived the writer of the list that contained ground coffee as being 'thrifty' and generally a 'good' homemaker. This research demonstrated the negative attitudes associated with convenience foods in the 1950s. A later replication of this study in 1970, when instant coffee was more widely accepted, no longer found these negative associations.

ACTIVITY 6.4

Third person technique

The picture is of a man called Dave Rodwell. He is a lecturer at the Oxford College of Further Education. He teaches 'consumer behaviour' on the CIM Marketing courses run at the college.

Without discussing your thoughts, or your answers, with your classmates please answer the following questions. Do not worry if you feel you cannot answer all the questions.

Q1: What sort of car do you think he drives?

Q2: What political party do you think he supports?

Q3: How old do you think he is?

Q4: What do you think is his favourite sport?

Q5: Which country do you think he was born in?

Q6: What do you think his father's job was/is?

Q7: What do you think is his favourite colour?

Q8: What sort of place do you think he lives in?

Q9: What pets do you think he has?

Q10: What newspaper do you think he regularly reads?

Once you have answered as many questions as you can, compare your responses with those of your classmates. Are there any similarities? Why do you think that is?

- *Thematic Apperception Test (TAT)* – respondents are asked to interpret an ambiguous picture or drawing or fill in a blank 'speech bubble' associated with a particular character in an ambiguous situation. A television recruitment advertisement for the UK police force showed a black man in casual clothes running followed by a white policeman running. The footage was presented in an ambiguous way (was the policeman chasing the man? or were they both chasing a third party?) to highlight the problem of racial stereotyping and the need for a multiracial police force. The advert was part of a campaign to increase the number of non-white police.

ACTIVITY 6.5

Thematic Apperception Test (TAT)

In not less than 50 words, describe this picture. Also, what might the woman be saying?

Now list the 'themes' in your response (what is happening, who is speaking, what they are saying etc.). Compare your themes with those of your classmates. What information could this technique provide?

- *Reperatory Grid (Rep Grid)* – a modification of the method first developed by Kelly in 1955 to support his theory of personality, the Rep Grid is useful as a projective technique in many marketing situations. Respondents are presented with a grid and asked to title the columns with brand names or types of a particular product (i.e. flavours of ice cream, types of car). They are then asked to take three of these products and think of a phrase which describes the way in which any two are different from the third. For instance, a Porsche and a Jaguar might be described as 'speed machines' when compared to a Volvo. This description is then used as a row title and each of the other products/brands rated accordingly. By repeatedly selecting and describing three items, the way in which an individual perceives the market is found. It might be that an individual perceives the car market as consisting of 'speed machines', 'safe but boring' and 'comfortable' cars. This information can be used in a number of ways for planning a promotion, identifying the attitudes associated with established products and identifying where gaps in the market exist. The Rep Grid technique is described in more detail in the unit on attitudes (Unit 12).
- *Role-playing* – respondents are asked to imagine that they are an object (a fridge or car, for example) or a different person (a bank manager or supplier, for example) and asked to describe their feelings, thoughts and actions. A variation on this technique is the 'friendly martian' role play where respondents are asked to imagine that they are a martian and told to describe what they would do under certain circumstances. For example, the following question could be asked to secure information about the appeal of different supermarkets: *'Imagine you are a martian who has just landed in a shopping centre close to Sainsbury's, Tesco, Asda and Budgen supermarkets. You need food. How would you decide which supermarket to visit?'*

ACTIVITY 6.6

Role-playing

Working on your own, answer the following question. Produce at least five ideas (no matter how 'silly' they appear).

Imagine you are a tin of cat food on the shelf at a supermarket. How would you make yourself more attractive to shoppers?

Compare your answers with those of your classmates. What similarities and differences exist? Have any new ideas emerged which could be applied to the selling of cat food (or any other tinned food for that matter?).

Comparison of different qualitative research methods

Depth interviews	Focus/discussion groups	Projective techniques
Very time consuming to administer	Moderately time consuming to administer	Relatively quick to administer (depending on technique)
Can only administer one person at a time	Can administer up to 10 people at a time	Can administer many people at a time (depending on technique)
Requires trained interviewers to administer	Requires trained facilitators to administer	Requires few specially trained staff to administer (depending on technique)
Danger of interviewer bias	Danger of group being biased towards opinions of stronger members	Low likelihood of bias

Depth interviews	Focus/discussion groups	Projective techniques
Time consuming to analyse	Time consuming to analyse	Relatively quick to analyse
Possible to obtain very detailed information	Possible to obtain very detailed information	Information limited by technique used
Indirectly useful for generating new ideas	Can be used for brainstorming new ideas directly	Indirectly useful for generating new ideas

QUESTION 6.1

You are asked to gather qualitative information quickly from around 100 customers. You have about three weeks for interviewing and analysis. What technique would you use and why?

Quantitative research

There are three basic ways of collecting primary data in qualitative research:

- Experimentation.
- Observation.
- Surveys (including interviews, telephone, diary and postal surveys).

These will now be discussed.

Experimentation

An experiment is a special form of research which sets out to examine the relationship between two factors by manipulating one whilst measuring changes in the other. For instance, we may test out three different packaging designs and measure the effect on sales. In other words, experiments are used to determine if a causal relationship exists. Experimental design is a well established scientific method (*see* Figure 6.1) with its own established rules and terminology. Many of these are 'borrowed' for use in other areas of market research. The main terms used are described below:

- *Hypothesis* – this is the 'big question' that your study is aimed at answering. For instance, does changing the packaging of electric toasters lead to higher sales?
- *Variables* – these are the factors under investigation. For instance, sales and packaging design.
- *Independent variable* – this is the name for the variable(s) we are manipulating. In the toaster example given, this would be the packaging design, but we might also change price, colour, product features and measure the effect on sales. These would also be independent variables.
- *Dependent variable* – this is the name for the variable(s) we are measuring. In the toaster example given, this would be the sales but we might also want to measure customer feelings towards the new packaging and other aspects of their purchasing behaviour as a result of changing the packaging design. These would also be dependent variables.
- *Intervening (or extraneous) variables* – these are those unwanted factors that 'interfere' with your research. For instance, you may be trying to assess people's attitude to changes in product price over a period where there are considerable fluctuations in the national economy. In this example, the economy is an intervening variable. Intervening variables contribute to experimental 'noise', that is, unavoidable variations in the study which affect the accuracy with which the effect of the independent variable can be assessed.
- *Experimenter* – this is the term used to distinguish the researcher from those he/she is studying (i.e. this would probably be you!).

- *Subjects* – these are the people being studied (i.e. shoppers, product users, potential purchasers and so on).
- *Control groups* – this is a group of subjects which is monitored for the purpose of providing a comparison only. For instance, if we are trying to assess the impact of a new mail order catalogue we might monitor two groups of subjects. One group would be sent the new catalogue whilst the other group would continue to receive the old catalogue. The group that receives the new catalogue is called the experimental group. The group that continues to receive the old catalogue is called the control group.
- *Field studies* – these are studies carried out in the 'real world'. They are the opposite of laboratory studies.
- *Laboratory studies* – these are studies carried out under controlled conditions such as in a laboratory or other 'mock-ups'.

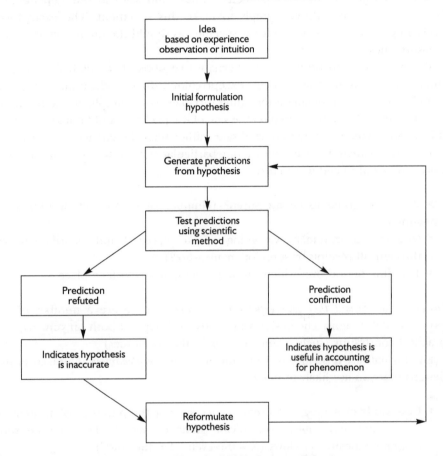

Figure 6.1 The scientific method. *Source:* Rice, C. (1993) *Consumer Behaviour,* Butterworth-Heinemann

British Telecom ask you to investigate customer satisfaction towards a new 'cheap rate' service for frequently called numbers which has been given on a trial basis to some of their customers.

In this example, who or what are likely to be the:

    Independent variable
    Dependent variable
    Experimenter
    Control group?

Would the study be classified as a field or laboratory study?

Experimental design

There are three main steps in the design of an experiment:

1 *Decide on your hypothesis* This must be expressed in a form which can be tested. For instance, 'some packaging is better than others' is *not* a good hypothesis. The use of the terms 'some' and 'better' are vague. An improved version would read something like 'Presenting tennis balls in green packaging leads to higher sales than presenting them in red packaging.'

2 *Select your dependent and independent variables* The variables must be clearly defined and measurable. The more accurately they can be measured the better. The actual variables used will depend upon the hypothesis. In the packaging example, we would probably choose packaging as our independent variable and sales as our dependent variable. However, it is not sufficient simply to make this statement. The exact form of the packaging to be used must be clearly specified as should the method that will be used to measure sales.

We may decide to produce two alternative versions of tennis ball packaging. These should be identical in all respects except colour. To introduce any other differences would be to risk introducing intervening variables. For example, if one of the packaging designs also had a motif printed on the side of the pack we would not know whether it was this design change that had affected sales rather than the change in package colour.

We may decide to measure sales at one particular store or across a number of different stores. We would need to be clear:

- What was going to be measured? (Number of packs sold or number of packs supplied?)
- How this measurement was going to take place? (Hand recording by sales staff, through till receipts or some other measure?)
- The time period over which this measurement was to take place.

3 *Decide on the format that your experiment will take* There are a number of alternative experimental designs. The design you choose will depend both on your hypothesis and practical constraints (such as time, cost and other resources).

Five formats are described by Chris Rice in *Consumer Behaviour.* These cover most of the designs that you are likely to need.

- **Case study or survey** An event occurs, such as the purchase of an item, which we later examine by means of a case study or survey. This can be represented diagrammatically as follows (X = the event, T = the study):

$$X \longrightarrow T$$

An example would be the purchase of a mountain bike. This style of bicycle became unexpectedly popular in the early 1990s. To try to find out the reason for this we may decide to survey those persons that purchased mountain bikes during this period. It may be that the result of such a survey would help us to develop a new bicycle and/or predict futures sales of existing styles of bicycle.

- **One group pre-test/post-test design** Sometime referred to as a test-retest design, a group of individuals are surveyed, an event occurs such as a change in our product, and then we retest the same group. This can be represented diagrammatically as follows (X = the event, T1 and T2 = are tests):

$$T1 \longrightarrow X \longrightarrow T2$$

Suppose we wished to determine opinions on how well a 'new formula' washing powder is performing. It would be sensible to test opinions of the washing powder before the change to the new formula as well as afterwards so that a comparison could be drawn.

- **Time series design or survey** In a time series survey, individuals are repeatedly surveyed before and after an event. This can be represented diagrammatically (for 8 surveys) as follows (X = the event, T1 to T8 = the tests):

$$T1 \longrightarrow T2 \longrightarrow T3 \longrightarrow T4 \longrightarrow X \longrightarrow T5 \longrightarrow T6 \longrightarrow T7 \longrightarrow T8$$

A common use of time series surveys is in political opinion polls. The event may be, for instance, the resignation of an MP due to impropriety or a change of party leader. The aim of a time series survey is to understand how responses change over time. The individuals tested may be the same on each occasion, as with consumer panel testing, or different as in the random sampling most commonly used in political polls.

- **Non-equivalent control group design** This is similar to the one group pre-test/post-test design already described except that two groups are involved. One group, called the experimental group, is exposed to the event, the other group, the control group is not. This can be represented diagrammatically as follows (X = the event, T1 and T2 = the tests):

Experimental group: $T1 \longrightarrow X \longrightarrow T2$

Control group: $T1 \longrightarrow T2$

By using a control group it is possible to eliminate the effect of many intervening variables. Suppose in our washing powder trial we split users of the original formula washing powder into two groups. Both groups were told that they were then going to be given a pack of 'new formula' powder but, in fact, only one group (the experimental group) received packs containing the new formula powder, the other group (control group) were given packs containing the original powder. In other words, the control group were fooled into thinking they were testing the new powder.

When opinions were retested we could therefore be more certain that any difference in opinions was really due to the powder and not to any effects due to the intervention of the experimenter. This type of experiment is often called a 'blind' or 'double blind' trial (depending on whether or not the experimenter was also unaware of the distribution of the powder).

Problems with this method relate to the matching of the groups. We must be sure that the experimental and control groups are similar in all respects otherwise it may be possible to attribute any changes in the dependent variable as an artefact of the group characteristics rather than the manipulation of the independent variable.

- **Classic experimental design** This design is similar to the non-equivalent control group design but overcomes the problem of matching groups by randomly assigning subjects to the experimental and control groups at the outset. The experimental format is identical in all other respects to the non-equivalent design.

Experimental group (random): $T1 \longrightarrow X \longrightarrow T2$

Control group (random): $T1 \longrightarrow T2$

To comply with this design, the respondents in the washing powder example would have to have been randomly assigned to the experimental and control groups.

You have been asked to test the effectiveness of a regional TV advertising campaign for 'Shine On', a shampoo whose sales have been flagging. What experimental design(s) could you use? Who would constitute the experimental and control groups?

QUESTION 6.3

You have been asked to make a prediction as to whether the Labour Party will win the next general election. What experimental design(s) could you use?

Observation

We all learn by observing the things that happen around us. Observation, as a market research method, is the formalization and refinement of this process.

We can clearly observe the behaviour of individuals, for instance which shoppers buy lottery tickets, but what observation cannot tell us is what people are thinking or feeling. For instance, when buying a lottery ticket it may be that some shoppers are thinking; *'If I don't win this week I'll stop'* and others *'I'm going to keep buying tickets until I win'*. These alternatives are obviously of interest because they will affect future behaviour, but observational techniques are not able to distinguish these two groups of shoppers. Observation is therefore quite limited as a technique but, nonetheless, can be useful under those circumstances where we are interested in behaviour than any mental processes.

There are three basic types of observation:

1 *Secretive* – where the subjects of the study are unaware that they are being observed. For instance, the behaviour of shoppers is observed via a hidden camera or by an experimenter pretending to be another shopper. This may pose ethical problems.
2 *Non-participatory* – where the subjects of the study are aware that they are being observed but the experimenter takes no part in the behaviour being observed. For instance, shoppers are observed by an experimenter with a clipboard sited prominently, perhaps near the checkouts. It is possible that the presence of the experimenters may affect the behaviour of the subject.
3 *Participatory* – where the subject and experimenter interact. A shopper might be approached by an experimenter and asked what they are buying and why. This can provide useful additional information but the behaviour of the experimenter may actually change the behaviour of the subject they are trying to observe.

Observations can be carried out in the field or in the laboratory. The latter overcomes many of the ethical problems associated with such studies but risks interfering with naturally occurring behaviours and can appear contrived. It may be, for instance, that meeting friends has an influence on supermarket buying behaviour. This aspect of shopping would be difficult to recreate in a laboratory.

Observational data is usually collected using recording sheets. A predetermined set of behaviours are identified and printed on these sheets. The experimenter is then able to mark down quickly the behaviours as they occur. Suppose we are trying to determine the order in which shoppers visit the various areas within a supermarket (wet fish, deli counter, fruit and veg, tinned food, etc.) as part of a study to reorganize shelving. In this instance we would be wise to prepare our recording sheet with a list of the various areas we are interested in. It is then easy to indicate, with a number, the order in which they were visited. It is also good practice to prepare for the unexpected by adding space on the recording sheet for behaviours which were not anticipated. For instance, it might be that a shopper visits an area more than once. You may wish to record which area they revisited as well as the reason why.

Observations that are difficult to record in 'real time' because they happen too fast or are obscured can be first recorded on video for later analysis.

Observational research by the Postal Service in the United States found that most people were on first-name terms with their postmen and women. This led to a successful promotional campaign which prominently featured post deliverers.

Observe students in your college canteen. In what order do they make decisions about what they are going to eat and drink? Are these decisions influenced by the people they are with? When and where do they pick up their cutlery, condiments? Where and how do they pay?

On the basis of the answers to these questions, how might the canteen improve its image and the degree to which it meets the needs of its customers?

Survey

A survey is the most commonly-used method of gathering quantitative data. It is essential to approach the design and administration of surveys in a structured way to avoid errors, wasted time and poor quality responses. The process of undertaking a survey project is similar in many ways to that for an experiment.

Steps in a survey project

1 Decide on your survey goals – what you want to learn.
2 Determine your sample – who you will ask.
3 Select interviewing methodology – how you will ask.
4 Design your questionnaire – what you will ask.
5 Pre-test the questionnaire, if at all practical – (known as piloting).
6 Administer interviews – ask the questions.
7 Enter the data.
8 Analyse the data.
9 Present the data.

Deciding on your survey goals

The first step in any survey is deciding what you want to know. This will determine whom you will survey and what you will ask them. If you are unclear about what you want then your results will be unclear. Researchers rarely take the time necessary at this stage of the project to consider their survey goals properly. Some general goals could include finding out more about:

- Consumer ratings of current products or services.
- A company's corporate image.
- Customer satisfaction levels.
- Television viewer opinions.
- Employee attitudes.
- Opinions about political issues.
- The potential market for a new product or service.

These sample goals represent general areas of investigation only. The more specific you can make your goals, the easier it will be to get usable answers. Specific goals are usually phrased as questions:

- What do the supporters of the different political parties feel about the level of defence spending?
- What do the employees of UserData Limited feel about the new salary scales?
- Do consumers prefer the services offered by Mercury or British Telecom?
- Which washing powder do customers think washes their clothing best: Persil or Ecover?

Even at this stage, it may be necessary to get clarification on certain concepts. For instance, in the last question, what is meant by 'washes their clothing best'? The person commissioning the research should be consulted on such questions of interpretation. The 'best' in this context may mean 'cleanest' or 'whitest' or may be to do with how the powder handles sensitive or coloured fabrics.

Determining your sample

In determining your sample you need to decide whom you will survey and how many people you will survey. Researchers often call this group the target population. In some cases, when doing an employee attitude survey for instance, the population is obvious. In other cases, such as when prospective customers are involved, determining the target group is more difficult. Correctly determining the target population is critical. A poorly defined target population will result in unrepresentative results.

Suppose we are commissioned to find out people's opinions of the recent architectural changes to the entrance of the Ashmolean Museum in Oxford. How would we go about determining our target population? If we were looking for a relative appraisal of the changes then we would need to find people that had seen the museum entrance before and after the changes. If we were only asked to find out visitors' general opinions of the new entrance then it would not matter whether or not they had seen the original architecture. Clearly, in this example, our survey goal determines the target population.

To decide how many people need surveying is both a statistical and commercial decision. Surveying more people costs more money but does increase the accuracy, or precision, of the results (up to a point). To increase a sample from 250 to 1,000 requires four times as many people, but it only doubles the precision. The statistical issues are dealt with in detail in Unit 7.

Sampling methods

There are two basic types of sampling:

- *Probability (or random) samples* – where individuals are drawn in some random fashion from among the population.
- *Non-probability (or non-random) samples* – where individuals are selected on the basis of one or more criteria determined by the researcher.

Probability samples Within this category there are four sampling methods which are commonly employed in market research:

- *Simple random sampling* – individuals are randomly drawn from the population at large (for example, by selecting from the electoral register).
- *Systematic sampling* – individuals (or households) are sampled at intervals based on a random start point. For instance, it might be decided to visit every tenth person on the electoral register starting at number 4. In this case the sampling interval is 10. The individuals that would be sampled are thus numbers 4, 14, 24 and so on.
- *Stratified random sampling* – the population is first divided into groups based on one or more criteria (say age, gender, or other affiliation) and, from within these groups, individuals are randomly selected. For this method to be possible the data available on each individual must contain information about the criteria to be used to stratify the groups. This is not always the case.
- *Multistage sampling* – the population is first divided into quite large groups, usually based on geography. A random selection of these large groups is then selected and sub-divided again. A random selection of groups is again made from the resulting sub-divisions and the process repeated as many times as required by the survey. Eventually, individuals are randomly sampled from the small groups arising as a result of the final subdivision.

To select individuals on a random basis it is necessary to construct a sampling frame. This is a list of all the known individuals within the population from which the selection is to take place. Each individual is assigned a unique number then, using random number tables or the computer equivalent, individuals are selected on the basis of random numbers produced.

Obviously, to list all the individuals within the UK would take forever. Luckily, such a list is already produced by the Government. It is called the electoral roll (or register). Its primary purpose is to record those persons eligible to vote. Unfortunately, the electoral roll has several drawbacks:

- Those under 18 years old are not listed (as they are not eligible to vote).
- Many people choose not to register to vote and are thus not listed.
- Mobile individuals – such as students – are frequently not registered where they live.
- Newly weds are not listed correctly – the wife's maiden name may appear and, if they have recently started living together, only one name may appear on the register.
- The register may be up to a year out of date.

In an attempt to overcome some of these problems, the Postal Address File (or PAF) is often used. This is the most comprehensive list of addresses in the UK. Addresses are then randomly selected from the list and the interviewer tries to interview one person from each household. Recently, more and more people are failing to register to vote which has led to increased use of the PAF. Unfortunately, the PAF too has several problems:

- There is no way of knowing who lives at the address.
- There is no way of knowing how many people live at the address.

It is thus left to the interviewer to select a person to interview based on an extensive set of rules provided by the research organization. This can result in error.

Non-probability samples   When a sampling frame cannot be established, or would prove too expensive or time consuming, one of the following four non-random methods are usually used:

- *Judgement sampling* – the researcher uses their judgement to select people that they feel are representative of the population or have a particular expertise or knowledge which makes them suitable. For example, business leaders, top scientists and so on. This method is commonly used with small sample sizes.
- *Convenience sampling* – the most convenient population is chosen, which may be the researchers friends, work colleagues or students from a nearby college. This method is often used to save time and resources.
- *Cluster sampling* – the population is repeatedly divided into groups rather like the process for multistage sampling. However, cluster sampling is different in that all individuals from the remaining small groups are interviewed rather than just a random sample of those remaining.
- *Quota sampling* – the researcher selects a predetermined number of individuals from different groups (i.e. based on age, gender and so on). This is perhaps the most popular non-probability sampling method used.

Setting quotas

Rather than randomly selecting individuals, you may wish to enforce balance in your population by setting quotas for certain subgroups. For instance, if you are surveying for a product that you know will mostly be used by under-35s you can set a quota for this age group in your survey sample. You may decide as a result that 90% of your sample should be in this age group.

To give another example, if you are interviewing users about a particular product brand, you may wish (depending on your project goals) to select your sample based on their current brand preferences to approximate current market share. Alternatively, you may decide to interview only those individuals that currently use a competitive brand or those that use no brand at all!

Quotas are usually specified to a research organization in the form of a grid. For example, if we have a requirement to interview fifty shoppers we might specify that:

Twenty five of them under 45 years old

Twenty five aged 45 or older

Fifteen in the AB social classes

Thirty five in the CDE social classes.

Alternatively we might specify how many of a particular age group should come from each social class grouping:

	AB	CDE
Under 45	13	12
45 or over	2	23

The structure of the sample is therefore fixed by the researcher.

Comparison of different sampling methods

Simple random	Systematic random	Stratified	Multistage	Convenience	Judgement	Cluster	Quota
Requires sampling frame	Requires sampling frame	Requires sampling frame	Requires sampling frame	Does not require sampling frame	Does not require sampling frame	Does not require sampling frame	Does not require sampling frame
High cost	Moderate cost	Moderate cost	Moderate cost	Low cost	Low cost	Moderate cost	Moderate cost
May not be representative	May not be representative	Representative	May not be representative	May not be representative	May not be representative	May not be representative	Representative
Low likelihood of bias	Low likelihood of bias	Low likelihood of bias	Low likelihood of bias	High likelihood of bias	High likelihood of bias	Moderate likelihood of bias	Moderate likelihood of bias

Avoiding bias

If you select a sample population which is not representative then your results may be biased. That is, they will not represent responses in the wider population. For example, if you asked Ford employees whether they preferred Ford cars you would probably get biased results. Totally excluding all bias is extremely difficult but should be the goal in any survey. However, just being aware of bias will allow you to avoid the more obvious sources and interpret certain results more cautiously. There are three main sources of bias:

1 *Incomplete coverage* – there may be a number of reasons for this:
   (a) sampling frame is incomplete
   (b) certain outlying areas are excluded (it is common in UK surveys to exclude counties north of the Caledonian canal in Scotland)
   (c) the survey method used may place constraints on those that can be sampled, i.e. a telephone survey requires ownership of a telephone!
2 *Non-response* – low response rates are a problem in any survey. Whether it is a street, telephone or postal survey a significant proportion of those approached will refuse to answer questions.
3 *Overrepresentation* – some sampling methods deliberately overrepresent certain groups (the non-probability sampling techniques already mentioned). Although this allows detailed examination of a certain subgroup of the population, there is no way of knowing how else the group characteristics might affect the survey responses.

The list below shows the ways in which overrepresentation can introduce bias:

Sample	Possible source of bias
Existing customers	Customer loyalty may mean that more favourable responses are given.
Ex-customers	Possibly no longer customer because of dislike of product/ service – may give less favourable results.
People in city-centre shopping street	Depending on shopping area, may only capture data from certain social classes. May be that only certain members of the family shop.
People in out-of-town shopping centre	Unlikely to be used by those without a car or those that have good local shops.

> You are asked to gather opinions on a new design of carry cot for babies. What problems might you experience using your classmates as a convenience sample?

Interviewing methods

Once you have decided on your sample you must decide on the method of data collection. The main methods are:

- Personal interview.
- Telephone surveys including CATI.
- Computer assisted interviewing (CAI).
- Postal surveys.

These will now be described.

Personal interviews What distinguishes this type of survey is that the questionnaire is administered 'face-to-face' with the interviewee. Such interviews are often categorized according to where they take place. The following examples are given:

- *Household survey* – the surveyor goes door-to-door, either randomly or according to some prearranged sampling method, and interviews people on the doorstep.
- *Home survey* – takes place in the interviewee's home. They are normally arranged in advance. This is obviously time consuming but guarantees a response. Advantages are that, in the comfort of their own home, conversation is likely to be freer and the interviewee will be more tolerant of a longer interview.
- *Hall survey* – as their name suggests, these take place in a hall or hired room. Individuals are invited to attend or called in off the street to take part.
- *Shop surveys* – these take place in shopping centres, inside a particular shop, at the entrance to a particular shop. In many cases a 'stall' is set up for this purpose and/or individuals are approached to participate.
- *On-street surveys* – otherwise known as 'clipboard' surveys, individuals are approached in the street. In busy, hectic streets this can be problematic. Surveying at busy times, such as lunchtime, is difficult as many people would rather have something to eat! On-street surveys need to be particularly short and to the point.

The use of a prompt card is common in personal interviewing. These are usually a verbal or pictorial representation of the response choices. For example, an interviewee might be asked which political party they intend to vote for. In this case, the response card would contain a list of political parties. The advantage of the prompt card is that it reduces the bias that can be introduced as a result of the changing voice intonation of the interviewer and, by having a number of different cards with different arrangements of responses, the effect of response ordering can be reduced (see Unit 14 on primacy and recency effects).

Telephone surveys (including CATI) Telephone surveys are probably the most popular interviewing method. The majority of homes and businesses have a phone which makes coverage almost complete (although about 10% of people are not on the phone – most notably students and old people, but also those who are ex-directory).

Sampling is easy using a telephone directory. Most libraries carry a full set of telephone directories for the whole of the UK. The telephone also makes the sampling of international interviewees easy.

Increasingly popular is computer assisted telephone interviewing (CATI) where the interviewer reads questions from a computer screen and enters the responses directly into the computer. In this way, results can be analysed rapidly. CATI can also assist the interviewer in structuring their interview by only displaying those questions which are relevant based on earlier responses.

Unfortunately, the growth of 'junk' phone calls is increasing refusal rates amongst potential interviewees.

Computer assisted interviews (CAI)   These are interviews in which the interviewees enter their own answers directly into a computer. They are popular at exhibitions and in large organizations where 'electronic mail' is used to send out the questionnaire. This method is convenient and, as with CATI, no post-survey data entry is required allowing for a rapid analysis. Obviously, CAI is limited by the availability of a suitable computer. The novelty and convenience of CAI leads to moderately high response rates.

Postal surveys   These surveys are generally the least expensive type. Postal surveys are seen as less intrusive than personal interviews and telephone surveys but response rates are generally the lowest of any survey method. More often than not, responses rates are less than 10% which provides an opportunity for considerable bias. In an attempt to boost return rates, all manner of offers and incentives are used. One American researcher found that enclosing a one dollar bill massively increased response rates (and no doubt also cost!).

Low levels of literacy are no doubt one reason why responses are reduced – a good reason to keep questions simple. English is not always the first language and, in areas where problems are envisaged, it may be worth producing multi-lingual questionnaire variants.

However, much of the low response rate is simply due to the high volumes of 'junk' mail people receive. Try to make your survey look as little like junk mail as possible. Better still, and wherever possible, save some trees and use the phone!

Comparison of different interview methods

Postal survey	Telephone (including CATI)	Computer assisted interviewing (CAI)	Personal interviews
Respondents can see, feel and/or taste	Respondents can hear	Respondents can see and hear	Respondents can see, feel, hear and/or taste
Moderately long interviews tolerated	Moderately long interviews tolerated	Moderately long interviews tolerated whilst still novel	Longer interviews tolerated when in comfortable surroundings (i.e. own home) otherwise only short interviews tolerated (on street)
Long time to receive responses	Quick to receive responses	Quick to receive responses	Quick to receive responses
Analysis time moderately fast when survey is electronically readable, otherwise slow	Fast analysis (CATI) Slow analysis (non-CATI)	Fast analysis	Slow analysis
Easy to survey random sample	Easy to survey random sample	More difficult to survey random sample	More difficult to survey random sample
Full coverage (including international)	Good coverage (including international)	Poor coverage (have to go out and find individuals)	Poor coverage (have to go out and find individuals)

Postal survey	Telephone (including CATI)	Computer assisted interviewing (CAI)	Personal interviews
Requires certain level of literacy	Requires comprehension of spoken language (usually English)	Requires certain level of literacy	Requires comprehension of spoken language (usually English)
Allows respondants to answer at their leisure	Forces respondants to answer at time of call	Forces respondants to answer at time of interview	Forces respondants to answer at time of interview
Low response rate	Medium response rate	Medium response rate	Medium response rate
Virtual elimination of interviewer bias	Possibility of interviewer bias	Virtual elimination of interviewer bias	Possibility of interviewer bias
Low cost	Medium cost	Medium cost	High cost
No special interviewer training required	Special interviewer training required	No special interviewer training required	Special interviewer training required
People more likely to answer sensitive questions	People less likely to answer sensitive questions	People more likely to answer sensitive questions	People less likely to answer sensitive questions

What are the advantages of postal surveys compared with telephone surveys?

What are the advantages of CAI compared with personal interviews?

QUESTION 6.6

Comparison of different quantitative research methods

Experimentation	Observation	Surveys
Moderately time consuming to undertake	Time consuming to undertake	Relatively quick to undertake (depending on technique)
Can administer many people at a time (depending on experimental design)	Are restricted in the number of people by the circumstances of the observation	Can administer many people at a time (depending on technique)
Requires trained experimenter and assistants to collect data	Requires trained observers to collect data	Require no specially trained staff to collect data (depending on technique)
Generally, low likelihood of bias	Danger of responses being biased by presence of observer	Generally, low likelihood of bias (depending on technique)
Time consuming to analyse	Time consuming to analyse	Relatively quick to analyse (depending on technique)

Ethical responsibilities of interviewers

The Market Research Society publishes a code of conduct which specifically addresses the responsibilities of those carrying out interviews. In summary interviewers shall:

- Be honest and not mislead the interviewee in order to procure information.
- Not use the information collected for any other purpose without the consent of the interviewee.
- Take steps to ensure that interviewees are not embarrassed or adversely affected as a direct result of an interview.
- Carry an identity card or badge including a photograph, name and organization.
- Send a leaflet, card or letter to the interviewee thanking them for taking part in the interview.
- In the case of telephone surveys, at the end of the interview the name of the survey organization, a name and contact number should be given.
- Provide a means by which the interviewee may verify that the survey is genuine without incurring any cost.
- Allow an interviewee to withdraw from a survey. Where appropriate, the research organization shall confirm that their data has been destroyed.
- Make no calls in person or by telephone before 9 a.m. weekdays, 10 a.m. Sundays, or after 9 p.m. on any other day unless an appointment has been made. Those carrying out research overseas should respect the equivalent customs of the host country.
- Only interview children under the age of 14 with the permission of their parents, guardian, or other person responsible for them (i.e. teacher). The responsible person shall be informed of the general content of the interview before the interview itself take place.

Questionnaire design

The primary data collection tool is the questionnaire. Whether you are conducting an interview by post, telephone, face-to-face, or even via computer, you will be need to design a questionnaire.

There are two important concepts in the design of measurement methods: reliability and validity.

Validity

If a data measurement tool actually measures what it purports to, then it is said to be valid. For example, time over a 100 metre sprint is not likely to be valid measure of intelligence. On the other hand, a well designed Intelligence Quotient (IQ) test *is* likely to measure intelligence accurately. The IQ test is therefore said to be a valid measure of intelligence.

Poorly designed questionnaires are often not valid measures – they purport to measure things that they do not. For example, the question, how many times a week do you watch television may seem – on the face of it – a valid way of measuring television viewing time. This is not the case. All the question actually does is measure the number of times the television is viewed and not the length of time it is viewed for. This question would therefore not be a valid measure of television viewing time.

Similarly, surveys on sample populations are said to be invalid if their findings are not to be generalized to the whole population.

Reliability

If a measurement tool consistently measures the same thing then it is said to be reliable.

For example, the IQ of a person changes only slowly. Therefore, if we measured it two weeks in a row we would expect it to be approximately the same. A good IQ test would indeed give a similar score week after week. Such a test is said to be reliable. A poorly designed IQ test might give widely differing scores each time is was administered. Such a test is termed unreliable, it cannot be relied upon to give an accurate answer.

Good questionnaires are both reliable and valid; they measure what they purport to and they do so reliably. Repeat testing of questionnaires, and comparison with other data sources are methods used to check both validity and reliability.

Golden rules on questionnaire design

The following rules are provided as a general guide to the design of questionnaires:

1 Keep the survey short – long surveys are often indicative of poorly defined survey goals. As a rule of thumb, keep the number of questions below forty. Go through each question. If you do not know, or care, what you will do with the result then leave the question out.

2 Design the questionnaire to match the survey method being used – for example, CATI and CAI are able to 'branch' to different questions depending on the responses given to earlier questions which can increase the amount of data collected with the same number of questions and make errors less likely.

3 Keep the questionnaire simple – do not mix topics – for example, combining a survey on smoking with one on political issues simply serves to confuse the interviewee.

4 Do not combine two questions in one – for example, 'How do you feel about John Major and the Government?' should be asked as two questions (a) 'How do you feel about John Major' (b) 'How do you feel about the Government?'

5 Avoid unnecessary terminology, abbreviations, technical words and jargon – these should only be used where questions are intended for a specialist group that would be expected to understand. For example, 'Do you own a PC 486DX 66 computer?' is probably an acceptable question for a computer buff but not a member of the general public.

6 Do not present biased questions – for example, 'How satisfied are you with your new, super fast, hi-tech Swan toaster?' assumes that people already have a positive perception of the toaster and thus is likely to bias their response. A more correct way of phrasing this question would be to ask 'How satisfied or dissatisfied are you with the Swan toaster?' – a suitable response scale would then be provided.

7 Make sure your questions are grammatically correct – poor grammar can lead to confusion, annoys certain people, and creates a poor impression.

8 Each question should have a 'Don't know' or 'Not applicable' response unless you are absolutely certain that you have covered all possibilities – for example, in response to the question 'What make of car do you own?' 'Don't know' and 'Not applicable' response categories should be provided. Some people may not actually know, or care, about the make of their car. Similarly, some people do not own a car. You would rarely want to include 'Don't know' or 'Not applicable' in a list of choices being read over the telephone or in person, but should usually accept them when given by respondents.

9 Provide example questions at the beginning of the questionnaire to demonstrate the method of completion. If a number of different question formats are used, provide examples of each and instructions for completion within the body of the questionnaire to avoid confusion.

10 Be specific in your questioning – 'woolly' questions lead to 'woolly' results. For example, 'Have you recently bought a can of cat food?' might be better rephrased 'Have you bought a can of Possum cat food in the last two weeks?'

11 Always allow for the interviewee to make their own comments at the end of the questionnaire – this will often provide useful leads for follow-up studies or allow you to interpret more accurately the data you collect.

12 Take care when laying out your questionnaire – a neat and tidy layout creates a good impression and reduces error.

13 Take care with the ordering of your questions – make sure that the response on a question is not affected by a previous answer or pre-empts a response to a later question. For example, a question which mentions blue packaging should not be succeeded by a question which asks for preferences on packaging colour.

14 Always start your questionnaire by explaining who you are and what you intend to do with the data you collect. This is polite as well as being ethically correct.

15 Always include a question asking whether the interviewee would mind being contacted further – you never know when a quick follow-up study may be required.

You are stopped in the street by an interviewer. The first thing they say is 'Good afternoon Sir (or Madam), where have you come from?' What is wrong with this?

Question types

Researchers use three basic types of questions:

- Multiple choice – where the interviewee has to select from a set of responses (also called closed questions)
- Open-ended – where the interviewee is allowed to enter anything
- Hybrid – a combination of the above two

Examples of each of these follow.

Multiple choice

Which destination would you choose for your ideal holiday?
(please tick one response only)

London	☐
Paris	☐
Caribbean	☐
None of the above	☐
Don't know	☐

Sometimes more than one response is required. This needs to be made abundantly clear to the respondee as in the following question example:

Which of the following qualifications do you possess? (please tick *all* the responses that apply)

CSE	☐
O-level	☐
A-level	☐
Diploma	☐
Degree or equivalent	☐

Open-ended

What destination would you choose for your ideal holiday?
(please write response below)

_____

Again, it might be that more than one response is required, as in the following example:

Please list the three things you like *best* about your new toaster:

1 _____

2 _____

3 _____

Hybrid

Which destination would you choose for you ideal holiday? (please tick or write one response only)

London ☐
Paris ☐
Caribbean ☐
Other (please specify) _____
Don't know ☐

Comparison of question types

Multiple choice	Open-ended	Hybrid
Easy to analyse	Difficult to analyse	If choices well researched then moderately easy to analyse
Likelihood of bias	Low likelihood of bias	Likelihood of bias
Difficult to design	Easy to design	Difficult to design
Suitable for quantitative data collection	Suitable for qualitative data collection	Suitable for quantitative data collection

Response scales

Depending on the sort of data you are collecting, you may need to use one of following types of response scales:

- *Likert scale* – developed in 1932 this scale is perhaps the most commonly used attitude response scale. A series of statements are rated in the following five-point scale: *strongly agree, agree, undecided, disagree, strongly disagree.*
- *Semantic differential* – developed by Osgood, Tannenbaum and Succi in 1957 this scale is commonly used where an attitude object rather than a statement is being rated. The semantic differential consists of 9 pairs of bipolar adjectives or opposites. Each is given a seven point scale. The adjectives used vary but typically consist of pairs such as good/ bad, active/passive, strong/weak and so on.
- *Rank order scales* – here the interviewee is asked to rank items in terms of some specific property or attribute. Rank ordering can provide useful competitive information and is therefore used in product positioning.

Examples of the scales are given below.

Likert scale

A number of different formats are favoured for Likert scales. Two examples are given below:

Using the scale given indicate how strongly you agree or disagree with the following statement (please circle your preferred response):

I enjoy studying marketing

Strongly Agree   (Agree)   Neither Agree   Disagree   Strongly Disagree
                      nor Disagree

Place a cross in the box which best indicates how strongly you agree or disagree with each of the statements given:

	Strongly Agree	Agree	Neither Agree nor Disagree	Disagree	Strongly Disagree
I enjoy studying marketing	X				
I enjoy attending College			X		
I think the College canteen food is over-priced				X	

Semantic differential

As noted, various adjective pairs are used as rating scales. Research has found that the scales used fall into one of three categories:

- Evaluation – examples are good/bad, clean/dirty.
- Potency – examples are weak/strong, large/small.
- Activity – active/passive, fast/slow.

Sometimes the scales seem rather unusual when applied to certain objects or ideas but, being able to apply similar adjectives across a range of items is one of the strengths of the technique. One example question is given below. Here attitudes to nuclear weapons are being measured.

Place a cross on one of the seven scale points for each of the adjective pairs given:

Nuclear Weapons

Bad	____ ____ ____ ____ ____ ____ ____	Good
Fair	____ ____ ____ ____ ____ ____ ____	Unfair
Clean	____ ____ ____ ____ ____ ____ ____	Dirty
Worthless	____ ____ ____ ____ ____ ____ ____	Valuable
Active	____ ____ ____ ____ ____ ____ ____	Passive
Cold	____ ____ ____ ____ ____ ____ ____	Hot
Fast	____ ____ ____ ____ ____ ____ ____	Slow
Large	____ ____ ____ ____ ____ ____ ____	Small
Weak	____ ____ ____ ____ ____ ____ ____	Strong

You may wish to fill this in yourself.

One of the attractions of the semantic differential is that the results can be graphically represented by joining up the crosses on the scale points. This is called a profile. Figure 6.2 is an example of how this is done.

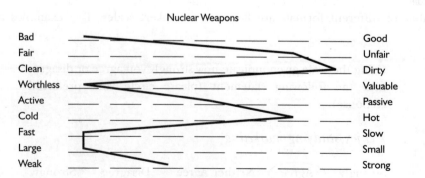

Figure 6.2   A sample profile derived from a semantic differential scale: attitudes to nuclear weapons

Using this profiling method it is easy to compare two 'objects' that have been rated on the same scales. This is particularly useful for brand comparisons. Figure 6.3 shows a profile comparing attitudes towards nuclear weapons with conventional weapons. With more than one line a key is required.

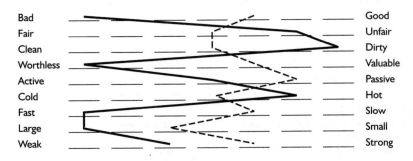

Figure 6.3 Profiles derived from a semantic differential scale: attitudes to nuclear (solid line) and conventional (dashed line) weapons

Rank order scale

Rank order scales can be used for rating anything from political parties to chocolate bars. Any number of items can be ranked but it is usual to keep the number below 10, and ideally below 7, to reduce the effort required to answer the question. Figures 6.4 and 6.5 are two examples of rank order questions.

Rank the following political parties in terms of their honesty. Place a 1 alongside the party you believe to be the most honest, a 2 alongside the party you believe to be the next honest, and so on until all the parties have been ranked.

Liberal Democrat	3
Conservatives	5
Labour	4
Green	2
Plaid Cymru	1

Figure 6.4 Rank ordering political parties by honesty

Rank the following washing powders according to their ability to keep white cottons clean. Place a 1 alongside the powder you believe to be the most effective, a 2 alongside the powder you believe to be the next most effective, and so on until all the powders have been ranked.

Persil	
Ecover	
Tide	
Ariel	

You may wish to fill this in.

Figure 6.5 Rank ordering washing powders by their ability to clean white cotton clothing

Real questionnaires

To conclude the discussion on questionnaires, it is only right to include one or two examples of questionnaires that are in use. Figure 6.6 is an excerpt from the National Savings Survey which appears in the third edition of the *Consumer Market Research Handbook* edited by Worcester and Downham. This is part of the interviewer's sheet. Figure 6.7 is a recruitment advert for a US *Family Circle* consumer panel which appears in *Consumer Behavior* by Schiffman and Kanuk.

No.	Question	Answer	Code	Skip to
36	SHOW CARDS 5 Can you tell me, very roughly, how much money you have saved or invested altogether in these forms of savings?	£50 or less £51–£200 £201–£500 £501–£1000 £1001–£3000 More Don't know	(69) 1 2 3 4 5 6 7	37
37	In which form of saving do you have *most* money?	Only one form held Premium Bonds National Savings Certificates Building Society P.O.S.B. Ordinary Account P.O.S.B. Investment Account Bank Deposit Account National Development Bonds Defence Bonds Unit Trusts Stocks and Shares Trustee S.B. Ordinary Account Trustee S.B. Special Investment A/c Local Authorities Other	(70) 1 2 3 4 5 6 7 8 9 0 X V (71) 1 2 3	38
38	SHOW CARD 6 What is this saving for? For any of these purposes (CARD) or for other purposes?	For emergencies For meeting large household bills For holidays, Christmas, etc. For security in later life To provide an income Other	(72) 1 2 3 4 5 6	39
39	Why did you choose that particular form of saving? PROBE!		(73) (74)	40

	IF ONLY ONE FORM OF SAVING,
	   GO TO 41.
	IF MORE THAN ONE, ASK FOR EACH
	   REMAINING IN ORDER OF SIZE.
	ASK SEPARATELY FOR ALL OTHER TYPES
	   OF SAVING HELD
		(WRITE IN TYPE)
		
		Type of saving ....
			(10)	

40a	SHOW CARD 6 What are the savings in .... for?	For emergencies For meeting large household bills For holidays, Christmas, etc. For security in later life To provide an income Others	(11) 1 2 3 4 5 6	

Figure 6.6 National Savings Survey (excerpt)

Join Our Consumer Panel!

Dear Reader:

We are about to form the 1994 FAMILY CIRCLE Consumer Panel. The 1993 panelists answered two very lengthy questionnaires over the year and received samples of our advertisers' products to evaluate. The 1994 panelists will be asked to do the same – to tell us about yourself, your home, family, work, likes and dislikes.

Please take a few minutes from your busy schedule to answer all the questions below. Although we cannot select everyone who responds, I can assure you that those readers who are scientifically selected will have an interesting and rewarding year. When you've answered all the questions, mail the completed questionnaire by March 1, 1994, to:

FAMILY CIRCLE
6400 Jericho Turnpike
Synosset, New York 11791

Thank you and I hope to hear from all of you!

Jackie Leo, Editor

1. Which of the following do you regularly buy? (Please "X" all that apply.)

Cold/flu/cough remedies (06) ☐1
Hand/body lotion ☐2
Home permanents ☐3
Low-calorie products ☐4
Haircolouring products ☐5
Low-fat products ☐6
Athletic shoes ☐7

Cigarettes (07) ☐1
Feminine hygiene products ☐2
Children's food products ☐3
Children's clothing ☐4
Home fix-it materials ☐5
Jeans ☐6

2. Where do you ususlly buy cosmetics and fragrances?

	Cosmetics	Fragrances
Drug store	(08) ☐1	(09) ☐1
Department store	☐2	☐2
Discount department store	☐3	☐3
Supermarket	☐4	☐4

3. Please indicate below which activities you regularly do.

Bake from scratch (10) ☐1
Cook from scratch ☐2
Watch pre-recorded videos ☐3
Exercise at club/spa ☐4

Cook using convenience foods ☐5
Read romance novels ☐6
Exercise at home ☐7
Buy collectibles ☐8

4. When will your household most likely purchase/lease your next vehicle?

0–3 months (11) ☐1
4–6 months ☐2
7–12 months ☐3

1–2 years ☐4
No definite plans ☐5

5. What will your next vehicle most likely be?

Full size (12) ☐1   Midsize ☐2   Minivan ☐3

6. Do you own a   Dog (13) ☐1   Cat ☐2

7. Do you have children?

Under 6 years (14) ☐1   No children under 18 ☐3
6 years or older ☐2

8. Are you: Female (15) ☐1   Male ☐2

9. Please "X" group that best describes your age.

18 to 24 (16) ☐1
25 to 29 ☐2
30 to 34 ☐3
35 to 39 ☐4

40 to 44 ☐5
45 to 49 ☐6
50 to 54 ☐7

55 to 59 ☐8
60 to 64 ☐9
65 or older ☐0

10. What is your current marital status?

Married (17) ☐1   Widowed ☐3
Single (never married) ☐2   Divorced/Separated ☐4

11. What is the highest level of education you have completed?

Some high school or less (18) ☐1
Graduated high school ☐2
Some college ☐3
Graduated college ☐4
Post-graduate study or more ☐5

12. Are you employed either full-time or part-time outside your home for a wage?

Employed full-time (30 hours or more per week) (19) ☐1
Part-time (less than 30 hours per week) ☐2
Not employed/Retired ☐3

13. Please "X" the box below that best describes your total estimated household income before taxes in 1994 for ALL family members. (Please include your own income as well as that of all other household members. Income from all sources such as wages, bonuses, profits, dividends, rentals, interest, etc., should be included.)

Less than $20,000 (20) ☐1
$20,000 to $24,999 ☐2
$25,000 to $29,999 ☐3
$30,000 to $34,999 ☐4
$35,000 to $39,999 ☐5

$40,000 to $45,999 ☐6
$46,000 to $49,999 ☐7
$50,000 to $74,999 ☐8
$75,000 to $99,999 ☐9
$100,000 or more ☐0

14. Have you participated in a consumer *panel* or *council* in the past 12 months?

Yes (21) ☐1   No ☐2

15. Do you currently subscribe to FAMILY CIRCLE?

Yes (22) ☐1   No ☐2

Name _____

Address _____

_____

Phone # (_____) _____

Figure 6.7 A recruitment advert for a US *Family Circle* consumer panel

Cut out and keep any questionnaires you find in magazines or newspapers. Act as 'devil's advocate' and list the flaws in each. Decide how these flaws might have affected the accuracy of the data collected.

You are working in the marketing department of a large software company.

One of the directors has asked that you design a study to find out whether your existing users are 'satisfied' with your new database product which was launched six months ago.

He has expressed interest in finding out about the following:

- usability
- reliability
- performance
- competitiveness

Think about the issues that need to be considered and prepare an outline questionnaire design.

Question 6.1

With limited time, a group discussion is likely to be the most productive technique. It would be possible to gather information from approximately twenty people per day (two groups of ten) which would take approximately one week to survey 100 people. However, analysis time is likely to take at least another week (depending on the information you require).

Depth interviews will provide more information but take approximately twice as long. Projective techniques may be an option where only a limited amount of information is required allowing use of one of the techniques described.

Question 6.2

It is most likely that:

- Independent variable is whether or not a customer has the 'cheap rate' service.
- Dependent variable is the measure of customer satisfaction. This could be obtained via questionnaire.
- Experimenter is most likely to be you.
- Control group is most likely to be those customers that have not had the service installed. They are the best persons to act as a comparative group.
- The study is a field study as the experiment is carried out in people's own homes.

Question 6.3

There are a number of experimental designs that can be used to test the effectiveness of an advertising campaign. The exact choice would depend on financial limits, resource constraints and the broadcast pattern of the advertisement. It is most important to test before and after the advertisement is broadcast and, presuming time series data is not available, you are left to decide between pre-test/post-test, non-equivalent control group and the classical experimental designs. First choice would be the latter which provides more opportunity to eliminate the effect of intervening variables. However, if the advert was on trial in a particular region (as is usually the case) it will not be possible to select people randomly from this region (as some may have seen the advert and some may not have). We would thus be forced to use one of the other two designs. Of these, the non-equivalent control group is preferred because of the presence of a control group to eliminate the effects of intervening variables.

Question 6.4

It is certain that time series data will be available from past political opinion polls. In this case all that is required is a single test (case study or survey design) which can be compared with secondary data from previous polls. You could determine from this whether the trend in voting is up or down and thus make your prediction on the likely outcome of the next election (you might also wish to take other historical trends into account which could be picked up from the secondary data). Of course, if the resources were available, we might wish to commence your own time-series survey.

Question 6.5

Your classmates may be a biased sample. Certainly, they are both unlikely to be representative of the population in general, and would probably not match any quotas for this sort of survey (which would require a high number of parents as subjects).

Question 6.6

Postal surveys are generally lower cost than telephone surveys and the respondee can be sent literature (such as photographs, fabric swatches, perfume samples) which could not be provided over the phone. Postal surveys also have better coverage than telephone surveys (not all people have a phone), interviewer bias is eliminated, and respondees can complete the survey form at their leisure.

CAI allows more personal questions to be asked than with a face-to-face interview. Responses are also quicker to analyse and interviewer bias is eliminated.

Question 6.7

They broke rule 14 – by failing to introduce themselves and the purpose of the survey first.

SUMMARY

In this unit you have learned about:

- Qualitative and quantitative primary research methods
- Survey methods
- The ethical responsibilities of interviewers
- Sampling methods (especially quotas)
- Questionnaire design
- Avoiding bias in sampling and in the design of questionnaires

Presentation and interpretation of research findings

OBJECTIVES

This unit covers the analysis and presentation of the results of your research findings. In this unit you will:

- Learn how to describe data.
- Examine the characteristics of data distributions.
- Appreciate the relationship between data samples and populations.
- Be introduced to the different methods of presenting information.
- Consider the advantages and disadvantages of these methods.
- Look at the possible sources of bias in data presentation.

By the end of this unit you will be able to:

- Understand the circumstances under which it would be appropriate to use the various measures of location and dispersion.
- Calculate the measures of location and dispersion for simple data sets.
- Interpret the meaning of different distributions.
- Determine from sample data the likely population statistics.
- Critically appraise the research of others on the basis of its use of the statistics discussed.
- Understand the circumstances under which it would be appropriate to use the various presentation methods for primary and secondary data.
- Present your own research findings in a meaningful and accurate way.
- Appraise the way in which third party data is presented.

An understanding of the use and abuse of basic statistics is essential to the interpretation and evaluation of research data. Much of the material will already be familiar to any student who has brushed with statistics in the past. Students new to the subject should not be put off by the thought of manipulating numbers or calculating formulae. A step-by-step approach and reference to the examples given will guarantee steady progress through this unit.

It is NOT necessary for students to develop 'hands-on' familiarity with statistical techniques, as the examination will NOT include questions requiring the manipulation of data. Nonetheless, students should acquaint themselves with the broad principles behind the presentation of statistics and should also be aware, again in general terms, of the way in which quantitative information may be misinterpreted, either accidentally or deliberately, through poor presentation and/or wilful manipulation of the evidence.

Presenting your data in a clear and compelling manner is about communicating ideas in a way which is both accurate and interesting. People can comprehend information presented graphically much more easily than lists of numbers or paragraphs of text. The old adage that '*a picture is worth a thousand words*' is certainly true. Most of the methods of data presentation demonstrated in this unit rely on the use of graphics to communicate information which would otherwise be difficult to summarize.

Remember that a graph or report is usually the culmination of your research effort and often the only evidence of all your hard work! It is worth taking the time to get them right.

Organize your study materials from the beginning of the course:

- Use file dividers to keep broad topic areas indexed and relevant materials and articles with the relevant notes.
- Have a pocket calculator to hand (any simple model will suffice although 'scientific' ones will have dedicated buttons for the direct calculation of many of the basic statistics described).
- Prepare a supply of scrap paper for rough 'workings-out'. When you are confident of your rough notes transfer these to a notebook
- Prepare a supply of squared graph paper and plain paper for use in drawing the various types of graphs and tables described in this unit. Keep all of these in your file.

Working through this unit's content is expected to take around three to four hours. The activities will take a further three to four hours to complete. Answers to all questions are at the end of the unit.

Characteristics of data

Each piece of data you collect, whether it be the response to a question on a questionnaire or the weight of produce purchased by a shopper, is called an 'observation'.

Each of these observations has a 'value' associated with it. This may be numerical or non-numerical; 'Yes', 'No', 207, 11 kg, 110 mm, 493 widgets, are all valid values. Sometimes non-numerical responses are converted (or coded) into numbers to make them easier to handle and store. For instance, a response of 'Yes' may be converted to the number 1; 'No' may be converted to the number 0.

The observations you collect in the course of a particular study, are called a data set. You may collect one, or more data sets from a series of studies and compare them for changes in attitudes, buying behaviour and to identify trends.

Data which has not been altered in any way (that is, it remains unchanged from when it was collected) is called raw data.

The observations in each data set are 'distributed' across a spread of values. This is called a data distribution.

In most cases, the raw data you collect will simply be pages of numbers or questionnaire responses. This, in itself, is fairly meaningless. Before raw data can be interpreted it must first be summarized. Three main methods are used to describe and present summarized data:

1 Tables
2 Graphics
3 Statistics

As an example, let us imagine that you have conducted a small survey of 10 marketing students to find out how many of the recommended textbooks they actually read. You find that 1 student admits to having read only one book, 2 students admit to having read two of the recommended books, 4 students say they have read three books, 2 students say they have read four books and 1 diligent student claims to have read five books.

Using tables

We could represent the data from the books examples in tabular form (Table 7.1).

Table 7.1   Numbers of recommended books read by marketing students

Number of books read	Number of students
1	1
2	2
3	4
4	2
5	1

This sort of table is called a *frequency table* because it records the frequency with which particular values occur.

Using graphics

We also represent the same books data graphically (Figure 7.1):

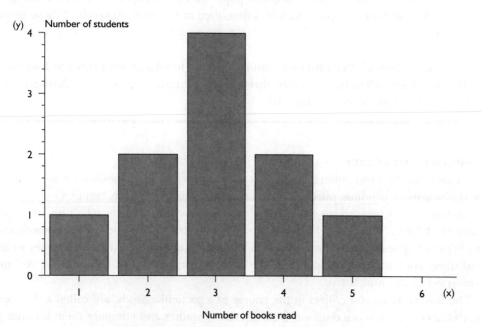

Figure 7.1   Numbers of recommended books read by marketing students

This representation of data is called a *frequency distribution*. Like the tabular equivalent it represents the frequency of unique values found in the data. You will also notice that this particular frequency distribution is symmetrical around the mid-point. That is, the left and right sides or the distribution are mirror images of each other. This situation is quite rare in market research but important nonetheless as symmetrical distributions (also called normal distributions) have certain special properties.

Using statistics

In this unit we will first concentrate on the third method of representing raw data using measures of location and measures of dispersion. Later on we will also look at the issues surrounding sampling and data presentation.

Measures of location

The commonest method of summarizing raw data is to calculate the 'average' response.

There are three 'averaging' statistics. These are called:

1 The arithmetic mean.
2 The mode.
3 The median.

Collectively, these statistics are known as *measures of location.*

A *measure of location* is a single figure used to represent the 'average' of a distribution or series of values. As such, it is said to anchor or locate the distribution on a scale of all possible values.

It is sometimes called a *measure of central tendency* because the 'average' tends to be centrally located in the data.

DEFINITION 7.1

The arithmetic mean

This is the most frequently used type of 'average'. It is calculated by adding together all the raw data values and then dividing this result by the number of values collected.

For instance, if a woman earned £16,000 per year and her husband £14,000 per year their mean annual salary would be £15,000. This can be calculated by the formula:

$$\text{mean} = \frac{\text{sum of values}}{\text{number of values}}$$

In the above example, the values are 16,000 and 14,000 and the number of values 2.

$$\text{mean} = \frac{16,000 + 14,000}{2} = \frac{30,000}{2} = £15,000$$

The mode

With ungrouped data the mode can be determined easily from a frequency table or frequency distribution without the need for any calculation!

To find the mode in a frequency table:

1 Look down the frequency (f) column to find the largest figure (which, of course, represents the most frequent response).
2 Read off the corresponding X value for that row. This value is the mode.
    Note: If you find two or more values of X with the same high frequency then:

    (a) If the values are adjacent then calculate the arithmetic mean of the values. This is the mode.

(b) If the values are not adjacent then the data has more than one mode. All the *X* values relating to the high frequencies should be reported.

Now try it for yourself!

Refer back to the frequency table presented for the books example at the beginning of this unit (Figure 7.1). Reading along the *f* column (number of students) we find that the largest figure is 4. Reading left along the row we find that this corresponds to an *X* (number of books) of 3. This is the mode for this set of data.

An alternative method is to find the mode from a frequency distribution:

1 Find the highest point on the frequency distribution.
2 Read off the corresponding value on the lower (*X*) axis. This value is the mode.

The mode calculated for the books example is the same as the arithmetic mean calculated earlier. With large data sets it is, in fact, quite unusual to find the mode equal to the mean. This only occurs on the rare occasion where there is an exactly symmetrical distribution of data. More commonly data contains more high values than low values (or vice versa) and the frequency distribution looks a bit lop-sided. This is called a skewed distribution.

Skewness

If a frequency distribution is *asymmetrical* (or lop-sided) it is said to be *skewed*.

If distribution has a longer 'tail' to the right it is said to be positively skewed (a). A distribution with a longer 'tail' to the left is said to be negatively skewed (c).

A distribution with equal length 'tails' is said to be symmetrical or normally distributed (b).

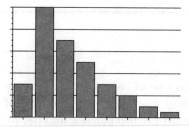

(a) Positive skew

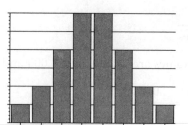

(b) Symmetrical

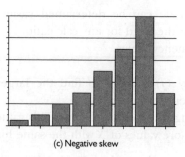

(c) Negative skew

Figure 7.2

Imagine we re-ran the books survey with a group of 10 science students and, from the raw data, produced the following frequency table:

Table 7.2 Frequency table showing the number of recommended books read by science students

Number of books read	Number of students
1	0
2	1
3	2
4	3
5	3

Referring back to the original table for marketing students (Figure 7.1), you can see that science students would appear to read more books than the marketing students. The frequency distribution of this data is markedly skewed to the right (there are more high values of X than low values). This is called a negative skew. When a distribution skews to the left (more low values of X than high values) it is said to be positively skewed.

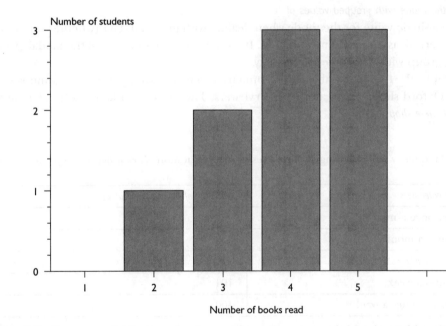

Figure 7.3 Frequency distribution showing numbers of recommended books read by science students

The *mode* is extremely useful because, unlike the mean, it can be used with non-numeric data (such as attitude data).

As part of your research for a software company, you test a prototype on 100 users. After they have used the system for several hours you give them an attitude questionnaire which contains the question '*How satisfied or dissatisfied are you with the 'user-friendliness' of the software you have just been using?*' The possible responses are: Extremely dissatisfied; Very dissatisfied; Dissatisfied; Neither dissatisfied or satisfied; Very satisfied; Extremely satisfied.

The data you collect is displayed as a frequency distribution in Figure 7.4.

The mode of this data is found in exactly the same way as described for numerical data. The highest point on the distribution (the most common response) is found and the corresponding 'value' read off the X axis. In this example, the mode of the distribution is 'satisfied'. It is impossible to calculate a mean for this distribution as the labels on the X axis have no intrinsic numerical value.

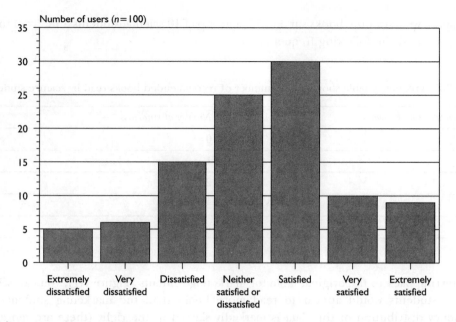

Figure 7.4 Attitude survey of 100 users of new prototype software. Response to the question: '*How satisfied or dissatisfied are you with the 'user-friendliness' of the software you have just been using?*'

Calculating the mode with grouped values of X

To provide a single value for the mode when dealing with grouped data (whether numerical or non-numerical) is somewhat meaningless. It is usually sufficient to quote the modal group, that is the group with the highest frequency.

For example, the frequency table below contains data from a shoppers survey administered in an east Oxford shopping area using interviewers. The question asked was '*How frequently do you visit these shops?*'

Table 7.3 Frequency table showing shoppers responses to question '*How frequently do you visit these shops?*'

Response categories	Number of people responding
Less than once a month	17
About once a month	13
More than twice a month	15
1 to 3 times a week	104
More than 3 times a week	100

The modal value in this example is '1 to 3 times a week' as this is the most frequently occurring response (but only just!).

QUESTION 7.1

What else would you say about the distribution of data in Table 7.3?

What could you deduce about the respondents' shopping behaviour in this area of Oxford? The answers are to be found at the end of this Unit.

The median

The final measure of location we will be looking at is the *median*. It is defined as the value (*X*) of the middle observation when the values are ranked in order of magnitude. In other words, the median is a value chosen so that it has as many observations above it as below it.

If we asked five households how many cars they owned, we might get the following five responses (each number representing a response from a single household):

2, 0, 1, 2, 1

Rearranging these in order of magnitude, we get:

0, 1, **1**, 2, 2

The median is most simply found by counting to the middle observation. In this case the middle observation is the third, which has a value of 1. Where there is an even number of responses it is necessary to calculate the mean of the two middle observations.

If we doubled our sample size on the car survey, we might get the following ten responses:

0, 0, 1, 1, **1, 2**, 2, 2, 2, 2

As there are an even number of observations we must calculate the mean of the two middle observations. In this case these are the fifth and sixth observations which have values of 1 and 2 respectively. The median in this instance is the arithmetic mean of these two values, in other words 1.5.

To avoid counting to the middle observation we can use the following formula:

$$\text{Middle observation} = \frac{n + 1}{2} \text{ where } n \text{ is equal to the sample size.}$$

So, with a sample size of 5, the middle observation is the third observation. Where the sample contains an even number of observations the above formula will not yield a whole number. If this happens take the mean of the values above and below the middle point provided by the formula.

For example, with a sample size of 6, the formula provides an answer of 3.5 (between the third and fourth observations). To find the median simply calculate the mean of the values of the third and fourth observations.

Comparison of measures of location

Now that we are familiar with the arithmetic mean, mode and median, it is time to sit back and review the similarities and differences between these three measures:

Arithmetic mean	Median	Mode
The common meaning of 'average'	Refers to the middle observation	Refers to the most frequently occurring response
Every value in the distribution is used in calculating the mean	The median is not affected by extreme values	No other value except the modal value is taken into account
Can be used in further calculations	Cannot be used in further calculations	Cannot be used in further calculations
The result from calculating the mean may be an 'impossible' value (i.e. 2.5 children)	The result of calculating the median is usually a 'real' value	The mode is always a 'real' value
Open-ended groups can affect calculations of the group mean	Open-ended groups less likely to affect the calculation of the median	Open-ended groups do not affect the calculation of the mode

Which measure of location should you use?

The mean is most suitable if:

- You want to present a statistic that is widely understood.
- You want to consider the influence of 'extreme' responses.
- You need to go on to use more complex statistics.
- It is not necessary to provide a 'real' value as a result.
- Your data is numerical.

For example, the mean can be used to determine the 'average' for most continuous variables (variables where every number has a meaning), such as weight, distance and psychological variables such as intelligence.

The median is most suitable if:

- Your research attaches some significance to the middle value.
- You want an 'average' which is not affected by extreme values.
- You do not need to do further detailed statistics.
- You want a more realistic representation of the 'average'.
- Your data is numerical.

For example, the median can be used to analyse changes in market trends. In this instance we may only be concerned with the movement of the 'middle' value.

The mode is most suitable if:

- You are only interested in determining the most frequent value.
- You do not need to do further detailed statistics.
- Your data is numerical or non-numerical.

For example, the mode can be used with non-numeric attitude survey data or to determine the price for a product or service which most people would accept.

EXAM HINT

Common mistakes

- A common error is to treat coded non-numerical responses as if they are numbers. Beware of falling into this trap. If one person says they shop at Tesco (coded as 1) and another says they shop at Sainsbury's (coded as 2), it is tempting to quote the 'average' response as being half way between the two coded numbers (i.e. 1.5). However, the value of 1.5 has, of course, no meaning in this context. To represent the 'average' of such data it is best to take the modal value.
- Under exam conditions it very easy to confuse X values with their frequency of occurrence f. Ask yourself what is being measured – this is the X variable – and how frequently these X responses occur – this is f.

Measures of dispersion

In addition to knowing about the 'average' of a distribution it is also useful to know about the 'spread' of values in the distribution.

There are three statistics which are commonly used to describe 'spread'. These are called:

1. The range.
2. The interquartile range.
3. The quartile deviation.
4. The mean deviation.
5. The standard deviation (and variance).

Collectively, these statistics are known as *measures of dispersion*.

Measures of dispersion summarize the 'spread' of values present in a distribution

The range

The range is the simplest measure of dispersion. It is defined as the difference between the highest value observation and the lowest value observation in the data.

For example, consider the following data observations:

1, 3, 2, 2, 2, 5, 7

The highest value is 7; the lowest value is 1. The range is therefore: $7 - 1 = 6$.

Quartiles

Before we go further, we need to know a bit about quartiles.

Earlier we defined the median as the value of the middle observation in a distribution of data. In other words, 50% of observations have values above the median and 50% have values below. The median thus divides the distribution in two.

Dividing the distribution into four equal parts creates what are known as quartiles.

If the observations are arranged in ascending order of size, the lower quartile (Q_1) is the value which cuts off the lowest 25% of observations. It can be calculated using the formula:

$$\left(Q_1 = \frac{n}{4} \right)$$

If the observations are arranged in ascending order of size, the upper quartile (Q_3) is the value which bounds the highest 25% of observations. It can be calculated using the formula:

$$\left(Q_3 = \frac{n}{4} \times 3 \right)$$

Note 1: You may have spotted that these formulae bear a close resemblance to those for determining the median. In fact, the median is merely the 'middle' quartile (it is sometimes referred to as Q_2).

Note 2: As with the calculation for the median, if the quartiles fall between two observations the mean of these observations is used.

Example: the following 10 observations were collected in response to the question: 'How far is your place of work from your home (in km)?' (the data has already been sorted into ascending order):

2, 3, 3, 14, 16, 23, 27, 28, 40, 64

The median of this data is the mean of the middle two observations (16 and 23) which equals 19.5 km.

The lower quartile (Q_1) is the mean of the second and third observations (3 and 3) which equals 3 km.

The upper quartile (Q_3) is the mean of the seventh and eighth observations (28 and 40) which equals 34 km.

Quartiles can also be used to determine the direction of skew in a distribution.

If ($Q_2 - Q_1$) is greater than ($Q_3 - Q_2$) then the distribution has negative skew.

On the other hand if ($Q_2 - Q_1$) is less than ($Q_3 - Q_2$) then the distribution has positive skew.

Interquartile range

The interquartile range is similar to the range but measures the difference, not between the two extreme observation values, but between the lower and upper quartiles. It is calculated with the formula:

Interquartile range = $Q_3 - Q_1$

Thus in the 'distance from home' example just given, the interquartile range is $34 - 3 = 31$ km. This compares with a calculated range for the same data of 62 km.

It can be seen from this example that the interquartile range is less sensitive to extreme values.

The smaller the value of the interquartile range, the less dispersed the data.

Quartile deviation

The quartile deviation (sometimes called the semi-interquartile range) is another measure of dispersion which makes use of quartiles. It is defined as being the mean distance of the upper and lower quartiles from the median. The smaller the value of this measure, the less dispersed is the data. The formula for calculating it is slightly different from the one used to calculate the interquartile range as it is measuring the mean deviation from the median rather than the spread of the data directly:

$$\text{Quartile deviation} = \frac{Q_3 - Q_1}{2}$$

Thus the quartile deviation in the 'distance from home' example is the interquartile range divided by 2 = 15.5 km.

Mean and standard deviation

These two methods of measuring dispersion are not included in the CIM syllabus, though you need to be aware of their potential benefits.

Comparison of measures of dispersion

Range	Interquartile range	Quartile deviation	Mean deviation	Standard deviation
Easy to find and calculate	Reasonably easy to find and calculate	Reasonably easy to find and calculate	More difficult to find and calculate	More difficult to find and calculate
Affected by extreme values	Less affected by extreme values	Less affected by extreme values	Less affected by extreme values	Less affected by extreme values
Only takes extreme values into account	Ignores 50% of values	Ignores 50% of values	Takes all values into account	Takes all values into account
Gives no indication of spread within distribution	Gives no indication of spread within distribution	Gives average spread from median	Gives average spread from mean	Gives indication of spread from mean
Cannot be used for further statistical analysis	Cannot be used for further statistical analysis	Cannot be used for further statistical analysis	Cannot be used for further statistical analysis	Can be used for further statistical analysis

Which measure of dispersion is appropriate?

The *range* is most suitable if:

- You want to present a statistic that is easy to understand.
- You want an indication of dispersion that is easy to compute.
- You want to consider the influence of 'extreme' responses.
- You know that 'extreme' values do not occur in your data.
- You do not need to do further detailed statistics.
- It is necessary to provide an indication of the 'real' values as a result.

For example the *range* can be used when determining the number of 'sale or return' products you need to stock. Taking into account the range of units likely to be purchased will ensure that you neither have too few in stock nor unnecessarily large quantities to return.

The *interquartile range* and *quartile deviation* are most suitable if:

- Your research attaches some significance to the middle value (you most likely used the median as your measure of location).
- You want a measure which is not affected by extreme values.
- You do not need to do further detailed statistics.
- If it is necessary to provide an indication of the 'real' values as a result, use the interquartile range.
- If it is necessary to provide an indication of the spread from the median, use the quartile deviation.

For example, these measures can be used to analyse changes in market trends. In this instance we may only be concerned with the change in values associated with the middle 50% of the population.

The *mean deviation* and *standard deviation* are most suitable if:

- You need to consider the influence of all values and their spread from the arithmetic mean (you most likely used the mean as your measure of location).
- If you need to do further statistical analysis and want a measure which is widely understood then use the standard deviation.
- If you do not need to do further statistical analysis then use the mean deviation as a measure.

For example, these measures are commonly used to calculate the spread of continuous variables (where every numerical value has a meaning) such as weight, height, time and so on.

Proportions, fractions and percentages

Often it is useful to represent values, not in terms of their absolute numerical 'worth', but in terms of their relative value in comparison with other observations. For example, it is all very well knowing that your product sold 250,000 units this month, but of more interest is how it performed in comparison to the competition. For instance, what market share do you have?

There are three ways of representing such information:

- As a percentage.
- As a fraction.
- As a proportion.

All of these are in common usage.
As an example, we may say that:

1 Your sales of 250,000 represent 50% (a *percentage*) of the overall number of units sold (500,000).
2 Your sales of 250,000 represent ½ (a *fraction*) of 500,000 units sold.
3 Your sales of 250,000 represent 0.5 (a *proportion*) of the 500,000 units sold.

All have the same meaning and can be used interchangeably to describe the relationship of the value 250,000 to the value 500,000. Twenty five and 50 would have the same relationship, as would 500 and 1000, 10 and 20 and 5 and 10. In each case the first value is half the second value.

Percentages are all around us: bank interest rates; mortgage rates; exam marks and so on. You may already be familiar with the method for calculating percentages.

For example, to find 10% of £50 you would multiply 50 by 0.1 (10 divided by 100):

$$10\% \text{ of } £50 = £50 \times \frac{10}{100} = £50 \times \frac{1}{10} = £5$$

You may also wish to find the relationship between two values. To find what percentage £5 is of £50 (the reverse of the above example) we divide the value whose percentage we are trying to find (in this case £5) by the value of the whole (£50) and multiply the result by 100:

$$£5 \text{ as a percentage of } £50 = \frac{5}{50} \times 100 = \frac{1}{10} \times 100 = 10\%$$

We can also find percentages for values greater than the whole. For example, a product which originally cost £10 now costs £15. What is this new price as a percentage of the previous price:

$$£15 \text{ as a percentage of } £10 = \frac{15}{10} \times 100 = \frac{3}{2} \times 100 = 150\%$$

We can also represent this as being a price *increase* of 50% as £5 (the increase) is 50% of £10 (the original value).

Proportions are merely a different way of representing the same percentage information. You can think of 1 as representing 100% (or the whole); 0.5 as representing 50% (a half); 0.25 as representing 25% (a quarter) and so on. To obtain the proportion from a percentage we divide by 100. For example, 10% represented as a proportion is 0.1.

Out of 100 purchasers of a product, 23 are men. What is the proportion of women buying the product?

First we must find the number of women = 100 − 23 = 77

$$77 \text{ as a proportion of } 100 = \frac{77}{100} \times 100 = 77\% = 0.77$$

As with proportions and percentages, fractions are merely another way of representing the relationship between two values. For instance, the relationship between £1 as a portion of £4 is represented by the fraction ¼ which is equivalent to ¼ × 100 = 25% which is equivalent to a proportion of 0.25.

QUESTION 7.2

Following a successful promotion, sales of 'White Wash' toothpaste jump from £1.4 million to £2.1 million per month. What is the percentage increase in sales?

QUESTION 7.3

Your customer panel is split in their opinion of a new butterscotch flavour soft drink you are test marketing. Out of the 80 members of your panel, 32 say they do not like the taste, 40 say they like it and the remainder are not sure. Express the size of these three groups as a proportion of the whole.

Sampling theory

Sampling theory is about understanding how well the data we collect from sample groups represents the 'real world'. This is important if we are to place any faith at all in the ability of our data to predict the information from the target population as a whole.

Suppose we wish to find out the monthly insurance premium that would be acceptable to our target population (which we estimate in this case to be about ½ million people). A decision is made to set the premium equal to the arithmetic mean (the company does not want to set the premium so high that it scares people off or too low so that it does not make any money). Given limits on our time and resources we might only get to question a sample of 200 people. Clearly, the data we collect can only be an estimate of the premium that the population, as a whole, would accept. In other words, we would expect some error in our findings.

Deciding the sample size for your survey

There are many factors which affect the size of a sample apart from the statistical considerations.

- *The survey method used.* Large sample sizes are easier to achieve with some methods (i.e. postal surveys; telephone surveys) than with others (i.e. face-to-face interviews; observation).
- *Time and resources may be limited.* This will involve a trade-off between sample size and the amount and accuracy of the information to be collected.
- *Precision required.* There is no point using large sample sizes when only a rough estimate of a population mean is required. Decide on the precision you require and use the formula provided for determining the sample size required.
- *Number of groups sampled.* If you plan to sample a number of groups you may be able to merge the group data to provide a better overall estimate of the population mean.

Presenting research findings

We turn our attention to the presentation of research data. In particular we will look at:

- Tables.
- Charts (including tally charts, bar charts and histograms).
- Graphs (single and multi-line).
- Pie charts.
- Pictograms and other uses of pictures in data presentation.

We will then turn our attention to bias in the presentation of data and, finally, report writing.

Tables

As we have seen earlier in this unit, tabulation is one of the most basic methods of presenting data in a summarized form. The size of a table is defined by the number of rows and columns it contains.

For example a 3 × 2 table would contain 3 rows and 2 columns. The intersection of these rows and columns creates cells. Each cell holds a piece of data. A 3 × 2 table would contain 6 cells and would look something like this:

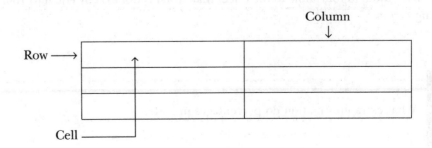

It is important to label the rows and columns so it is clear what data is being presented. Part of the skill in constructing a table is to identify which information is best presented in columns and which is best presented in rows. It is most usual to present the values, individual data or other measures in the rows and the elements being compared or contrasted as columns.

For instance the following table (Figure 7.5) compares the weekly sales of four different ice cream flavours across three London outlets. You will notice that the table has been captioned and totals have been added to the end of each row and column. The total in the lower right hand corner should (if you have got your sums right!) be equal to both the sum of the 'total' row and 'total' column:

Ice cream flavours	Outlets			Total
	Oxford Street	Tottenham Court Rd	Kensington High St.	
Nutty Choc	1345	1310	1100	3755
Mint Delight	500	324	106	930
Almond Surprise	2005	1987	1024	5016
Double Choc	3375	3405	2876	9656
Total	7225	7026	5106	19357

Figure 7.5 Sales figures for different ice cream flavours (number of portions sold). A comparison of three London outlets

We can also add summary information (as well as, or instead of, the summarized raw data) as necessary to make the data more meaningful and easier to interpret. In the example below (Figure 7.6), percentages have been added for each cell:

Ice cream flavours	Outlets						Total	
	Oxford Street		Tottenham Court Rd		Kensington High St.			
	Number	%	Number	%	Number	%	Number	%
Nutty Choc	1345	18.6	1310	18.6	1100	21.5	3755	19.4
Mint Delight	500	6.9	324	4.6	106	2.1	930	4.8
Almond Sunrise	2005	27.8	1987	28.3	1024	20.1	5016	25.9
Double Choc	3375	46.7	3405	48.5	2876	56.3	9656	49.9
Total	7225	100.0	7026	100.0	5106	100.0	19357	100.0

Figure 7.6 Sales figures for different ice cream flavours (number of portions sold). A comparison of three London outlets

Sometimes when percentages are calculated the total does not equal exactly 100% due to rounding errors when calculating the individual percentages. Try to avoid this by rounding figures to the nearest decimal place. For instance round 23.55 up to 23.6 and 23.54 down to 23.5. Most errors should 'cancel out'. If you are still left with a total slightly above or below 100% then add a footnote to your table to the effect that 'Total is not exactly equal to 100% due to rounding errors'.

What extra information do percentages provide?

- The table should have a clear caption so that its purpose is clear.
- The table caption should carry a reference (such as Table A, Table 3.2, Figure 3.2 etc.) so that it can easily be referred to from a report or in a presentation.
- Columns and rows should be clearly labelled and distinct from the data.
- Where it is meaningful to do so, subtotal each row and column (as shown above) and provide an overall total in the lower right hand corner.
- Do not be afraid to include other extra rows or columns with summary data (such as percentages) where you feel it adds meaning to the data.
- Make sure the figures in the tables are properly aligned. This is particularly important where the data contains decimals. This makes the information easier to read.
- Try not to pack too much data into one table. If possible, summarize the data into a smaller table.
- If you are trying to draw attention to one or two figures, highlight these (using bold type or whatever other method you have at your disposal).
- Tables do not always have to show every row and column outlined. Sometimes the table appears less cluttered if some of this detail is omitted (see the different table styles below).

Table styles

Nowadays, word processing and spreadsheet computer software packages allow a wide variety of table styles. The following give a flavour of the range of styles available:

Attitudes towards product X	Group A	Group B	Total
Favourable	23	10	33
Unfavourable	12	23	35
Undecided	2	1	3
Total	37	34	71

Figure 7.7   Results of attitude survey of two different user groups towards product X

Attitudes towards product X	Group A	Group B	Total
Favourable	23	10	33
Unfavourable	12	23	35
Undecided	2	1	3
Total	37	34	71

Figure 7.8   Results of attitude survey of two different user groups towards product X

Attitudes towards product X	Group A	Group B	Total
Favourable	23	10	33
Unfavourable	12	23	35
Undecided	2	1	3
Total	37	34	71

Figure 7.9   Results of attitude survey of two different user groups towards product X

Which of the above table styles do you think best represents the data and why?

Figure 7.10 shows a table from the *Financial Times*. Notice the amount of information that has been displayed in just one table.

TOP 10 ADVERTISERS

Rank 1994	Rank 1993	Company	Spending 1994 £m	Spending 1993 £m	% change
1	1	Procter & Gamble	118	95	24
2	4	BT	103	61	69
3	2	Unilever (Lever Bros)	72	70	3
4	5	Ford	70	57	23
5	3	Kellogg UK	69	62	11
6	6	Vauxhall Motors	60	51	18
7	9	Procter & Gamble (health and beauty)	55	39	41
8	11	Dixons Stores	49	38	29
9	10	Unilever (Birds Eye Walls)	44	39	18
10	13	Peugeot Talbot	41	37	11

Source: *Marketing Week*

Figure 7.10   Top ten advertisers. Table from *Financial Times*, April 1995

Charts

Whereas tables provide a numerical summary and representation of data, charts can add a visual dimension which can help to add more impact and make comprehension easier.

Tally charts

Perhaps the simplest visual representation of data uses tally marks. These are normally used as a rough indication of frequency and are usually hand drawn. If they are drawn carefully they show the shape of the frequency distribution. They are related to the pictogram, bar charts and histograms described later.

For instance, ten households say they possess 1 television; eight households say they possess 2 televisions; fifteen households possess 3 televisions and four households say they possess 4 televisions. A tally chart for this data would look like this:

Number of televisions	Number of households
1	╫╫ ╫╫
2	╫╫ ///
3	╫╫ ╫╫ ╫╫
4	////

What is the modal value in the television example?

Bar charts and histograms

These two terms are often used interchangeably to describe charts where data is presented as a series of bars. The length of the bar usually indicates the magnitude associated with the corresponding X value but can also be used to represent proportions and percentages.

There are three main types of bar charts, all are commonly used in representing a wide range of different types of data:

- Simple bar charts.
- Component bar charts.
- Compound bar charts.

The following data (Figure 7.11) was collected from an attitude survey concerning the satisfaction of customers with a new software package.

Customer responses to new software package	Number of customers
'very dissatisfied'	4
'dissatisfied'	8
'neither satisfied nor dissatisfied'	4
'satisfied'	8
'very satisfied'	6

Figure 7.11   Attitude data from software survey

This could be represented as the following simple bar chart (Figure 7.12).

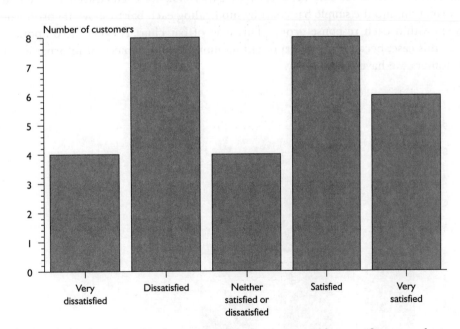

Figure 7.12   Simple bar chart showing satisfaction of customers with new software product

Note: The vertical scale could just as easily show the percentage of customers responding within each category.

Figure 7.13 shows a simple bar chart reproduced from the Guardian. Note the information that has been added and the impact afforded by the three-dimensional representation.

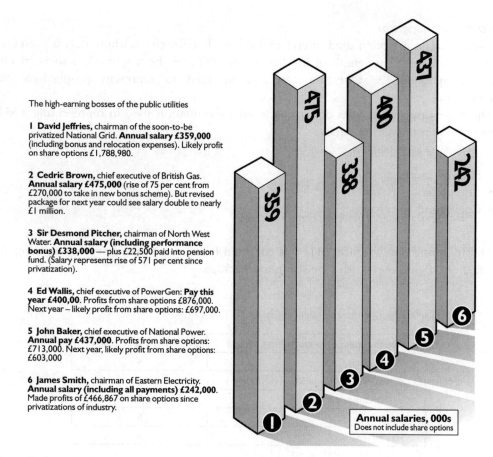

Annual salaries, 000s
Does not include share options

Figure 7.13 A simple bar chart from the *Guardian*, April 1995

Component bar charts

If we had also recorded the amount of software experience for each customer, we could add this information into the simple bar chart by subdividing each bar to show the proportion of customers within each response group. This type of bar chart is called a component bar chart. In this case, because we are representing more than one piece of information about our customers, we have to add a key.

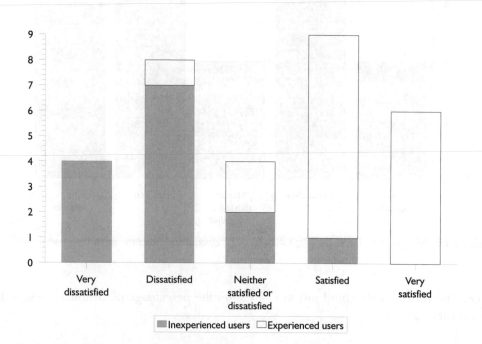

Figure 7.14 Component bar chart showing satisfaction and experience of customers with new software product

What does Figure 7.14 tell you about the relationship between experience and satisfaction?

As with simple bar charts, the vertical axis could indicate percentage but, if this were the case, the bars would all be the same length with only the components changing their proportions. This is called a percentage component bar chart. If we were trying to represent the change in customer response rates over several trials, a percentage component bar chart would be of use. An annual customer satisfaction survey might produce a chart similar to Figure 7.15.

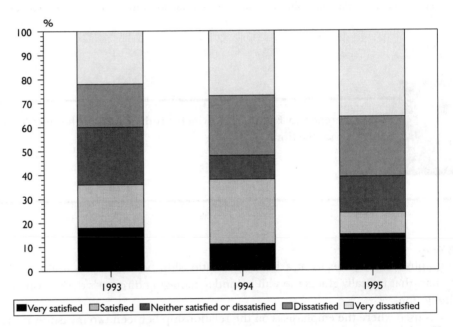

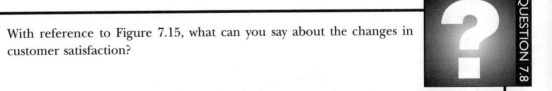

Figure 7.15 Percentage component bar chart showing customer satisfaction with product X. Surveys carried out in 1993, 1994 and 1995

With reference to Figure 7.15, what can you say about the changes in customer satisfaction?

Compound bar charts

Compound bar charts are characterized by having multiple bars associated with each value of *X*. If, referring back to our original customers' satisfaction data, we wished to compare customer satisfaction rates on our software with those of the competition we might use a compound bar chart in the following way:

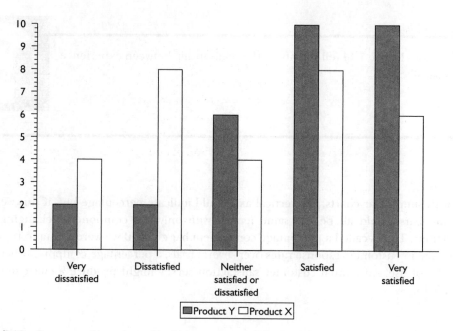

Figure 7.16 Compound bar chart showing customer satisfaction with product X and competitive product Y

QUESTION 7.9

With reference to Figure 7.16, which product has the highest levels of customer satisfaction?

Line graphs

These graphs show, by means of a line, the relationship between two variables. The sales figure chart that typically graces the wall behind a managing director's desk, is one example of a line graph.

A line is used where the emphasis is on the relationship between two measures rather than their actual values. In a sales graphs, for instance, we want to know whether sales are increasing or decreasing week by week. It is not as important to know the actual sales.

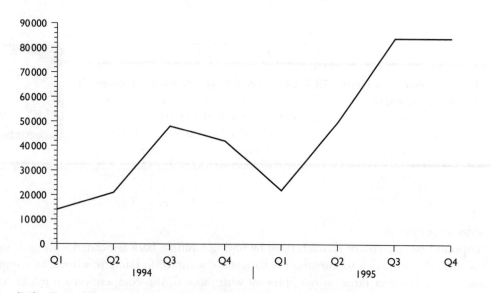

Figure 7.17 Typical line graph showing relationship between sales and financial quarters

Constructing a line graph

A line graph has a vertical scale (called the Y axis) and a horizontal scale (called the X axis). We covered, in an earlier unit, the concept of dependent and independent variables. The dependent variable is the variable being measured, the independent variable is the one we are measuring against. If we were measuring week-by-week sales, the dependent variable is the number of products sold and the independent variable is time. It is most common to place the dependent variable (the variable we are most interested in which could be sales, number of customers) along the Y axis and the independent variable (time, questionnaire response categories, and so on) along the X axis.

Constructing a graph involves a number of distinct stages:

1 Draw the horizontal (X) axis and vertical (Y) axis.

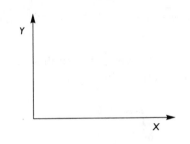

2 Decide on the scale for each axis. The intersection of the X and Y axes is called the origin and is usually labelled '0'. However, if the data you are representing consists only of very large numbers you can save a lot of space by starting your Y axis (or X axis) at a higher value. If this is the case then clearly label the lower end of the Y axis.

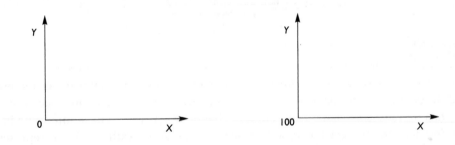

3 Clearly label each scale and indicate the units being represented.

4 Plot the data. Each piece of data has an X value and a Y value associated with it. For instance, recorded sales in 1994 of 100,000 units would constitute one data point. For this data point draw a light pencil line (or use a ruler) from the X value ('1994') and a horizontal line from the Y value ('100,000') and place a '+' where the lines intersect on the graph. Do this for all your data points.

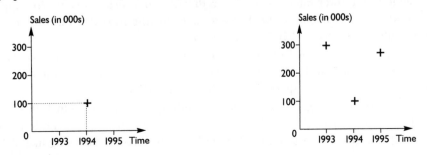

5 Join up the centres of the data points with a line, working from left to right. There is also a type of graph, which is less commonly used, where the data points are left unconnected. This is called a scattergram.

For neatness, you can erase your original '+' markers once the line has been drawn.

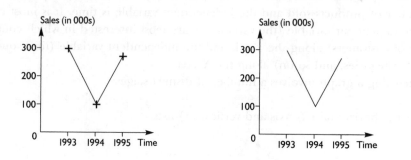

6 Last, but not least, it is necessary to give your graph a caption and number so that it can be referred to easily in presentations and reports.

Graph 1 International sales 1993–5

Let us work through an example. We wish to find the relationship between our company's investment in advertising over a particular period and sales to find out whether the two are related. If we spend more on advertising does this result in more sales and vice versa?

The data we have collected is shown in the table below. As we are most interested in sales (this is the dependent variable) we will construct a line graph with the Y axis representing 'Sales' and the X axis representing 'Investment in Advertising'.

Sales (in thousands of units) from data collected 1992–1994	*Investment in Advertising (in thousands of £s) from data collected 1992–1994*
210	50
120	10
80	80

Following the steps outlined earlier, we would first draw the Y axis and X axis. As the lowest values for sales is 80,000 units, it is sensible to start the lower end of the Y axis at a value other than '0'. Let us choose 50,000 as a round number. Choosing a round number helps us to construct an easy-to-read scale.

The selection of a lower value for the Y axis dictates, to a certain extent, the upper value. Let us 'round up' the top end of the Y axis to 250,000 (the next nearest 50,000 step above the highest value given for Y (210,000) in our table).

The values given for X range from 10,000 to 80,000. Although a number of alternatives are possible, let us choose a scale of 0 to 100,000 for our X axis. This accommodates all the X values in our table with some space to spare at either end of the scale.

As the values for both sales and advertising spending are given to us in 1000s, it is easiest to mark the scales accordingly. The Y axis label should therefore read something like 'Sales (in thousands of units)'. The X axis label should therefore read something like 'Advertising

Spending (in thousands of £s)'. As space is often limited for the labelling of axes, it is common practice to abbreviate labels. If this is necessary, you should add information to the graph's caption so that the reader is in no doubt as to the units being used. For this example, we will abbreviate the *Y* axis label to 'Sales (000s units)' and the *X* axis label to 'Advertising (£k)'.

Our caption should clearly present all the information needed to make sense of the graph even if this information is duplicated in any accompanying material.

So far, our graph looks something like this:

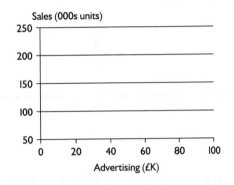

ACME Corporation: A comparison of sales (in thousands of units) with advertising spending (in thousands of £s). Annual data collected during period 1992–1994

The next step is to plot the data as described earlier. The graph below shows the lines for 'working out' the positions of the three data points in this example:

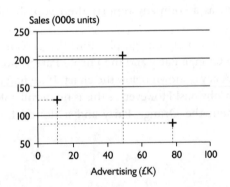

ACME Corporation: A comparison of sales (in thousands of units) with advertising spending (in thousands of £s). Annual data collected during period 1992–1994

Finally, join up the data points erasing your workings-out as you go. The final graph should look something like this:

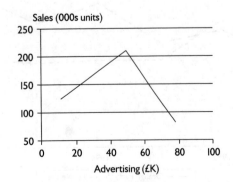

ACME Corporation: A comparison of sales (in thousands of units) with advertising spending (in thousands of £s). Annual data collected during period 1992–1994

Draw a line graph using the data in the following table:

Sales	Week Number
100	1
250	5
200	9
320	13

Multi-line graphs

We can represent more than one set of data on a line graph. This is useful for comparing information. It might be that we want to compare this year's sales with last year's or the performance of different products over the same time period. The method for producing these graphs is the same as has been described for single line graphs. Obviously, it is important to distinguish the lines. This is usually done by using colour or a pattern to differentiate them. It is important to provide a key to the colours, or any other coding used, where there is any danger of confusion. Keys are commonly found on maps and architectural drawings. If your graphs are likely to be photocopied or printed in a single colour publication (such as a company report) then you should not rely on colour as a means of coding!

The following example of a multi-line graph shows the percentage of the vote obtained by two political parties (the Orange Party and the Purple Party), over the course of three years' elections (Figure 7.18). A key is shown below the chart. If we had colour capability the choice of colours would be fairly obvious! However, as this is not a full colour publication, we will use a dashed line to represent the Orange Party and a dotted line to represent the Purple Party.

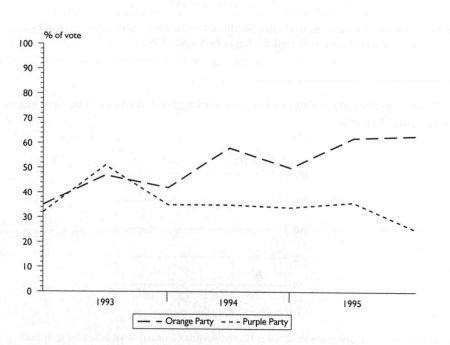

Figure 7.18   Performance of Orange and Purple political parties over period 1993–1995

Pie charts

Pie charts, so called because they are round and divided into pie-like slices, are commonly used to represent percentages and proportions. Suppose we wanted to represent the percentage of males and females in a particular survey sample. We are probably not interested in the absolute number of males and females but more the proportions involved; whether the number of males outweighed the number of females or vice versa. This can most easily be seen from a pie chart. If our survey sample had consisted of 33 males and 99 females, a pie chart would look like this:

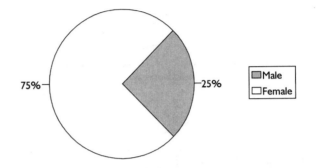

Figure 7.19 Pie chart showing percentage of males and females in survey X

The key shown is not necessary where space can be found to place labels next to the pie slices. The other information which can be shown as well as, or instead of, the percentage information given, is the absolute values that the pie slices represent. What information is shown will depend on the purpose of your chart. Unnecessary information can clutter the chart and confuse your audience.

Pies charts are frequently used for showing market share. Here we are less interested in the overall size of the market (which may be affected by a number of external factors such as the economy) but how much of the market we are selling to in comparison with our competition.

Emphasizing data in a pie chart

It is common practice to emphasize the data in a pie chart by 'detaching' the relevant slice (rather like serving up a portion of cake). It may be that we wish to highlight the percentage of satisfied, or dissatisfied, customers or the market share of our company (see Figure 7.20). This method of emphasis is particularly effective when combined with a three-dimensional pie chart as can be produced from most of the popular computer graphing packages.

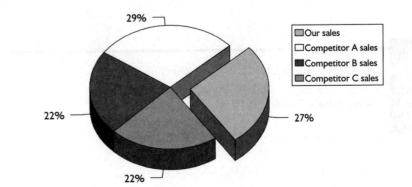

Figure 7.20 Pie chart showing our market share compared with competitors A, B and C

Drawing a pie chart

To draw a pie chart (without a computer!) you will need a compass, or a round object you can draw around, and a protractor (to measure angles).

1 Using the compass (or round object) draw a circle of the size required.

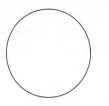

2 Draw a straight line horizontally from the centre of the circle to the outside edge.

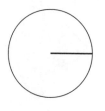

3 You will now need to calculate the position of the pie slices according to your data. Place your protractor on the horizontal line you have just drawn, with the centre of the protractor positioned on the centre of the circle.

4 Convert your data into percentages. The size of your slice (in degrees) can be calculated using the following formula:

$$\text{Slice angle (in degrees)} = \frac{\text{percentage}}{100} \times 360$$

For example, 25% would be represented by a slice of $\frac{25}{100} \times 360 = 90°$

(which is equal to ¼ of a pie)

5 To transfer the angle to your pie, read off the degrees on the protractor and place a mark on the outside edge of the circle. Draw a straight line from this mark to the centre of the circle to create your slice.

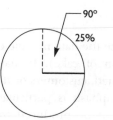

6 To create further slices, place your protractor on the line representing your last slice and repeat steps 4 and 5.

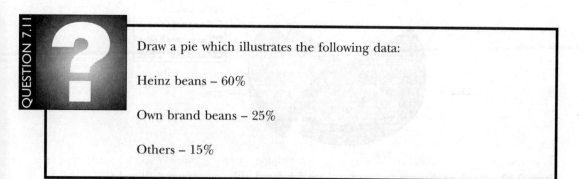

Draw a pie which illustrates the following data:

Heinz beans – 60%

Own brand beans – 25%

Others – 15%

Pictograms

Pictograms are charts and graphs which use pictures to convey information.

The most common style of pictogram is a variant of a bar chart where pictures are 'stacked' or 'stretched' in place of the bars. Some computer programmes are available which automatically display pictograms based on the data and pictures you specify.

Not all pictures are suitable for use in this way, they must have clearly defined edges so that their height can easily be determined. Pictograms should differentiate by numbers and not area. For example, to show that sales of one brand of television are 10 times that of another, we should show 10 times as many televisions and *not* two televisions – one ten times the size of the other.

The following example of a stacked pictogram shows sales of 'Possum' brand canned cat food. Each can represents sales of 100,000 units. Sales do not exactly equal multiples of 100,000 units in each quarter so it is necessary to show part-cans also.

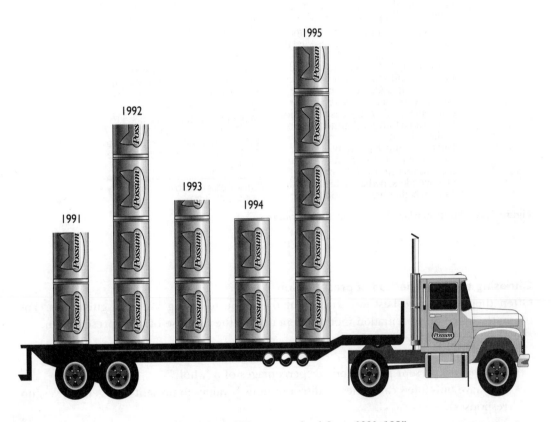

Figure 7.21   A pictogram showing sales of Possum cat food from 1991–1995

As they have a vivid impact, pictograms are particularly suitable for popular presentation.

Other uses of pictures

Pictures can also be used to add interest and enliven the display of otherwise 'boring' numbers. Pictures should not be used where their use confuses, misleads, or otherwise distracts from the point of the presentation.

Clever use of graphics can add a whole new dimension to the presentation of data which, with the advent of readily available computer 'clip-art', you do not have to be an artist to produce. Having made this statement, you will find that the most professional and imaginative graphics are still produced by trained graphic artists.

Here is one example of the imaginative use of pictures to present data (taken from the *Guardian* newspaper). You can see how it is a modified version of one of the standard pie chart methods of data presentation we have discussed.

Guinness's claims that there is no difference between its Irish brewed and London brewed stout, despite generations of drinkers proclaiming the Irish product to be a different animal.

This Friday, Bass brewers will introduce its own Irish contender, though in the form of a sort of hybrid between bitter and stout. Caffrey's was launched a year ago to the pub trade and now moves into the canned market, with help of the ubiquitous 'widget'.

Jane Sabiney, of Bass, says that the success of Caffrey's has exceeded the brewer's expectations. 'At the moment, through the on-trade it is selling £1.75 million worth a week and will take off-trade by storm. We're aiming very much at the repertoire drinkers who do not necessarily stick to the same thing each time they go to the pub,' she says. The retail launch is being backed by a campaign from WCRS which dwells in the Antrim origins of the product. One wonders, perhaps a touch cynically, whether brewers would have

Stout market
Estimates

Beamish 9%

14% Murphy's

Guinness 77%

been so anxious to wave the green, white and orange in less political harmony.

The question of nationality and authenticity has permeated much of the beer market, largely because considerations of health and moderated drinking patterns have meant that, of late, quality rather than quantity has driven the brewing figures. For instance, cask conditioned ales, or 'real ales' as they are more commonly known, have taken an increased market share between 1989 and 1993, with the feeling the the mass-produced beers are loosing fashionability.

Guinness, perhaps the strongest beer brand in the world, has remained untroubled, if not unaware of the competition for authenticity.

Whether it will feel the need to wave the Shamrock beyond March 17 will be a test of how resilient – not to say Irish – the boys from the black stuff are feeling.

Emily Bell is the Observer's business correspondent

Figure 7.22   Stout market share: from the *Guardian*

Choosing the best method of presentation

Often there is no one best way to present data. The following are only guidelines. The ultimate choice of presentation method depends on the purpose of your presentation.

Consider using a *pie chart* when:

- You wish to present proportions or percentages of a 'whole'.
- You have only a few categories or discontinuous X values to present (i.e. gender, yes/no responses).
- You wish to present market share or market segment details.

Consider using a *line graph* when:

- Your X-values are continuous (e.g. time, height, weight, etc.).
- You are more interested in absolute values than percentages or proportions.
- You want to present more than one data set on a single graph.
- You wish to present time series data.

Consider using a *bar chart* when:

- You have many categories or discontinuous X values to present (i.e. responses to multiple choice questions).
- Where the profile or distribution of your X values is of interest . For instance, response to a multiple choice question may range from 'very good' to 'very bad', with three or more categories in between. The distribution of these responses can be seen and interpreted most readily from a bar chart.
- When you need to show a lot of information on one chart. Stacked and multiple bar charts are used for this purpose.

Consider using a *pictogram* or other picture-based chart when:

- The data to be presented is relatively straightforward.
- You are making a popular presentation.

QUESTION 7.12

Which presentation method would you use in the following cases:

1 Displaying responses to an attitude survey.
2 To display market share information.
3 Simple data to be used in a presentation open to the general.
  public.
4 To display variations in the packed weight of your product.
5 To display complex information about percentage changes in data over separate
  trials.

Bias in the presentation of data

Data which is presented in a misleading fashion is said to be biased. Bias can be introduced unintentionally or, in certain cases, on purpose.

The Market Research Society's Code of Conduct states that:

a member shall not knowingly communicate conclusions from a given research project or service that are inconsistent with, or not warranted by, the data. (paragraph B.3)

There are four main ways in which bias can occur:

1 Omission of information.
2 Manipulation of graph axes.
3 Failure to present comparative data.
4 Using an inappropriate presentation method.

Omission of information

Omitting certain important information from a graph is not only bad practice but can mislead your audience. Three examples are given below:

1 *Number of respondees* – Your audience should be told both the number of respondees to a survey and the proportion of those questioned who responded. Different importance would be attached to a survey where only 20 people where questioned, and one where 2000 people were surveyed. Similarly, if a postal survey of 2000 attracted only 20 replies, we might suspect that the responses represented the opinions of some special interest group only.
2 *Who the respondees are* – Whether your respondees are potential buyers of your product, potential users, randomly selected members of the public, or some other subset of the population, may change the interpretation of the results. For instance, comments on price are more relevant if they originate from potential buyers. Other respondees may have no idea of the market value of a particular product.
3 *Scale units* – Your audience can be mislead by the omission, or incomplete labelling of, the units used in your graph. For example the vertical axis on a sales graph should be clearly labelled with the units used. It may be that this axis represents some monetary value or unit sales. If monetary, it should be clear whether the figures given represent turnover, profit, or some other financial indicator.

Manipulating graph axes

Sometimes called 'stretching the truth', expanding or contracting the scales on chart axes can make small changes in values seem larger, or smaller, respectively. For example, the three sales graphs in Figure 7.23 all show the same data, the sales of 'Possum' cat food during the four quarters of 1994. Which do you think looks most impressive?

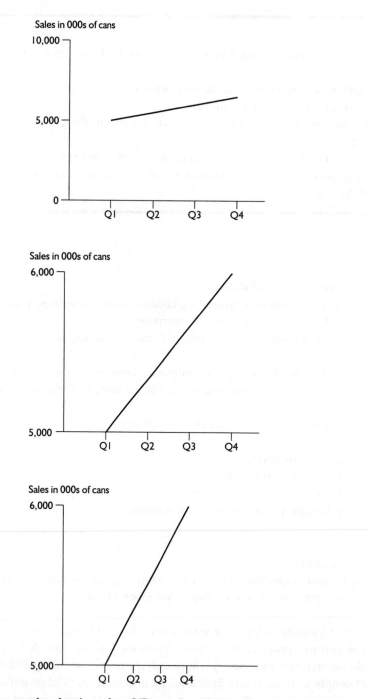

Figure 7.23 Three line graphs, showing sales of 'Possum' cat food, which demonstrate how expanding or contracting scales can mislead

All the graphs are technically correct but give very different impressions of 'Possum' sales. To avoid misleading your audience, always present your data in a consistent fashion. For example, in the above example, a scale should be used which allows the data from a number of years to be plotted on the same chart. Thus one could not be accused of exaggerating this year's sales. Also the zero point on the vertical (*Y*) scale should be labelled even if part of the vertical scale is then omitted, as long as this is clearly shown. In such an example, it may be more appropriate not to show absolute sales figures but give an indication of the percentage increase in sales during 1994 or moving averages.

Failure to provide comparative data

Often data can only be accurately presented when a comparison is made with some 'base line' or other comparative data. This may require one, or more, sets of data to be displayed on the chart or the inclusion of a caption.

Suppose we wish to represent the number of shoppers using the 'Shop-Til-You-Drop' (STUD) chain of supermarkets. We would probably use a line graph:

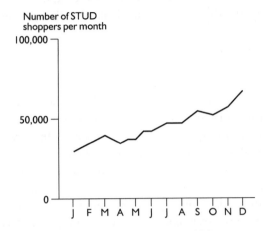

Figure 7.24   Number of STUD shoppers per month during 1995

On the face of it, this increase looks promising. However, if, over the same period, the number of shoppers using supermarkets had risen greatly, the increase shown on the graph might actually represent a decrease in market share. Of course, the reverse is also possible. If there had been a general decline in the number of shoppers using supermarkets, the figures shown would indicate that STUD was doing very well indeed 'bucking the trend'. To assist in the interpretation of this data, and to avoid being misleading, it is therefore best to provide some comparative data, perhaps the performance of the competition or an indication of the general market trend.

Using an inappropriate presentation method

Using an inappropriate method of presentation can, under certain circumstances, mislead your audience. Suppose a survey is conducted to find out the most acceptable cost for annual tickets to a new leisure centre. Responses fall into a number of categories, the results could be shown with either a pie chart or bar chart:

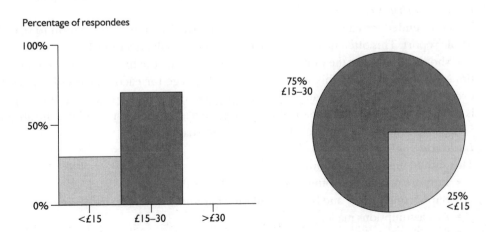

Figure 7.25   Bar chart and pie chart showing responses to survey on leisure ticket cost

The pie chart is, in a sense, misleading because it does not show the response categories where no one responded (in this case none of the respondees thought that more than £30 was an acceptable price). This information is lost in the pie chart presentation but appears, or should do, in a bar chart.

Report writing

Invariably, the presentation of research data requires the writing of a report. This will include the graphical presentation of data as described in the first part of this unit along with a description of your research and recommendations for further action.

A report is usually the only full record of your research; the purpose of the work, the sample used, all the results, the method of analysis used, the conclusions reached and so on.

Characteristics of a good research report:

1 Objectives of the research are well defined.
2 Structured and logically ordered. The report should be broken down into sections, each with their own informative title. These sections should be ordered in such a way as to lead the reader through the research. For example, data should be presented and the analysis method described before any conclusions are presented.
3 Comprehensive (it covers all aspects of the research) but concise (should not be unnecessarily wordy or cover irrelevant areas). A summary or abstract should be provided which summarizes the important findings for casual readers.
4 Accurate, clear and precise language is used throughout (terminology should be appropriate for the intended audience).

These four characteristics can be remembered from the acronym: O – S – C – A (Objectives, Structure, Comprehensiveness, Accuracy).

Structure of a research report

In the scientific community, a 'standard' report structure has evolved. Whilst this is not suitable for all purposes, it provides a useful guide under most circumstances.

1 *Title page(s)*
  This should include the following:
  - Title of the report.
  - Name of sponsor and/or customer for the report.
  - Title of researcher and organisation.
  - Date of publication.
2 *Table of contents*
  This should include page references for each heading contained with the report.
3 *Executive summary or abstract*
  This is intended for casual readers who may not have the time or inclination to read the whole report. This often includes the person that makes the decisions!

  It should summarize the whole of the report, including the findings and recommendations. As a rough guide, this should not exceed $\frac{1}{8}$ page for each 5 pages of report. For example, the summary for a 40 page report should be less than a page long. If your paper is added to an electronic database often the only text available to the reader is the abstract. Some systems limit the 'on line' abstract to 250 words.
4 *Introduction or background*
  This should include the following:
  - Purpose of research (often this is referred to as the 'brief').
  - Supporting history and background information (i.e. other relevant studies).
  - Any assumptions made.
  - Specific aims of research.
5 *Methodology*
  Should include the following:
  - Details of any material used (questionnaires, interview forms, special equipment).
  - Sample population (numbers and profile).
  - Design of study.
  - Procedure used (the sequence in which the study was conducted).

6 *Results and analysis*
   Should include the following:
   - Details of analysis method(s) used.
   - Descriptive statistics for raw data.
   - Any advanced statistics.
   - Tabular and/or graphical presentation of data.

7 *Discussion and conclusions*
   Should include the following:
   - Discussion of research findings.
   - Conclusions to be drawn from findings.
   - Self-critique of study (i.e. unexpected problems that arose, why not enough people could be surveyed, flaws discovered in a questionnaire, etc.).
   - Additional graphical presentation of summarized or combined data to support discussion or conclusions.

8 *Recommendations*
   Should include the following:
   - Actions to take as a result of research.
   - Recommendations for future research.

9 *Acknowledgements*
   Should include the following:
   - Thanks to organizations that have funded/supported research.
   - Thanks to individuals that have helped in the preparation of the report (i.e. they may have given useful advice or provided administrative support).

10 *References*
    Should include full references for all materials and other research studies referred to.

11 *Appendices*
    Should include all information, such as the full questionnaire text, which, if included in the main body of the text, would have interrupted the flow of the report.

Find a copy of the *Journal of the Market Research Society*, or one of the many other journals in this field, and examine the structure of three papers. How do these compare with each other and with the 'ideal' structure outlined in this unit.

Report writing tips
The following tips are presented to assist in the writing of a good report and help assess the reports of others.

- Does the report contain enough information to allow another researcher to replicate the work? If not, then the report should contain more detail. This is, of course, unless the writer wishes for certain aspects of their research method to remain secret.
- The introductory sections to a report, should address at least the following questions:

  - Why is this report being written?
  - What does it hope to achieve?
  - Who is this report aimed at?

- The results and analysis sections of a report should not contain any discussion or conclusions only an impartial description of the data.

- Conclusions should be based solely on the data reported combined with the findings from other, fully referenced, studies. A clear distinction should be made between the results themselves, the interpretation of the results (which may be contested), and the recommendations being made.
- Recommendations should be concrete and specific, not 'woolly'.
- Are all the graphs and tables properly titled, clearly presented and referenced in the body of the text?
- Does the summary include all the important information from the report?

EXTENDING ACTIVITY 7.2

If your organization undertakes any research, find out how the data is presented.

Better still, if you have access to computer software capable of producing tables, charts or fancy graphs, try reproducing some of those shown in this unit or make up your own from any of the example data contained in this workbook.

EXTENDING ACTIVITY 7.3

Search through newspapers and magazines and cut out any graphs or charts that you find.

Decide whether you think that the presentation of information is clear and meaningful. Note down any problems. Do you think that the graph or chart is biased in any way? Does it over-emphasize the significance of certain data in an attempt to 'prove a point'?

Think what method you would have used to present the same data.

EXTENDING ACTIVITY 7.4

If your organization undertakes any research, find out how the data is analysed. Better still, if you have access to statistical computer software (many spreadsheet packages are capable of basic statistical analysis), try analysing, interpreting and forecasting from example data sets.

ANSWERS

Question 7.1

The data in Table 7.3 is skewed. The data indicates that the shoppers use this shopping area on a regular basis ('1 to 3 times a week' or 'more than 3 times a week' are by far the most frequent responses). Most likely, it is an area of local shops, perhaps within walking distance, which sells perishable goods which are bought every few days (bread, milk, etc.).

Question 7.2

We wish to find the percentage increase in sales. Sales were originally £1.4 m then jumped to £2.1 m an increase of £0.7 m. We need to find what percentage £0.7 m (the increase) is of £1.4 m (the original sales).

$$\text{Percentage} = \frac{0.7}{1.4} \times 100 = 50\%$$

Question 7.3

First determine the size of all three opinion groups on your customer panel: 40 like the taste; 32 don't like the taste; and 8 are unsure.

'Like' group: 40 as a proportion of 80 $= \dfrac{40}{80} = 0.5$

'Dislike' group: 32 as a proportion of 80 $= \dfrac{32}{80} = 0.4$

'Unsure' group: 8 as a proportion of 80 $= \dfrac{8}{80} = 0.1$

Question 7.4

Percentages provide us with information about relative sales. Thus the sales of 'Nutty Choc' (Figure 7.6) at the Kensington High Street branch are less than at the other two branches but are a *greater proportion* of the overall sales at that branch.

Question 7.5

When it is the column data that is being compared then a style which emphasizes the columns is to be preferred (such as Figure 7.8). Figure 7.7 is a 'cleaner' presentation more suited to a technical report or presentation.

Question 7.6

The modal value is 3 (the most frequently occurring response).

Question 7.7

It suggests that the inexperienced users are less satisfied than the experienced users. This would warrant further investigation.

Question 7.8

Customers seem to be getting increasingly dissatisfied with the product. This could be because of increased competition on price or features, for example, or a general increase in customer expectations.

Question 7.9

More people seem to be satisfied with product Y than product X.

Question 7.10

The graph should look something like this:

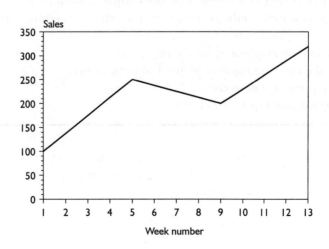

Question 7.11

The pie chart should look something like this:

It should be fully and clearly labelled.

Question 7.12

1 A bar chart or histogram would be most appropriate as it can display a number of discontinuous responses.

2 A pie chart is probably the most appropriate as it indicates the overall portions of the market share.

3 A pictogram or other chart-type which uses pictures is likely to be the most interesting and compelling for this audience.

4 A line graph would be the most appropriate as it can display values on a continuous variable (such as weight).

5 Bar charts are generally the best at showing complex information. A percentage component bar chart is likely to be most suitable.

SUMMARY

In this unit you have learned about:

- The characteristics of data.
- Calculation and use of the mode, median and mean as measures of location for individual and grouped data.
- Normal and skewed distributions.
- Which measures of location are appropriate when.
- Calculation and use of spread, quartiles, interquartile range, quartile deviation, mean deviation and standard deviation as measures of dispersion.
- Which measures of dispersion are appropriate when.
- Proportions, fractions and percentages and their usage.
- sampling theory and how to calculate the sample size required.
- Presenting research findings using tables, charts, graphs, pie charts and pictograms.
- Constructing line graphs and pie charts.
- Choosing the most appropriate method of presentation.
- Bias in the presentation of data.
- Report writing and report structures.

What does it cost?

OBJECTIVES

In this unit you will:

- Clarify the relationship between economics and marketing.
- Explore the concepts of opportunity cost, utility and demand.

By the end of this unit you will be able to:

- Identify the value and relevance of economic theory to your business activities.
- Apply the concepts of opportunity cost, utility and demand.

STUDY GUIDE

This unit will help you appreciate the contribution economics makes to understanding customer behaviour.

There are two aspects of economics: microeconomics, which covers the economic interrelationships of individual markets, consumers or producers; macroeconomics which considers the behaviour of broad aggregates affecting the economy as a whole. The two areas are not separate and what is happening in the economy as a whole affects the smaller aggregates and vice versa.

You must be able to ensure that their future business decision making is undertaken in the context of the wider and rapidly changing economic environment. You should be able to incorporate economists' viewpoints into the marketing discipline in order to justify their decision making.

This unit will take approximately 3 hours to read through and understand. The activities you have been asked to carry out will take another 2 hours.

STUDY TIPS

Organize your study material from the beginning of your course:

- Use file dividers to keep broad topic areas indexed and relevant materials and articles with the relevant notes.
- Look out for relevant articles and current examples, you will find these useful to illustrate examination answers.

The economist's view of human economic behaviour

The nub of microeconomic theory is the way in which prices work. Almost all theories of motivation make some assumptions about individual needs and drives. Economists have also chosen to make certain assumptions about the way in which people behave. Other theories of motivation are covered in Unit 12.

Economists say that people are rational-economic and that:

- They try to get as much satisfaction out of their purchases as they can – in economic terminology goods, services and leisure give utility.
- People will consider which course of action will give them the greatest utility – generally speaking they are willing to substitute one good for another provided the price is right.
- People are primarily economic creatures.
- People are individualistic.

The price system

A market price is the result of an interaction between the consumers' demand for a good and the supply of that product by producers.

Factors affecting pricing decisions

If costs set the floor for prices, market demand sets the ceiling. Competition is also an important determinant of price. When economists classify firms it is usually with respect to the type of competition under which they exist.

There are two types of competition, perfect competition and imperfect competition:

Perfect competition (many producers, identical products)

People are trading a uniform commodity. No single buyer or seller will affect the price. There is no point in increasing the price because buyers can get as much as they want at the going rate. For a state of perfect competition to exist the following conditions must be present:

- There must be a large number of buyers and sellers so that no one firm is able to affect the market price, all participants in the market must have roughly the same buying power.
- There must be freedom of entry into and exit from the market for both buyers and sellers.
- All the goods being sold must be the same.
- Perfect communication exists so that buyers and sellers have perfect knowledge of the market.
- It must be possible to buy or sell any amount of the commodity at the market price.
- The buyers and sellers will act rationally and maximize their satisfaction, buyers will try to maximize their utility and sellers will try to maximize their profits.

This example shows you the ideal functioning of a market; in practice commodity markets come close to the ideal. However, in real life a perfect market would be hard to find so markets are said to be imperfect.

Imperfect competition

- Markets are imperfect because sellers and buyers do not have complete information about competitors' prices.
- Customer loyalty prevents rational decisions from being made.
- Product differentiation is achieved not only by product design and quality but by branding and advertising (this topic is discussed in more detail in Unit 10).
- Markets are not always perfectly competitive as groups of suppliers and buyers can influence supply or demand, and price.

In this type of competition it is possible to distinguish three types:

Monopoly (single producer, no close substitutes). This literally means there is only one seller. Pricing would depend on whether it is a government monopoly (like the post office), or a private regulated monopoly, or a private non-regulated monopoly.

Oligopoly (few producers with product differentiation). The market here consists of only a few large dominant suppliers. The production of detergent is almost entirely divided between Proctor and Gamble and Unilever. Oligopolys rarely compete on price as price changes downward will be followed by other firms, whereas price increases may not be followed.

Competition through promotion and product differentiation is more common.

Monopolistic competition (many producers with product differentiation). In this market there are many buyers and sellers with a range of prices rather than one single market price because sellers are able to differentiate themselves, using price and non-price variables.

It is called monopolistic competition because, due to imperfections in the market, each organization has a small degree of monopoly power. The branding of consumer goods is an attempt to break the chain of substitution. The marketer needs to be aware that the type of competition an organization faces will affect the way in which prices are set.

Opportunity cost

Every decision has a cost and economists use a term – opportunity cost – to cover what has been sacrificed in order to make a purchasing decision.

If a person decides to go on holiday they may have to give up something else, perhaps having their house painted or buying new clothes.

The opportunity cost of going on holiday can be measured as having the house painted or the new clothes.

> *Opportunity cost* is the cost of one option expressed in terms of giving up the next best alternative.

The answer to how people assess value and costs is one that all marketers would like to know.

When a decision is made the person making the decision will obviously want to choose the one that gives them the greatest value – this is called optimization. Different people evaluate gains and costs differently.

In order to follow these ideas we need to consider:

- How consumers think about price and value and how they go about maximizing utility.
- The economic factors that influence their behaviour.

How consumers think about price and value and how they go about maximizing utility

Consumer perceptions of price and value

Both industrial buyers and consumers balance the price of a product/service against the benefits of owning it. When a customer buys something they are exchanging something of value (the price) to get something of value back (the benefits or satisfaction of having or using the product or service). Economists call this the concept of utility.

> Utility is the psychological worth a person associates with a course of action or an object. The task of decision theory is to find out how people assign utility to objects and how it influences their decision making.

It is difficult to measure utility and normally economists simply have to assume that consumers are rational and therefore do maximize utility.

Marginal utility

The marginal utility is the additional utility derived from the consumption of an additional unit. For example, if a person has three cups of coffee and then has a fourth, *total utility* (the overall experience) refers to the satisfaction from having all four cups, while marginal utility refers to the additional satisfaction from drinking the fourth cup of coffee while already having drunk three.

The law of diminishing marginal utility

What is interesting for the marketer is that when more and more of a commodity is consumed in any given time period, instead of becoming more satisfied, consumers become less satisfied *with each additional unit*. This is called the law of diminishing marginal utility. And although the total utility (satisfaction) they get will continue to increase as each successive unit is consumed, it will do so at a decreasing pace. The consequence of this is that total satisfaction/utility will be rising but more slowly/at a diminishing rate, which can be seen in Figures 8.1 and 8.2.

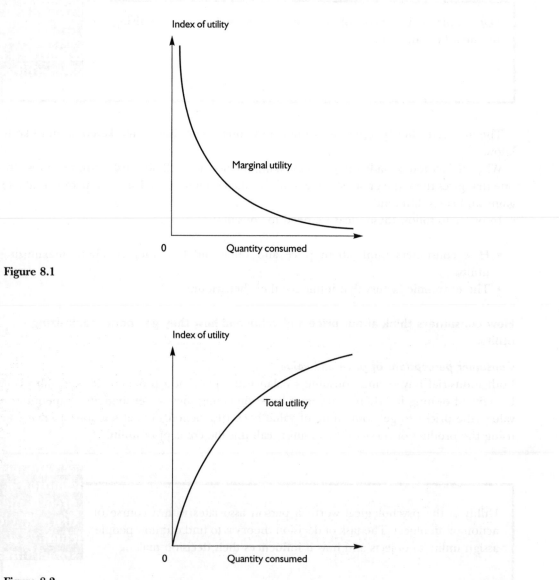

Figure 8.1

Figure 8.2

> *The law of diminishing utility* states that:
>
> Other things being constant, as more and more units of a commodity are consumed the additional satisfaction, or utility, derived from the consumption of each successive unit will decrease.

In considering this law it is important to think about the phrase 'all other things remain constant' – these would be:

- *Time* – the law only operates over a short period of time.
- *Income* – the utility that someone gets from a product may change if their income goes up.
- *Addiction* – the nature of the successive units will not be changed.

If the product had been free the person would have continued buying up to the point where the marginal utility (total satisfaction gained) had reached zero. This is because the goods are free. However, in the marketplace this does not apply because products have to be paid for. Marginal utility will be compared to price in determining consumption.

If there was only one product, the person would consume up to a point where marginal utility = the price. If the marginal utility was greater than the price, the person would consume more. If the extra satisfaction was less than the price then the person would consume less.

In reality, the consumer has a limited income and has to allocate their money between several products. For example when a purchase is made the consumer will:

- Put a value on it.
- Take into account any alternative products on which the same money can be spent.
- Compare the utilty they would get.

Equi-marginal utility

To maximize the total utility, the consumer will spend their money in such a way that the extra utility per £1 on the last unit of a product (a) is equal to the extra utility per £1 on the last unit of a product (b).

If the last cup of coffee per £1 gave you more satisfaction than the last cup of tea per £1, then you would switch to more coffee. As you switch to more coffee the extra utility of each cup will start falling and become less satisfying but you will keep switching provided the marginal utility per £1 is higher than for tea. When the last cup of coffee and tea are equally satisfying per £1 you will have no further desire to switch from one to the other, and that particular combination of coffee and tea will be maximizing your utility.

Hints for the marketer

It is therefore essential for the marketer to keep the marginal utility above that of other brands as this will encourage switching. Symbolically this could be expresses as:

$$\frac{\text{Marginal utility b}}{\text{Price a}} = \frac{\text{Marginal utility b}}{\text{Price b}} = \frac{\text{MU n}}{\text{P n}}$$

where a, b - - - n represents the range of products bought.
What this shows is:

1 When the price of a product is higher than that of another product (or increases), the marginal utility per £ would have fallen and therefore the consumer switches away, i.e. less of the more expensive product will be bought.
2 If the price decreases (perhaps because the prices of other goods have risen) the marginal utility per £ has risen therefore the consumer will switch towards this product.

A typical demand curve is therefore downward sloping from left to right.

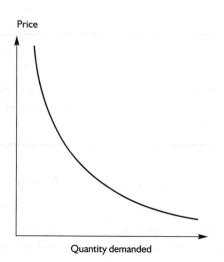

Figure 8.3   A typical demand curve is downward sloping from left to right

This law assumes that all other factors apart from price remain the same and that price alone affects the satisfaction because a reduction in price creates better value for money which leads to a rise in quality demanded and sales. This can be seen in Figure 8.3.

DEFINITION

Price refers to the real price of a commodity as distinct from the money price. For example, if because of inflation all prices rose by the same amount, there would be a rise in money price, but real prices would stay the same because their comparative value would not have changed.

Consumer behaviour and rises in income

When the household income increases in real terms, there is an increase in purchasing power. Utility theory would therefore predict the following:

- Consumers will buy more goods.
- Goods previously outside the income resources of the household will now be bought.
- The actual extra goods that are bought will depend on their marginal utilities and price.
- Luxury items will have a higher marginal utility than necessities as income rises above subsistance level.
- As more expensive goods become more attractive the marginal utility and demand for inferior goods (see later) will fall.

Points for the marketer to reflect on:

1   The concept of opportunity cost supports the theory that all goods are in competition for scarce income resources, and it is not just brands competing for a share of the same sector. Instead of competing for market share, marketers should concentrate on increasing the overall value/size of their generic market through industry-wide campaigns.

ACTIVITY 9.1

- If all goods are in competition how could you go about increasing the share of your organization's generic market?

2   Utility or satisfaction with the brand will depend on added value and perceived value. Always identify and assess the benefits that give the highest customer utility – this will give the company a competitive advantage.

Always make sure that features are translated into benefits.

Although lowering the price should produce a better utility/price ratio, price reduction often sends negative signals to the customer about quality and value. This change in perception may mean they buy less, not more.

ACTIVITY 9.2

- Are the features of the product/service that your organization sells translated into benefits?
- Which of these benefits provide your customers with the greatest utility?
- How do these compare with your competitors?
- How would you go about assessing them?
- Will lowering the price produce a better utility/price ratio and increase sales for your organization, or will it send negative signals to customers about quality and the overall value of the product/service and induce them to buy less?
- If you increase your price will you sell more?
- Instead of lowering price are there any other ways in which you could increase your customers' perception of value?

EXAM HINT

Remember that cost-driven (own label) brands often reflect what the target market wants, they do not cut back on quality, but eliminate services not relevant to the target market. Before following a cost-driven brand strategy the marketer must consider:

- Is the price-sensitive segment likely to grow?
- How will buyers respond when competitors launch low price alternatives?
- Is the culture of the firm geared to reducing costs?

ACTIVITY 9.3

What marketing techniques can you use to stop the marginal utility from declining?

Economic factors that influence behaviour

Demand

Consumers want to buy a range of goods. The goods they choose to buy will depend on:

- The price of the good.
- The price of other goods.
- The household income.
- The income distribution of households.
- Taste, changes in fashion and expectation.

Each of these points will be considered in turn.

Demand and the price of the good

Market demand represents the cumulative response of all customers and potential customers to a product, and it indicates the collective quantity demanded. Demand consists of three elements: price, quantity and time.

In marketing we look at demand in three ways:

1 *Effective demand* – demand backed by the ability to pay.
2 *Potential demand* – where there is the ability to pay but demand has not been aroused.
3 *Latent demand* – demand for goods not backed by the ability to pay.

Economists look at demand as:

1 *Ex-ante demand* – which is the quantity consumers will wish to purchase at a particular price.
2 *Ex-post demand* – is the amount they actually purchased.

Economists concentrate on looking at ex-post demand whereas marketers take a longer view and accept that there is often a period of time between becoming aware of a need and carrying out the purchase.

Demand is generally lower at a higher price. Each price the organization might charge will lead to a different level of demand. The relationship of the price charged to the level of demand can be shown in a demand curve.

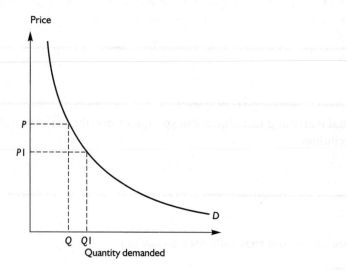

Figure 8.4   A simple demand curve

There are some exceptions:

Goods demanded for their price (Veblen goods or goods of ostentation)
With some goods price is part of the attraction of the article and a rise in price will make it more attractive. The article acquires snob value. A Rolls Royce, jewellery, wine or perfume are good examples.

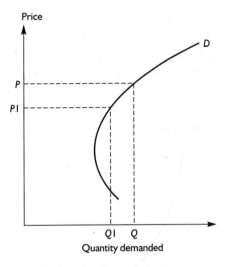

Figure 8.5 Demand for Veblen goods (goods of ostentation)

Giffen goods

Sir Robert Giffen, a nineteenth-century statistician and economist, observed that a fall in the price of bread caused the labouring classes to buy less bread and vice versa. When a price is decreased, and a proportion of the family income is freed, the money would be immediately spent on other foods to vary the diet, therefore less bread was needed. Once the price was increased the family would go back to living on bread.

The price of other goods

Although the price a competitor charges is outside the control of the marketer, it is important to gauge the impact a competitor will have on demand and be able to measure how sensitive the demand for one product is to a change in the price of other goods.

The demand for all goods is interrelated because they compete for consumers' limited income. Two aspects of this can be quantified: where goods are substitutes for one another or are complementary.

Substitutes

Where demand decreases as a result of a price reduction in the other products the substitute products would be competitive and the relatively cheaper product would then replace the more expensive product thereby giving better value for money.

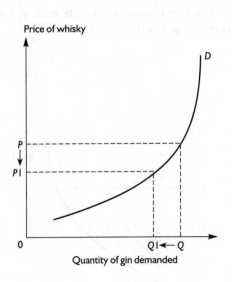

Figure 8.6 Substitutes

Marketers can reduce the impact of low pricing strategies by adding value to their products so that customers perceive them as having no direct substitutes.

Complementary or joint demand

In the case of complementary or joint demand there is a direct relationship between the price of one commodity and the demand for the other. Examples of these would be cars and petrol, gin and tonic, strawberries and cream, compact disc players and compact discs.

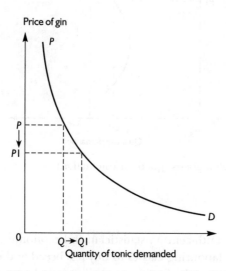

Figure 8.7 Complements: a fall in the price of gin from 0P to 0P1 will increase the quantity of tonic demanded from 0Q to 0Q1

The household income

Demand for a product is backed by the ability to pay for it (effective demand). Purchasing power is therefore linked to income. The nature of the relationship between income and demand will depend upon the nature of the product and the level of the customer's income.

Products can be categorized into normal goods and inferior goods.

Normal goods

In the graph (Figure 8.8) you can see as income rises demand rises and then tends to get steeper at the higher level. This is because there is a limit to how much people will want – there are only so many cars one can buy, so many fresh vegetables that can be eaten, so much milk that can be drunk. With inexpensive foodstuffs such as salt the demand tends to stay constant at all but the very lowest levels of income.

Figure 8.8 Income and demand – a normal good

Inferior goods

As income rises the demand for a product may go down as consumers switch to better alternatives which they can now afford.

When disposable income falls because of inflation or a rise in taxes demand for basic brands may increase as customers trade down. This effect can be seen as consumers switch between products such as cheap cuts of meat to expensive cuts of meat, or taxis and buses and so on.

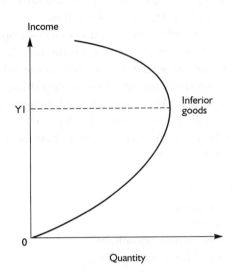

Figure 8.9 Inferior goods

In the diagram if income rose above Yl the quantity demanded would fall.
If the product is inferior and the income levels are rising the marketer should:

- Reposition the product and add benefits.
- Look for new markets where income levels are lower.

ACTIVITY 9.4

1 Income levels have risen and there is a decline in public transport because people are buying more cars. How would you propose to go about adding utility to the use of public transport?
2 Income levels have risen and there is a decline in the use of margarine because people are buying more butter. How would you go about adding utility to the use of margarine?

The income distribution of households

If there is an uneven distribution of income there will be a different demand pattern and a different distribution of normal and inferior goods.

Other factors that would influence demand are:

- Taste.
- Changes in fashion.
- Marketing techniques.
- Economic conditions, e.g. the impact of taxation, interest rates and inflation.
- Changes in population.
- Expectations – when consumers believe that prices will rise or that shortages will occur they tend to stock up.

SUMMARY

In this unit you have seen that:

- Economists have chosen to make certain assumptions about the way in which people behave.
- It is important to think about the demand and supply of goods and how prices in the market are formed.
- The type of competition an organization faces will affect the way in which prices are set and the way in which customers see prices.
- Every decision has a cost and economists use a term – opportunity cost – the cost of one option expressed in terms of giving up the next best alternative.
- Marketers have to be able to set price according to the value consumers assign to the exchange and economists consider this process using the concept of utility.
- Utility or satisfaction with the brand does not only depend on price, it depends on other less tangible variables that add value (utility) to the product/service. It is the utility/price ratio that forms the basis for a purchase decision.
- Consumers' choice will depend on:

1 The price of the good.
2 The price of other goods.
3 The household income.
4 The income distribution of households.
5 Taste, changes in fashion and expectation.
6 Marketing techniques that add value and alter perceived value.
7 Economic conditions, which can have a strong impact on the way in which consumers respond to prices. The impact of taxation, interest rates, boom, inflation, unemployment and recession will influence consumer behaviour and not only because of the objective nature of the economic context but rather the way that context is perceived and interpreted.
8 Changes in population.

EXTENDING KNOWLEDGE

Hatton, A. and Oldroyd, M. (1992) *Economic Theory and Marketing Practice*, Butterworth-Heinemann. This book, written by two CIM Senior Examiners, contains useful hints on how to apply economic theory to marketing practice.

Cyclical fluctuations

In this unit you will:

- Examine trade cycles.
- Examine the use of economic indicators.

By the end of this unit you will:

- Understand how variations in economic activity have a direct effect on derived demand products.
- See that there are many different explanations for trade cycles.
- Understand that inventory cycle refers to the fluctuations brought about by changes in stock levels.
- Appreciate that the cycle can be traced and may even be predicted by the behaviour of economic indicators.

certain. dem
lefinition *n.* s
precise meai
distinct, clea
lefinitive *a.* fi
something: ı

Derived demand refers to something which is not demanded for itself but for the use to which it can be put. Bread is bought for direct consumption, but a company will demand labour because it wants to produce something else which it can eventually sell. The demand for labour is said to be derived from the demand of the final product. Variations in economic activity have a direct effect on derived demand products.

This unit will take you about 2 to 3 hours to read through and think about. The activities you have been asked to carry out will take you about 4 or 5 hours.

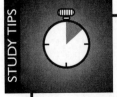

Organize your study material from the beginning of your course:

- Use file dividers to keep broad topic areas indexed and relevant materials and articles with the relevant notes.
- Look out for relevant articles and current examples; you will find these useful to illustrate examination answers.

The business cycle

This refers to the periodic fluctuations in economic activity that occur in industrialized countries. At times we have economic growth and at other times we have high unemployment and falling production. The word cycle implies that there is something regular about it.

Many different cycles have been identified by various economists, for example Kuznets highlighted a 15–25 year cycle, while Kondratieff identified a 50–60 year cycle. For much of the post-war period most advanced economies have suffered fluctuations of economic activity that last about 4–5 years, these are called business cycles.

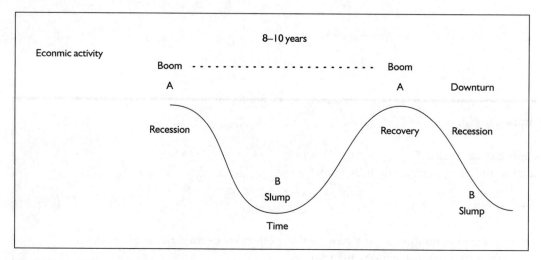

Figure 9.1 Phases of the business cycle

Terminology associated with the business cycle

Slump

A slump is a depression where we can expect to find:

- heavy unemployment
- deflation
- a low level of consumer demand
- low capital utilization
- low profits
- low business confidence.

Recovery

The recovery is where we can expect to find:

- expanding production
- replacement of old machinery
- rising consumers' expenditure
- increasing profits
- some increase in prices
- buoyant business expectation.

Boom

The boom is where we can expect to find:

- investment high
- profits high
- consumer spending rising fast
- prices rising rapidly
- labour in short supply
- production bottlenecks.

Downturn leading to recession

The recession (the downswing) is where we can expect to find:

- falling consumption
- decreasing profits
- decreasing expectations
- rising stocks of unsold goods
- firms become unprofitable
- firms go into liquidation
- inflation falls
- unemployment rising.

The marketer must be able to try to anticipate fluctuations, especially the stages at which the economy is moving into or out of recessions and booms.

The stage of the cycle will determine the policies you should be pursuing:

- *Downturn* Control stock in line with order slowdown, analyse weak products and channel outlets (Pareto analysis), stop recruitment and further long-term commitments.
- *Recession* Retain skilled core staff and upgrade their skills, order capital equipment for future installation.
- *Recovery* Orders start coming in, start building stock and encourage distributors to do likewise, start hiring and prepare new products for launch.

What causes a business cycle?

Business cycles are influenced by external factors, internal factors or a combination of both. External factors include wars, weather, population changes, etc.

Internal factors would be factors inside the economic system. Briefly these are due to:

The multiplier-accelerator

The multiplier describes how an initial rise in demand in the economy leads to rounds of spending which give a larger overall increase in output and income.

If, for example, you decide to spend £100 more on your shopping this will increase the income of retailers. Of this £100 a proportion will be spent again, e.g. £50 may be spent on buying more goods. The income of the manufacturers will now have risen by £50 and they will also spend some of this, e.g. £25, on supplies. The result is that there is a series of increases in demand which is known as the 'multiplier process'.

The multiplier can also interact with the 'accelerator'. As demand increases firms may have to invest more to make sure they can produce enough output. If demand is growing at an accelerating rate this extra (net) investment will also have to rise; this will set off a multipliers process which leads to further increases in demand which can then result in firms investing even more. As a result the economy moves into a boom.

If, however, demand grows at a slower rate firms will not need to increase their capacity as much. Net investment is therefore at a lower level than before and this fall in investment sets off a downward mulitiplier, and the economy moves towards a recession.

The inventory cycle

The inventory cycle refers to the stocking and destocking process in industry.

If demand falls in the economy firms will find that their stocks will increase, over time they will reduce their production levels leading to even less output and income in the economy.

Once stocks are used up firms need to increase their production again which will boost demand in the economy.

Businesses will also start to restock, which further increases the level of activity. However, once their stocks are replenished they will not need to produce as much and this reduction of output leads to a reduction of income in the economy and sets the cycle off again.

The 'just-in-time' method of ordering stock is a recent trend which may change the inventory cycle.

Politics

One explanation of business cycles is that they operate as a result of political activity. An early suggestion of the political aspect came from Karl Marx and was developed by Michael Kelecki (1899–1970). He suggested that in a boom period workers become economically powerful and demand higher wages – the subsequent recession is engineered by capitalists in order to create unemployment and reduce the power of the workers.

More recent political theorists ascribe the cause to the desire of political parties to achieve re-election; it is easier for a party to impose hard decisions shortly after an election and then stimulate demand in the run-up to the next election, thus creating a business cycle.

A Concise Dictionary of Business, Oxford University Press, 1990.

Government action has an effect on the economic environment and policies are likely to affect the economy in the short term. These policies affect consumer spending and the marketer needs to take them into account.

In boom period

1 *Objectives* Reduce or control inflation

Policy used
1.1 Increase taxes.

Possible short-term consequences:
* reduction in demand, leading to lower growth and rising unemployment;
* higher wage demands to compensate for tax increase;
* possible deferred investment;
* reduction in rate of growth of imports because there is less spending.

Policy used
1.2 Reduce government spending.

Possible short-term consquences:
* lower growth and rising unemployment;
* less government investment;
* decline in public services.

Policy used
1.3 Tighter credit.

Possible short-term consequences:
- rising unemployment;
- lower growth;
- corporate borrowing difficult;
- interest rates higher.

Policy used
1.4 Higher interest rates.

Possible short-term consequences:
- rising unemployment;
- lower growth;
- depressed housing and related markets;
- investments deferred;
- overseas capital attracted and exchange rate strengthened, this makes exporting harder.

In slump period

2 *Objectives* To reduce unemployment

Policy used
2.1 Reduce taxes.

Possible short-term consequences:
- increased demand leading to more jobs and output, possibly leading to higher inflation;
- increased government borrowing to finance the tax cuts.

Policy used
2.2 Increase government spending.

Possible short-term consequences:
- more jobs;
- increased output;
- higher inflation;
- increased government borrowing;
- improved services;
- increased government debt.

Policy used
2.3 Easier credit.

Possible short-term consequences:
- increased demand;
- increased jobs;
- increased output;
- increased inflation;
- increased imports;
- inflationary housing market.

Policy used
2.4 Reduce interest rates.

Possible short-term consequences:
- same effect as tighter credit;
- more investment by industry.

In boom period

The balance of payments position often gets worse in a boom. With higher levels of income, spending on imports tends to rise, and higher prices in the economy can make exports less competitive.

3 *Objectives* To improve balance of payments – see 1.1–1.4.

In slump period

4   *Objectives*   To stimulate economic growth – see 2.1–1.4.

Other reasons for the business cycle may include
- Changes in the money supply (Friedman).
- Technical innovation (technological life cyle) (Schumpeter and Hansen).
- Underconsumption (e.g. public values related to consumerism, environmentalism, life style and so on).
- Overinvestment (Hayek and Mises).
- Bouts of optimism and pessimism among consumers and producers (psychological theorists such as Pigou and Bagehot).

Forecasting the cycle
Unfortunately no way has been found to do this accurately. However, the marketer can take a careful note of present trends of the following:

- GDP
- volume of retail sales
- level of unemployment
- changes in stocks, and so on.

Surveys of business opinion such as the CBI survey can help. The marketer may also be able to predict trends from changes in statistics. There are a number of statistical trends that are thought to be significant in measuring business cycles – these are called economic indicators. Some react ahead of the trend and are known as leading indicators (housing starts), others lag behind the business cycle (investment and unemployment).

In the UK a range of indicators are published quarterly by the Central Statistics Office in the journal *Economic Trends*.

SUMMARY

In this unit you have seen that:

- Derived demand refers to something which is not demanded for itself but for the use to which it can be put. Variations in economic activity have a direct effect on derived demand products.
- There are four phases to the traditional cycle: slump, recovery, boom and recession. There are different economic characteristics associated with each cycle.
- There are many different explanations of the trade cycle, both internal and external – these interact with each other.
- The inventory cycle refers to changes in stock levels.
- The cycle can be traced and may even be predicted by the behaviour of economic indicators.

The importance of perceived benefit – 'what is it worth?'

OBJECTIVES

In this unit you will:

- Understand the difference between a brand and a commodity.
- Examine the part sensation and perception play in the branding process.
- Examine additional aspects of the total branding process.

By the end of this unit you will:

- Understand how marketing techniques can add value and change the perceived value for money.
- Understand how the integrated use of the whole of the marketing mix is used in the branding process.

STUDY GUIDE

Winning and retaining customers demands a unified, consistent marketing approach.

It is extremely important that a company thinks of its business in terms of customer benefits rather than solely in terms of features and functional capacity. Products/services offer customers a large number of benefits, functional and psychological.

In this unit you will learn about perception and the way in which we select and organize sensory data presented by our environment. An understanding of perceptual processes is important to the marketer as a customer's decisions to purchase will be influenced to a large extent by the way the product/service is perceived. Perception will be affected not only by the product/service itself, but also by the attributes which the marketer is able to give to the product/service through the integrated use of an augmented marketing mix. The use of the marketing mix extends beyond the 4Ps and includes service and corporate values, including relationship management.

Organize your study material from the beginning of your course:

- Use file dividers to keep broad topic areas indexed and relevant materials and articles with the relevant notes.
- Look out for relevant articles and current examples, you will find these useful to illustrate examination answers.

This unit will take you about 2 hours to read through and about 2 hours to carry out the various activities.

A brand or a commodity?

Before looking at how marketing techniques can change perceived value for money, a distinction must be drawn between a brand and a commodity.

Commodity markets

Commodity markets such as iron ore, sugar and milk are characterized by a lack of perceived differentiation. Decisions to buy are based on price and availability.

Branded markets

A brand can be a product, service, person, organization or place. A successful brand is a one that the buyer or user identifies as having relevant and unique added values which most closely match their needs.

The positioning of a brand in a market segment and the marketing mix differentiates it from competitor products. This process of differentiation does not rely solely on the core product, but also on aspects that add value and develop a distinctive perception in the mind of the consumer.

EXAM HINT

Collect together examples of brands and adverts after you have read this unit. Use them to illustrate your exam answers wherever possible. Specific marks are allocated for originality.

The difference between a brand and a commodity can be summed up in the phrase 'added values'. A brand is more than the sum of its component parts. It embodies, for the purchaser or user, additional attributes which, whilst they may be considered by some to be 'intangible', are still very real.

The influence of external and internal factors

Successful brands do not use one aspect of the marketing mix, they develop a holistic approach to communicate the relevant added values for which buyers are prepared to pay a price premium.

Perceived benefit and added value

Perceived value can be thought of as consisting of three levels. The first only contains the physical product, with no services attached. The second level includes support services that must be provided to meet customer satisfaction, the third level includes the intangibles. The intangibles and service element, as de Chernatony and McDonald point out in *Creating Powerful Brands*, have 80% of the impact and 20% of the costs.

Core product

- Function.
- Packaging.
- Design.
- Price.
- Efficacy.
- Features.

Services

- Before sales service.
- During sales service.
- After sales service.
- Delivery.
- Availability.
- Advice.
- Finance.
- Add-ons.
- Warranties.
- Guarantees.

Intangibles

- Quality perceptions.
- Value perceptions.
- Organization.
- Brand name.
- Corporate image.
- Reputation.
- Other user recommendations.

ACTIVITY 10.1

Using your own organization, which of the intangible aspects does your organization value most? Do you know if this fits with what your customers value most?

QUESTION 10.1

What is the difference between a commodity and a brand? How would a marketer turn a commodity into a brand?

A competitive weapon

The added value of the brand image is one of the most competitive weapons in the marketplace. A large amount of money is spent by marketers in communicating with consumers but some of it may be wasted.

Sensation and perception

The manner in which a product/service is perceived depends upon both internal and external factors. External reality and internal reality are intertwined and we carry all of our experiences in our minds and we bring our own interests, needs, motives and expectations into the way in which we relate to the world.

Research shows that for a number of products where there is strong brand loyalty, and where taste would appear to have a strong influence on the buying decisions, there is little sensory difference between products.

Over the last years a commodity, water, has been taken and made into a brand. Conversely, strong brands have been turned into commodities. Orange juice is an example, where price cutting and promotional methods have switched from above the line to below the line activities, the intangible aspects of the brand that add value to it have been eroded. Quite clearly the way in which marketers use and integrate the whole of the marketing mix has a part to play in this process.

To illustrate the power of these added values consider the results of a blind test (i.e. where the brand identity is concealed) in which Diet Pepsi was compared against Diet Coke by a panel of consumers:

- Prefer Pepsi 51%.
- Prefer Coke 44%.
- Equal/can't say 5%.

When the two brands were given to a matched sample in an open test (i.e. the true identity of the brands was revealed), the following results were produced:

- Prefer Pepsi 23%.
- Prefer Coke 65%.
- Equal/can't say 12%.

As de Chernatony and McDonald say in their book *Creating Powerful Brands* (Butterworth-Heinemann, 1994), 'How can this be explained if not in terms of the added values that are aroused in the minds of consumers when they see a familiar Coke logo and pack?'

External and internal factors

External factors relate to the physical character of the stimulus, while internal factors include our motives and expectations, these are considered below:

External factors influencing attention

Physical properties

Physical properties of the stimulus include: intensity, size, position, contrast, novelty, repetition and movement.

Intensity and size

The brighter the light or the louder a sound the more likely a person is to attend.

Position

In magazines greater readership is obtained by putting advertisements on the covers or within the first 10% of the pages. An advertisement placed next to compatible editorial in both newspapers and magazines is thought to attract more readers.

Contrast

- A black and white advertisement with a spot of colour in it will attract attention because of the contrast.
- Colour advertisements are thought to be more effective than black and white advertisements.
- Alternating the use of large and small sizes, loud and soft tones, and primary and pastel shades will attract more attention than using only one stimulus.
- A quiet commercial after a loud programme can attract attention.
- Showing an object out of its normal setting will also attract attention such as a car travelling across sand dunes or along a beach.

Novelty

Anything which is different from what we would normally expect will tend to attract our attention. For example, an unusual bottle shape, a perfume strip in a magazine and so on.

Repetition

Advertisements are repeated over and over again.

Movement

Advertisers use moving billboards, mobiles at point of purchase displays and artwork that is created to inject a feeling of movement into it.

Collect a number of advertisements and think about whether you can see how the above techniques are applied to attract the attention of the reader. Place them into your file with your comments. The more you look the more you will be able to apply your understanding.

ACTIVITY 10.2

Internal factors

Customers do not receive messages passively. Customers take the messages marketers give them and then actively use them to fit into their own internal world and also to give them clues about the brand's capability. It is what customers do with the marketing mix in their minds that needs to be assessed. The marketer has constantly to say, 'What is going on in there?'

The brand becomes the consumer's idea of the product/service, not the marketers. It is what customers perceive, interpret and believe the values of the brand to be. When a brand acquires a personality that is well recognized, even products with very little functional difference are seen as being different.

Selective attention

People may only choose to listen to certain aspects of the advertising message and only decide to see and hear a part of what is being communicated.

Selective exposure

Through selective exposure people avoid coming into contact with anything that may contradict strongly held beliefs and attitudes.

Selective reception, comprehension and retention

This means that only certain aspects of the advertising message will then be retained in memory in order to support existing beliefs and attitudes.

Perceptual vigilance or defence

This refers to the way in which people maintain their prior beliefs, for example: dealing with a customer who is upset with the way they have been treated by customer service, even though it is the customer who behaved badly.

Expectation

Expectation refers to the way people respond in a certain way to a given situation or set of stimuli. This may be the result of either known or unknown past experiences.

People often perceive what they expect to perceive rather than the message they actually receive.

Subliminal perception

This is the expression used to describe something that is below the level of perception.

Brands and self-image

One of the most important aspects of self-concept is the individual's level of aspiration.

Possessions, brands, people and places have symbolic value for them and are judged on the basis of how they fit with their own personal picture of themselves. There are different types of self-image:

1   Actual self-image – how consumers see themselves.
2   Ideal self-image – how they would like to see themselves.
3   Social self-image – how consumers feel others see them.
4   Ideal self-image – how consumers would like others to see them.
5   Expected self-image – how consumers expect to see themselves at some specified future time.

Studies show that consumers prefer brands which relate to their self-perception and to their subjective images of brands.

Advertising

Advertising techniques take symbols and use them as metaphors, implying there is a similarity between the brand and the symbol.

EXAMPLE

i

> The crown is used as a sign on a brand of paint to indicate quality. Flowers are used as sign of love, an apology and so on – Say it with Flowers.

Advertising techniques also link existing concepts or images that people have in their minds, to a sense image. The sense image is then linked to an object or event in the outside world. The value of a brand is increased by linking it to favourable and pleasurable events and places. For example, a Bounty chocolate bar is linked to a beautiful exotic beach and Oxo is used as a sign of happy family life and good motherhood.

Stereotyping in advertising

Market segmentation techniques build up typologies on which advertising is created.

The general inclination is to place a person in categories according to some easily and quickly identifiable characteristic such as age, sex, ethnic membership, nationality or occupation. Stereotyping follows this process of reasoning:

1   On the basis of their physical appearance we assign someone to a group.
2   We then imagine that all members of the group share certain characteristics.
3   We then infer that the particular individual must possess these characteristics.

People do use stereotypes as a form of simple generalization as it would be impossible to store the details of every individual experience. The question that needs to be asked is how do they affect the way stereotyped people feel about themselves and their behaviour, and also the way they are treated by other people?

Marketers need to think about the ethics of stereotyping.

The perception of quality

Consumers may try to evaluate a product's attributes directly by physical cues such as taste, smell, size and shape. In many cases the consumer is unable to make a judgement purely on the basis of the product's physical characteristics. The reasons for this are:

- The physical differences that exist between competing products may not exceed consumers' sensory thresholds.
- The consumer may not be experienced enough to know which product differentiations are important.

Extrinsic factors

Consumers assess products on the basis of certain clues or indicators. In some cases these are extrinsic, external to the product itself such as price, brand name, promotion, display and the retail store. For example, many disinfectants are purchased on the basis of smell.

Intrinsic factors

Others are intrinsic, due to the actual characteristics of the product itself – size, colour, feel, functional effectiveness.

Both intrinsic and extrinsic cues will affect the person's perception of the product and the perceived value. For example, as consumers realize how much sugar is in some products they will question some of the perceived value.

Consumers' use of surrogate indicators in product choice means that research needs to be done in order to find out which indicators or attributes are used to make product decisions for particular products.

Which indicators do your customers use to assess quality?

ACTIVITY 10.3

The perception of price and its relationship to quality

Consumers perceive value in brands when:

- It costs less to buy them than competing brands offering similar benefits, i.e. cost-driven brands.
- They have unique benefits which offset their premium prices, i.e. value-added brands.

A number of research studies confirm the view that consumers rely on price as an indicator of product quality. This happens particularly when they have little information to go on or they are not confident of their own ability to make the decision on other grounds such as familiarity with the brand name, experience with the product. This also applies to services although the price/quality relationship will depend on the particular category of service.

Reference pricing

Consumers carry reference prices in their minds. This knowledge may come from previous experience, remembering and noting prices or analysing prices within the context of the current buying situation. Department stores are known for separating products by price and quality. Retailers often put expensive items next to less expensive items. Sale prices will show the original price.

A reduction of just one penny can make a difference – £1.99 as opposed to £2.

What reference prices do your customers carry in their minds?

Corporate image

A corporate image doesn't simply refer to the design of a company's letterhead. In reality a corporate image goes much deeper and cover the way a business relates to its whole social and cultural context.

A corporate image adds value. It is not only brands that customers create a relationship with, but the organization itself. As much as brands become 'in the mind' so do organizations – both for the people working within them and for their customers.

If the people working within an organization feel bad about it, you can be sure their colleagues and customers will feel the same way. If customers feel bad about an organization, the employees will feel the same way as well. This phenomenon is also called a parallel process.

1   How do people working in your organization feel about it?
2   What effect do your customers have on their feelings?
3   How do customers feel about your organization?
4   Does the culture of your organization allow employees to talk about their good and bad feelings? How is this managed?

Advertising and perceived benefit

We come to our decisions as a result of what has been called the 'principle of competitive persuasion'. Advertising helps to create images in people's minds. A brand's image is what people believe it is.

Advertising turns a product into a brand by adding psychological intangibles as well as the functional tangible value. The intangible values are self-image, lifestyle and benefits.

It uses images and feelings to create equity for the brand. It takes a product and makes it into an asset, something that has 'cash value'. Brands form the basis of a company's assets and are valued on them.

Jim Young, in *How to Become an Advertising Man* (Advertising Publications Inc. 1963), says that there are five ways in which advertising works. These are:

1   By familiarizing – that is as the dictionary says by 'making something well-known; bringing into common use'. We will see that this is the absolutely basic value created by advertising, the one underlying all others.
2   By reminding – a function alone, in some cases, it makes advertising pay.
3   By spreading news – not only in the newspaper sense, but a special kind of news that only advertising, in the commercial field, can most widely deal with.

4 By overcoming inertias – the great drag on all human progress, economic or non-economic, as represented in the sociological term 'cultural lag'.
5 By adding a value not in the product – the most challenging field for creativeness in advertising.

Most advertising will involve at least two or more of these uses. The main value of these points is to be able to answer the following question, 'What is the advertising trying to achieve?', and also 'Which role is the primary role?'

Sales promotion and perceived value
Below-the-line promotions can be split into price- and non-price-related activities:

Price-related

- Consumer price promotions.
- Trade advertising allowances.
- Dealer promotions.
- Free goods.
- National accounts discounting.
- Over-riders.
- Trade bonuses.

Non-price-related

- In-store display.
- Merchandising.
- Competitions.
- Self-liquidating premiums.

As John Wilmshurst says in *Below-the-line Promotion* (Butterworth-Heinemann):

Some promotions, such as price reductions, do not reinforce the belief that the brand is worth paying for and draw particular attention to price as a choice determinant.
   Continuous, indiscriminate and badly executed price-cutting is clearly dangerous. However, to ignore the role of normal price and short-term price reduction as a key weapon in the marketeer's armory is equally dangerous at a time when more and more purchasing decisions are being made at the point of sale.

Wilmshurst also makes the following points:

1 With some brands price reductions can *devalue* the brand so as to cheapen its character.
2 A difference must be made between strategic long-term decisions to cut the price in order to undercut the competition (for example, if one wanted to establish a reputation for low prices, or promoting the fact that your store offered the best prices in town.), and short-term tactical pricing to encourage new buyers or persuade lapsed buyers to return to you.

The role of promotion is to encourage purchase by temporarily improving the value of the brand. Added-value promotions can enhance people's perception of the brand, whereas price reductions may reduce it.

Public relations and perceived value
Good business is based on achieving good relationships within the environment it operates. Good relationships alter the perceived values. Public relations is a marketing technique which is used to add value not only to a brand but also to the organization. Public relations influences opinion in a way that people who have a stake in the business are happy to support it.

The public relations universe

Organization

- Customers.
- Opinion formers.
- Local communities.
- Central and local government.
- The media.
- Shareholders and the City.
- Suppliers.
- Employees and their families.
- Trade Unions.
- Competitors.

Selling

A sales force is one of the most effective marketing tools that a company can use to create and keep customers, particularly in industrial marketing. Personal selling has a number of specific advantages that can increase the perceived value:

1 The customer is able to talk about their needs. This can lead to a more intimate relationship with the customer.
2 Although the marketing strategy and marketing mix has been established, the salesperson can personalize and tailor the offer.
3 The salesperson can help the customer articulate their needs more clearly, and modify the offer to make a closer fit with the perceived needs of the customer.
4 When objections arise to price and interfere with the perceived value of an offer, the salesperson can deal with them on a functional level and also on an emotional level.

QUESTION 10.2

How do marketing techniques alter perceived value?

SUMMARY

In this unit you have seen that:

- There is a difference between commodity and branded markets.
- Perception involves the selection and organization of data coming from the senses in a way that it creates meaning for people.
- Attention involves external factors such as intensity and size, position, contrast, novelty, repetition and movement. These factors are used to gain attention.
- Attention also involves internal factors such as interests, needs, motives and expectations and that we perceive what we want to perceive.
- The branding process takes place in the mind and should be considered as an output process.
- Consumers, in order to simplify their decision making, create sets and group products according to their perceived attributes.
- Marketing techniques can add value to a brand and alter the perceived value. The techniques should be used in an integrated way. The marketing techniques that were considered covered quality, price, corporate image, advertising, sales promotion, public relations and selling.

Social and cultural influences on buying behaviour

This unit deals with those influences on our buying behaviour which arise from social and cultural aspects of the society. In this unit you will:

- Be introduced to the concept of culture and explore its constituent elements.
- Consider the nature of culture – how we acquire it, what membership means, and the cultural consideration required when marketing to different cultures or sub-cultures.
- Look at group influence – how it can occur and its impact on buying behaviour.

By the end of this unit you will:

- Understand the importance of culture in shaping buying behaviour.
- Be able to anticipate the problems which can occur when marketing across cultures or sub-cultures.
- Understand the importance of group influence in shaping behaviour and how this influence is used in marketing.

Organize your study materials from the beginning of your course:

- Use file dividers to keep broad topic areas indexed and relevant materials and articles with the relevant notes.
- Look out for relevant articles and current examples, you will find these useful to illustrate examination answers.

This unit will take you about 1 to 2 hours to read through and think about. The activities you have been asked to carry out will take you about 2 hours.

What is culture?

Sociologists use the term to describe the physical and social environment which results in shared attitudes and behaviours, a fact which is of interest to marketers.

Culture

The values, attitudes, beliefs, ideas, artefacts and other meaningful symbols represented in the pattern of life adopted by people that help them interpret, evaluate and communicate as members of a society.

Culture can be represented graphically as in Figure 11.1.

Influences from institutions and other elements of society (such as education, politics, and the law) combine in complex ways to provide us with culture, customs and rituals which are expressed as attitudes and behaviours.

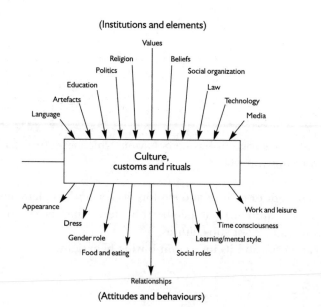

Figure 11.1

Keith Williams, *Behavioural Aspects of Marketing* (1990) describes five main characteristics of culture:

1 It exists to serve the needs of a society. For example, most cultures have some form of 'wedding' ceremony.
2 It is acquired socially. That is, we are not born with any cultural knowledge but acquire it throughout our lifetime.
3 It is learned by interacting with other members of the culture.
4 It is cumulative. Culture is transferred from generation to generation with new influences constantly being added to the cultural 'soup'.
5 It is adaptive. Culture changes in response to the needs of the society.

Importance of culture in marketing

By understanding the nature of culture, and the cultural differences that exist in the population, the marketer can do much to prevent potential problems arising when marketing to different cultural groups. A thorough understanding of a particular culture can also be used in a positive way to market more effectively within that culture.

Apart from the more obvious aspects of culture, such as language, there are many cultural differences that need to be taken into account. These will be discussed in this unit. By way of an introduction, here are some specific examples of cultural differences that have adversely affected the marketing of products.

- Austin Rover (as it then was) produced a speaking car. A polite, demure female voice informed the driver when the doors were open, the seat belt undone and so on. This was found to be unacceptable to Italian males for whom their car was very much a male preserve.
- White teeth are a sign of health in western countries, but not in certain sub-cultures within southeast Asia where the chewing of betel nuts, which discolours the teeth, is associated with status. Toothpaste manufacturers relying on a 'white is good' message have not had much success!

National cultural characteristics are frequently used to market products, not just within that culture, but to other cultures:

- The German reputation for quality engineering has been used to market a range of products from cars to cans of beer.
- The Japanese reputation for producing value-for-money consumer electrical goods has been exploited by one clever European manufacturer who gave themselves a Japanese-sounding brand name ('Matsui').
- French 'chic' has been used in marketing make-up, fashion and food.

Culture is also important in the conduct of business dealings. Business etiquette in Japan, for instance, is very different to that in the West. It is considered polite in Japan to exchange gifts with a new business colleague, exchange business cards as part of an introductory ritual and for the chair of any meeting to sit facing the door. Many Western companies provide training for those executives undertaking business abroad.

Elements of culture
Culture is exhibited by the customs, language, symbols and rituals within a society. These are the observable elements of the culture.

- Customs are the established 'rules' of behaviour within a society. They define what is, and what is not, acceptable.
- Language and symbols are the means by which members of a particular culture communicate with one another. This communication can be verbal (using words) or non-verbal (using images which convey ideas directly or indirectly).
- Rituals are patterns of behaviour, often quite complex, which a society shares. Ritual behaviours include religious services, attainment parties (18th birthday, retirement, engagement, etc.) and private routines such as the Saturday morning shopping trip and the Sunday walk in the park.

Customs
Williams (1990) defines four classes of customs:

1 *Folkways* – these are the everyday customs of the culture. Greetings are one such example.
2 *Conventions* – these are more formally observed folkways, ones which might start to cause more long-term offence if ignored. For example, the sending of Christmas presents.
3 *Mores* – these are formally recognized rules of behaviour such as respect for your parents. Adherence to them is seen as being of wider significance within a culture.
4 *Laws* – those mores which society wishes to control are governed by laws.

Languages and symbols
Marketers involved in multi-lingual operations must be aware of the implications of selling their products to speakers whose native language is not English. The use of language in advertising copy also requires attention.

The use of language 'tricks' is extremely common in advertising where a short phrase or 'word play' is used to convey the promotional message.

- *Word rhyming* – 'Let the train take the strain' was a phrase used by British Rail to promote their InterCity service. It 'works' because of the similarity of the words train and strain. This is unlikely to be the case in other languages.
- *Double-meaning* – 'Labour isn't working' was a slogan generated, as part of a general election campaign, by the agency Saatchi and Saatchi for the UK Conservative Party. The slogan, paired with the image of a long dole queue, was used on poster boards up and down the UK to extremely good effect. The two meanings of the phrase provided a strong and lasting message. Again, this double-meaning would not be possible to exploit in other languages.
- *Colloquialisms* – Toys 'Я' Us – the toy store chain – makes use of a backwards 'R' to suggest a childlike quality, and as an informal shorthand for the word 'are'. This colloquial use of the language is usually known only to native speakers. It is rarely taught and does not appear in dictionaries.
- *Culturally-bound* – A UK Barclays Bank Connect Card advert proudly promoted that its card was 'used by ex-chequers'. The advert showed the distinctive eyebrows of Sir Denis Healey. The play on words here relies on the knowledge that Denis Healey was an ex-Chancellor of the Exchequer, as well as an understanding of the double-meaning of the word 'Exchequer' in this context. Even fluent English speakers are unlikely to understand this play on words unless they know of Denis Healey and his historical position in the government.

The word-plays described are very much surface features of a language. It is also common for language, and objects, to have other meanings and associations other than those that might appear in a dictionary. For instance, a crudely drawn heart (♥) conveys a meaning of innocent love. The phrase '*he fought like a tiger*' only makes sense because of the symbolism we associate with the word '*tiger*' (courage, cunning, stealth). Such words and objects are said to be 'symbolic'. Symbols add richness to communication within a culture.

Symbols can be simple and blunt or subtle and complex. The richness of symbolic meaning can be used in marketing to associate certain qualities with your product or convey more complex meanings in a shorthand form (which can thus be understood and absorbed more quickly). For example, the UK Conservative Party used the lion as a symbol in their 1977 election campaign to represent the qualities of nobility, power and sovereignity in the hope that these values would enchance their public image.

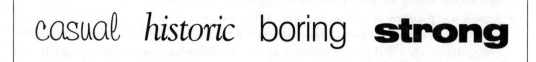

Figure 11.2 Even different typefaces can have different symbolic associations.

Symbol	Associations
Dolphin	Intelligence
Tick	Correctness
Gold	Wealth
Crown	Superiority
Swan	Grace
Owl	Wisdom

Figure 11.3 Some common symbols and their associations in European culture

Rituals

From a marketing perspective, rituals and rites represent a substantial opportunity. In particular, if it is possible to associate an object or other event, known as artefacts, with a ritual then the persistence of the ritual will ensure the continuing use of the artefact.

One example is the red and white Santa Claus costume. This has become so closely associated with Christmas that many people believe it to be historic. In fact, the red and white costume was 'invented' by Coca Cola as a marketing promotion. It has ensured that the combination of red and white (the Coca Cola colours) has a continuing positive association with fun and jollity.

Rituals	Typical artefacts
25 years service*	Award ceremony, clock/plaque
Friday night at home	Video, take out meal, beer
Saturday night out	Meal, cinema/theatre/disco/concert
Valentine's day	Red rose, card
21st Birthday*	Key, card, presents

Figure 11.4 Common UK rituals and typical artefacts. *Indicates rites of passage

If you have ever been abroad, think of the things you found strange about the host country's culture. Try to list 5 things. Were these customs, language/symbols or rituals?

ACTIVITY 11.1

Macro- v micro-culture: the cultural onion

At any one time we are influenced by many different cultures. A person living in England is most probably influenced by 'Western', 'European' and 'English' cultures. The customs and rituals of these cultures are shared with many other people. Such widespread cultures are frequently referred to as macro cultures. Imagine peeling an onion. The well-defined outer layers are rather like macro cultures, with one nesting neatly inside anther. However, if we were to peel the onion further we would find that the layers become less distinct. It is rather the same with culture. As we examine smaller and smaller cultural groups the dividing lines become less distinct. A single individual may well be a 'member' of 10 or more overlapping sub-cultures, or micro-cultures, as they are known (see Figure 11.5).

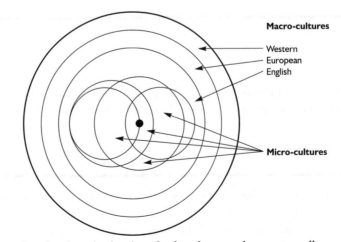

Figure 11.5 The cultural onion. As the size of cultural groups becomes smaller and smaller the separation between them becomes less distinct. The position of a hypothetical individual is represented by a black dot

There are six broad sub-cultures in the UK based on ethnicity, age, geography, religion, gender, occupational and social class.

- **Ethnicity** – This includes not only indigenous population groups, such as the Welsh and Scots, but also from those groups that have settled in the UK.
- **Age** – Within society there are certain values and attitudes which are shared by persons of a similar age. For instance, people brought up during the war years shared some very extreme changes in society such as rationing and life-threatening situations which few persons have since experienced.
- **Geography** – The physical separation of peoples can lead to the development of distinct cultures in different regions.
- **Religion** – Those who subscribe to a particular religion are strongly influenced by its customs and practices. Most religions dictate rules which their followers must abide. These often include dietary, social and ethical requirements.
- **Gender** – Traditionally, in our culture, women have been considered 'home makers' whilst men have been considered the 'bread winners'. Whilst these descriptions are no longer accurate or relevant, many advertisers perpetuate, or otherwise use these stereotypes, and other gender differences to market products.
- **Occupation and social class** – These characteristics of UK culture are often used interchangeably. Many organizations, such as the Market Research Society, define social class in terms of occupation. Occupation is a product of many things such as the occupation of one's parents, education, intelligence, aptitude and opportunity. People with similar occupations tend to share similar lifestyles and incomes. It is common for insurance companies, for instance, to target specific occupations which have been proven to be of a lower risk. Police officers are one such occupational group.

Market segmentation using culture

It is possible to segment a market according to the micro-cultures that exist within the target population.

You might decide to market to women, for instance, to try to increase their consumption of lager. You could get more specific and decide to target businessmen under 35 in the south-east to increase sales of a new cure for baldness.

Look back to Unit 3 for further information on the use of sub-cultures for segmentation purposes.

ACTIVITY 11.2

Think how you might use sub-cultures in the UK to market a new dating service.

Learning culture

As has been stated, all culture is learned. The process of learning one's native culture is termed *socialization*. The learning of a new culture is termed *acculturation*.

DEFINITION 11.2

certain. defi
definition *n.* s
precise mean
distinct, clea
definitive *a.* fi
something: r

Socialization is the process by which the culture of a society is transmitted from generation to generation so that each individual not only understands and follows the 'rules' of their culture but is able to pass these on to others.

There are three main mechanisms by which culture is learned:

- *Social modelling* – where a culture is learned by copying an existing member of the culture. It may be that this learning is direct (i.e. from a peer or family member) or indirectly from media (i.e. from television or a magazine). Fashion, for example, is often adopted from the pages of a magazine and rarely from other members of the family.
- *Role-playing* – A form of social modelling where imitation is allowed to develop further.
- *Conditioning* – whereby certain behaviours are rewarded or punished according to their conformance with the rules of the culture. Eating food without cutlery is likely to be admonished by parents.

Social modelling is the mechanism of most use to marketers in gaining acceptance of their product. Showing a prominent member of a culture behaving in a certain manner (Naomi Campbell wearing a new fashion, for example) can increase the acceptability of this behaviour amongst other members of the culture.

Conditioning can also be used. If purchasers are rewarded for buying a product, through discount vouchers or cash-back offers, the purchasing behaviour is more likely to be repeated.

Dynamic nature of culture

Culture is constantly changing but we are so much part of it that these changes often go unnoticed. It is only when we compare our current culture with that of the past that the differences become apparent.

Marketers should be aware of cultural trends so that they do not get 'left behind' or, conversely, do not miss the opportunity to be the first in the field to market based on a emerging cultural characteristic. Promotions aimed at young people must be particularly careful in this respect.

Cross-cultural marketing

We have already seen how mistakes can be made, and benefits gained, from an understanding of the cultural differences between markets.

Basically, the aim of cross-cultural marketing is, as with all customer-driven marketing, to give the customer what they require. Some products, such as televisions and computers, have an almost worldwide appeal whereas other products, such as many foodstuffs, require the marketing activity to be tailored to local cultures.

There are two strategic approaches to cross-cultural marketing:

1 *Global marketing* – which uses common cultural characteristics of consumers.
2 *Local marketing* – which makes uses of differences in consumers from different cultures.

Local v global marketing

At its most extreme, global marketing is the selling of world brands using the same marketing strategy worldwide. Ohmae, in the *Harvard Business Review* (1989), suggests that the products most amenable to such treatment are 'modern' electronic products which, because of their novelty, transcend traditional cultural boundaries. It is easier to create a global cultural image for a product which has not existed before than one which has already become ingrained in the individual cultures. Similarly, those products that appeal to a specific world micro-culture, such as the very rich or younger generation, are also amenable to global marketing. Examples of these include expensive designer clothes and accessories (Pierre Cardin, Ray Bans, Gucci) for the rich and music for the young (artists such as Michael Jackson and George Michael have been marketed in this way).

Cars are often marketed with a similar message worldwide but the product itself is often modified to meet local legal requirements. UK cars exported to the USA have to be fitted with larger bumpers (or fenders as the Americans say) to meet Federal laws. Cars imported into the UK from Europe have to be modified for right-hand drive. McDonald's, on the other hand, sells a similar product worldwide but localizes its marketing message.

Examples of truly local marketing, where both the product and message are modified, are more difficult to find. One example is the way in which many foreign lagers are marketed in the UK. With their history of drinking draught bitter and stout, the British have a very different perception of 'light' beers to many of our European neighbours. Much of the promotion of lagers within the UK is aimed at establishing a market position for lagers, a form of marketing not required abroad where lager drinking already predominates. Figure 11.6 summarizes the sorts of products more suitable for both global and local marketing.

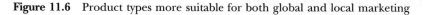

Product types more suitable for global marketing
Products aimed at a specific global micro-culture (e.g. the 'jet-set')
Products which are easy to tailor (e.g. foodstuffs)
Products which are novel (e.g. electronics)

Products which are difficult to tailor (e.g. furniture)
Products which appeal to a specific culture only (e.g. greeting cards)
Product types more suitable for local marketing

Figure 11.6 Product types more suitable for both global and local marketing

In support of the scheme presented here, some marketers label the products most suitable for global marketing as 'high tech' and 'high touch' (Schiffman and Kanuk, 1994). By this they mean that high technology products (such as computers and cameras) and high touch products (perfumes, wrist watches) are more likely to transcend cultural differences and are thus more amenable to global marketing. In contrast, products which are low technology or low touch are more suitable, it is claimed, for a local marketing strategy.

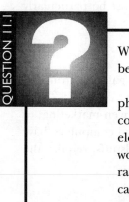

QUESTION 11.1

Which of the following are suitable for global marketing and which are better suited to local marketing?

photocopiers
cordless phones
electric guitars
work clothes
radio cassette players
camera film
pre-cooked meals
gold, precious jewellery

Measurement of culture
The multifaceted nature of culture necessitates that a range of measurement techniques are used. With the exception of content analysis, these are described elsewhere in this book.

- *Projective tests* – These are frequently used to assess motivation and personality.
- *Attitude measurement* – This is frequently used to determine believes and values.
- *Depth interviews and group discussions* – These are useful to discover emerging cultural characteristics.
- *Observation* – This can provide valuable insights into the more obscure aspects of culture which may not be amenable to direct questioning. For instance, a consumer may not be aware that certain of their behaviours are ritualized.
- *Content analysis* – As the name implies, this technique uses an analysis of past and present media to identify cultural changes. This can also be undertaken on a cross-cultural basis. Such a survey carried out in the early 1990s found a shift in trends in household furnishings away from greys with primary spot colours towards pastel tones.

People in groups

People are naturally sociable. There is a strong desire amongst most people to form part of a group. This group may be a family, a department at work, or a social club.

> A group may be defined as *two or more people whom interact together and share some common attitudes and/or behaviours.*
>
> This definition is by no means comprehensive. It is perhaps easier to define a group in terms of its characteristics. A collection of people which possess most of the characteristics listed are usually deemed to constitute a group:
>
> - More than 1 person.
> - Sufficient interaction between members.
> - Perception of themselves as a group.
> - A certain set of agreed/accepted values (called norms).
> - Allocation of specific roles (different activities) to members.
> - Social (affective) relations between members.
> - Shared aims.

Group influence

Most research work by psychologists has shown that groups exert a strong influence on the way we behave.

Undoubtedly, the most quoted experiment – performed by Professor Mayo – was the Drawing Office experiment. Chris Rice (1993) explains:

> Here the problem lay in low morale which was blamed on the lighting. Mayo split the department into two – the first group was the experimental group, the second group acted as the control group and their lighting remained unaltered throughout the experiment. When the intensity of the lighting of the experimental group was increased the expected improvement in morale and output occurred. What was unexpected was that the morale and output of the control group rose in exactly the same way. This puzzled Mayo who proceeded to reduce the intensity for the experimental group – output of both groups again rose! His conclusion was that the changed behaviour was nothing to do with the intensity of the lighting, but was a group phenomenon.

Interestingly, culture plays a strong part in the degree of conformance exhibited by an individual. Isolated members of a culture within a group (for example, a white man in a group of black females) are more likely to conform than if they are in a group with members of their own culture. It also seems that certain cultures are more likely to conform than others. Norwegian students have been found to conform more than the French; similarly Russian children were found to conform more than their Israeli counterparts (Gross *Psychology*, 1989).

Consumer reference groups

> A reference group is a group (or possibly individual) used by a person as a reference point in the formation of their own attitudes and behaviour.

From a marketing perspective, reference groups are useful in that they are influential in the formation of consumer behaviour. A teenager may, for instance, decide to dress in a certain way because of the influence of his, or her, schoolmates. In this example the schoolmates are the reference group.

There are two general types of reference groups:

- *Normative groups* – These are groups which shape the basic attitudes and behaviour of an individual. The most prevalent normative group is the individual's family.
- *Comparative groups* – These are groups which are used to compare and contrast one's existing attitudes and behaviours. In UK common parlance if you are doing well, in comparative terms, it is often said that you are 'keeping up with the Joneses'. That is, your lifestyle is comparable to others that you perceive to be in the same social class.

Reference groups are frequently categorized on the following dimensions:

- *Ascribed versus acquired groups* – Ascribed groups are those to which an individual naturally belongs, e.g. gender, family unit. Acquired groups are those to which an individual actively seeks membership, e.g. health club.
- *Formal versus informal groups* – A formal group is well-defined in terms of its structure and purpose, e.g. parliament. Informal groups are less well-structured and exist primarily to fulfil a social function, e.g. a group of drinking 'buddies'.
- *Primary versus secondary groups* – Primary groups are usually small and associated with more personal contact, e.g. close friends, colleagues at work. Secondary groups are usually larger with communication which is generally less personal, e.g. colleges, large work groups.

There are two important reference groups to which an individual does **not** belong:

- *Aspirational groups* – These are groups which an individual aspires to join, e.g. rock musicians, artists.
- *Dissociative groups* – These are groups which an individual actively avoids membership of, e.g. for some people the Hell's Angels motorbike club might be such a group, others might actively avoid working in the arms industry.

From a marketer's viewpoint, informal, primary groups are of most interest as they are likely to exert the most influence on an individual's consumer behaviour. In addition, aspirational groups are the most important non-membership groups for the same reason.

List five reference groups that you belong to. For each of these decide whether it should be classed and a normative group, comparative group or whether it fulfils both functions.

The influence of reference groups is summarized in Figure 11.7.

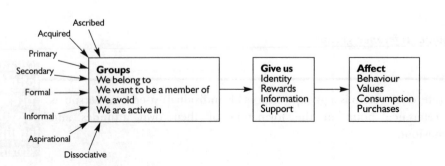

Figure 11.7 Reference groups and their influence

An experiment by Rule *et al.* (1985) tried to assess the influence that various groups exert. US students were asked to record, both when they felt that someone was trying to influence them and, when they were trying to influence someone else. Whereas such experiments are unlikely to be completely accurate (are students exposed to the same influences as others? would they recognize all attempts to influence them?), they do provide a useful guide. The results are summarized in Figure 11.8. Perhaps not surprisingly, immediate family and close friends were perceived as the groups who made the most attempts to persuade. These groups were also those that the student tried most to persuade.

	Who tries to persuade you (%)	Whom do you try to persuade (%)
Immediate family	27	35
Extended family	7	5
Close friends	18	24
Occasional friends	7	12
Instructors	13	7
Sales people	11	2
Other professionals	10	3
Trait defined – religious. etc.	5	9
Goal defined – trying to impress them, etc.	2	3

Figure 11.8 Groups that US students perceived as trying to persuade them and whom they tried to persuade. Figures given are percentages

QUESTION 11.2

Categorize the following groups on the dimensions: ascribed/acquired, formal/informal, primary/secondary. Note whether they might also be aspirational or dissociative.

Dance troupe
Local branch of political party
Your college class

Group membership: roles and norms

I would never be a member of any group that would have me as a member.

paraphrased from Groucho Marx

When you join a group you accept certain norms, which govern the behaviour of the group, and take on a certain role (whether it be active or passive).

Norms may apply to any aspect of the behaviour of the group. If you joined Greenpeace, the environmental action group, you would be expected to agree with their 'direct action' method of campaigning. You might also be expected not to buy environmentally-unfriendly products, where alternatives were available, to avoid unnecessary car travel, and to vote for the Green Party.

As a member of a local Greenpeace group you might also be given, or take on, a number of roles: as organizer of a door-to-door collection, as press officer and so on.

Norms commonly affect the following aspects of the group culture:

- Physical appearance and dress.
- Social and leisure activities (even when these are not the main business of the group).
- Language and gestures used.
- General opinions, attitudes and beliefs.
- The way in which the group carries out its own business.

Roles within a group are decided, primarily, on how we see ourselves and what others expect of us. If we see ourselves are a leader we are likely to try for this role. Alternatively, if others see us as 'leadership material' we are likely to be offered this role.

Within any groups a number of role types commonly exist. Most roles inevitably fall into the first two categories:

- *Task roles* – a member or members concerned with pursuing the goals of the group (often referred to as the members who 'get things done').
- *Maintenance roles* – a member or members concerned with keeping the group operational and efficient (these may be the group administrators or act as emotional supports for the group).
- *Comedy role* – a member who is a joker or the willing butt of jokes.
- *Observer role* – a passive observer of proceedings.
- *Deviant role* – a member who constantly disagrees and challenges the group norms.
- *Specialist role* – a member who is held as being a specialist in the technical activities of the group.
- *Spokesperson role* – a member who communicates the activities of the group to non-group members.

Turn to Unit 1 for further information in the roles assumed within a decision making unit.

Communication within groups

The way in which group members communicate with one another is important to marketers. The direction and density of communication affects how quickly decisions are made, the satisfaction of group members and the quality of the decision. Study of communication patterns might also help you to market your products more effectively and efficiently.

The sociometric method is the technique most used to determine communication patterns. Individuals are asked where they obtained advice or information on a certain subject or product and whom they provided with advice or information. Lines are then drawn on a diagram between circles representing the individuals involved to form what is called a sociogram. It might be that you wish to know how knowledge of a particular book spread within a community or how consumers found out about a special offer.

For instance, Afzal, Bev, Craig and Don all state that they bought a new book because of a recommendation from their mutual acquaintance Elise. We could represent this communication as the sociogram shown in Figure 11.9.

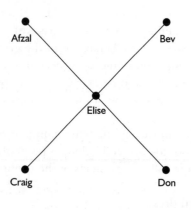

Figure 11.9 A sociogram

When such studies are undertaken, three common sociogram patterns emerge; circle, wheel (or star) and all-channel. These are illustrated below for a five person group. Each line represents a channel of communication, each dot represents an individual.

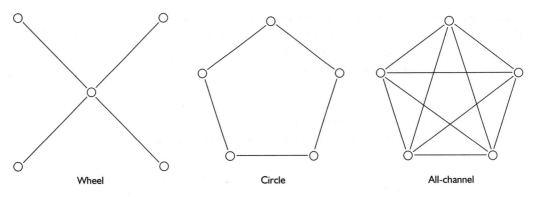

| Wheel | Circle | All-channel |

Figure 11.10

In Unit 14 we will look in more detail at the spread of information within a group of people. In particular, we will look at the role played by opinion leaders.

How do you communicate within your class? Pick a subject which has been discussed at a recent break time and draw out a sociogram. Describe the various structures you discover.

Consumer-referent groups
Marketers have identified the groups which have the most impact on consumer behaviour:

Family – In an earlier unit we discussed the family as a decision making unit.

Peer groups – Through school, our teenage years and on into adulthood we are constantly surrounded by people of our own age and social class. These are usually informal and often social groups of friends. In conjunction with the family, close friends are the biggest influence on our consumer behaviour.

Consumer or lobbying groups – In recent years consumers who feel that they are getting a 'bad deal' have formed groups with the specific purpose of bringing pressure to bear on manufacturers and service providers. Such groups may address a single issue or provide a more general service as a 'watchdog'.

Work groups – People at work form both formal groups (departments, divisions and so on) as well as more informal groups (company sailing club, after-work drinking 'buddies', office squash league, and so on). The amount of time that people spend at work in the company of their work colleagues provides ample opportunity for influence.

How the mass media uses referent groups
The appeal of certain types of referent groups is used in advertising to influence the consumer. Three general approaches are:

Aspirational appeal – present the product in a situation, or use a celebrity or type of person, to which the consumer aspires. Examples include showing the product in the context of a beautiful house or using an athletic actor.

Peer appeal – present the product by a person to whom the consumer can relate. For instance, an advert aimed at selling car phones to working women may show a business women stranded in the middle of nowhere with a broken down car.

Expert appeal – the product is endorsed by an expert, who may be known or unknown, with the aim of convincing the consumer that the product does the job for which is was designed. The more trustworthy the expert, the more convincing the appeal. Ex-police officers have been used on several occasions for this very reason.

The benefits of using reference groups in the ways described is that they reduce the perceived risk of purchase and increase product awareness. As we have seen in earlier units, these are two of the most important barriers to successful marketing.

Appeal element	Product	Type of appeal
Michael Jackson	Soft drink	Inspirational
Exotic locations	Cars	Inspirational
Ex-police chief Markham	Car tyres	Expert
Ex-police chief Stalker	Alarm systems	Expert
Head of company post room	Courier service	Expert
Scientists	Washing powder	Expert
Driver in broken down car in unsafe or remote area	Car breakdown and recovery service	Peer

Figure 11.11 Some examples of referent group appeal

ACTIVITY 11.5

Watch (or video record if you are able) three or four commercial breaks and identify those where referent group appeal has been used. Identify which type of appeal.

Elements of persuasive communication

There are various attributes of the reference group that affect its power to influence. These are covered in detail in Unit 14.

SUMMARY

In this unit you have learned about:

- The nature and importance of culture.
- The elements of culture – customs, language and symbols, rituals and rites.
- Macro and micro cultures.
- Market segmentation using culture.
- The process of socialization.
- Cross-cultural marketing.
- Local and global marketing.
- How culture can be measured.
- The nature of group influence.
- Consumer reference group types and categories.
- Group membership – roles and norms.
- The sociometric method and its application to group communication.
- Consumer-referant groups.

Question 11.1

All but the work clothes and pre-cooked meals are 'high-tech' or 'high touch' items and are thus more suited to global marketing.

Question 11.2

Dance troupe – If you are a member then it is an acquired group most likely to be fairly formal (with people appointed to specific roles) and primary (people are likely to be friends). If you are not a member then is may be that you aspire to join (aspirational)

Local branch of a political party – This is an acquired group, formal (with appointed officers) and could be either primary or secondary, depending on the degree of social contact between its members. Non-members (from other political parties) would be most likely to avoid the group (dissociative).

College class – This is an acquired group which is quite informal (the only strict role belongs to the teacher who arguably is not a class member). The group is likely to consist of primary and secondary groupings depending on its size and the length of time it has been together.

Attitudes and behaviour

This unit describes the link between attitudes and behaviour and the application of motivation theories. In this unit you will be:

- Introduced to the concept of attitudes.
- Presented with the different models of attitudes and how they can be used to explain behaviour.
- Introduced to the concept of motivation and the various issues surrounding its application in a marketing context.

By the end of this unit you will be able to:

- Understand the use and application of attitudes within marketing.
- Understand the use and application of motivation within marketing.
- Conduct a study to measure attitudes.

Most of the qualitative data we collect as market researchers relates to the attitudes of current or potential consumers to the products or services we offer. To gain acceptance from customers we must present a favourable image and avoid unfavourable associations. How favourable impressions translate into active endorsements of a product or service is a matter of some conjecture. The attitude theories described in this unit all approach this problem in a slightly different manner.

The motivations that drive customers are also important. To provide what the customer needs requires an understanding of their goals and aspirations. Whereas proven theories of customer motivation are thin on the ground, the general theories of motivation that exist provide useful guidance to marketers.

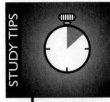

Organize your study materials from the beginning of your course:

- Use file dividers to keep broad topic areas indexed and relevant materials and articles with the relevant notes.
- Look out for relevant articles and current examples, you will find these useful to illustrate examination answers.

This unit will take you about 2 to 3 hours to read through and think about. The activities you have been asked to carry out will take you about 3 to 4 hours.

What are attitudes

I know what I like and I like what I know

lyrics from the Genesis album 'Selling England by the Pound'

Most of us have at some time been asked what we 'think' or 'feel' about a particular object, issue, activity, or person. Our responses to such questions are an expression of our attitudes. That is, whether we generally like or dislike the object, issue, activity or person under discussion.

Formal definitions of attitude try to capture this notion of 'liking and disliking' but, as much of what we say and do can be interpreted as expressing an attitude, such definitions are often broad and/or uninformative. Examples of the more popular definitions are given below.

'A learned orientation or disposition, toward an object or situation, which provides a tendency to respond favourably or unfavourably to the object of situation.' (The learning may not be based on personal experience but may be acquired through observational learning and identification.) Rokeach, 1968.

'Attitudes are likes and dislikes.' Bem, 1979

'An overall evaluation that allows one to respond in a consistently favourable or unfavourable manner with respect to a given object or alternative.' Engel *et al.*, 1990

Characteristics of attitudes

Attitudes are held by individuals. When similar attitudes are held by many individuals they become embedded in that society's culture (see previous unit). The following are generally held to be characteristics of attitudes:

- They can be held about any object, person, issue or activity – referred to as the attitude object.
- They may be strongly or weakly held – an attitude is not simply something that is turned on or off, it is an assessment based on a continuous evaluation.
- They are learned – we acquire attitudes in much the same way we acquire culture, through conditioning and social modelling (see previous unit).
- Attitudes change – they are dynamic. We no longer have the same attitudes as we did when we were younger. We are constantly modifying attitudes based on our experiences and acquiring new attitudes as we encounter new attitude objects.
- Some attitudes are more fundamental than others and more resistant to change – certain opinions stay with us throughout our lives, whilst others change from week to week.

Marketers are most concerned with understanding attitudes (for instance, does a brand have a favourable or unfavourable image), modifying attitudes (to make them more favourable towards certain attitude object and/or less favourable towards others), and turning positive attitudes towards an object into action, usually involving the purchase of the item in question.

Understanding attitudes

An attitude is not a simple entity but is formed from a combination of mental processes and expressed by actions.

Most psychologist agree that, at some level, attitudes contain three components:

1 *A cognitive component* – the knowledge and perceptions about an object. For instance, its shape colour, price and so on.
2 *An affective component* – what a person subjectively feels about the attitude object – whether or not they are favourably disposed towards it. For instance, is the colour of the product a 'favoured' colour?
3 *A behavioural component* – how a person responds to the attitude object (based on 1 and 2 above).

Suppose we are interested in customers' attitudes to washing powder. The cognitive component to their attitudes may relate to the fact that the powder cleans, is environmentally friendly and so on. These are what they believe to be the 'truths' about the product. Whether they are favourably disposed to the product overall will depend on how they feel about the cognitive components of the product. If they value both cleaning ability and environmental friendliness highly, then they are likely to feel positive towards the product overall. As a result of assessing the cognitive and affective components of their attitude they may decide to purchase one brand of powder instead of another (the behavioural component).

Attitudes, beliefs and values

Attitudes are normally thought of as resulting from a combination of beliefs and values.

- *Beliefs* – the body of knowledge we hold about the world (may be incomplete or inaccurate). Beliefs are often expressed in sentences where the word 'is' appears. For example, the information that 'Guinness is good for you' was presented as a fact in a clever advertising campaign. Undoubtedly, this view now forms part of many peoples' belief system.
- *Values* – these are deeply held views about what is good, desirable, valuable, worthwhile. Unlike beliefs, these are usually ideals to which we aspire and may be expressed in sentences were the words 'should be' appear. For example, 'Health care should be free to all' is an expression of the value of social justice.

The relationship between attitudes and our beliefs and values is a complex one. People typically have thousands of beliefs about the world, hundreds of attitudes although probably fewer than fifty values.

It is interesting to see how advertisers use these values to sell products. Typically, a product is associated with a particular value dimension to give it appeal.

For example, pharmaceutical products are typically sold using the dimension of (theoretical) truth. Facts and figures, often in the form of a graph, are shown to demonstrate the effectiveness of the product being sold. It may be that X brand of toothpaste prevents the formation of plaque for six hours or that a shampoo bonds extra proteins to your hair, and so on.

Relationship between attitudes and behaviour

As marketers, we are most interested in being able to predict and alter the behavioural component of attitudes. We want people to like our products but also buy them, remain loyal and recommend the products to others. All these involve action of some sort.

Figure 12.1 represents a simple model of the relationship between attitudes and behaviour. In this simple model positive cognitive and affective perceptions of an object lead to positive behaviours and vice versa.

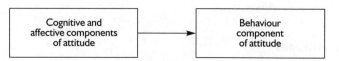

Figure 12.1 A simple model of the relationship between attitudes and behaviour

Unfortunately, psychological research has found that there is no clear relationship between measured attitudes and behaviour. Perhaps this is not surprising as many of the factors which also influence our behaviour are outside our own control. It might be, for instance, that we would like to take a 3-week holiday in Portugal. We are extremely favourably disposed towards the idea but there are a number of reasons why we might not be able actually to book the holiday. Some examples of outside influences, in this instance, might be:

- We have no money.
- We cannot get the time off work.
- The are no more bookings available for Portugal this year.
- Spain has an air traffic control strike on at the moment which is stopping flights to Portugal.
- A family member is ill and needs our support.

Some of the apparent difference between what we think and what we do may be due to measurement difficulties. We may observe a person buying a product but are they doing so because they are favourably disposed towards that product or because it happens to be the nearest on the supermarket shelf? Similarly, interview is the only way of securing attitudes, in isolation from behaviour but, as we have seen in previous units, such methods also have their problems.

Some elegant experiments have been undertaken by psychologists and sociologists to try and determine the factors affecting the link between attitudes and behaviour. Perhaps most famous of these is the Travelling Chinese Experiment.

In the early 1930s strong feelings existed against the Chinese in the United States. Around this time Richard LaPiere, a sociologist, took a Chinese couple on a tour of America. The trio stopped at 250 hotels and restaurants during their trip. On only one occasion were they refused entry. After returning from his trip, he wrote to each of the establishments he had visited asking them whether they would accept Chinese patrons. Somewhat surprisingly, of the half that responded to his letter, 90% said they would not.

This experiment demonstrates a rather large gap between what the various proprietors said they would do and what they actually did. In other words, their attitudes (as secured by letter) were strikingly different to their behaviour (as demonstrated by Mr LaPiere's visits).

There are a number of methodological problems with LaPiere's informal experiment, for example was the same person that answered the letter been in a position to refuse service, but nonetheless the results are strongly suggestive of a real discrepancy between attitudes and behaviour.

Can you think of any other factors in LaPiere's 'experiment' that may have weakened the link between attitudes and behaviour?

QUESTION 12.1

As a result of LaPiere's study and the experiments of others, it is generally agreed that attitudes are only one factor in behaviour. It is said that they are a predisposing factor. In other words, without any other interventions, the attitudes would lead more directly to behaviour. The following intervening factors are said to affect the degree to which attitude leads to behaviour:

- *Unforeseen events* – it may be that unforeseen events lead to a change in behaviour. For instance, you may wish to go to a football match but it starts raining so you reluctantly make alternative arrangements.
- *Elapsed time* – as attitudes are dynamic, the longer the elapsed time between measurement of the attitude and the behaviour you are trying to predict, the less likely there is to be a link.

- *Situational factors* – it may be that the situation you find yourself in precludes action. For example, a consumer may wish to buy a tub of ice cream but the shops have just closed or they may not have enough money to hand.
- *Stability* – a particular attitude may be unstable in that you keep changing your mind. For example, one day you may feel like wearing jeans, the next day more formal wear.
- *Conflict of attitudes* – it may be that more than one attitude is applicable to a certain situation, the resultant behaviour will inevitably lead to a compromise behaviour. For example, you go into a shop to buy a tub of ice cream. You and your partner both want a different flavour. You equally well want to keep your partner happy and you want your favourite flavour. The behaviour you exhibit will be a compromise between these two contradictory aims (the exact compromise will depend how selfish you are!).
- *Strength* – the strength with which an attitude is held can determine behaviour. Also one attitude can be expressed in many different ways. For example, if you support a particular political party you may or may not become a member depending on the strength of your support.
- *Specificity* – the accuracy with which attitudes are measured also affect the degree to which they are able to predict behaviour. This is discussed in more detail below.

We are left with a more complex view of the relationship between attitudes and behaviour than suggested earlier. Figure 12.2 is more representative of the relationship that exists:

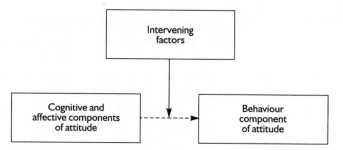

Figure 12.2 Most likely relationship between attitudes and behaviour

Specificity of measurement

Fishbein and Ajzen argue that you can predict behaviour from attitudes if the attitudes you are investigating are measured accurately enough. In other words, you need to ensure *specificity* of measurement. This has implications in the design of attitude surveys. Most importantly, questions must ask precisely about the behaviour you are trying to predict. The Pill Experiment, carried out by Davidson and Jaccard in the late 1970s, on women's attitudes to the contraceptive pill illustrates this quite point well.

A group of women were asked a question about their general attitudes to birth control. There was found to be a very low correlation between positive attitudes towards birth control and their actual use of the pill.

When the question was changed to something more specific – it asked about their attitudes to oral contraception – the correlation between attitudes and usage was much higher (0.32). When the question was made more specific again – asking about their use of oral contraceptive over the next two years – an even higher correlation between attitudes and behaviour was found (0.57).

When measured attitudes are similar to the observed behaviour, they are said to correspond.

Consistency theories of attitude

There are three prominent attitude theories which address how attitudes change and adapt to changing circumstances:

- Balance theory (Heider, 1958).
- Congruity theory (Osgood and Tannenbaum, 1955).
- Cognitive dissonance theory (Festinger, 1957).

These are all based on the assumption that people seek consistency in their attitudes. That is, one cannot simultaneously hold two contradictory beliefs. Suppose a reliable friend recommends a restaurant which you subsequently visit and find disappointing. In general terms, consistency theories state that you cannot simultaneously believe both that your friend is reliable yet that his recommendation was wrong. You would, according to consistency theorists, be 'forced' to either change your opinion of your friend or make some excuse concerning the performance of the restaurant on the occasion you visited.

Balance theory and congruity theory are described in this unit. For a description of cognitive dissonance theory refer to Unit 15.

Balance theory

Balance theory is mainly concerned with the transfer of information between people. This is of use to marketers investigating ways in which recommendations, as well as negative information, are communicated.

Consider a person (A) that receives information from another person (B) concerning an attitude object (O). Depending on the whether this information is positive or negative, the following four scenarios are possible. The interactions are represented as triangles, the nature of the communications as positive (or favourable) (+) or negative (or unfavourable) (–):

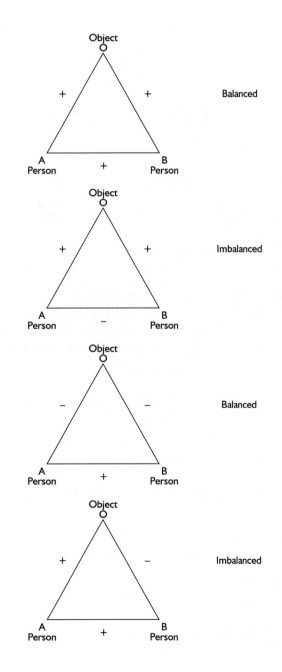

Figure 12.3

The top triangle (1) is balanced. Persons A and B have a positive attitude, both towards each other, and the object. There is no inconsistency.

Triangle (2) is unbalanced. Persons A and B have a negative attitude towards each other yet they both have a positive attitude to the object. Although their views of the object are consistent (both positive), their views of each other are negative. This is inconsistent.

Triangle (3) is balanced. Persons A and B have a positive attitude towards each other and share the same (negative) attitude towards the object. There is no inconsistency.

Triangle (4) is unbalanced. Persons A and B have a positive attitude towards each other but their attitudes towards the object are different. This is inconsistent.

According to balance theory, where there is inconsistency (situations B and D) this must be resolved either by changing the attitude to a person or the object.

A selling situation is one context where balance theory can be applied. Suppose a salesman (let us called him David) visits you at work and tries to sell you a new photocopier. He can show you pictures of the copier and talk about its benefits but, ultimately, you are placing your trust in him. After all, the photocopier could turn out to be unreliable, noisy, smelly and expensive to run. How do you decide whether or not to be positive towards the copier? Let us represent this as a balance triangle:

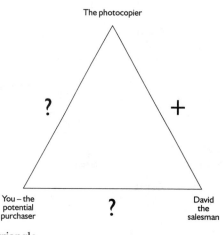

Figure 12.4 Initial balance triangle

Initially, only the salesman's view of the photocopier copier is certain. Over the course of his sales pitch we will undoubtedly make our mind up about David. If we feel favourably towards him then the situation shown in Figure 12.5 is most likely, if we do not feel favourably disposed towards him the situation shown in Figure 12.6 is more likely.

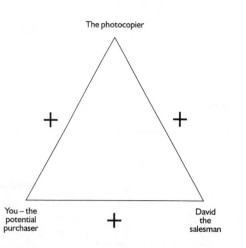

Figure 12.5 Favourable towards David so, to be consistent, we are most likely to feel favourable towards copier

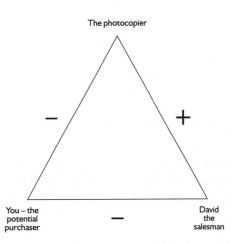

Figure 12.6 Unfavourable towards David so, to be consistent, we are most likely to feel unfavourable towards photocopier

These scenarios can be applied to any marketing situation where customers do not have direct contact with the product but rely on intermediaries for information. Where a service, rather than a product, is being marketed, the only way in which quality is 'sold' is via the salesperson. There is an old marketing saying which goes 'people buy people first'.

Congruity theory

This theory builds on the notion of positive and negative attitudes and adds the concept of attitude strength. Congruity theory allows us to rate our attitudes towards an object from −3 (highly unfavourable) to +3 (high favourable) with a middle zero point. To reduce consistency (to obtain congruity), we take into account not only the direction of the attitude (as in balance theory) but also its strength. An example will serve to demonstrate. Let us return to David, our copier salesman.

Suppose we gain the impression from David that the copier is extremely good and meets all our requirements. We might rate it +3 (high favourable). However, we also take a mild dislike to Dave, let us say a rating of −1 (slight unfavourable). To achieve congruity we must adjust both of these ratings. Congruity theory states that the final attitude towards an object is calculated by halving the difference between the ratings. Therefore we would give the copier a rating of +1 (slightly favourable), the mid-point between −1 and +3. This is illustrated in Figure 12.7.

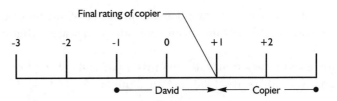

Figure 12.7 Congruity theory

Alternatively, suppose we took a mild liking to David (rating +1). This would result in a more positive rating of the copier of +2. See Figure 12.8.

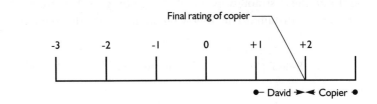

Figure 12.8 Congruity theory

 Pick four television commercials that involve celebrities. For each advert, rate the celebrity using a –3 to +3 scale. Now, using the same scale, rate the products or services that they are promoting. See activity debrief.

Multi-component models of attitude

These models aim to predict attitudes from any evaluation of their component parts. According to Fishbein, one of the most prominent researchers in this field, an attitude towards an object is a function of:

- strength of belief that object has certain attributes
- the desirability of these attributes
- the number of attributes.

Attributes are those elements of an object that define it. Some of the attributes of a vacuum cleaner might be:

- has mains cable storage
- can clean-up liquids
- colour
- is floor standing (rather than upright).

Fishbein model

Fishbein's model states that if a consumer believes strongly that an object has many positive, desirable attributes then it will be rated more favourably. This model can be summarized by the formula:

$$\text{Attitude towards an object} = \sum_{i=1}^{n} (b_i e_i)$$

where
b_i = strength of the belief that object contains attribute i
e_i = evaluation of the desirability of attribute i
n = number of attributes.

This can be described as the sum of the multiplication of the belief and evaluations for all attributes.

Usually b is rated on a scale of 1 (strong belief of presence of attribute) to 3 (uncertain of presence) and evaluation of desirability of the attitude on a scale 1 (highly desirable) to 7 (undesirable).

Suppose we are asked to assess attitude towards a particular brand of CD player. These generally have, amongst others, the following attributers:

- Sound quality.
- Portability.
- Ease of use.

We might then ask a sample of potential purchasers for their opinion on these attributes. If an individual strongly believed that the sound quality was good they might rate it with a 1 (strong belief of presence of attribute). If sound quality was only moderately important to them then they might rate the desirability of it as 4. Continuing in this fashion it is possible to build up data for each attribute. The following table shows the data from a single individual:

Attribute	Belief (b)	Evaluation (e)	$b \times e$
Sound quality	1	4	4
Portability	3	2	6
Ease of use	3	1	3
			Total = 13

The attitude score for this particular brand of CD player is thus 13. The higher the figure, the less favourable the attitude towards the object. The maximum (i.e. worst possible) score can be calculated by multiplying the number of attributes by 21. Thus the worse score for a three attribute assessment is $3 \times 21 = 63$.

This method is particularly useful to marketers wishing to do brand comparisons.

ACTIVITY 12.2

Find two differently designed telephones – the more different the better. Pick four attributes and assess the phones separately against your chosen attributes. To get you started, one attribute might be 'volume of ringer' another could be 'has dial memories'.

Which phone came out better?

Extended Fishbein model

As we have already discussed, attitudes do not necessarily lead to corresponding behaviour. In an attempt to improve the accuracy of Fishbein's original model Williams (1981) modified it so that the ratings referred not to an object but to the behavioural outcomes of taking a particular action. Statistically, the same formula is used but the meaning is very different.

$$\text{Attitude towards an action} = \sum_{i=1}^{n} (b_i e_i)$$

Where

b_i = strength of belief that action will lead to particular outcome i

e_i = evaluation/desirability of outcome i

n = number of outcomes.

If a consumer believes that purchasing a product will lead to a large number of desirable outcomes, then they are more likely to purchase it.

For example, you may buy a fast car not because it is fast but because of the outcomes of speed: getting from A to B quicker; to impress friends; to overtake easily on motorways. According to the extended model, we can predict behaviour accurately only if we rate these outcomes rather than any attributes of the car. Based on our earlier concerns about the link between behaviour and attitudes, this model is likely to give more reliable results.

The difference between the standard and extended Fishbein models is best illustrated with an example. Suppose we have been asked to predict voting intentions at the next general election. According to the standard Fishbein model we would find out those attributes of the various political parties that were important to people and then rate the political parties against these attributes. The ratings that the parties received would then be seen as indicative of people's voting intentions, i.e. the party that got the best rating with the majority of those surveyed would win. Figure 12.9 is an example of some of the attributes we might use in our survey.

Attributes	Conservative		Labour		Liberal Democrat		Green	
	b	e	b	e	b	e	b	e
Good leadership								
Honest								
Stable/consistent								
Environmentally aware								
Total sum b × e for each party								

Figure 12.9 Prediction of voting intentions using Fishbein model

According to the extended model, we would look at the outcomes that are important to people and how likely voting for each of the parties might bring about the desired outcomes. Figure 12.10 is an example of some of the outcomes we might use if we decided to use the extended model.

Outcomes	Conservative		Labour		Liberal Democrat		Green	
	b	*e*	*b*	*e*	*b*	*e*	*b*	*e*
More jobs								
Better environment								
Less homelessness								
Lower taxes								
Total sum *b* × *e* for each party								

Figure 12.10 Prediction of voting intentions using extended Fishbein model

Fill in both the political rating grids (Figure 12.9 and Figure 12.10) for the Fishbein and extended Fishbein models.

Do the models predict different voting intentions? If so, think why that might be.

Which do you think most accurately predicts your own voting behaviour?

Measuring attitudes

There are numerous methods which have been devised for the measurement of attitudes. The most significant are:

Likert scales

Semantic differential

Exotic methods – such as repertory grid

All but the Kelly's repertory grid technique have been mentioned elsewhere. Look back to Unit 6 if you need to.

Repertory grid

The work of George Kelly has found widespread use in the application of psychology. His theory, called Personal Construct Theory, crossed many traditional boundaries within psychology and has been considered of relevance to the study of perception, personality and attitudes.

At the heart of Kelly's theory is the notion that people are fundamentally inquisitive and that we explore and explain the world using what he called constructs. These constructs are, essentially, definitions of the parts of the world – a way of compartmentalizing it – to make sense of it and predict what is likely to happen in the future. Kelly himself said of constructs:

Man looks at his world through transparent patterns and templates which he creates and then attempts to fit over the realities of which the world is composed. (Kelly, 1955)

Perhaps the biggest contribution to marketing is the repertory grid (rep grid) technique which Kelly developed for the measurement of constructs. The technique has found use beyond what Kelly originally intended and is frequently used in marketing in the comparative study of attitudes.

In the original format rep grid, Kelly would present a series of cards with occupations written on them (known as elements). Subjects would be asked to pick any three occupations and describe the way in which any two were different from the third. The resulting response was used as a construct. The actual constructs generated can be extremely broad in nature such as 'wears a hat' or 'government worker'. The subject can describe the differences between the elements in any manner that they like. The generation of construct is repeated using any other three occupations and repeated until either no more constructs can be originated or a predetermined limit has been reached.

Clearly, such a technique can be applied to a range of marketing problems where more than one product or service is being compared. It has been used in:

- market segmentation
- brand comparison
- identification of marketing/branding opportunities.

Suppose we have been asked to investigate the various ice cream flavours in the marketplace and determine what characteristics any new flavour should have to be successful. We know the sales figures for the various flavours but we do not know what it is about the ice cream flavours that people like. This is where the rep grid technique can help.

A rep grid is a table with the columns as elements and the rows as constructs. If we were investigating different ice cream flavours, the flavours themselves would be the elements. In this example we will limit ourselves to four flavours although, of course, a real study would take into account all the flavours on the market. To start with, our rep grid would look something like Figure 12.11.

Constructs	Elements			
	Nuts and cookies	Strawberry	Roast peanut	French chocolate

Figure 12.11 Rep grid for ice cream example

To generate the constructs we take any three flavours (elements) and find a way in which any two are different from the third. If we took Strawberry, French Chocolate and Roast Peanut we may decide that the Strawberry is different from the others in that it is 'fruity'. We would therefore write in 'fruity' as a construct and place a tick against 'Strawberry' and any other of the elements which we consider to share the 'fruity' construct. In this example, none of the others would probably be considered 'fruity'. By taking another three elements and comparing them we might come up with the following additional constructs: 'has bits in', 'doughy', 'chocolate-taste' and so on. It must be emphasized that constructs are a very personal thing. No two persons' will look the same. After three constructs are generated, the grid may end up looking something like Figure 12.12.

Constructs	Elements			
	Nuts and cookies	Strawberry	Roast peanut	French chocolate
Fruity		√		
Has bits in	√		√	√
Doughy	√			

Figure 12.12 Rep grid for ice cream example with three constructs added

By comparing the high-selling flavours with others we can determine what constructs are the most popular and use this information to determine what constructs any new flavour should match. For instance, we might decide that it should 'doughy' and 'have bits in'. From this information we might decide to test cookies and chocolate as a combination.

As noted, rep grids can also be used as a tool for determining how consumers segment a market. In this type of analysis columns are compared to determine the relationship between different elements (products) and a comparison of rows to compare the relationship between different constructs.

An element analysis will provide information on how the consumer segments products, whereas a construct analysis will determine which constructs are used for this segmentation.

Chris Rice (*Consumer Behaviour*) provides the following example, using people as elements, which explains the process of construct analysis.

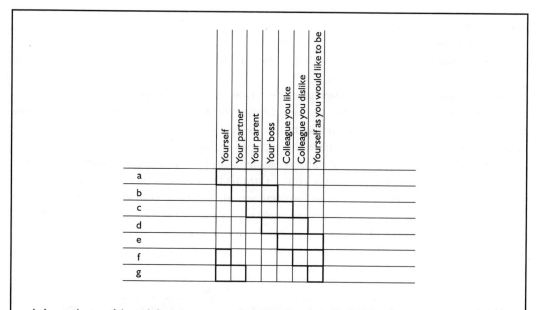

1 Across the top of the grid above you see a number of 'people-types' set out at the top of the columns – yourself, your partner, your parent, your boss, a colleague you like, a colleague you dislike, yourself as you would like to be. Pencil in the space provided the names of the real people who fit those descriptions in your life (do it in pencil so that you can rub the names out when you have finished).

2 You will see that three boxes have been picked out in heavier print in the first horizontal row – corresponding to the characters 'yourself', 'your partner', 'your parent'.

3 Think of the three people you have identified – which one is different?

4 Place a tick in the box of the one you have chosen.

5 Write in the right hand column the characteristic that makes that person different from the other two.

6 Write in the left-hand space what you perceive as being the opposite of that characteristic. It will help if you avoid using 'closed' constructs such as male, female, bald, etc. wherever possible and use more open, personality type adjectives.

7 Now work along the remainder of the row, consider each of the persons you have identified and put a tick in the appropriate box for any of those persons who also share the characteristic you listed in the right-hand column.

8 Complete the rest of the grid, row by row, following the same procedure – the only limitation is that you should not use the same construct more than once.

You should now have a grid that looks something like this:

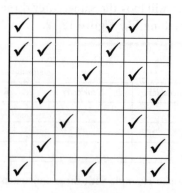

9 To score the grid we need a measure of how similar or different two rows are. Let us imagine that the first two rows are:

We count a point for each pair that match – i.e. whenever there is a tick in both rows we score a point; and whenever there is a tick in neither row we also score a point. So the example above would get a matching score of:

$$1 + 0 + 1 + 1 + 1 + 0 + 1$$

=5 for the comparison score for rows 1 and 2.
As you can see the scores will always lie between 0 and 7.

10 Repeat stage 9 for rows 1 and 3, 1 and 4, 1 and 5, 1 and 6, 1 and 7.
11 Then work out the scores for rows 2 and 3, 2 and 4, and so on to 2 and 7.
12 Complete the remainder of the comparisons – 3 and 4, 3 and 5, 3 and 6, 3 and 7, 4 and 5, 4 and 6, 4 and 7, 5 and 6, 5 and 7, 6 and 7.
13 Put the values into the appropriate 'holes' in the diagram.

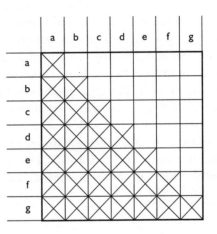

14 As mentioned above the scores can vary from 0 to 7. The higher the score, the more similar the two constructs are until we reach a score of 7 when it might suggest that the two constructs are identical. Similarly scores of 0 or 1 suggest the constructs may be opposites.
15 In our example grid above the comparisons scores might produce a grid that looks like this:

	a	b	c	d	e	f	g
a		5	2	6	5	2	1
b			2	4	5	2	1
c				3	4	7	6
d					4	3	2
e						4	3
f							6

Interpretation of this data would suggest that constructs (a) and (d) are similar and constructs (c), (f) and (g) form another, separate cluster of constructs which are similar. Construct (g) seems to be nearly opposite to both (a) and (b).

Figure 12.13 Construct analysis

What purchasing decisions have you made recently where you have had to consider alternatives? Using this as an example construct a rep grid with at least five constructs and five elements. If you cannot think of an appropriate purchasing decision, consider newspapers. You might wish to use the following as elements: the *Guardian*, *Financial Times*, the *European*, the *Sun*, *The Times* and a local newspaper.

Motivation

Do not buy what you want, but what you need; what you do not need is dear at a farthing.

Marcus Porcius Cato (234–149 BC) *Reliquae*

The study of motivation is concerned with *why* people choose to behave in a certain way. In particular, it is concerned with:

- The most basic human requirements – referred to as 'needs'.
- How these needs translate into behaviours – referred to as 'drives'.
- What these behaviours aim to achieve – referred to as 'goals'.

In an organization context, understanding what motivates a workforce is of prime importance to ensuring their continued productivity and satisfaction. In a marketing context, understanding what motivates a consumer is equally important. It enables products to be produced which are both desired and satisfying. An understanding of what motivates is also of use in preparing promotions and can be used for market segmentation purposes.

Certainly, this is a broad area of study. The great psychologist George Miller described the study of motivation as covering all things 'biological, social and psychological that defeat our laziness and move us, either eagerly or reluctantly, to action' (1957).

At a basic level, our body has a need (hunger, for instance) which translates into a drive (in the case of hunger, this is a drive to obtain food). The goal is to satisfy the need (in this example, to feel full). This can be represented diagrammatically as shown in Figure 12.14.

Figure 12.14

Achievement of the goal satisfies the initial needs thus completing the circle. Of course, next time that need surfaces (in the case of hunger, the next meal time) then the whole circular process will start again.

Perhaps the most popular theory which links needs and drives with goals is that of Hull. His Drive-Reduction Theory attempts to explain both motivation and learning. He was mostly concerned with the operation of primary needs but principles he presents are of general interest. Hull's theory is illustrated in Figure 12.15. As we have discussed, a need gives rise to a drive and corresponding behaviour aimed at reducing the drive and thus the need.

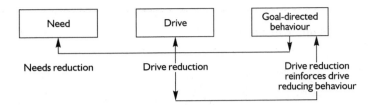

Figure 12.15   A simplified view of Hull's Drive Reduction Theory

According to Hull, this act of reducing the drive (drive reduction) reinforces the drive-reducing behaviour thus making the behaviour more likely to occur again in response to recurrence of the need.

Suppose we are on a beach and feel thirsty. We will go to find the nearest source of refreshment, a beach bar perhaps. According to Hull's theory we are most likely to drink a product which has satisfied our thirst in the past, Perrier water for instance. If this is not on sale, we may pick something similar, or try something new, and this (if it satisfies us) is then more likely to be selected next time we are thirsty.

As well as positive motivations (in the above example, the drink) we can also experience negative motivations or avoidance of certain items or situation. If we are thirsty, for example, we are likely to avoid salty things, which are likely to make us even more thirsty. To give another example, if we are cold we will avoid situation which will make us colder (avoidance of cold) and seek out situation, that make us warmer (approach warmth).

On this basis, we can classify objects as either approach objects (contact with these will satisfy our need) and avoidance objects (contact with these will make our need worse). Let us now look in more detail at needs.

Needs

These fall into three broad categories:

- *Physiological (or primary) needs* – these are the needs that sustain life. They include the need for food, air, sex and self-preservation.
- *Psychological needs* – these are the needs that relate to our competence to deal effectively with the outside environment, often termed personal competence.
- *Learned (secondary or cultural) needs* – we have already seen the influence that culture can have on an individual's behaviour. Learned needs are those needs which arise as a result of our socialization. As the name suggests, they are learned and are dependent on the culture we grow up in. Some cultures value power and status, others humility and a structured life. These are all learned needs.

These different categories of needs are related in complex ways. For example, the food a consumer purchases (a primary need) will depend on secondary needs. If you are hungry at breakfast time in the UK, you are most likely to eat cereal and toast. In the US you may well satisfy your hunger by eating pancakes or even cake – the culturally acceptable breakfast foods in that country. In addition, psychological needs may play a part – does the food look palatable, pleasant and well-presented?

The following are examples of how learned and psychological needs interact with primary needs:

- donating a kidney to save another life
- fasting for the purpose of protest or religious 'cleansing'
- giving up one's life for the greater good (such as with the Japanese kamikaze fighter pilots in World War II).

Needs arousal

We are aware of our needs only when they are aroused. They can be aroused by four distinct stimuli: physiological, cognitive, environmental and emotional. The following table contains examples of all four stimulus types.

Stimulus type	Example of mechanisms	Need aroused
Physiological	Drop in blood sugar levels	Hunger
	Testosterone release in men	Sex
Cognitive	Remembering a loved one	Affection
	Seeing an advert which reminds you to phone a friend	Social
Emotional	Fear of being burgled	Security
	Chaotic life	Stability
Environmental	Finding a dream home that you can afford	Success
	Walking past a clothes shop and seeing clothes you want to buy	Prestige, self-respect

There at least two prominent theories that address motivation needs which are of use to marketers.

- Maslow's hierarchy of needs.
- McClelland's three motivating needs.

Before discussing these we will turn to a description of goals.

Goals

As already noted, these are the end-points of motivated behaviour. Goals can be generic or specific. If you are thirsty, you may want any liquid or you may want a specific brand of drink (see Figure 12.16). Some psychologists distinguish between *wants* and *goals* referring to the specific want as the object of desire (the brand of drink in this case) and the goal as the behaviour required to obtain the specific want.

GENERIC   SPECIFIC

←———————————————————————————————→

Any drink ––– Any cold drink ––– Any carbonated cold drink ––– Any carbonated cold water ––– Perrier

Figure 12.16

From the marketer's point of view, we are interested in making goals specific to our products. Different levels of specificity are appropriate to different types of products. For example, many foods are unbranded – potatoes, for example. In the case of this food, the Potato Marketing Board presents the purchase of potatoes as a fairly generic goal.

Choice of goal chosen to satisfy a certain need depends on a number of things:

- *Personal experience* – If a particular goal has satisfied a need in the past then it is more likely to be selected again. As we have seen with Hull's Drive Reduction Model, the success of a goal in satisfying a need actually reinforces its use again. For example, if a particular washing powder has been successful in cleaning our clothes we are more likely to buy that same washing powder in the future.
- *Cultural norms and values* – We have seen in the previous unit how cultural norms and values affect behaviour. To give an example, it may be that we shun the purchase of a new washing machine liquid (as opposed to powder) because using such a product is not the 'done thing' in our culture.

- *Personal norms and values* – Our own personal norms and values, possibly religious or ethical, can also affect the goals we select for the achievement of a particular need. For example, if we are 'green minded' we might choose to select an environmentally-friendly washing powder.
- *Physical and/or intellectual capacity* – It might be some goals are unachievable due to our own personal limitations. Suppose we want to own a cat but are allergic to fur. Our need for companionship must find an alternative goal.
- *Accessibility of goal* – It may be that the goal we select is determined on the basis of accessibility. We may wish, for example, to go to a particular play but the distance of the theatre precludes us going.

Maslow's hierarchy of needs

Maslow categorized human needs in five groups which he arranged into a hierarchy of importance (see Figure 12.17). These five groups, arranged from lower to higher importance are:

- *Physiological needs* – such as hunger, thirst, sex and activity.
- *Safety needs* – freedom from threat, health but also security, order and stability.
- *Social, or belonging needs* – relationships, affection, sense of belonging (identification).
- *Esteem needs* – such as prestige, success and self-respect.
- *Self-actualization needs* – the fulfilment of personal potential.

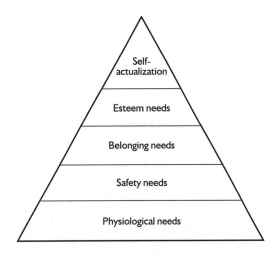

Figure 12.17 Maslow's hierarchy of needs

He also introduced two other categories of 'enabling' needs which provided the channels through which the five categories of needs could be achieved:

- *Freedom of enquiry and expression needs* – for social conditions permitting free speech and encouraging justice, fairness and honesty.
- *Knowledge and understanding needs* – to gain and order knowledge of the environment, to explore, learn and experiment.

Marketing applications of Maslow

As a theory, Maslow's hierarchy of needs has proved useful in applying a more behaviour-oriented structure to the market. As such, it has found use in market segmentation and brand/product positioning.

Each product/service has a 'natural' needs category which it addresses. Most products only actually address the very basic physiological and safety needs. For example, all the foodstuffs sold actually only address our physiological need for sustenance. However, it is possible to position products to appeal to just about any needs category which broadens the appeal and can be used to create a brand image.

The following table provides some examples of positioning by needs category:

Needs category	Products appealing to this category
Physiological	'Ready Brek' breakfast cereal provides you with a protective 'barrier' against the cold
Safety	AA Rescue Service stops you being stranded at night in a hostile environment
Social	British Telecom adverts – the telephone keeps you in touch with absent family and friends
Esteem	Rolex watch adverts suggesting that ownership of a Rolex is a sign of success
Self-actualization	Adverts for adult education courses encouraging you to further yourself

As already stated, we can also segment a market using Maslow's needs categories. The table below gives examples.

Needs category	Potential target groups
Physiological needs	Teenagers eager for sexual experience
	Old persons worried about health problems
Safety needs	Wealthy people with valuable possessions to protect
	Families worried about safety of children
Social needs	New arrivals in an area looking for social affiliations clubs, societies, etc.
	Single parents looking for company
Esteem needs	Recent high income earners eager for outside signs of prestige
	High status groups, e.g. company directors
Self-actualization	Those in higher education – likely to be looking for additional education
	Health-conscious teenagers eager to conform to perfect body image

Needs also translate into benefits which form the basis of benefits segmentation. Furthermore, motivation is also used in psychographic segmentation (see Unit 3).

In terms of Maslow's categorization of needs (physiological, safety, social, esteem, self-actualization), how would you segment the following products/services?:

Headache tablet
Cream cake
Household burglar alarm
Computer
Church service
Wedding ring
Typing course

For each of the above, think of a way you might position them in at least one other segment. Write this down and explain your decision.

Evaluation of Maslow's hierarchy of needs

Maslow's theory certainly has intuitive appeal. If you are desperate for food you are unlikely to be concerned about social niceties or self-fulfilment. His ideas are also useful in that they consider much of what drives us as individuals. Unfortunately, there are a number of problems with the theory as Rice (1994) explains:

- Lack of empirical evidence to support it. Physiological and safety needs are not always the predominant factor in determining behaviour.
- The absence of money from the list of needs worries some people.
- Self-actualization and esteem needs are likely to be a function of each individual's self-perception.

Notwithstanding these problems, Maslow's work has provided a framework which is easy and useful to marketers.

McClelland's theory of need achievement

Unlike Maslow, some psychologists, such as McClelland and his colleagues, believe in the presence of just three main needs. Whereas these can be subsumed within Maslow's hierarchy, considered as separate entities they are useful for marketers to consider.

- *Affiliation* – this relates to a desire to belong, to be part of a group and to have friends.
- *Power* – this relates to control over both people and other objects in the environment.
- *Achievement* – this relates to the need to achieve.

Think of work colleagues, friends and family that you know. How would you classify them in terms of McClelland's three needs theory? Which need motivates them most?

Other theories of motivation

There are two other theories which are occasionally referred to in a marketing context. A brief explanation will suffice for each of these.

Alderfer's ERG hierarchy of needs – This proposes a hierarchy of just three needs: existence, relatedness and growth (hence ERG). While similar in many ways to Maslow, Alderfer introduces the useful notion of frustration. That is, if a need is not satisfied it results in frustration which may result in other behaviours. In a marketing context, we may find consumers dissatisfied with a particular product settling for an alternative or complaining at what they have purchased. It is important to accept that frustration can occur in any buying situation and to plan for it.

Vroom's expectancy theory – This theory is strongly related to the extended Fishbein model of attitudes. Essentially, the strength of an individual's motivation is based on the expectation that a behaviour will lead to a certain outcome and the preference (or valence) for that outcome. For a worked example see Activity 12.7. From a marketing viewpoint, it is clear that to increase the motivation to buy we must increase the perceived value of our products/service and raise the expectancy of satisfaction that will result from its purchase.

In a previous unit we have discussed probabilities. Working through an example of the use of Vroom's expectancy theory is a good way of exercising this knowledge.

1   List five outcomes that you might expect from going on holiday to the West Indies. To get you started, outcomes 1 and 2 have already been completed:

   1: Feel relaxed
   2: Get a sun tan
   3:
   4:
   5:

2   Now give each of these outcomes a value (this is known as the valence (V)), +1 if you like them; 0 if you feel neutral towards them and –1 if you dislike them.

3   Estimate the probability of attaining each outcome. You will remember that a probability of 1 is equal to absolute certainty while 0 is equal to no chance at all. 0.5, for example, represents a 50% chance of the outcome being achieved. This value is the expectancy (E).

4   Now place your values in the table provided below and calculate $E \times V$, placing this value in the last column. Now add up the values in the $E \times V$ column. The result is called the F score and relates to the motivational value of the holiday.

Outcomes	Expectancy (E)	Valence (V)	$E \times V$
1: Feel relaxed			
2: Get a sun tan			
3:			
4:			
5:			

You might want to experiment with this technique as a way of comparing the F scores from different product brands.

Measuring motivation

The most popular techniques for motivation research are undoubtedly projective techniques such as those discussed in the earlier unit on primary data, such as the word association and thematic apperception tests (TAT). However, depth interviews and group discussions are also used. Unlike other uses of these methods, the focus is to uncover *why* a particular behaviour took place. The group discussion can yield more information than individual in-depth interviews but is not suitable for the discussion of certain topics such as those that might embarrass, are difficult to discuss in company or require very individual consideration.

Try interviewing fellow students about their motivation for undertaking the marketing course. Start by asking the question:

Why did you decide to apply for this particular course at this particular college?

Make notes as they answer. After each answer your aim is to ask another why question about some detail of their previous answer. It is likely that a number of opportunities for further questioning will arise, make sure no opportunity is missed. Note each question, returning to it if necessary.

If you have a tape recorder available, you may wish to use this to record the interview to ease later study.

What needs do you identify?

Question 12.1

In case of La Piere's experiment it may have been that the quality of clothing, politeness, the presence of LaPiere himself, financial considerations, all played a part in creating a discrepancy between attitudes and behaviour.

Activity 12.1: Are the products promoted by the higher scoring celebrities rated more highly?

If so, then this could be explained by congruity theory. Alternatively, it may just be that, by chance, the products promoted by your favourite celebrities are those that appeal to you more. If so, then do you think that the advertisers have done this intentionally?

In this unit you have learned about:

- Attitudes – their characteristics and component parts.
- The relationship between attitudes and behaviour.
- The importance of specificity of attitude measurement.
- Balance and congruity theories of attitudes and attitude change.
- Multi-component models of attitudes – the Fishbein and extended Fishbein models.
- Measuring attitudes.
- The repertory grid technique.
- Motivation – including needs and goals.
- Maslow's hierarchy of needs and its application to marketing.
- McClelland's theory of needs achievement.
- Measuring motivation.

Consumer modelling

This unit describes the principles underlying consumer modelling and discusses the relevance and value of various approaches. In this unit you will:

- Be introduced to consumer decision models.
- Learn about the classification and construction of models.
- Learn how to evaluate models.
- Be informed about simple and comprehensive models.
- Be presented with a number of specific examples of consumer behaviour models and a model of organizational buying.

By the end of this unit you will be able to:

- Understand how models are classified, constructed and evaluated.
- Understand the main differences between different types of models.
- Explore a purchasing decision using one of the models presented.

STUDY GUIDE

The emphasis in this unit is very much on understanding the principles and techniques behind consumer modelling rather than slavishly learning specific models by rote. The only way to gain a thorough understanding of modelling techniques and their application is to try working examples and relate these to your own purchasing experiences.

EXAM HINT

The Understanding Customers examination paper will *never* include questions on consumer modelling, which provide students with the opportunity to earn marks by reproducing complex diagrams. In particular, therefore, painstaking memorization of the 'grand' models of consumer behaviour will be a worthless exercise. Any questions on modelling will require students to know why models are used, how they are designed, and what their benefits are.

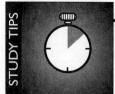

Organize your study materials from the beginning of your course:

- Use file dividers to keep broad topic areas indexed and relevant materials and articles with the relevant notes.
- Look out for relevant articles and current examples, you will find these useful to illustrate examination answers.

This unit will take you about 2 to 3 hours to read through and think about. The activities you have been asked to carry out will take you about 3 to 4 hours.

Consumer decision making

We all make decisions every day of our lives. *'What shall I have for breakfast?' 'What sort of career do I want?' 'What brand of potatoes should I buy?'* We are so used to making decisions that we rarely think about them. In fact, making decisions has become so automatic that we sometimes have difficulty explaining why we made a particular choice!

The aim of consumer decision-making research is to understand why decisions are made. Not surprisingly, this is not always easy. An understanding of the decision-making process requires a knowledge of consumer behaviour. The contents of this unit tie together many of the basic psychological and social processes that have been described in the earlier sections of this book.

Ask a friend or colleague (politely!) why they chose the clothes they are wearing. The response may well be *'I just liked them'* or something quite specific. List the reasons they give for each item of clothing (underwear excepted!).

This should give an idea of the range of possible reasons for a buying decision being made.

What is a model?

certain. dem
lefinition *n.* s
precise meai
distinct, clea
lefinitive *a.* fi
something: i

Model

A physical, visual or mathematical . . . simplified representation of a complex system.

Macmillan Dictionary of Retailing

A model is an abstract representation of a process or relationship. A simple example: if we believe that raising the price for crossing a toll bridge will reduce the number of cars using the bridge we have expressed a model which can be represented in one of three ways:

- Verbally – 'as price increases, cars decrease'.

- Mathematically – $C = K (1/P)$ where C = number of cars, P = toll price, K = constant.

- Pictorially – | Price increase | $\longrightarrow$ | Reduction in cars |

We all hold numerous models in our heads, most of which we give no thought to, but which allow us to make sense of the world and predict the likely course of events. Consider gravity. We all have a notion about gravity – we know that if we let go of something it will fall to the floor. This allows us to predict what is going to happen when we accidentally knock something over, drop kick a football, or throw something.

It is possible to have totally different models of the same phenomenon. Keith Williams (1990) gives the example of an atlas where one might find the same country on different pages modelled on its topography, climate, geology, population and zoology.

Models are of assistance in a number of ways:

1   They assist in the development of theories.
2   They aid the understanding of complex relationships.
3   They provide a framework for discussion and research.

We will now turn our attentions to the modelling of consumer behaviour.

Consumer decision models

In this unit, we are primarily concerned with the use of models to understand consumer behaviour. In most cases, what is being modelled is the behaviour leading up to a purchasing decision.

We are most interested in understanding how and why certain decisions are made. As such, our models will usually include consideration of many of the topics that we have discussed in earlier units:

- Attitudes.
- Perception.
- Learning.
- Motivation.
- Social and cultural influences.

In most cases, consumer models are expressed pictorially and, in this unit, we will discuss the basic principles underlying consumer modelling as well as looking at several specific models.

Classification of models

In 1974, the Market Research Society presented the findings of a study group which had been established to look at modelling. They agreed a classification system for assessing models which identified 11 dimensions:

- *Micro or macro.* In a micro-model each individual or unit in the market or database is represented and processed at the individual level. The output may or may not be a result of the aggregation of individual data. In a macro-model the total market is considered as a whole and the model's output is a global market response.
- *Data-based or theory-based.* Data-based models are the logical outcome of the process of data analysis used. Theory-based models are developed through the application of reason and have their basis in theories adopted from the behavioural sciences.
- *Low, medium, or high level models.* This relates to simplicity or lack of it. At the lowest level simple models can be devised that require few variables but they inevitably have certain limitations because of their narrow coverage. They are better regarded as sub-models or component parts of some larger, more comprehensive model. At the other extreme there are 'grand' models that seek to orchestrate all relevant market variables and represent the full range of marketing stimuli. The medium category lies somewhere between the two.
- *Descriptive (historical or current), diagnostic or predictive.* Here the distinction is made between models that describe market behaviour, those that seek to explain or diagnose why consumers behave as they do, and those that set out to predict how consumers will behave under specified circumstances.

- *Behavioural or statistical.* In behavioural models reference is made to underlying assumptions about how the individual behaves. They seek to relate to the total process of consumer responses to a given stimulus. With the statistical model there are no implicit assumptions about how or why consumers behave as they do. The internal parameters are hypothesized as a function of the analytical procedures employed.
- *Generalized or ad hoc.* Here a distinction is made between models that are intended to be, or can be, applied to a wide range of markets and those that are developed in the context of, and for use in, one market only.
- *Functional or intellectual.* The functional model represents the actual function of the object; it is meant to have real world application. The intellectual model need not be rooted in practicability.
- *Static or dynamic.* The static model represents a particular system at a given point in time and cannot take account of time effects. The dynamic model is able to represent systems over time. It can take account of changing values of parameters and even changes in basic relationships between parameters over time.
- *Qualitative or quantitative.* In the case of qualitative models no explicit variables are measured. In the case of quantitative models they are. A quantitative model is therefore more likely to be helpful in predicting behaviour as it should provide an indication of the weighting of importance that should be given to individual variables.
- *Algebraic, sequential/net, or topological.* In algebraic models summation or other manipulation is independent of the order of the variables. With sequential or net models the order of the variables is explicitly taken into account by the model. Topological models are based upon field theory concepts involving space and geometry, forces and motion. They are *Gestalt* models, that is they are concerned with the total situation.
- *Successful or unsuccessful.* These concepts are indefinable. What constitutes success or lack of it will differ among different people. Nonetheless it was felt to be a useful criterion.

We would all like a simple model which accurately predicts all consumer behaviour under a variety of circumstances. Unfortunately, the perfect model does not exist and the best we can hope for is to be able to understand the behaviour that most people will conform to under a restricted set of circumstances. Nonetheless, this is better than 'whistling in the wind' and, gaining a better understanding of behaviour, does have other benefits as we have seen in earlier units.

Construction of models

Before looking at models in detail, we must identify the variable types which form the 'building blocks' of these consumer models. You may remember some of them from an earlier discussion in the unit on statistics:

stimulus	*or*	*response*
These act as inputs to the consumer's behaviour. Examples include: advertising, environmental factors, reference group influence and physiological factors.		These are the observable responses of individuals which may be directly due to certain stimuli or arise as a result of internal processes.

internal	*or*	*external*
These are variables which arise as a result of either internal physiological or psychological processes. Examples include: attitudes, learning, motivation, hunger and sex.		These are variables which arise as a result of external influences. Examples include: economic factors, situational factors, weather.

endogenous	*or*	*exogenous*
These are variables which have a clearly defined effect. These are included in the model.		These are variables which have a poorly defined effect. For example, a change in future circumstances, price changes by competitors and so on. These are usually not included in a model.

To these categories we must add intervening variables which act between stimulus and response. They modify the relationship between the stimuli received and the responses made but, by definition, cannot be observed or measured. They are thus exogenous variables which can be both external or internal in origin.

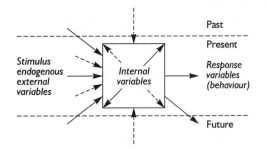

Figure 13.1 Showing effect on consumer of variable types. Dotted lines represent the possible influence of exogenous variables

Figure 13.1 illustrates the action of the various variables, the box representing the consumer. In particular, it should be noted how response variables can impact future behaviour and that past and future considerations can be considered as stimuli. The possible action of exogenous variables is represented by the dotted arrows.

Evaluating models

Before considering specific models in detail, it is worthwhile to consider the criteria to be used in their evaluation. The following were proposed by Williams (1990) as being indicative of a 'good' model:

1 *Simplicity* – whether the model is of high or low level, it should seek to break down complex behaviour patterns into simple easily understandable components.
2 *Factual basis* – a model should be consistent with the facts as far as they are known.
3 *Logic* – to be plausible a model must make sense and be internally consistent.
4 *Originality* – if a model is to advance knowledge it should be original, either in its basic construction or in the way in which it links together previously separate areas of knowledge.
5 *Explanatory power* – a model should seek to explain how, and why, specified behaviour takes place.
6 *Prediction* – a model should aid the prediction of a consumer's reaction to a given stimulus.
7 *Heuristic power* – this refers to a model's capacity to suggest new areas of research.
8 *Validity* – if a model is to have validity is must be verifiable. This means that it should be possible, at least in theory, to test the relationships proposed between variables.

It would be unrealistic to expect every model to satisfy all these criteria. However, they do provide a useful framework for assessing the importance and significance to be attached to a particular model. If, for example, a model lacked any factual basis, failed to explain observed behaviour and did little to enlighten our thinking, then we would be justified in dismissing it.

Of course, no set of criteria can be comprehensive or pertain to every situation. As with all such problems, a common-sense assessment, against the background of a general understanding of the components of consumer behaviour, will go a long way.

Simple models

Simple models of consumer behaviour take a 'broad brush' approach to understanding consumers. In contrast to the comprehensive models to be discussed later in this unit, they consider only the main influences on behaviour. Simple models fall into four general categories:

- *Black box* – this is the generic name for models which do not consider internal processes but rely solely on directly observable stimulus variables and responses.
- *Decision process* – these types of models enjoy widespread use within marketing. They illustrate the various decision stages a consumer progresses through to arrive at a particular course of action. An example is the AIDA (Attention→Interest→Desire→Action) promotional model.
- *Personal variable* – these, in contrast to black box models, focus on internal variables. They attempt to model particular internal processes. One example is Fishbein's attitude model.
- *Hybrid decision/personal* – these attempt to combine the features of decision process and personal variable models. In this unit, we will consider Chris Rice's PV/PPS model.

Black box models

Perhaps the simplest black box model of behaviour is the stimulus-response (SR) model which is typically illustrated by the experiments of Pavlov. Pavlov found that when a dog was presented with meat it salivated. In this case the stimulus was the meat, the response the salivation. Simple SR relationships also exist in people. For example, a short tap just below the knee (stimulus) will cause the leg to move in a reflex action (response). The basic SR model can be represented as in Figure 13.2.

Figure 13.2   The simplest black box model

More complex black box models typically consider more variables and more entities (whether they be single consumers or organizations).

Figure 13.3 is an example of a 'consumer-centric' black box model of a consumer's decision environment. It shows the stimuli which can influence purchasing behaviour. Note that some of the influencing variables can themselves be influenced by the consumer resulting in a two-way interaction.

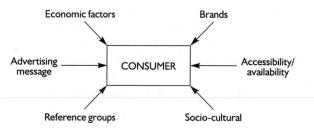

Figure 13.3   Consumer-centric black box model of consumer decision environment

Figure 13.4 shows Kotler's model of the buying process showing inputs and outputs. It presents a more considered view of buying behaviour. It takes into account more influences and details more of the responses.

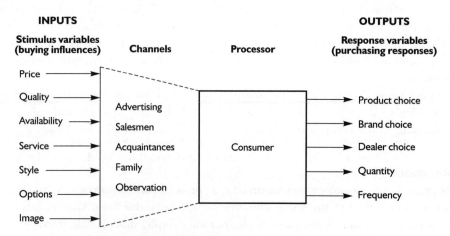

Figure 13.4   Kotler's model of the buying process. A complex black box model

As black box models concentrate solely on the action of external variables, they are only useful in the investigation of behaviour where internal variables are not deemed significant. When considering black box models researchers are primarily interested in the relative importance of the stimuli involved.

For example, cigarette advertising is banned on British television so, unless a particular consumer is known to be regularly exposed to other sources of advertising (magazines, cinema, etc.), then reference groups and cultural influences, and brand experience are more likely to play a part in the brand of cigarettes chosen. Similarly, someone who lives in a big city is less likely to be influenced by accessibility/availability restrictions than a consumer living in a remote village.

Decision process models

Unlike black box models, decision process models represent a process flow. They are derived from the general decision-making/problems solving models of researchers such as Newell and Simon. Figure 13.5 illustrates such a generic model. This was also discussed in Unit 1.

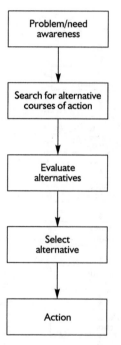

Figure 13.5 Generic decision process model

Decision process models occur in many areas of marketing (both with reference to behaviour and other fields) and form the core of most of the comprehensive models discussed later in the unit.

Process flow models usually follow certain conventions:

1 Flow is usually top down or, less frequently, left to right.
2 Actions, or identifiable states, are represented in boxes.
3 Decisions points are broken down into binary (Yes/No) decisions and represented with a diamond. The decision question appears in the diamond.
4 Direction of flow is indicated by an arrow, optional flows by dotted or dashed lines (usually accompanied by an explanatory legend).
5 Outside processes – which link with the process being represented – are usually indicated by a circle.
6 Termination states – which end the process – are usually indicated by an oval or lozenge shape.

To explore the concept of decision process models further we will consider a real example from the work of Lunn, Blamires and Seaman which illustrates in some detail the decision process involved in buying an electric razor (dry shaver). Figure 13.6 represents the overall structure of the decision process only. The original text provides supplementary models for various stages but these will not be considered in this text.

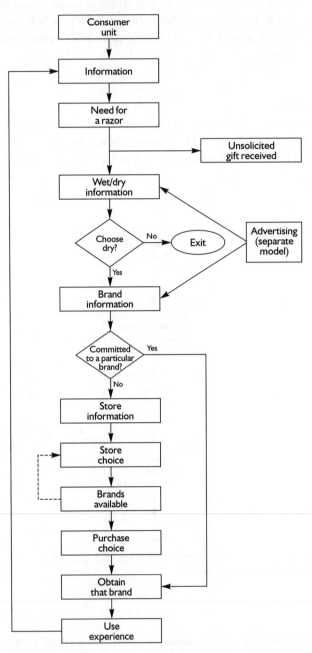

Figure 13.6 Overall structure of electric razor purchasing decision. Adapted from Lunn, Blamires, and Seaman (1988), *Consumer Market Research Handbook*, 3rd edn, McGraw-Hill

The benefit of this form of modelling is that it allows marketers effectively to structure their approach to marketing around consumer behaviour. They also allow the marketing process to be investigated with a series of 'what if' type analyses. Typical questions include:

- What product changes would increase the likelihood of our product being selected?
- What product attributes should be stressed in the advertising of the product?
- What is the likely effect of the introduction of more competition or changes in the competitive market?
- Is there a case for improving any of our marketing strategy?

Such models can be predictive but this requires the additional collection of other psychological measures such as attitudes, motivations and so on.

Personal variable models

As noted, these focus on modelling specific internal processes such as attitudes, perception and motivation.

The rise in the 1980s of information processing theory has been influential in the development of personal variable models. Information processing theory is mostly concerned with the mind and the way it is organized. It has provided another perspective on the way in which decisions are modelled and particular in the area of rule development – the rules used in arriving at a decision where alternatives are being considered. There are four basic personal variable models, classified according to the decisions rule types used within the model:

- *Compensatory, or trade-off rule* – this assumes that consumers trade off products against each other considering all the features of the products against some hypothetical ideal. The rule implies that sacrifices are made as part of the decision process but that each alternative is considered thoroughly. For example, you may be willing to compromise on the appearance of a new stereo system if the sound quality is good.
- *Threshold rule* – this assumes that products can be totally rejected on the basis of just one undesirable characteristic, without further consideration. For example, you may reject the purchase of a new set of kitchen pans out-of-hand if their colour clashes with the rest of your kitchen despite the fact that the other characteristics of the pan may have been ideal.
- *Disjunctive rule* – this assumes that a product can be chosen simply because it excels on one characteristic. Returning to the pans example, it may be that a sub-standard set of pans is chosen simply because they are the 'right' colour.
- *Lexicographical rule* – this assumes that a product can be selected on the basis of considering just a few characteristics in a predetermined order. Taking house buying as an example, you may have a set of criteria such as number of bedrooms, access to shops, size of garden and so on, which you have prioritized to determine your choice of residence. If these are satisfactory, then you may not bother considering any further characteristics (for instance you may not mind if it does or does not have a garage, how many bathrooms or if it is a maisonette or house).

Hybrid model – Rice's PV/PPS model

In an attempt to overcome the weaknesses of the personal variable and decision process models, Chris Rice synthesized the two approaches to develop, what he calls the perceived value/perceived probability of satisfaction (PV/PPS) model.

The central notion in this model is that the subjective utility (*SU*) of a particular decision alternative can be calculated from:

1 the value attached to the outcomes (perceived value or *PV*)
2 the perception of the probability of each outcome occurring (perceived probability of satisfaction (or *PPS*).

The formula for calculating *SU* is:

$$SU = PV \times PPS$$

The model therefore predicts that the highest utility option will be that where the outcomes are valued highly and are most likely to be satisfied.

This can be illustrated graphically as in Figure 13.7, neatly dividing purchases into four categories.

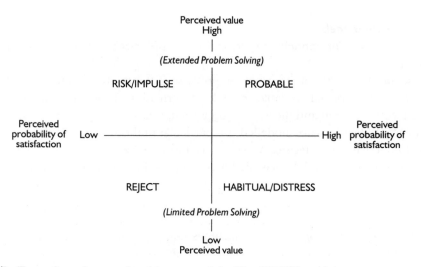

Figure 13.7 Type of purchase analysed in terms of the Rice PV/PPS model

The following explanation is adapted from Chris Rice (*Consumer Behaviour*):

The lower right-hand quadrant is concerned with purchases which are of low perceived value in themselves, but which have a high probability of satisfaction. Here an example might be the situation of running low on petrol when travelling down a motorway. Government quality standards ensure that there is little to choose between brands so the car is filled with whichever brand is sold in the next service station. Many petrol companies attempt to increase the perceived value of their brand by offering air miles, tokens or similar. This example could be classed as a *distress purchase*, but a similar process would be predicted in *habitual buying* at supermarkets. Low involvement purchases are often made on the basis that there is little or nothing to choose between brands.

The top left-hand quadrant is interesting (high value, low probability) as it may go some way towards explaining otherwise apparently irrational behaviour. An example might be gambling on the UK lottery despite the chances of winning a fortune being extremely small. Here the hypothesis would be that, for many people, the very high value of winning a very large sum of money (with its attendant outcomes of travel, giving up work and being able to afford luxuries), more than compensates for the very low probability of that outcome occurring. This can be classed as a *risk or impulse purchase*. The top right-hand quadrant is the marketer's dream – high values and high probability of satisfaction – the combination that is most likely to result in *probable purchase*.

Thus in practical terms this model clearly identifies two key objectives of marketing effort and communication:

1   to raise the perceived value of the outcomes of purchase.
2   to raise the perceived probability of satisfaction following purchase.

An example will illustrate the model.

Suppose, we are trying to decide which type of food to purchase on our way home from work. We have two alternatives: either pre-cooked or fresh. However, we are unsure what our partner has planned for this evening. We may be 'watching a video' (in which case we might want something quick and convenient to cook) or we may be having 'a romantic meal' in which case a well-cooked, tasty meal is called for. Obviously, a real situation may consider many more characteristics and/or alternatives

To assess perceived value we could rate the value of each characteristic on a scale of 1 to 10. We might arrive at the results similar to those in Figure 13.8. It is important to remember that these are only perceived values and may bear no resemblance to an objective assessment.

Food	'Romantic meal at home'	'Getting a video'
Pre-cooked	3	8
Fresh	9	5

Figure 13.8 Rice PV/PPS model – perceived value table

We must then assess the probability of each of the conditions occurring. We may perceive that 'getting a video' is more likely and give this a probability of 0.8 (an 80% likelihood of happening). This leaves us with a probability of 0.2 (or 20%) for the 'romantic meal at home' (you may remember from the statistics unit that the complete set of probabilities must add up to 1.0).

To calculate the subjective utility scores (SU) we must now multiply each cell in the value table by its perceived probability. Therefore, all the entries in the 'romantic meal' column are multiplied by 0.2; and all the entries in the 'getting a video' column are multiplied by 0.8. The resulting table will look like this:

Food	'Romantic meal at home'	'Getting a video'
Pre-cooked	0.6	6.4
Fresh	1.8	4

Figure 13.9 Rice PV/PPS model – subjective utility scores

According to PV/PPS theory we will act on the outcome that will result in the highest SU score. In this example, we are certain to buy pre-cooked food.

In this context, the pre-cooked meal is seen as relatively the most probable purchase – it would thus occupy the top right-hand quadrant in Figure 13.7 in that it has both perceived high value and perceived high probability of satisfaction.

Comparison of simple models

	Black box	Decision process	Personal variable	Hybrid decision/ personal
Considers internal variables	No	Yes	Yes	Yes
Considers external variables	Yes	Yes	No	Yes
Good for explanation	No	No	Yes	Yes
Good for prediction	Yes	Possibly	Yes	Yes
Good for structuring marketing strategies	No	Yes	No	No
Simple to understand	Yes	Yes	No	No

Comprehensive, or grand, models of consumer behaviour

In this last part of the unit we will discuss some of the so-called grand models of consumer behaviour which attempt to explain comprehensively all those aspects of the buying situation which their creators deem to be significant. In particular, we will look at:

- Nicosia model.
- Howard–Sheth model.
- Engel, Blackwell and Miniard model (which you may see referred to as the Engel, Kollat and Blackwell model – an earlier derivative).

The purpose of this text is not to explain these models in detail – such an explanation would take a whole book in itself – but merely to introduce you to the basic concepts underlying each. For a full description of each model, you are referred to the further reading list at the end of this unit.

Nicosia model

This model focuses on the relationship between consumer and supplier. It is represented in Figure 13.10. The middle shows how the supplier influences the consumer through its promotional and advertising activities which are, in turn, influenced by customer feedback and involvement. The model is divided into four fields:

- *Field 1* This deals with the communication flow between supplier and consumer. This stage is open to social, cultural and individual influence. Much of what has been written about these topics is relevant to this field. As a result of these influences, the consumer forms a positive or negative attitude. A favourable attitude will lead on to Field 2.
- *Field 2* This deals with the search and evaluation of alternatives. A decision to proceed with a particular alternative will provide the motivation to proceed to Field 3.
- *Field 3* This field represents the actual act of purchase.
- *Field 4* This considers the post-purchase feedback to both the supplier and consumer. The former occurs via sales data, the latter through the influence of experience.

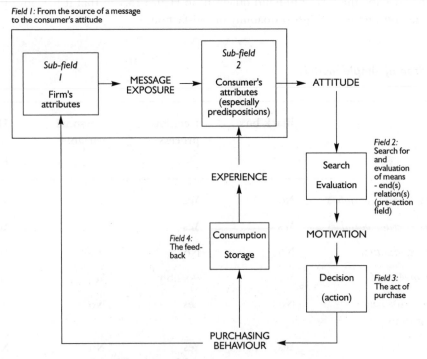

Figure 13.10 Summary of the Nicosia model

The model is useful in that it considers customer feedback and considers consumer behaviour very much as a process, rather than an outcome of a process, which makes it therefore more amenable to investigation.

Critics of the model express doubts over its predictive abilities and claim it to be more descriptive in nature. Some empirical testing has been done which supports the model.

Howard–Sheth

This has already been referred to in Unit 1.

This model is essentially similar to the simple SR model described earlier in this unit except, of course, unlike a black box approach, an attempt has been made partially to explain the action of internal variables. A highly simplified outline of the Howard–Sheth model is shown in Figure 13.11.

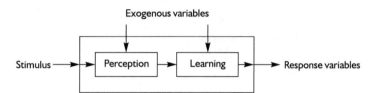

Figure 13.11   Highly simplified top level structure of Howard–Sheth model

The model identifies three types of stimulus variables:

- *Significative* – physical characteristics of the potential purchase.
- *Symbolic* – those attributes of the product communicated to the consumer by the marketer.
- *Social* – arising from the consumer's social environment (reference groups, family, social class etc.).

The distinction between significative and symbolic warrants further explanation. Take, for example, the weight of a chocolate bar. A measurement of the chocolate bar using scales would provide significative information on its weight. However, the marketer may choose to give the consumer a different symbolic message by showing the chocolate bar in an advert being held by someone with small hands (making it appear bigger) or designing the packaging/shape in such a way as to make the bar seem more substantial. Thus the same information (weight) make have both a significative and symbolic interpretation.

The central perception and learning component of the model are referred to as constructs. These are considered as abstract processes which are not directly amenable to measurement or defined in detail within the model. The proposed linkage between the perceptual and learning constructs gives this model its distinctive character.

The responses variables are the observable behaviours resulting from the internal constructs. An attitude, for instance, has both internal components (cognitive and affective) and an external behavioural component. Those parts of perceptual and learning constructs that are thought to have observable behaviours are thus represented in the response variables (known in this model as the outputs). The outputs are themselves linked in sequence, ultimately leading to the actual purchase. The broken lines in the model represent possible feedback links.

The full model is presented in Figure 13.12.

Consider the purchase of a computer (you should read this example with reference to Figure 13.12). The consumer sees a computer advertised in a magazine (the stimulus) but does not know enough about computers to contemplate a purchase (stimulus ambiguity). To remedy this lack of information they instigate an 'overt search' which may require reading more specialist magazines or asking an 'expert' friend. They attend to the additional information received (attention) although this information may well, subsequently, be biased (perceptual bias). This bias can be due to a number of factors (the work of exogenous variables) such as forgetting or misinterpreting some information. The process then moves to the learning constructs.

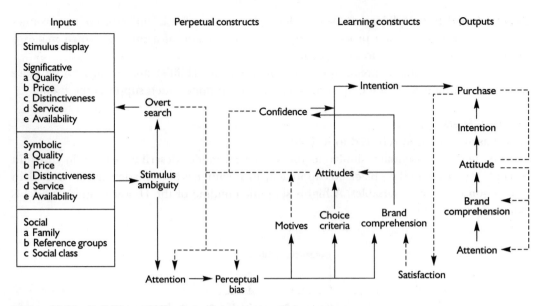

Figure 13.12 Full Howard–Sheth model

The perceptual constructs influence motivation, choice criteria and brand comprehension. This results in the formation of an attitude. Choice criteria will be affected by the consumer's motives and lead to an evaluation of how the alternative brands match up to the criteria. The choice criteria for a computer may include colour screen, floor-standing processor and so on. Some brands may be available with these options, others not (brand comprehension). On the basis of an understanding of choice criteria and the brands, an attitude towards each specific brand is formed.

The consumer then evaluates the certainty with which a particular product will meet perceived needs (confidence). For example, will the IBM computer meet my requirement for speed. This, in combination with the attitude, leads to an intention to purchase (intention) which results in the actual observable purchase (an output variable).

A particular feature of the Howard–Sheth model is that it assumes that there are three types of buying situations. Those that require:

- *Extended problem-solving (EPS)* – where the consumer has little, or no, prior brand knowledge and where the perceived risk associated with the purchase is high. This may be the case with high value, one-off purchases such as a first home. In such cases, the consumer is likely to spend some time collecting and assimilating information about alternatives.
- *Limited problem-solving (LPS)* – where there is some prior brand knowledge but no brand preference has yet emerged. Information gathering is therefore limited to those brands which are actively being considered for purchase.
- *Routinized response behaviour* – where sufficient information has been collected in the past for the consumer to be certain of the brand they wish to purchase (the evoked set). Other brands are unlikely to be considered unless some unforeseen events occurs (such as the demise of a favoured brand).

These all affect the way the criteria for choice are determined.

Overall, the Howard-Sheth model gives great emphasis to internal variables although their relationship to one another is poorly defined. It is most useful in the evaluation of different brands of product, rather than different alternatives, and this can be considered both a strength and weakness.

It accepts that consumers do not always consider all alternatives in detail but rather work from a limited sub-set of evoked brands. However, fundamentally, it assumes a rational consumer.

Since the model was first proposed in 1969 it has undergone a number of refinements as a result of empirical evaluation. This has, undoubtedly, increased its utility.

Engel, Blackwell and Miniard (EBM)

This is a development of the original Engel, Kollat and Blackwell model first introduced in 1968. Not surprisingly, it shares much with the Howard–Sheth model. Both have a similar scope and are of, approximately, the same level of complexity. There are, however, some distinctive differences. Primarily, the core of the EBM model is a decision process, much like the decision process model mentioned earlier, which is considerably augmented with inputs from information processing, and considers other influencing factors.

The complete model consists of four sections (see Figure 13.13):

- Decision process.
- Information processing.
- Input.
- Variables influencing decision process.

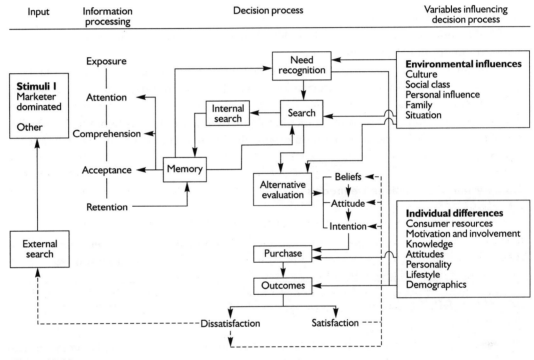

Figure 13.13

Decision process

This consists of five basic stages:

- *Need recognition* – this is an acknowledgement that a problem does exist. That is, an awareness by an individual that they have a need to be satisfied. For example, the theft of a friend's bicycle may cause us to recognize the need for a better bike lock for our bike.
- *Search* – where enough information is available in memory to make a decision then an internal search is all that is required. Where such information is scarce, an external search for information is undertaken.
- *Alternative evaluation* – here an evaluation of the alternatives found during the search is undertaken. As can be seen from the model, this takes into account our attitudes and beliefs. Some of the rule types described under personal variable models are likely to be involved in the reduction of alternatives.
- *Purchase* – a purchase is made based on the chosen alternative.
- *Outcomes* – these can be either positive or negative depending on whether the purchase satisfies the original perceived need. Dissatisfaction may result in post-purchase dissonance.

225

Information processing

Before information can be used in the rest of the model, the consumer must first be exposed to it, attend to it, understand the information, accept it and, finally, retain it in memory. Any selective attention or exposure mechanisms (such as those that occur in post-purchase dissonance) would operate at this stage.

Information input

Information from marketing and non-marketing sources feeds into the information processing section of the model. The model prompts for additional information to be collected as part of an external information search which results where not enough information is available from memory or post-purchase dissonance occurs.

Variables influencing decision process

This section considers the individual, social and situational factors which influence the decision processes.

Assessment of EBM model

The EBM model is undoubtedly the most flexible described. It is also more coherent than the Howard–Sheth model in its presentation of consumer behaviour.

It includes human processes not considered in the other models, most notably, it specifically introduces memory, information processing and consideration of both positive and negative purchase outcomes.

Critics of the model focus on the somewhat vague definition of the role of the influencing variables. Others feel that the separation of information search and alternative evaluation is somewhat artificial.

Comparison of comprehensive models

	Nicosia	Howard–Sheth	Engel, Blackwell and Miniard
Verified by empirical investigation	Some	Some	Some
Descriptive, Explanatory, Predictive	Descriptive but can be used to predict	Explanatory but can be used to predict	Explanatory but can be used to predict
Concerned with relationship between consumer and supplier	Yes	Not specifically	Not specifically
Suitable for brand comparison	Yes	Yes	Yes
Suitable for comparison of unrelated alternatives	Yes	Not as good	Yes
Assumes rational consumer	No	Yes	Yes
Includes concept of different levels of problem-solving based on evoked sets	No	Yes	Not explicitly – claim that same process is involved
Considers post-purchase dissonance	Not explicitly	Not explicitly	Yes

Other consumer models

Other popular consumer behaviour models are:

- *Bettman's information processing model* – As the name suggests this presents an information processing model of consumer choice. Its key feature is that it assumes that minimum effort is expended in the decision process employing simple decision rules wherever possible.
- *Sheth–Newman–Gross model* – This attempts to explain 'why' consumers make the choices they do. It compares the influences of five 'consumption' values and the degree to which the purchase of the product is perceived to address these values. The model is simple and has proven itself to be most useful in real-world applications.
- *Sheth family decision making* – Whereas most models concentrate on individual decision-making, this model addresses how decisions are made by a family unit.

Taking any one of the grand models, work through the decision-making process for an item you have recently purchased. If nothing comes to mind, choose one of the items from the list below:

- Books for your marketing course.
- A loaf of bread.
- Birthday card for a friend.
- A new stereo system.

Try to identify the variables involved and how they impact on your final decision. You should draw out the model adding your own notes as appropriate.

Did following the model provide you with any insights into how the consumer environment could be improved?

Industrial buyer behaviour models

The American Marketing Association model

This model, published by the American marketing association (AMA), describes the main influences and players in the process. It is usually displayed as below.

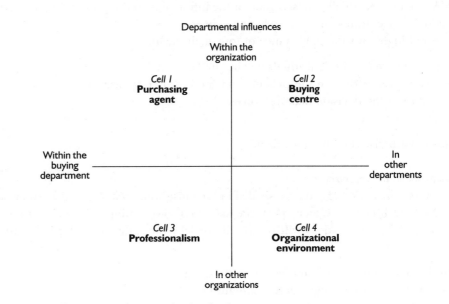

Figure 13.14 Influences on the organization buying process

Cell 1 – The purchasing agent
This model identifies the following factors which influence the buying behaviour:

- *Social factors* – relationships, friendships and antipathies that exist between the buyer and suppliers and the extent to which they affect the buying decision.
- *Price and cost factors* – level of competition amongst other suppliers, the cash flow situation, how much money the organization is willing to pay for a better quality product, any cost/benefit analysis that might have been conducted, the professional background of the buyer (for example accountancy may make a buyer more cost conscious than a buyer from another professional background).
- *Supply and continuity* – some organizations may mulitsource their supplies in case a shortage will affect the production capacity of the buying organization.
- *Risk avoidance* – the purchaser will want to know whether the supplier is financially stable, whether they can produce what is promised in the time available at the quoted price.

Cell 2 – The buying centre
This is the DMU that has previously been discussed. The key factors here are:

- *Organizational structure and policy* – this will determine how purchases are made within the organization, how they are co-ordinated and communicated.
- *Power, status and conflict procedures* – this will determine who makes the purchasing decisions.
- *Gatekeeping* – who allows information into the organization and disseminates it.

Cell 3 – Professionalism
This is within the buying department but also looks at professional standards and practice in other organizations.

- Specialist journals, conferences and trade shows.
- Word of mouth communication between purchasing specialists.
- Supply–purchase reciprocity as part of co-operative trading relationships.

Cell 4 – The organizational environment
This deals with factors outside the organization.

- PEST factors (political/legal, economic, social, technological), commercial and competitive factors.
- Nature of the supplier.
- Co-operative buying.

The Sheth model of industrial buying

The AMA model is essentially a description of the influences on the purchasing decision, the Sheth model concentrates on the purchasing process.

This model highlights the importance of four main factors:

1 The expectations of the individuals making up the DMU.
2 The characteristics of both the product and the buying organization.
3 The nature of the decision making process.
4 The situation variables.

These factors are discussed in more detail:

Expectations within the organization

These elements are coded (1) and are shaded in the illustration. Sheth says that every person in the DMU will bring to their performance their own unique set of attitudes and orientations. Their expectations will be conditioned by the individual's background (1a). These are:

- education – general and commercial/professional
- role orientation – e.g. engineer, accountant etc
- life style – more general values

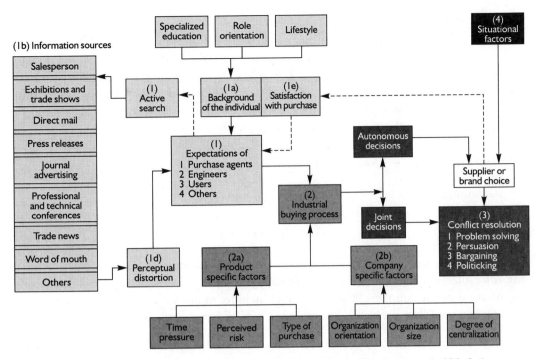

Figure 13.15 Model of industrial behaviour. Adapted from Sheth, J.N., in *Journal of Marketing* (1973), **37**(4), pp. 50–56

Their expectations will also be influenced by:

- The sources of information (salesperson, exhibition and trade shows, direct mail, press releases, journal advertising, professional and technical conferences, trade news, word of mouth – these are listed in the diagram under 1b) and the process they have gone through to get the information.
- Perceptual distortion (1d), which is always possible in any form of communication.
- The person's previous experience (1e), which will mediate the incoming information.
- The active search (1c) may be carried out by the someone in the DMU listed in the diagram as purchasing agents, engineers, users, others.

Characteristics of the product and the buying organization

These elements are coded (2) and are shaded in the illustration. In this section Sheth considers the actual buying process and contends that it is affected by:

1   Product specific factors (2a) such as:
- *Time pressure* – group decisions take longer than individual ones.
- *Perceived risk* – when a decision is risky more members of the DMU will be involved.
- *Type of purchase* – extensive problem solving will involve more members of the DMU than simple repeat purchases which are more likely to be given to an individual to carry out.

2   Company specific factors (2b) such as:
- *Organizational orientation* – the internal power balance and influence in the DMU will depend on how the organization sees itself. For example: is it heavily sales and marketing oriented? is it production oriented? or does technology dominate it?
- *Organization size* – the smaller the organization the more likely it will be that a single buyer will possess all the relevant information, the larger the organization the greater the likelihood there will be of group decision making.
- *Degree of centralization* – decentralized organizations involve a lot more people in the decision making than centralized organizations with a centralized buying function.

Nature of the decision-making process

These elements are coded (3) and are shaded in the illustration. Sheth discriminates between autonomous decisions and those taken jointly by the DMU. When a decision is taken autonomously it gets little attention and is relatively straightforward. When a group is concerned, because of the different goals and orientations of the people within the group, conflict is likely to arise. The model devotes a section (3) to how the conflict should be resolved:

- problem solving
- persuasion
- bargaining
- politicking

Situational variables

These elements are coded (4) and are shaded in the illustration. Here Sheth included unforeseen factors that are outside the control of the DMU and could affect the purchasing organization or the suppliers. Examples could include: industrial relations problems, major breakdowns, cash-flow problems, bankruptcy, changes in tax provisions.

SUMMARY

In this unit you have learned:

- The nature of consumer decision making.
- What constitutes a consumer decision model.
- How to classify and construct models.
- How to evaluate a model.
- About black box, decision process, personal variable and the PV/PPS hybrid model.
- About several grand models – Nicosia, Howard–Sheth and Engel Blackwell and Miniard in particular.
- The influences that affect organizational buying and buying behaviour – involving the study of two organizational buying models: AMA and Sheth.

Further reading

Nicosia model

Nicosia, F. M., *Consumer Decision Processes*, Englewood Cliffs, NJ, Prentice Hall, 1966.

Arsham, H, and Dianich, D. F., Consumer buying behaviour and optimal advertising strategy, *Computer and Operations Research*, **15**, 1988.

Howard–Sheth Model

Howard, J. A. and Sheth, *The Theory Of Buyer Behaviour*, New York, Wiley, 1969.

Engel, Blackwell and Miniard Model

Engel, J. F., Blackwell, R. D., and Miniard, P. W., *Consumer Behaviour*, 5th edn, Hinsdale, IL Dryden Press, 1968.

Engel, J. F., Kollat, D. T. and Blackwell, R. D. *Consumer Behaviour*, New York, Holt Rhinehart and Winston, 1968.

O'Brien, J. An empirical evaluation of the EKB model relative to the decision-making process, in Hawes, J. M. and Gilsan, G. B., eds, *Developments in Marketing Science*, Akron, OH: Academy of Marketing Science, 1987.

Innovation and communication

This unit describes two main topics: innovator groups and influences on customer behaviour. In this unit you will:

- Be introduced to the concept of innovation diffusion.
- Gain an understanding of how information about innovations is communicated.
- Examine in detail the communication process and how it can be made more persuasive.

By the end of this unit you will be able to:

- Identify and classify innovations and those consumers that adopt them.
- Understand what makes an innovative product, idea or service successful.
- Assess and increase the persuasive content of a communication.

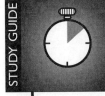

In Unit 11 we looked at some of the factors which influence consumer behaviour. We concluded by looking at the influence of opinion leaders and the processes involved in communicating information between referents and other group members.

In this unit these ideas are developed further as we look at how new ideas are communicated between persons, the role opinion leaders play in this process, and how communication – in general – can be made more persuasive.

Organize your study materials from the beginning of your course:

- Use file dividers to keep broad topic areas indexed and relevant materials and articles with the relevant notes.
- Look out for relevant articles and current examples, you will find these useful to illustrate examination answers.

This unit will take you about 2 to 3 hours to read through and think about. The activities you have been asked to carry out will take you about 1 to 2 hours.

Innovation

> An innovation is any new idea, product or service which is perceived, by the receiver of communication concerning its existence, to be new.

The definition of *innovation* has several important implications:

1 An innovation can be anything from a novel type of paper clip to a new postal delivery service.
2 The innovation is in the eye of the receiver:

- the 'innovation' does not have to be novel to the sender of the communication;
- the 'innovation' does not have to be new, it may have existed for some time before the receiver became aware of its existence.

It is often said that innovation is the key to success and, while this was certainly the case a decade or so ago, environmental concerns and legislation are sensibly creating a move towards products which last longer and are replaced less frequently.

Thus, although the pace of product innovation may be slowing, it is nonetheless still an important part of marketing, and will remain so, especially when applied to ideas and services.

Diffusion of innovations

The process of diffusion is concerned with how innovations spread within a market. There are four main parts to the diffusion process:

1 the innovation
2 the time taken for the innovation to be adopted
3 the channels of communication through which information about the innovation spreads
4 the social systems involved.

Most writers refer to the receiver of the innovation as the 'adopter'.

A simple 'one-step' communication is illustrated in Figure 14.1.

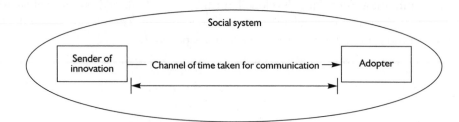

Figure 14.1   An illustration of a simple diffusion process

Adoption stages

The consumer does not adopt an innovation immediately. They may, indeed, not adopt the innovation at all. Rogers, in his book *Diffusion of Innovations*, identified the following stages in the adoption process:

- *Awareness* – the consumer is aware of the innovation but little is known about it.
- *Interest* – the consumers becomes aware that the innovation may satisfy a need.

- *Evaluation* – the consumer forms an attitude about the innovation which may be positive or negative. On the basis of this, they decide whether they are going to try it or reject it.
- *Trial* – if a trial is possible, and wanted, then the product is tried by the consumer.
- *Adoption* – the innovation is accepted or rejected. If accepted, the consumer becomes committed to the innovation (if it is a product, then this usually means purchase).

Types of innovation

There are generally acknowledged to be three types of product innovation:

- *Continuous* – the product is being continuously upgraded in small increments. 'New' products in this case are actually only slight modification on existing products. The use of the product changes little, the consumer does not have to adapt, or modify in any substantial way, their use of the product. Examples include 'new improved' washing powders, new versions of established software.
- *Dynamically continuous* – the product innovation is more disruptive on consumer usage patterns but still does not substantially alter them. Examples include disposable nappies, cordless phones.
- *Discontinuous* – the product requires the consumer to adopt new behaviour patterns entirely. Examples include the introduction of video recorders and computers.

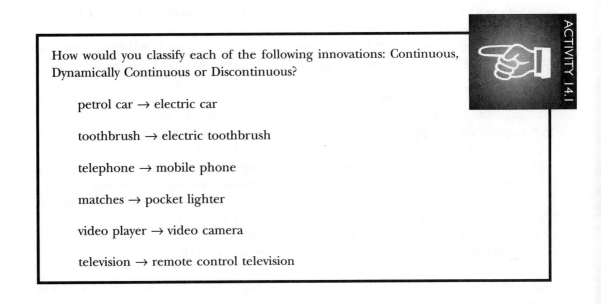

ACTIVITY 14.1

How would you classify each of the following innovations: Continuous, Dynamically Continuous or Discontinuous?

petrol car → electric car

toothbrush → electric toothbrush

telephone → mobile phone

matches → pocket lighter

video player → video camera

television → remote control television

What makes an innovation successful?

According to Rogers and Shoemaker, the following characteristics of the innovation influence the speed and extent of adoption:

- *Relative advantage* – the degree to which the innovation is seen as being superior to any comparable predecessor. Of course, some discontinuous innovations (such as the video camera) may have no single, or obvious, comparator.
- *Compatibility* – the degree to which the innovation is compatible with existing culture. Products which are not compatible with existing practices (the use of chop sticks in the UK for example) are likely to take longer.
- *Complexity* – the more complex the innovation, the longer it will take to adopt. A simple to understand innovation (such as the pump-actin toothpaste tube) will be more rapidly adopted.
- *Trialability* – if it is possible to sample an innovation it is more likely to be adopted rapidly. Free samples of a whole range of products and services are provided on this basis.
- *Observability* – products which are highly visible in the society in which the diffusion is taking place will be adopted more rapidly.

Thus a continuous innovation which is compatible with the culture, can be trialled, yet is simple and observable, is most likely to get broadly adopted most rapidly. The following table (Figure 14.2) rates several innovations on these criteria. It is important to realize that these are perceived values. One person might, for example, find the complexity of a particular pocket calculator 'high' whilst another might find it 'low'.

Innovation	Relative advantage	Compatibility	Complexity	Trialability	Observability
Compact discs	High	Low	Low	High	Medium
Sinclair C5	Low	Low	High	Low	High
Pocket calculator	High	High	Medium	High	Medium
Post-it notes	High	High	Low	High	Medium
Ford Sierra	Low	High	Medium	Medium	High

Figure 14.2 Rating of innovations on basis of Rogers and Shoemaker criteria

Multiplicative innovation adoption (MIA) model

The authors propose the following theoretical model of innovation adoption which is based on the Roger and Shoemaker criteria. It assumes that each of the criterion makes an equal contribution to the success, or otherwise, of the innovation. It also assumes that they combine in such a way that the presence of positive ratings on more than one criterion has a multiplicative effect on success.

To assess an innovation using the MIA model it is first necessary to rate the innovation on the Rogers and Shoemaker criteria using the following scheme:

- *Relative advantage:* rate the innovation with a 3 if the relative advantage is high, 2 if it is judged to be medium and 1 if it is low. This rating is referred to as RA.
- *Compatibility:* rate the innovation with a 3 if the compatibility is high, 2 if it is judged to be medium and 1 if it is low. This rating is referred to as CT.
- *Complexity:* rate the innovation with a 3 if it is simple, 2 if it is judged to be of medium complexity and 1 if it is judged to be highly complex. This rating is referred to as CL.
- *Trialability:* rate the innovation with a 3 if the opportunity to trial is high, 2 if it is judged to be medium and 1 if it is low. This rating is referred to as TR.
- *Observability:* rate the innovation with a 3 if the observability is high, 2 if it is judged to be medium and 1 if it is low. This rating is referred to as OB.

The ratings for each innovation are then multiplied together to obtain an overall prediction of the speed and extent (SE) to which the innovation will be adopted:

Speed and extent (SE) rating $= RA \times CT \times CL \times TR \times OB$

Referring back to Figure 14.2 and using the MIA rating scheme, we obtain the SE ratings seen in Figure 14.3. The higher the SE rating, the higher the predicted success of the innovation.

Innovation	Speed/extent (SE) rating
Compact discs	$3 \times 1 \times 3 \times 3 \times 2 = 54$
Sinclair C5	$1 \times 1 \times 1 \times 1 \times 3 = 3$
Pocket calculator	$3 \times 3 \times 2 \times 3 \times 2 = 108$
Post-it notes	$3 \times 3 \times 3 \times 3 \times 2 = 162$
Ford Sierra	$1 \times 3 \times 2 \times 2 \times 3 = 36$

Figure 14.3 Speed and extent (SE) ratings using the Simmons and Phipps MIA model

Based on the example ratings provided, it is predicted that the most successful innovation would be post-it notes and the least the Sinclair C5.

Assessment of success criteria and MIA model

- Success is a difficult concept to define and thus any criteria or model is open to criticism on the basis that what they attempt to describe is itself vague. To one person it might be high sales figures, to another high profit margins, high public profile or something else. For example, one-off designer label clothes may not sell in high volumes but may be valuable in that they build up the reputation of the designer. In a sense, they are therefore a success. We could redefine success as meeting the aims that the originator of the innovation themselves sets. However, this risks diluting the concept and it is probably best to accept a general definition based on cultural expectations.
- The MIA model presented is theoretical and requires validation. Tools do not yet exist to measure the five criteria but could no doubt be simply constructed.
- The model and criteria are powerful in that they are based on perceived characteristics. Thus different individuals could rate the same innovation in a variety of ways. This would make the application of the technique particularly suitable for target marketing.

Rate the following innovations using the MIA model:

electric car
electric toothbrush
mobile phone
pocket lighter
video camera
remote control television

On the basis of your analysis which would you have predicted was most likely to succeed? Does this match your current perceptions of these products in the market-place?

Categories of adopters

Research on the diffusion process (by Rogers) has found that adoption follows a curve of normal distribution amongst adopters (you will remember from the statistics unit that a normal curve is bell-shaped). This is illustrated in Figure 14.5. Initially, only a very few people adopt an innovation but the numbers steadily, then dramatically increase until they reach a peak. The number of people adopting over time then declines. This normal distribution has been approximately divided into 5 categories (see Figure 14.4).

This information can be most useful in targeting new product campaigns.

	Percentage (%) of population	Characteristics of group
Innovators	2.5	Risk-takers, more adventurous, more spending power, take most publications
Early adopters	13.5	Highest proportion of opinion leaders, above average education, tend to be younger than later adopters, well-respected, have greatest contact with sales people
Early majority	34	Slightly above average age, education, social status and income. Rely on informal sources of information.
Late majority	34	Above average age but below average education, social status and income. Rely on informal sources of information.
Laggards	16	Lowest group with respect to education, income and social status. Are the oldest group

Figure 14.4 Categories of adopters

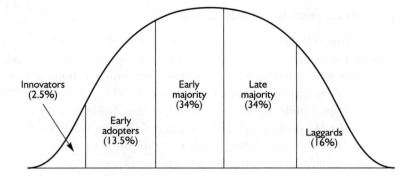

Figure 14.5 Adoption curve

Opinion leaders

As we can see from the characteristics of the adopter groups, opinion leaders are crucial in the diffusion of innovations.

Opinion leaders are those individuals who are instrumental in changing the consumer behaviour of others. If there were no opinion leaders then behaviour would stagnate with no new fashions, ideas or attitudes emerging. Marketers are interested in targeting opinion leaders as, once these are convinced of the benefits of a new product or service, the rest of the adopters will then follow.

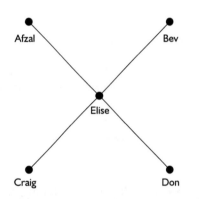

Figure 14.6 Sociogram of flow of information concerning recommendation of book

In the book example referred to in Unit 11 (see Figure 14.6), Elise was the opinion leader. Her knowledge of the book led to the purchase of four further copies. Obviously, you do not always buy everything that is recommended to you, the source of the recommendation must possess other qualities. Research has shown that opinion leaders generally possess certain similar characteristics:

- *Personality traits* – Opinion leaders tend to be self-confident individuals. They are confident about their own decisions and opinions and are thus more able to convince others. Leaders are also sociable, indeed they must be to enable the network of acquaintances required for communication.
- *Demographic characteristics* – Not surprisingly, people tend to seek information from those whom they perceive to be most knowledgeable in a particular subject matter. Thus if you were buying a computer you might seek the advice of a computer-literate friend.
- *Social class* – Most commonly the opinion leader is of the same social class as the people they are influencing. This may be because advice from those of a similar status is more valued or simply that we more regularly communicate with persons in our class.

What demographic characteristics would you imagine an opinion leader in the following purchasing decisions might posses?

Who would you consult about purchasing Top 10 chart music?

Who would you consult about purchasing a violin?

Who would you consult about purchasing a sewing machine?

Shiffman and Kanuk (1994) present a multi-step model of how an opinion leader receives and disseminates information (Figure 14.7). Most importantly it shows that some consumers receive information directly from mass media rather than 'consulting' an opinion leader. Note also that the communication between opinion leader and consumer is two way, accurately demonstrating that opinion leaders are themselves open to influence from other sources.

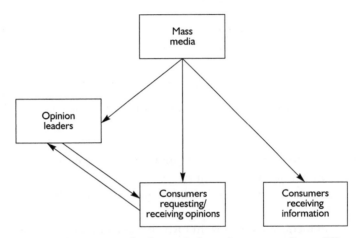

Figure 14.7 Diagram showing communication path from the mass media to different consumer groups via opinion leaders. Adapted from Shiffman and Kanuk (1994) *Consumer Behaviour*

Persuasive communication

We have seen in this unit, and earlier, how communication occurs between members in a group. We will now consider what affects the persuasiveness of that communication. For instance, if a lecturer told you to keep quiet in class you (probably) would. However, if a classmate told you, would you be as likely to obey?

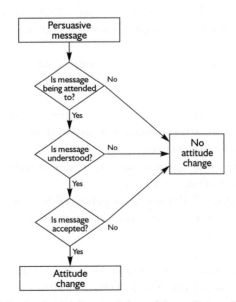

Figure 14.8 Hovland model of attitude change. Adapted from: Deaux, Dane, and Wrightsman, *Social Psychology in the 90s* (1993), Brooks/Cole

If a persuasive message is successful it leads to an attitude change (see Unit 12 for more information on attitudes). For attitude change to occur, a persuasive message on its own is not enough. During the early 1950s a social psychologist called Carl Hovland undertook a large volume of research in this area. With his colleagues he devised the process model shown in Figure 14.8 which shows the stages required for a message to lead to attitude change.

Figure 14.9 shows a communication model where a referent, one or more members from a reference group (possibly an opinion leader), is trying to influence a consumer. The content of the communication is the message with the whole discourse taking place within a particular context. You will notice the similarity with the earlier model of diffusion which is, essentially, the same communication process.

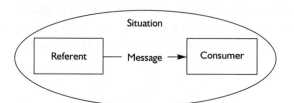

Figure 14.9   Communication model

The persuasiveness of the communication can be affected by the characteristics of all those elements shown in Figure 14.9:

- *Referent* – known as the source of the communication, the person trying to persuade.
- *Message* – the content of the communication.
- *Consumer* – known as the recipient of the communication, the person who is being persuaded.
- *Situation* – the immediate context within which the communication is taking place.

Source of communication

The following characteristics of the source affect its persuasiveness:

- **Status and credibility** – if the source is perceived as an expert then they are more persuasive. Thus stories in 'reputable' newspapers are more likely to be believed, as are endorsements from professionals in the topic being communicated. Experiments have shown a 'sleeper effect'. The difference between high credibility and low credibility sources is forgotten over time. However, when the recipient is reminded of source the original status effect returns.
- **Attractiveness** – the more attractive, charming, humorous the source the more persuasive (generally) they are likely to be. Of course, these characteristics are as perceived by the recipient.
- **Trustworthiness** – the more trustworthy the source is perceived to be the more persuasive they are. The trustworthiness is assessed on the basis of the perceived intentions and motives of the source.
- **Non-verbal behaviour** – non-verbal behaviour relates to trust. A 'shifty' disposition, for instance, does not instil trust.
- **Similarity with recipient** – if the source is perceived as being of a similar culture and social status as the recipient, then this can increase the persuasive power of the message.

Advertisers make use of all of these beneficial characteristics when formulating their advertisements. As we have already seen, certain individuals are used as experts or aspirational figures to gain appeal as are people from the same ethnic or social grouping as those in the target audience.

Content of communication (the message)

The following characteristics of the message affect its persuasiveness:

- **Non-verbal aspects** – Face-to-face communication is more effective than mass media. In this situation the source can react to the recipient (via eye contact, body posture, etc.) and are thus able to anticipate and modify their message accordingly.
- **Implicit or explicit** – This is concerned with whether the recipient is left to draw their own conclusion from the information provided (implicit) or presented with a conclusion by the source (explicit). Thus advertising aimed at people of high intelligence should not dictate choice but provide information for the recipient to make their own mind up.
- **Emotional appeal** – Emotions, such as fear, humour, sympathy and, of course, sex can be used to increase the persuasiveness of a communication. Experiments with smokers, concerning the danger of cancer, has shown that, somewhat surprisingly, 'high fear' messages are not the most effective way of persuasion. Scaring a smoker into thinking they are 'going to die' (high fear) is less likely to persuade them to stop smoking than a message with a lower fear content (such as 'smoking puts you at a high risk of cancer'). It appears that recipients 'switch off' when presented with high fear messages but are more receptive to messages where the fear content is more regulated.
- **One-sided versus two-sided arguments** – Whether a communication should make any reference to the competition (two-sided communication) seems to depend on the recipient.
- **Primacy–Recency** – The order in which information is presented can affect its persuasiveness. The first and last slots in an advert break are the most sought after as research has shown that they are more likely to be remembered.

Recipient

The following characteristics of recipients affect the persuasiveness of the communication:

- **Level of education** – The more educated respond better to more complex arguments.
- **Resistance to persuasion** – Resistance to persuasion is strongest when counter-arguments are available and weakest when they are not.
- **Latitude of acceptance and rejection** – It is easier to persuade people where large shifts in their existing attitudes are *not* required.
- **Compatibility with self-concept** – Related to the above, if we have a certain self-concept (that is we believe we possess certain attributes or characteristics) then messages which support our self-concept are more likely to be accepted.
- **Individual differences** – Opinions differ, but some psychologists believe that there is a personality factor which equate to 'persuasability' thus some people are, inherently, more difficult to persuade than others.

Situations

The following aspects of the situation affect the effectiveness of the persuasive communication:

- **Informal situations** – These are generally more effective than formal ones for persuasion. The example of 'Tupperware parties' and other home shopping is one common way that purchasing is made less formal and thus more persuasive.
- **Role-playing** – Trying to put the recipient in the 'shoes' of the source can increase persuasion.
- **Small groups** – As we have seen people are more likely to be persuaded if they are part of a small group that already shares these norms and values.
- **Public commitment** – Making a public commitment is more likely to lead to attitude change. Political parties make good use of this at election time.

Think of a recent decision you have made. What influencing factors can you identify from among those listed? Were there other influencing factors as well?

List them.

Similarly, can you remember any occasion when you resisted persuasion. What went wrong in the persuasive process? List the factors involved.

SUMMARY

In this unit you have learned about:

- What constitutes an innovation.
- How diffusion of innovations occur.
- The stages of innovation adoption.
- Different types of innovation.
- What makes an innovation successful.
- The MIA model for predicting innovation success.
- Categories of adopters.
- The characteristics and role of opinion leaders.
- Persuasive communication and the process by which it occurs.
- Those aspects of the source, message, recipient and situation that can increase persuasive power.

Cognitive reinforcement and dissonance

OBJECTIVES

This unit describes how learning is reinforced and post-purchase dissonance occurs. In this unit you will:

- Be introduced to the concept of reinforcement.
- Explore cognitive dissonance theory.
- Assess the evidence for the theory.

By the end of this unit you will be able to:

- Identify occurrences of reinforcement in marketing.
- Consider ways in which you might use reinforcement.
- Understand dissonance and how it can occur in the marketing function.
- Understand about post-purchase dissonance and how it can be avoided.

STUDY GUIDE

In Unit 12 we looked at some of the popular theories of attitude change. Perhaps most important is the theory of cognitive dissonance which is covered in this unit.

STUDY TIPS

Organize your study materials from the beginning of your course:

- Use file dividers to keep broad topic areas indexed and relevant materials and articles with the relevant notes.
- Look out for relevant articles and current examples, you will find these useful to illustrate examination answers.

This unit will take you about 1 to 2 hours to read through and think about. The activities you have been asked to carry out will take you about 1 hour.

Reinforcement

The concept of reinforcement lies at the heart of psychological theories of learning. It was first postulated by Thorndike in 1911 when he stated in *Animal Intelligence*:

> of the responses made to a situation, those which satisfy the organism's needs tend to be retained while those which fail to satisfy these needs tend to be eliminated.

In other words, responses which satisfy a need (see Unit 12 on motivation) are more likely to be perpetuated. This process is called *conditioning*. We have already looked at socialization, and the role that conditioning plays in acquiring culture, in Unit 11. However, the use of conditioning in other marketing contexts is worth further, brief exploration.

There are two prominent conditioning theories:

- Classical conditioning.
- Operant conditioning.

These will now be discussed.

Classical conditioning

Classical conditioning is said to take place when two stimuli are paired. That is, a stimulus is associated with an event. The work on this form of conditioning arose out of experimentation by Ivan Pavlov with dogs. Naturally, the dogs would salivate on sight of meat. But, by repeatedly preceding the arrival of the meat by a ring of a bell, Pavlov was able to get the dogs to salivate to the sound of the bell *without the presence of meat*. The dogs were therefore conditioned to produce salivation.

Classical conditioning is frequently used in advertising and promotions. By repeatedly associating a slogan, image or sound with a particular product it is possible to conjure up the memory of the product by the associated stimulus only. For example, colours have become associated with particular political parties so that the colour alone can evoke thoughts of the party. Similarly, a jingle or other tune associated with a product in an advertisement which goes on to become a 'popular hit' will continue to evoke images of that product (for free!). It is now quite common for music to be scored for commercials with just this goal.

The association between the conditioned stimulus and the original response slowly weakens until it is totally extinguished. This is known as *extinction*. A conditioned response that has been extinguished may, however, *spontaneously recover*, if the original association is again reinforced. In other words, the association will take less time to re-establish than the learning of a new association. It is as if the mind has retained some kind of 'memory' of the association which makes re-establishment easier. For example, offering petrol tokens will reinforce a driver to use that chain of petrol stations although the association will slowly weaken if the promotion is stopped. However, due to the action of spontaneous recovery, a reintroduction of the token scheme will make the original driver more easy to attract back when compared to a driver new to that chain of stations.

Operant conditioning

This is different from classical conditioning in that the learner is instrumental in producing the stimulus (in classical conditioning the stimulus – the bell in the case of Pavlov's dogs – was introduced by the experimenter). This can be explained using the experiments of Skinner on more animals, this time rats, in a cage which became known as the 'Skinner Box'. The box contained a lever which, when depressed, dispensed food pellets. After wandering around the cage for some time the rats eventually pressed the lever, either out of curiosity or by accident, which of course provided them with food (positive reinforcement). As a result, the pressing of the lever became associated with the production of food.

Both positive and negative reinforcement can occur. For example, if the lever delivered an electric shock, the rat would be unlikely to repeat the behaviour.

Sales promotions commonly make use of operant conditioning to reinforce certain behaviours. For example, the 'computers for schools' coupons scheme introduced by Tesco stores reinforces shopping at that store. Operant conditioning is also responsible for much brand loyalty. If a customer is satisfied with a brand or product their purchasing behaviour is reinforced.

Go to your local supermarket and try to identify at least three promotions. What type of conditioning is being used in each?

Cognitive dissonance theory

Cognitive dissonance is a motivating state of affairs. Just as hunger impels us to eat, so does dissonance impel a person to change his opinions or his behaviour . . . (Festinger, 1962)

According to Festinger, any two pieces of information (say A and B) contained in a person's mind can be related in one of three ways:

1 They can be consonant, or consistent. In this case A implies B.
2 They can be dissonant, or inconsistent. In this case A implies the opposite of B.
3 They can be unrelated or irrelevant to each other. A not related to B.

For example, the two pieces of information 'I like cream cakes' and 'cream cakes make me spotty' are dissonant. Presumably, one does not want to have spots yet one wants to eat cream cakes. On the other hand, 'I like Guinness' and 'Guinness is good for you' are consonant pieces of information.

As with the other consistency theories discussed, the aim of cognitive dissonance theory is to reduce the amount of dissonance, often defined as 'mental discomfort'.

The emphasis in marketing is on post-purchase dissonance. That is, when information about an accepted or rejected item is received following a purchasing decision. At this point, positive information about the rejected item will generate dissonance, as will negative information about the accepted item.

Suppose you have to choose between two alternative summer holiday destinations: South of France or Portugal. After a lot of thumbing through holiday brochures, you finally settle on the South of France. Just after booking the vacation you meet someone who has just returned from the South of France. A negative report from them is likely to generate dissonance as will a positive report from recent visitors to Portugal.

The magnitude of this dissonance will be proportional to:

- *The significance of the decision* – if you had spent a lot of money on the holiday or perhaps it was your only holiday for a number of years, the dissonance would undoubtedly be greater.
- *The attractiveness of the rejected alternative* – if your decision had been a narrow one then positive information from one of the rejected options is likely to create greater dissonance.
- *The number of negative characters of the choice made* – if the selected destination was seen to have a several things 'going for it' then a disappointing report about the weather, for instance, is less likely to create dissonance.
- *The number of options considered* – the more rejected choices the greater the dissonance. Trying to choose a holiday destination from ten alternatives makes it more likely that one of the rejected options would have turned out better.
- *Commitment to decision* – if the decision can easily be reversed and/or no public expression of the decision has been made then less dissonance is likely to result.
- *Volition or choice* – if the choice is 'forced' rather than voluntary then dissonance is minimized.

As with the other consistency theories considered, a person experiencing dissonance will act to reduce the discomfort. There are a number of ways this can be done. They can:

- Change their decision. This may not always be possible or practical.
- Actively seek positive information about the chosen alternative. This is called *selective exposure.*

- Concentrate on information presenting the positive features of the chosen alternative and ignore information presenting negative features. This is called selective attention.
- Change their attitudes.
- Actively avoid exposure to information that is likely to cause dissonance. This is called *selective avoidance.*
- Dismiss or devalue ambiguous information about the chosen option. This is called *selective interpretation.*

For example, the dissonance resulting from the information that 'I like cream cakes' and 'cream cakes make me fat' can be reduced by one or more of the following. We might:

- Stop eating cakes (change decision).
- Decide that cake eating does not cause fatness (change attitudes).
- Convince ourselves that enjoying a cream cake is worth the risk of putting on a bit of weight (selective attention).
- Question the link between cake eating and weight increase (selective interpretation).
- Eat a cake but then avoid information in magazines and papers which suggests cakes are bad (selective avoidance).
- Eat a cake but then seek information in magazines and papers which suggests cakes are good (selective exposure).

Marketers can use dissonance theory in several ways:

- *Post-purchase reinforcement* – continue to supply the purchaser with positive information about the product even after purchase thus reducing post-purchase dissonance. This will retain brand and corporate loyalty. This is common amongst car manufacturers who continue to send on glossy brochures and owner newsletters after the purchase is made. BMW are known to place car adverts aimed solely at existing owners of their cars.
- *Try and buy schemes* – offering limited trials, reinforced by coupons and gifts, will create a commitment and positive attitude towards the product which is then more likely to be purchased (to avoid dissonance when the product is returned). Book clubs are one example of sales organizations that operate in this way.
- *Anticipating and addressing dissonance in the advertising message and product branding* – a recent advert for cream cakes actually emphasized that they were a treat which, perhaps, wasn't the healthiest. The message given was 'Go on – you are worth it'. In the area of product branding, one cigarette manufacturer is actually trying to give a similar message with 'Death' cigarettes. Acknowledging the health problems with smoking but promoting a devil-may-care image.

ACTIVITY 15.2

Have you ever been aware of post-purchase dissonance? How have you coped?

Try to think of three examples.

ACTIVITY 15.3

Find one or more people who is intending to buy a lottery ticket. Ask them to rate their chances of winning on a scale of 1 to 10 where 10 is high, 1 is low.

After they have bought the ticket – get them to rate their chances again. Has their rating changed? If so, how can this be explained by dissonance theory.

Ratings should be higher after the ticket is purchased. Research suggests that the act of committing oneself to a bet creates dissonance and leads to a dissonance-reducing boost in confidence in one's choice.

In this unit you have learned about:

- Classical and operant conditioning and how this can be used in marketing.
- Cognitive dissonance theory.
- Marketing uses of the theory.

Forecasting changing behaviour and expectations

This unit introduces you to forecasting behaviour and expectations. In this unit you will:

- Consider changes in socio-cultural factors.
- Appreciate the effect of technology.
- Understand environmental concerns.
- Consider global and intercultural marketing.
- Appreciate how the economic environment can affect consumer spending and purchasing power.

By the end of this unit you will:

- Understand the importance of forecasting behaviour and expectations.
- Recognize the inter-relatedness of environmental factors.

STUDY GUIDE

Marketing strategy matches the capabilities of an organization with the demands of the environment. Marketing is a dynamic process and the ability to understand what is happening in the market and environment at all times is essential.

Marketers need to understand the increasing pressure to think strategically globally but to remember that marketing mixes need to be adapted to cultural requirements.

There is also an increasing need for marketers to consider their ethical behaviour and the role they can play to ensure that safe environmental practices and ethical business practices are carried out by their own organizations.

This unit will take you approximately 2 hours to read through. The activities will take you about another 3 hours.

STUDY TIPS

Organize your study materials from the beginning of your course:

- Use file dividers to keep broad topic areas and relevant materials and articles with the relevant notes.
- Look out for relevant articles and current examples, you will find these useful to illustrate examination answers.

Socio-cultural factors

The demographic environment

Demography studies populations in terms of age structure, geographic distribution, balance between males and females, future size and characteristics. Marketers need to know this for the following reasons:

1 *The demand side*
   The size, structure and trends of the population exert an influence on demand. There is a strong relationship between population growth and economic growth, and the absolute size of the population determines potential or primary demand.
2 *The supply side*
   Labour is an essential resource. For example, in retailing the decrease in young low-paid staff has already led to the employment of older people.

Size of population

The population in the UK is expected to have grown by 1.2% from 56.4 million in 1980 to 57.5 million in 1998. Although this is lower than many countries (the USA is expected to grow by 11% in the same period) there will be other significant changes in the structure of the population taking place during this period. Mintel has identified the most significant as being:

- 9% more children up to the age of 14.
- 18% fewer teenagers and young adults aged 15–29.
- 13% more 30–54-year-olds.
- 7% fewer 55–69-year-olds.
- 5% more 70-year-olds.

The key marketing factor to emerge from this is the swing from teenagers and young adults to middle-aged marrieds. The increased life expectancy has increased the demand for products and services catering for the elderly, such as entertainment, health products and holidays.

> How will these changes in demography affect the market you work with?

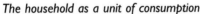

ACTIVITY 16.1

The household as a unit of consumption

Marketers focus attention on the household as a unit of consumption (DMU Unit 1). In household structure several changes have occurred:

- Growth in the number of one-person households. One-person households include single, separated, widowed and divorced. This section has grown over the last few years partly as more people are getting divorced and partly because more young adults leave home early. A UK government forecast expects that the number of one-person households will have increased by 30% in the period 1976–94. At the same time the number of pensioner one-person households is expected to have increased from 2.9 million in 1979 to almost 4 million by the mid-1990s.

  There has already been a demand for more starter homes, smaller appliances, food that can be purchased in smaller quantities and a greater emphasis on convenience products.

- Rise in the number of two-person cohabitant households. Several sociologists propose that cohabitation is the first stage of marriage. At the same time there is an increase in the number of households with two or more people of the same sex sharing. Married couples with one or two dependent children comprised 30% of households in 1961 compared with 20% in 1991.
- Rise in the number of group households with members of the same sex sharing expenses and living together, particularly in larger cities.

Geographical shifts in population
In Britain there is a north south divide which is characterized by different levels of economic activity and employment.

- There is a decline of over 5% in the number of people living in London, Surrey, the West Midlands, Yorkshire and the north west of England.
- There is an increase of 10% in the number of people living in Cambridgeshire, Buckinghamshire, Dorset and Cornwall in England and Down in Northern Ireland.

ACTIVITY 16.2

Is your market likely to be affected by geographical shifts in population?

- Family structure changes have come about through:
  - later marriages
  - fewer children
  - increased divorce rates
  - more working wives
  - careers for women

Changing role of women
The role of women has changed with many women working. Women now have more money but less time. This has led to opportunities for labour-saving consumer durables in the home, convenience food, new cars, changing shopping habits (Sunday shopping and catalogue buying) and child-care facilities.

An ageing population
People now live longer, one of the reasons for this is medical care. There is an increase in empty nesters (see family life cycle) who have more discretionary income.

Increased middle class
Higher levels of education have created more people who are middle class.

Slow down of birth in developed nations
Family size is decreasing as many families are only having one child.

Class consciousness and social mobility
For a discussion on class refer to Unit 3. Please note that class structures vary from country to country.

Influence of children in family purchasing
Taking children with you to the supermarket can affect what you buy, recent research has shown. Fathers spend on average 13% more when shopping by themselves with their children. Mothers spend less.

Since the number of under-15s will grow by 10% in this decade in the UK, with an estimated disposable income of £9 billion by 1998, this is a crucial influence on buying behaviour.

Marketing Week, 4/11/94

Education and achievement

It is likely that more and more people will become qualified. In 1977/78, 30% of school leavers left school without any GCE/SCE or CSE qualifications by 1987/88 this changed to 20%. Fewer girls leave school without qualifications than boys.

There will be a rise in the demand for the 'knowledge' workers, which has led to the Government expanding vocational and higher education in an effort to avert critical shortages in skills.

There is general correlation between academic achievements and occupation of the father with those of their off-spring between the ages of 25 and 59.

Ethnicity

About 5% of the UK's population belong to an ethnic minority. The concentration is around London and the south-east (9%) and in the north (1%).

Healthy living

There is an increased concern for healthy living which has led to a demand for sporting facilities, low-fat products and natural foods.

Quality of life

There are changes in lifestyle such as, for example, a demand for recycled products, gourmet foods, an increased demand for classical music.

Convenience and self-service

There is an increased demand for convenience such as more ready-to-use products, more convenient sizes and easier methods of payment.

Informality

There is a greater style of informality which has resulted in a demand for more casual clothing, less formal restaurants and less formal furnishings.

Local government

Services which have been traditionally provided by local government employees are having to go out for commercial tender. This has opened up a number of opportunities for the UK private sector.

Pensions

The Government is trying to get citizens to take responsibility for providing for their own pensions.

Private medicine

This area is still covered by the NHS although private medicine has increased. It is unlikely that the majority of people, while they are still being taxed for it, will want to pay for it twice.

Employment trends

- A growth in the number of people who are willing to travel long distances to work.
- A growth in the number of people who can work at home and remain in contact via computer terminals.
- A growth in contractual and temporary employment.
- A growth in part-time work (mostly women).
- A growth in self-employment.
- Flexible work times.
- A growth in the number of virtual companies where the workforce is decentralized and includes a majority of home workers.

Changes in lifestyle

Albrecht (1979) has distinguished five major lifestyle changes taking place which have increased the level of stress. These are:

- from rural to urban living
- from stationary to mobile
- from self-sufficient to interconnected
- from isolated to interconnected
- from physically active to sedentary.

Protection of consumer interests

Consumerism is the term used by the consumer movement to describe what they do and is concerned with the protection of consumers' interests. The consumer movement is concerned with protecting the publics interests. These range from:

- ensuring the availability of product and price information
- ensuring the labelling is correct
- ensuring that advertising does not misinform
- ensuring that products are safe
- ensuring that businesses do not indulge in sharp practices
- ensuring that businesses abide by the law
- encouraging government to intervene on consumers' behalf.

ACTIVITY 16.3

1 What consumer interests does the organization you work for have to take into account?
2 What does your organization do about ensuring that consumers concerns are met?

Changes in the marketing mix

Changes in lifestyle will create changes in the marketing mix. If this is so, then as culture and values change and people look more to understand themselves, the brands created today already contain the seeds for their own destruction.

Culture is dynamic, it changes and marketers must be aware of changes in society. If and when people change their ideas of who they are the social and political culture will change as well and there will be a demand for different goods/services and the marketing techniques across a whole range of dimensions will need to change as well.

ACTIVITY 16.4

Do you think people in the UK have the same response to luxury goods as people living in the US? Do you have any evidence for this? According to the box below something slightly different has happened in the UK but for different reasons.

People in the US are much more suspicious of the 'value' of luxury goods than they once were. The ostentatious parade of branded goods has been replaced in the 1990s by a desire for products and services of enduring value. According to *Fortune* magazine, these include microwave-safe porcelain, practical sports watches and classic suits.

Social and cultural changes.

You should be able to apply social and cultural changes to future changes in different types of markets.

1 What sort of social and cultural changes are happening in the UK today?
2 How would these factors affect:

- A supermarket?
- A construction company?
- A cosmetic company?
- A gym?

At the same time, major changes are taking place in the rest of the world; some of these may be similar to those that are happening in the UK, others are different, in order to understand this fully each specific country and context would need to be researched.

World markets
(Update given by Professor Douglas McWilliams at the CIM Conference 1995.)

The UK used to have 50% of world markets in 1860; this has dropped to 5% and is now remaining the same although it is hoped that this will grow to about 6%. The UK started to restructure earlier than Europe and is now a post-industrial society. The economy is less distorted now because of the decrease in state-controlled industries. The government instead of having to pay out enormous subsidies is now receiving taxes from privatized industries.

The UK's main trading partners (Europe) are not growing as fast and labour costs although less than in Germany are still higher than in Singapore. In China people work for 50 cents (US) an hour, in Czechoslovakia $2. This will put pressure on costs.

Structure of economic growth
In the past consumer spending has grown faster than GDP but now consumer spending is growing less than GDP. This is a new occurrence as it is rare to have a recovery with consumer spending lagging behind.

Major global changes
The balance between capital and labour is changing. This is happening because there has been a massive growth of people, skills, intelligence and education. The death rate is down and the birth rate up, this has created a labour surplus which worldwide means that profits are a more important aspect of world economy.

Politics
In the Pacific there is a three-handed game between US, Japan and China with China becoming a military superpower. Europe is turning in on itself and there is a widespread availability of lethal weapons.

- Profit is the key.
- Search for the fastest growing markets.
- Don't rely on inflation for growth, it must come from organic growth.

Population growth in under-developed countries

There is an annual and exponential growth rate of 1.8%. The world population will have grown from 4.4 billion in 1980 to 6.2 billion by the year 2000.

Contrary to what many might suspect, India boasts a large consumer class of around 550 million. Consumption is reported to be booming particularly in rural areas.

The Economist, 5/11/94

Choose two countries that you are interested in, a developed country and an undeveloped country, and over a period of time, collect articles on them that reflect social/cultural and demographic changes. Telephone the Department of Trade and Industry (DTI) for additional information.

In 1988, Hay Management Consultants took fourteen people – seven from their own organization and seven from a variety of other organizations (British Aerospace, The Civil Service, Eurotunnel, ICI, Prudential Corporation, Saatchi and Saatchi and Tesco), who are likely to be in a senior position in the year 2000 and asked them to think about the world as it might be in AD 2000. In doing this, they were looking for the inevitable, the unexpected, and the problems. Among their conclusions were:

1   Throughout Europe we are running short of young people. The number of 16 to 19-year-olds will have fallen by up to 15% by 1995 alone. The result will be a shortage of qualified people, which will have to be overcome by a combination of fewer retirements, more married women being wooed back into the workforce, the replacement of people with technology, an ever greater investment in education, and possibly a drawing of skilled labour from the old European empires, Africa, Asia and China.

2   The 50–54 age group will increase by a third, and the over-75 group by a quarter. Markets and tastes will be dominated by the middle-aged. A major problem, however, will be the costs to society of an ageing population; the cost per head of the health services is six times higher for the over 75s, and the cost of social services 26 times higher.

3   The further development of office technology will make the truly personal mobile office feasible.

4   The next scientific revolution will be biotechnology which will allow a far greater range of diseases to be cured, including cancer and AIDS.

5   In agriculture, biotechnology will be able to solve many of the world's food problems.

6   The family car will still exist but new materials and new manufacturing techniques will mean that every car can be different, with the driver effectively able to design a customized car. Components will be cheaper to replace than to repair.

7   In monetary terms the global village will have arrived, with notes and coins virtually obsolete.

8   A new mood of detente will result in a fall in defence spending, enabling the United States' double-deficit problem to be a single-deficit one.

9   The highly educated baby-boomers are increasingly likely to adopt a portfolio lifestyle in their later years doing a variety of jobs at the same time.

10 More and more information about our public and private lives will be stored on computer, with an increased ability to corrupt or misuse the information.

11 An even greater number of employees will be on short-term specific contracts with organizations, and pay will be more directly geared to outputs.

Headlines 2000: the world as we see it, *Hay Management Consultants*, 1989

Technology

Changes in technology have an impact on:

- the environment
- the types of products that are marketed
- methods of production
- the type of work that is done
- the way in which the work is carried out
- the way in which human resources are deployed
- techniques used for marketing
- consumers and society in general.

Marketers therefore need to be alert to watching their immediate competitors and also any emerging technologies, especially ones that are capable of being transferred from one context to another. For example technology that was first developed for the US space programme may now be found in many domestic and industrial situations.

ACTIVITY 16.6

Give examples of the way in which technology has affected techniques used for marketing.

ACTIVITY 16.7

1   Using your own organization as an example, in what way has information technology changed the way in which people do their work?
2   Give an example of a technological change in your own organization and show how people have benefitted from them.

EXAM HINT

Technology

You should be able to give examples of changes in technology and relate them to the social and cultural changes that have taken place because of them.

1 Give an example of how a change in technology has created social change on an individual level and at an organizational level.

Environmental priorities

The four major areas of concern are:

1 An impending shortage of raw materials.
2 Increasing costs of energy.
3 Increasing levels and consequences of pollution.
4 An increasing need for government to become involved in the management of resources.

The question facing us is how our need for products balances with our need to protect our environment, and how this need will be taken up by the rest of the developing world.

Behavioural aspects

Many opinion surveys show a clear growth in environmental consciousness among the public. In the UK, this has been substantiated by research carried out by Market and Opinion Research International (MORI).

However, the results of surveys only show a change of values on a global level, these are not always reflected in consumer purchase behaviour.

Private and social cost

The costs of production do not just include rent, rates, labour, material and transport costs – these are relatively simple and easy to calculate. The true costs are not borne by industry, the true costs are the social costs of production.

The costs that business impose upon society have included damage to the environment: global warning, acid rain, depletion of the ozone layer, waste, the catastrophes of oil spillages, nuclear incidents (e.g. Chernobyl), noise, congestion, air and water pollution, industrial pollution, to name but a few.

A corporate response

Change should not only be driven by law-making in Brussels or parliament, by environmental standards, by pressure groups and consumer demand. Businesses should become proactive and make care for the environment part of their core beliefs and values and these should form part of the mission statement.

Legislation

The UK is developing a range of legislation to cover most aspects of environmental pollution. This response has been driven by the demand of the electorate and the European Community. The European Community has already issued 200 regulations and directives relating to all aspects of environmental pollution. Halogens will be phased out by 2000 and CFCs must be phased out by mid-1997.

- The Department of Trade launched an environmental programme in May 1989. They also created an environmental unit to carry out work in this area. In addition, there is a hotline to provide businesses with all types of information relating to environmental issues.

- The White Paper, The Common Inheritance, was published in 1990. This sets out policy related to:
  - Minimizing energy use.
  - Ensuring labelling so that consumers can identify environmentally friendly products.
  - Reducing emissions from motor vehicles, cleaning up untreated discharges into the sea
  - disposal of sewage sludge into the sea will be banned from 1997.
- The Energy Conservation and Warmer Homes Bill was passed in 1995 and requires local authorities to take steps to improve the energy efficiency of their housing stock. It was introduced to Parliament as a Private Members Bill, a route which is becoming increasingly popular for piecemeal environmental legislation.
- The Environmental Protection Act was passed in 1991. Recognition is now being given to an integrated approach to pollution – damage to one part means damage to the whole. The Government is also responding to pressure to create an integrated transport policy.

International agreements

People are realizing that pollution is a matter of global concern. Agreements are being reached to do this. The UK signed the Montreal Protocol of 1987 (revised in 1990 to include CFCs) which will try to control the production of ozone-depleting chemicals throughout the world.

ACTIVITY 16.8

How does the following legislation affect your organization?

Manufacturers who claim that their products are environmentally friendly because their products do not contain a certain ingredient may be prosecuted under the 1986 Trades Description Act as a false claim.

Marketing 3/11/94

ACTIVITY 16.9

Would your organization benefit from using an ecolabel? What resistance would you have to overcome internally to get your ideas adopted?

Hoover is the first UK company to get an EC ecolabel. Their 'New Wave' washing machines use considerably less water, detergent and energy than the models they replace.

New markets

Green marketing is seen by some as a transparent marketing activity. To many consumers and business people it is not, it is marketing listening to and responding to customers' needs. People buy goods for material welfare, physic welfare and display. We all need recreation and work, to be fed, clothed, sheltered, and we need all this but we also need peace of mind. Green marketing, taken seriously and with honest intent, is part of this process.

A potential market exists for pollution control systems such as scrubbers and recycling systems. Demand from consumers is also creating a market for greener products.

In order to carry these programmes out businesses will obviously reduce some costs, but will need to in some cases increase prices as plant is changed, products redesigned to create less damage on the environment. Prices will have to be borne by the consumer.

ACTIVITY 16.10

How much of your organizations research and development budget is being spent on environmentally related research?

3M, the company that invented the Post-It pad, devoted over 15% of its research and development budget to environmentally related research in 1993.

ACTIVITY 16.11

Read the box below. Is there any way your organization could use recycled material in their manufacturing process?

Several US athletic shoe manufacturers use recycled materials in their shoes.

Three US jeans manufacturers think fashions made of recycled plastic bottles will keep sales buoyant.

Brandweek, 10/10/94

Training

Employees working for organizations will also have to change, for example, work practices. In some cases new technology and processes will result in redundancies and jobs becoming obsolete. This should open up areas for retraining. A major area of training is environmental management.

ACTIVITY 16.12

Carry out this activity within your own organization and find answers to the following questions:

1 How has the environmental movement affected the business?
2 What has it meant to your organization to have become more environmentally friendly?
3 If changes have been made were they brought about by a change in core belief and values, consumer demand or legislation?
4 Were there any costs involved in making the changes, or indeed any savings?
5 Have the changes been communicated internally and externally?
6 Does your organization only do business with environmentally friendly suppliers?
7 Are any more changes anticipated?

If it is at all possible try to present and discuss your findings in class. It is extremely interesting being able to get a picture of how other businesses are reacting to changes in this area.

If this is not possible and your organization is not doing anything in this area, contact a few major companies and ask them to supply you with some information.

Remember, the examiners will expect you to be able to relate your ideas to practical examples. The examples you may be asked to provide could be applied to the consumer and industrial markets.

EXAM HINTS

Global marketing and intercultural/international marketing

Globalization

The term 'Globalization of markets' (Levitt, 1983) relates to:

1 Tastes, preferences and price-mindedness becoming increasingly universal.
2 Products and services becoming more standardized and competition within industries reaching a worldwide scale.
3 The way in which organizations try and design their marketing policies and control systems for global products, consumers and competition on a global scale.

Jean-Claude Usunier writes in *International Marketing*, Prentice Hall, 1993:

Globalization means homogenizing on a world scale. The implicit assumption behind the globalization process is that all elements will globalize simultaneously. A central assumption of globalization is that the mostly artificial trade barriers (non-tariff, regulation, industrial standards, etc.) have kept many markets at the multidomestic stage. If these barriers are removed, which is the aim of 1992, 'insiders' who hold a large market share just in their home market may only be protected from new entrants by natural culture-related entry barriers.

Harold Clark (1987) of J. Walter Thompson argues the case against the existence of a global consumer:

1 Consumers are not 'global' themselves (national and cultural variance remains quite significant).
2 Consumers do not generally buy 'global' brands or products. They do not really care whether the brand is or is not available elsewhere in the world.
3 Since what consumers value is personal and individual, they will naturally let their individuality affect the values they place on the brands they buy. They contribute actively in this way to the persona of the brand in their own situation.

What is global strategy?

A global strategy implies a world view of competition and competitive advantage, not simply a belief that consumers and markets are themselves global.

McDonald's, Holiday Inns and Coca-Cola are global brands that provide their buyers with the possibility of cultural adaption to a way of life that they desire.

Most organizations would like to have truly global products as this would simplify the whole marketing process. In practice this is highly unlikely. Some companies refuse to adapt and have been successful, others have not adapted to local culture and as a result have faced difficulties (e.g. Euro Disney). Although, interestingly Disneyworld in Tokyo is flourishing.

Cultural identification

People within a cultural affinity class share common values, behaviour and interests and tend to present common traits as a consumer segment. Cultural affinity classes create a sense of belonging to a common group across different countries. Satellite television enables these groups to be contacted across different countries.

See Unit 11 for more information on social and cultural influences.

Think about the following issues:

1   Knowing that culture and micro-culture influence consumer purchasing, are there any ethical reasons, such as social disintegration, any injury to social tradition and so on which the marketer needs to consider before marketing goods and services to foreign countries?

2   Provided the marketer is convinced that the marketing system will 'design, deliver, and legitimate products and services that increase the material welfare of the population by promoting equity, justice, and self-reliance without causing injury to tradition' (Dholakia *et al.*, 1988), what resistance can they expect at local and/or social level?

Other factors to consider in intercultural marketing

Economic development

The level of economic development will have an influence in different countries.

Technological development

Each country would have developed to a different technological level. This factor covers a range of activities from the educational level and the use of technology down to man-power skills.

Political and legal decisions

Institutions such as the state, Church and trade unions will also have an influence. Some governments may be hostile to imports, even to foreign investment, others may encourage it. In politically unstable countries these attitudes may suddenly change. There is often much more legislation protecting the consumer against unfair advertising practices. The activity of consumer movements will also vary.

Business practices

The way business is carried out will vary. The marketer needs to study the social and cultural conventions of each country. This will range from the writing of letters, dress, time-keeping, giving of gifts, verbal and non-verbal communication, decision making.

Competitive activity

The international marketer will probably face different levels of competition in different countries. Sometimes local competition will be well established, at other times the country concerned may already have a preferential relationship with organizations from another country.

Consumer behaviour

Cultural projection

Cultural projection is a form of selective perception as people tend to project their own cultural background on to what they perceive in other cultures. To understand another culture it is important to understand your own first.

- The way purchasing decisions are taken within the family and the role of women in the buying process will be different. The influence of the extended family will also need to be taken into consideration. The cultural role of women will be different and decisions may well be taken by men in different product categories.
- Maslow's theory about the hierarchy of needs (see Unit 12) cannot be applied cross-culturally. Hofstede's research shows that it is based on American culture and is not universal. For example, in Hindu culture self-realization, which does not imply material consumption, is encouraged.

- Different cultures have varying levels of need for shelter and food. In Japan, German-speaking countries, some Latin countries and Greece, people are motivated by the need for personal security. In France, Spain, Portugal, Yugoslavia, Chile and other Latin and Asian countries, people are motivated by the need for security and belonging, while in north European countries, success and belonging are the main motivators.
- Cultural stereotyping
  A 'made in' label operates in a number of ways. These are summarized below:

  1 Consumers hold stereotyped images both of foreign countries and of their own country.
  2 These images are used as information cues in judging products originating from different countries.
  3 Buyers are not always aware of a product's true origin, yet they are always able to express preferences for product locations.
  4 Consumers in some countries prefer foreign brands.
  5 Like price or brand name, country of origin may serve as a proxy variable for product evaluation when other information is lacking.
  6 Country of origin identifications may serve as a surrogate for branding.

- Cultural conventions such as the structure of daily life.
- Other aspects of consumer behaviour will also need to be studied, such as brand loyalty, the use of rational price/quality comparisons, involvement in the purchase, perceived risk, the decision making process may be very different.
- Aspects of the marketing mix will need to be studied:
  - Physical attributes such as national regulations and standard, consumption patterns (e.g. these will affect pack sizes), climate and physical environment.
  - Service attributes (also dependent on culture).
  - Symbolic attributes such as brand name, packaging, use of colour, verbal and non-verbal communication and so on, which will be culturally determined.

ACTIVITY 16.14

Using your own organization, find out if changes have been made to the marketing mix in order to adapt them for non-domestic markets? If changes have not been made, are there good reasons why? Do you think changes should be made?

If your organization is not marketing outside the UK, find out whether it will be considered in the future and what changes will have to made to the marketing mix for the non-domestic market.

It would be helpful to use this as a discussion point with your colleagues in class as it will broaden your experience.

EXAM HINTS

Global and intercultural/international marketing

1 You should know the difference between these two approaches and be able to apply them.
2 You should be able to understand the behavioral differences when dealing with domestic markets as opposed to international ones.

Global and intercultural/international marketing

1 What is the difference between global marketing and intercultural marketing?

2 What behavioural differences should you be aware of when dealing with domestic markets as opposed to international ones?

3 How would you approach marketing:

- An international hotel?
- A food product?
- A beverage?
- A computer?

Economic environment

The economic environment can affect consumer spending and purchasing power.

Total spending power includes:

- current income
- savings
- credit
- prices.

A major determinant of demand income is widely used as a measure of potential demand.

1 Net disposable income is all earnings (earned from salaries) unearned (from investments) health and welfare benefits and so on, less tax.

2 Discretionary income is the amount available after all 'essential' (mortgage, rent, food, basic clothing, etc.) expenditure has been met.

Consumer behaviour and marketing strategy will influence whether a product/service falls in the discretionary or non-discretionary sector.

Marketers should be aware of:

1 Patterns of real income distribution.

2 Inflationary and deflationary pressure.

3 Changing consumer expenditure patterns.

4 Changes in the saving/debt ratio.

5 Concern over third world debt.

6 Different consumer expenditure patterns.

These changes must not be looked at in isolation but be viewed against a background of change in the political/economic balances of power – such as the rise of Japan and south east Asia, the collapse of the Soviet Union, developments in China and major changes in the physical environment. See above.

Economic factors

You should be able to understand how consumer behaviour is affected by economic factors both domestically and abroad. It is important to understand that it is not the objective nature of the economic context but rather the way in which that context is perceived and interpreted by consumers.

Economic factors

1   What economic factors should marketers be aware of when marketing at home and abroad?

Economic forecasting involves looking at the impact and relationship of the following:

- the industrial structure
- the income distribution
- GNP per capita
- rate of growth of GNP
- ratio of investment to GNP
- business cycles
- money supply
- inflation rates
- investment levels
- unemployment
- energy costs
- patterns of ownership
- exchange rates
- taxation
- currency stability
- export and so on.

Annual real GDP growth is rising. The world rate is set to rise from 2.4% in the last ten years to just under 4% within the next ten. Growth is not evenly spread, for example east Asia is expected to have an 8% growth. However, growth in the UK and Europe will be round about 4%.

Make sure that you read the quality press and trade and business magazines on a regular basis to keep track of what is happening in your market. Collect articles and put them into your folder. You will be expected to include up-to-date examples in the exam.

In this unit you have seen that:

- Forecasting changing behaviour and expectations will depend on a large variety of factors. We have looked at: size of population, the household as a unit of consumption, geographical shifts in population, changing role of women, class consciousness, influence of children in family purchasing, education and achievement, ethnicity, healthy living, quality of life, convenience, informality, declining role of the state, local government, pensions, private medicine in the UK.
- We have also considered some aspects of world population.

- Changes in technology have an impact on:
  - The environment.
  - The types of products that are marketed.
  - Methods of production.
  - The type of work that is done.
  - The way in which the work is carried out.
  - The way in which human resources are deployed.
  - Techniques used for marketing.
  - Consumers and society in general.
- Taking care of the environment is of increasing importance. Marketers need to be developing products to meet this need and to ensure their production methods do not contaminate the environment.
- Global and intercultural/international marketing is an area that the marketer needs to take into consideration, with an awareness of differences in consumer behaviour. The ethics involved in intercultural marketing need to be taken into account.

Marketing ethics could therefore be looked upon as servicing the needs of all the stakeholders – this includes society.

Demand forecasting

Forecasts are made on the basis of what is happening externally to the organization such as changes in the political/legal environment, economic environment local and overseas, social-cultural environment, technological environment, supplier environment, overseas environment, competitor activity. Consumer tastes and the results from any market research need to be taken into consideration. These are uncontrollable factors.

Internal factors such as past sales patterns, promotional budget availability, pricing policies, distribution spread and quality of outlets and personnel and the strengths and weaknesses within the organization will then determine what marketing objectives are set. These are controllable factors.

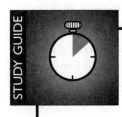

This unit will take you about 1 hour to read through and 1 hour to carry out the activities.

Organize your study material from the beginning of your course:

- Use file dividers to keep broad topic areas indexed and relevant materials and articles with the relevant notes.
- Look out for relevant articles and current examples, you will find these useful to illustrate examination answers.

Forecasting

There are three methods that are used:

1 Subjective methods:
   - consumer/user survey methods
   - panels of executive opinion/jury method
   - salesforce composite
   - Delphi method
2 Combined methods:
   - Bayesian theory
3 Objective statistical methods:
   - time series
       trends analysis
       moving averages
       z chart
       exponential smoothing
   - causal techniques
       leading indicators (correlation)
       simulation
       diffusion models

There are two basic approaches to sales forecasting:

1 Forecast the total market, then determine the market share.
2 Forecast the company sales directly.

As with any organization, the overall forecast can be calculated and broken down or it can be built up from products upwards.

Time-scale of forecasts

Short term – up to 12 months, these tend to be tactical and aimed at production planning. Sales forecasting is essential because over-production can lead to an increase in stocks which costs money; under-production leads to customer dissatisfaction and sales lost to competition. Short-term fluctuations are important here. They can be done on a 0–3, 0–6, 0–9, 0–12 month basis.

Medium term – These are usually between 1 and 5 years ahead and are very important as they are used as a basis for planning and budgets.

Long term – These are 5 years plus and are needed to plan resources in the longer term. They affect employment levels, production and the number of factories, warehousing and so on. They are usually based on macro-economic factors, government policies, economic trends and so on.

Subjective methods

Consumer/user survey methods

Consumer selling
This is done through market research. Its accuracy will depend on the quality of the market research.

Industrial selling
This is generally done via the salesforce because there are generally fewer customers. There is always the danger of overestimation.

Panels of executive opinion/jury method
Experts within the industry either internal to the organization or outside it are asked to prepare a forecast in advance. A discussion will then be held and the forecasts modified during the discussion. A broad industry-wide forecast will then be produced.

Delphi method

This method is similar to the above except that the forecast is done on the basis of a questionnaire to avoid the influence of the group.

Salesforce composite

In the 'bottom up' or 'grass roots' approach each salesperson is asked to forecast the number of sales they anticipate making within their territory. These results are then combined to create area/region/national forecasts. The danger lies in salespeople putting in lower estimates so that they are easier to achieve, not knowing that their area and sales forecasts tend to be based on recent actual performance rather than projected, future performance. The sales figures are then compared with the regional sales managers' reports and the two used to create a combined forecast.

Sometimes a realistic estimate may be put forward but management may want higher figures and as a result change the figures to something that may not be achievable.

Combined methods

Bayesian theory

This uses a combination of qualititative and quantitative methods. It is based on the use of probability; the probabilities are based on people's opinions and will be subjective.

Worked example

(taken from *Sales Techniques and Management*, Lancaster and Jobber)

Classical Reproductions Ltd.

This company is trying to decide whether to enter the US market now, in a year's time or in two years' time. The company's management feels that the US economy could either continue to be buoyant, could suffer a moderate downturn or could suffer a serious recession.

Factors and profits	X Now	X-1 year	X-2 years
Economy stays good	800,000	600,000	500,000
Moderate downturn	450,000	370,000	200,000
Recession	−324,000	50,000	80,000

The management decides the probability of each event is as follows:

(a) Economy buoyant   0.4
(b) Moderate downturn   0.3
(c) Recession   0.3

All this is incorporated into a decision tree:

Probability × Profit

	*Export now	(a) 0.4 × 800,000
		(b) 0.3 × 450,000
		(c) 0.3 × −324,000
Decisions	*Export in one year	(a) 0.4 × 370,000
		(b) 0.3 × 370,000
		(c) 0.3 × 50,000
	*Export in two years	(a) 0.4 × 500,000
		(b) 0.3 × 200,000
		(c) 0.3 × 80,000

Value expected

Export now
(a) 0.4 × 800,000 + (b) 0.3 × 450,000 + (c) 0.3 × –324,000 = 357,800

Export in one year
(a) 0.4 × 370,000 + (b) 0.3 × 370,000 + (c) 0.3 × 50,000 = 366,000

Export in two years
(a) 0.4 × 500,000 + (b) 0.3 × 200,000 + (c) 0.3 × 80,000 = 284,000

The maximum payout will be gained by delaying export until one year's time.

The above example is called prior analysis and is based on prior probabilities. Further information could be obtained through a survey.

Objective statistical methods

Time series

Trends analysis
In forecasting we are interested in identifying five main types of events:

- Trends
- Cyclical changes
- Seasonal variations
- Unpredicatable events
- Influence of marketing mix or sales and proft.

Trends
When we consider trends, we are trying to determine the general direction that data is going. Suppose we measure product sales at weekly intervals, we want to know whether sales are, generally, increasing week on week, decreasing, or following some other recognized pattern.

There are four main trends:

- Positive trend.
- Negative trend.
- S-trend.
- Zero trend.

These are illustrated in Figures 17.1–17.4. In all cases the horizontal (*X*) axis represents time and the vertical (*Y*) axis indicates the measures we are considering (which could be any statistic we are interested in monitoring: sales, number of products sold, mean age of customers for our products, attitudes and so on).

A positive trend (Figure 17.1) is seen where the value of the measure we are monitoring is steadily increasing. The rate of increase is shown by the slope of the line. The steeper the slope the faster the increase. Such a pattern might be seen in a expanding market. For instance, bicycle sales in the UK have shown a steady increase for a number of years.

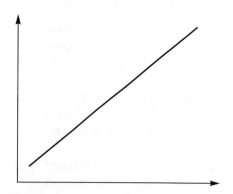

Figure 17.1 Graph showing positive trend

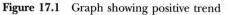

A negative trend (Figure 17.2) is seen where the value of the measure we are monitoring is steadily decreasing. The rate of decrease is shown by the slope of the line. The steeper the slope the faster the decrease. Such a pattern might be seen in a contracting market. For instance, the sale of vinyl records steadily decreased following the introduction of compact discs.

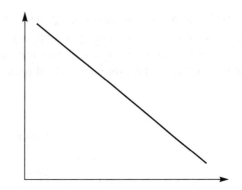

Figure 17.2 Graph showing negative trend

An S-trend (Figure 17.3) is seen where the value of the measure we are monitoring slowly increases, then increases more rapidly and finally slows down again. This pattern is commonly seen when examining sales of a product over its life cycle. When a new product is launched sales are initially slow, then gradually speed up until saturation point is reached when the sales remain steady or possibly decrease slightly.

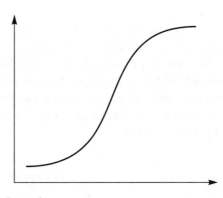

Figure 17.3 Graph showing S-trend

A zero trend (Figure 7.4) means just that. There is no discernable trend upwards or downwards. We may see this sort of trend in sales of products with a steady turnover and a stable market such as in the sales of light bulbs.

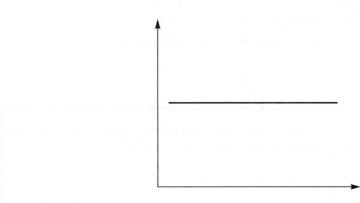

Figure 17.4 Graph showing zero trend

Seasonal variations

Measures are often subject to seasonal changes. These are defined as regular variations that occur within a period of up to twelve months. For instance, sales of ice cream peak in the summer months; sales of turkey increase at Christmas; most shop sales increase on Saturdays; traffic flows increase at the 'rush hours' and so on.

Cyclical changes

Overlayed on the general trends there are often long-term variations due to outside influences. The effect of the economy on overall spending is one example of a cyclical change which is likely to stretch over many years, sometimes masking and sometimes enhancing any underlying trends. Figure 17.5 shows a cyclical pattern which demonstrates a generally positive trend.

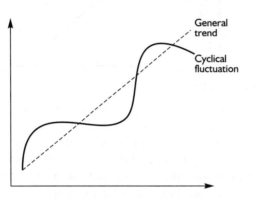

Figure 17.5   Cyclical changes

Unpredictable events

As well as the predictable seasonal and cyclical changes we have seen, unexpected, one-off events can occur which cause sudden changes in the measures we are monitoring. For instance, in 1992, the Gulf War caused a massive drop in the number of American tourists visiting the UK. This seriously affected a whole range of travel and tourist-related industries. However, unpredictable events can also enhance measures; the death of a famous singer will inevitably increase the sales of his or her back catalogue. Figure 17.6 shows the negative effect on a positive trend of an unpredicted event.

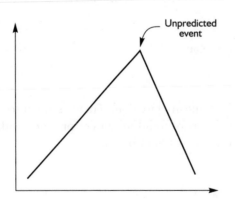

Figure 17.6   The effect of a negative, unpredicted event on a positive trend

You are launching a combined telephone/wrist watch into the UK market. What trend would you expect sales to follow?

Moving averages

The most common forecasting techniques use averaged data from the recent past to predict the near future. Averaging data has the benefit of smoothing out any small irregularities and thus increases the accuracy of the forecast.

Suppose we obtain the data shown in Table 17.1 on the number of weekly light bulb sales in the UK:

Table 17.1   Weekly light bulb sales in the UK over a five week period

Week number	Sales (number of units in 000s)
1	120
2	123
3	119
4	121
5	122

In this instance we will calculate moving averages based on the figure from weeks 1 to 4. This is called the four-week moving average and is commonly used although any period can be averaged. The forecast for week 5 is obtained by calculating the arithmetic mean for the preceeding four weeks (weeks 1 to 4):

$$\text{Forecast for week 5} = \frac{120 + 123 + 119 + 121}{4} = \frac{483}{4} = 120.75$$

As you can see, in this case the forecast was 1.25 less than the actual week 5 sales. This is known as forecast error. It is usual to experiment with different averaging periods to reduce the forecasting error. In this way the most accurate forecast can be made. Moving averages are only really going to be accurate where there is no substantial positive or negative trend present.

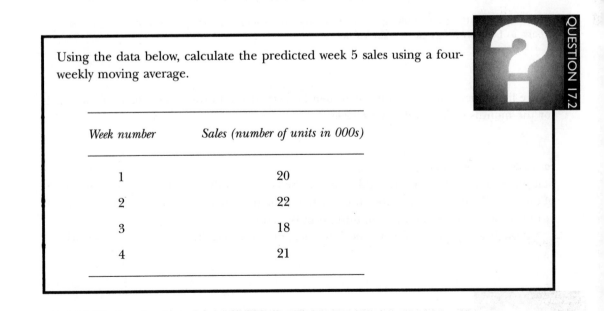

Using the data below, calculate the predicted week 5 sales using a four-weekly moving average.

Week number	Sales (number of units in 000s)
1	20
2	22
3	18
4	21

QUESTION 17.2

Forecasting with trends

When there is a trend in the data, a different forecasting technique is employed using linear regression. A full description of linear regression is outside the scope of this text but a straightforward graphical method called the 'line of best fit' will be explained.

Suppose we wish to predict the continuing upward trend in the number of passengers using the St. Albans to London Kings Cross train service. We have collated the following figures for the first part of 1995 and wish to predict the number of journeys in July and August 1995:

Month	Number of ticketed passenger journeys
January 1995	400,000
February 1995	400,100
March 1995	402,000
April 1995	401,500
May 1995	403,000
June 1995	403,300

To calculate the 'line of best fit' it is first necessary to draw a scattergram. This is a graph where each data point is represented individually.

Then, using your own judgement draw a straight line through the data points on the scattergram. Try to get as many points above the line as below it. A scattergram and 'line of best fit' for the train service data is shown in Figure 17.7.

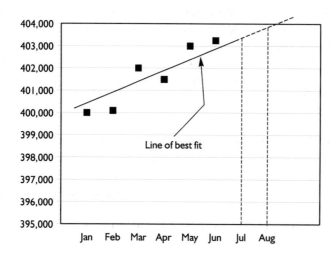

Figure 17.7 Scattergram showing number of ticketed passenger journeys per month on the St. Albans to London Kings Cross train service

The line which you have drawn can then be extended and the values read off the X axis for the months of July and August 1995.

Forecasting: a health warning!
Statistical methods for forecasting depend on the belief that the future is always an extension of the past. Of course, this is rarely the case but through judicial use of the statistical methods at our disposal we can aim to minimize forecast error.

Although forecasting will never be 100% accurate, it is usually better than guesswork!

If your organization undertakes any research, find out how the data is analysed. Better still, if you have access to any statistical computer software (many spreadsheet packages are capable of basic statistical analysis), try analysing, interpreting and forecasting from example data sets.

Z chart

This method is based on the moving average technique but is usually carried out for a year using monthly sales figures. They are done as follows:

- Moving annual sales are calculated by adding up the sum of the past twelve months at any one time.
- These are plotted on a graph with actual monthly sales. Cumulated sales are also calculated and added to the graph.

You will be able to see that part way through the year one look at the graph will give you a reasonable guess as to what the end of year figures will be as both the moving total line and the cumulative sales line will have to meet at year end.

Exponential smoothing

This is a computer technique which uses moving averages but is able to weight and use different parts of historical data according to how typical these are thought to be.

Causal techniques

leading indicators

Leading indicators are based on finding a correlation or relationship between the sales of the product and data such as population statistics and so on.

Simulation

This is a computer method which allows the marketer to play around with different variables so that a lot of different alternatives can be looked at.

Diffusion models

This method is used for new products as the other techniques are based on past sales data.

Using your own organization, find out what forecasting methods are used. Compare these with the methods used by your class colleagues.

ACTIVITY 17.1

Possible exam question

Briefly describe the methods used in micro forecasting.

QUESTION 17.3

In this unit you have covered the following forecasting methods:

1 Subjective methods:
    • Consumer/user survey methods.
    • Panels of executive opinion/jury method.
    • Salesforce composite.
    • Delphi method.
2 Combined methods:
    • Bayesian theory.
3 Objective statistical methods:
    • Time series.
        – Trends analysis
        – Moving averages
        – Z chart
        – Exponential smoothing.
    • Causal techniques.
        – leading indicators (correlation)
        – simulation
        – diffusion models.

Question 17.2

The forecast for week 5 sales is:

$$\frac{20 + 22 + 18 + 21}{4} = 20.25$$

Specimen exam questions and answer guidelines

Some of the answers have been produced as a short list of points the Examiners would expect to find within answers that were capable of attracting high marks. Others have been presented as answers.

With most of the questions there is no one best response, but a variety of viewpoints which could all be acceptable, providing they were reinforced by supporting evidence, cogent argument and relevant examples.

Look at the answers with a critical eye and think about how you could improve on them.

EXAM HINT

1 You will notice that some of the questions require a good deal of thinking about, others merely ask you to repeat what you can find in this book – the questions requiring memory will obviously be easier and quicker to do as you will not have to think about them in so much detail.
2 Make sure that you choose a question that will allow you to write a sufficient amount, that you plan and structure your work and that where asked, use a report-form style.
3 Attempt the full number of questions you have been asked to do, do not spend too much time on one answer.

Specimen exam paper 1   5 December 1995

Part A – Compulsory

You should read the following material and answer the questions beneath. The material is taken from *Marketing Strategy* by Paul Fifield (Butterworth-Heinemann, 1992, p. 110).

'Attitude research has been a popular academic pastime for over eighty years, with important work having been produced by people such as Fishbein, Festinger, Ajzen and others. Today, there is still nothing conclusive to show that attitude is linked to behaviour. Nevertheless this doesn't apparently stop many organizations spending millions and millions of pounds, dollars, francs or marks with advertising agencies world-wide in an attempt to change the attitudes of their customers. Even if we assume that advertising and the communication process is able to change attitudes (a separate area of research which is still current – and still inconclusive) what do we know about the effect that a change in attitude has on actual consumer behaviour, in other words, will a positive attitude lead to a purchase of our products and services? Certainly the research is able to show equally forcefully that a behaviour change creates an attitude change as well as the other way around. Now, you must understand that I am not out simply to knock advertising ... but it never fails to amaze me how much we can take simply on faith, especially in the more glamorous aspects of marketing such as advertising.'

Question 1

(a) To what extent do you agree with Fifield's views about the unreliability of the assumed link between attitudes and behaviour, and the possibility that behaviour change causes attitude change rather than the other way round? **(10 marks)**

(b) Imagine you report to the marketing director of an organization whose products or services are viewed with hostility by some sections of their potential market place. The marketing director wishes to win over at least some of these hostile people and groups, in order to turn them into customers; he has asked for your views on which of the following general strategies would be preferable:

Either

(i) Changing the attitudes of the currently hostile people and groups, in the hope that they would then purchase the products or services supplied by your organization;

Or

(ii) Changing their behaviour first in the expectation that modified attitudes would subsequently ensue.

Write a memo to your marketing director, outlining the arguments for and against each of the above options, followed by a reasoned statement of your own preferences.

(20 marks)

(c) How might you use (market) research techniques to enable you to choose sensibly between alternatives (i) and (ii) above? **(10 marks)**

Part B

In the exam you only have to answer THREE questions from the second part of the paper. Each answer is worth 20 marks.

Question 2

Write a report to your management team, discussing the merits and weaknesses of the statement (taken from a marketing text) that 'Several organizations appear to have pinned their hopes for future success on customer service and/or total quality Management; they believe that by offering more service and more quality, they will create competitive advantage and customers will flock to them.' Ensure that your report incorporates some recommendations appropriate to the future of customer service and/or TQM as sources of competitive advantage.

Question 3

Produce a systematic checklist showing the principles which should govern the construction of market segments. Illustrate your material with examples of segmentation systems relevant to various kinds of product/service and to various kinds of customers, both individual and organizational.

Question 4

Foxall has attacked consumer models for (a) their high level of abstraction, and (b) their inability to describe or predict actual consumer behaviour with accuracy. Produce a discussion document, as if targeted towards marketing colleagues, in which you assess the accuracy of Foxall's views and evaluate the degree to which the construction of consumer models can still be regarded as a worthwhile exercise.

Question 5

Imagine you have been asked to give a presentation on the ways in which customer behaviour and expectations may change over the next ten years. Outline your notes for this presentation, in which you propose to address three principal themes:

(a) Changes in the marketing for existing products and services.
(b) The appearance of new products and services.
(c) The disappearance of some products and services currently on offer.

Question 6

'The economic factors influencing the behaviour of people as customers' is the title of a chapter you have been asked to write as a contribution to a book of readings about consumer behaviour. Summarize the principal factors you would discuss in your chapter, and apply your material to any two of the following:

- Home improvements like the installation of a new kitchen, central heating or air conditioning.
- Purchase of a new car.
- Willingness to send children to private (fee-paying) schools.
- Acquisition of 'Old Masters' paintings.
- Consumption of instant coffee.

Question 7

If you were invited to give a talk to business studies undergraduates under the title, 'What Can Market Research Do? What Can't It Do?', what points would you make?

Question 8

Your Marketing Director believes that customers are selfish people motivated solely by self-interest. Write a memo in which you discuss the accuracy of this view in the light of your knowledge about motivation and theory.

Question 9

You have just read a newspaper article which is highly critical of many industrial/organizational buyers because they are too passive and simply react to the supplier's marketing mix. Compose a 'Letter to the Editor' in which you assess the accuracy of the criticism and identify the features of a more accurate model for industrial buying.

Question 10

Imagine that you are responsible for designing a marketing campaign to promote an entirely new music-and-video reproduction system which represents a complete departure from existing technology but which offers superb performance standards. Answer the following questions related to your task:

(a) Towards which segments of the population would your marketing efforts be principally targeted, and why? **(10 marks)**
(b) What methods of influence and persuasion would you recommend, in order to make it more likely that the product will be successful? **(10 marks)**

Answer 1(a)

NOTE: There are two parts to section (a) asking for comment on Fifield's views. You must first address the relationship between attitudes and behaviour and then the possibility of behaviour causing attitude change.

1   *The unreliability of the assumed link between attitudes and behaviour*

NOTE: This is covered in Unit 12.

You should include the following points, ordered similarly to the list set out below:

- Summarize Fifield's views on the relationship between attitude and behaviour as you understand them to be (taken from the quote).
- Explain why marketers are interested in predicting behavioural change.
- Present the simple model of how attitudes lead to behavioural change.
- Discuss why we might expect this link to be unclear due to intervening variables.
- Refer to an experiment, such as the Travelling Chinese Experiment by Richard LaPiere, by way of example.
- You may also refer to any other experiences you might have had which demonstrate the action of intervening variables.
- List the categories of intervening variables.
- Present the more complex model of the relationship between attitudes and behaviour showing the role of intervening variables.
- Discuss how some survey methods have been able to predict behaviour from attitudes more accurately by asking specific questions. You may refer to the specificity of measurement arguments put forward by Fishbein and Ajzen and the Birth Pill Experiment by Davidson and Jaccard.
- Return to Fifield's views and comment on them accordingly. You would probably wish to:
    - disagree with his fatalism;
    - accept that an imperfect relationship between attitudes and behaviour exists;
    - urge caution when interpreting research because of the presence of intervening variables;
    - highlight the importance of well-designed research methodologies and tools to reduce the impact of intervening variables.

2   *Possibility that behaviour change causes attitude change rather than the other way round*

NOTE: This is covered in Unit 15.

You should include the following points ordered similarly to the list set out below:

- Summarize Fifield's views on the subject (as presented in the quote)
- Describe that Cognitive Dissonance Theory (Festinger), a popular theory of attitude change does accept attitude change can arise out of a change in behaviour as does Attribution Theory.
- Briefly describe Cognitive Dissonance Theory.
- Describe in more detail post-purchase dissonance giving an example from your own experience or use the holiday example given in Unit 15. Explain the factors which affect the degree of dissonance experienced.
- Explain strategies a person uses to reduce dissonance. Note that a change of attitudes is one of these.
- Return to Fifield's views and comment on them accordingly. You would probably wish to:
    - accept that behaviour change can cause attitude change where dissonance occurs;
    - propose that this process is complimentary to the attitudes change behaviour view;

- suggest that such a mechanism is essential if attitudes are to be at all modifiable by behaviour and this is merely one way in which learning takes place;
- describe how dissonance theory can be used by marketers to good effect.

Answer 1(b)

NOTE: This is to be represented in a memo format giving the marketing director views on which general strategy to adopt to win over hostile but potential customers. It should be divided into sections giving for and against arguments for each option then a reasoned statement of your preference. The topics are covered in Units 12, 13, 14 and 15. The answer would also benefit from more wider reading, especially on Attribution Theory.

The structure of your answer should look something like this:

To: Marketing director
From:
Title: Strategies to win over hostile potential customers
Date:

Theory suggests that there are two possible general strategies for winning over hostile customers. These are:

- Trying to change the attitudes of the hostile group so that they are more favourably disposed towards our product/service and thus more likely to purchase.
- Modifying their behaviour first in the expectation that this will lead to modified attitudes.

The main sources of influence are:

- Personal experience
- Influence of family and friends
- Promotional methods such as direct marketing
- Advertising, public relations, sales promotions and personal selling

Personality factors also play a role. Certain personality types are more influenced by novel products, other personality types respond better to certain types of advertising than others.

These will now be discussed considering the pros and cons of each alternative.

NOTE: At this point you might wish to give an example of the sort of product/service that we might be dealing with to make explanation easier. An example might be the attempts of the nuclear electric companies to change the public's attitude to nuclear power for which a number of methods have/are being tried (advertising, literature, seminars, free tours around power plants, reasoned arguments and public debate).

Option 1: Changing the behaviour of a hostile group by changing their attitudes
The process of bringing about an attitude change is well understood. Pressure to change can arise from internal or external sources.

NOTE: At this point you could explain a bit more about the nature of attitudes and their component parts (beliefs and values as well as cognitive, affective and behavioural components, see Unit 12).

NOTE: You might also outline theories of behaviour-from-attitude change such as that of Hovland (Unit 14) and the elements involved in persuasive communication.

Strategies for behaviour-from-attitude change

The main behaviour-from-attitude change strategies are:

- Changing the consumer' basic motivations by making certain needs more prominent.
- Associating the product or service with an individual, group, object or event towards which the consumer has a positive attitude thus causing some of the positive feelings to 'rub off' on the product /service in question.
- Relating two conflicting attitudes – for example, offering a service which satisfies two, or more, previously held beliefs which the consumer thought were irreconcilable.
- Altering components of the multi-attribute model. Models of attitudes, such as that of Fishbein, provide an insight into how attitudes can be changed by manipulating the attributes of a product/service, the beliefs in the presence of these attributes and evaluation of these attributes.
- Changing consumer beliefs about competitors brands. It is also possible to use attitude models to change the perception of competitive products by manipulating the beliefs associated with them.

Advantages of behaviour-from-attitude change

This section should cover the following points:

- The mechanisms for attitude change are readily understood and accessible to investigation.
- Attitude change is generally thought to follow a pattern with easily identified stages.
- A number of models exist for explaining and predicting attitude change under changing circumstances (i.e. Fishbein).
- The use of attitude change is generally agreed to be an ethical way in our society of converting consumers to your point of view.
- Change can be achieved through a number of channels – through the influence of family and friends and promotional methods.

Disadvantages of behaviour-from-attitude change

This section should cover the following points:

- Behavioural changes do not always follow from attitude change due to the possibility of intervening variables.
- There are risks involved in certain strategies, such as changing beliefs about competitor products, which may 'backfire'.

Strategies for change

The main attitude-from-behaviour change strategies are based on two theories:

- Cognitive Dissonance Theory
- Attribution Theory

Each provides an explanation why behaviour might reasonably precede attitude change. Cognitive Dissonance Theory suggests that the doubts that follow a purchasing decision might initiate a change of attitudes in the purchaser to make these consonant with their actions. Attribution Theory focuses on how people assign causality to their actions. For example, if someone purchases and eats a banana they might reasonably infer that they like bananas. Main strategies include:

- Obtain a commitment to buy a product/service (this relates to the reduction of post-purchase dissonance).
- Reward existing customers to induce loyalty by reinforcing their purchasing decision (i.e. air miles).
- Foot-in-the-door technique where compliance to a small request (a demonstration or trial promotion for example) makes compliance to a larger request (i.e. a purchase) more likely.

- Attribution towards others – if a friend or colleague had purchased a product we might ask why? If we concluded that this was as a result of the benefits offered by the product then we would be more likely to purchase ourselves. If we thought it was most likely to have been as a result of, for example, their liking of gadgets, then we would be less likely to purchase.

Advantages of attitude-from-behaviour change

This section should cover the following points:

- Changing behaviour is a more direct way of assuring sales.
- Easier to measure than attitude-from-behaviour change.
- Provides more opportunity for face-to-face contact with potential customer which could increase the likelihood of persuading them.

Disadvantages of attitude-from-behaviour change

This section should cover the following points:

- Need to target customers more directly (direct marketing).
- Costs due to provision of demonstrations/samples might prove prohibitive.
- Might be seen as 'manipulation' of behaviour (ethical concerns).
- Could backfire as bad experience with product/service might reinforce customer hostility.

Statement of own preferences

This could cover the following points:

- Behaviour-from-attitude change is the most suitable strategy where potential customers would have had little experience of product/service.
- Behaviour-from-attitude change is a lower risk approach in terms of offending hostile customers further.
- Attitude-from-behaviour change strategies can be a useful complement once trial purchase, or actual purchase, has been made.
- It might be useful to do some direct marketing to hostile group to gauge effect.
- Behaviour-from-attitude change is likely to be less expensive as mass media could be used more effectively but monitoring of progress is likely to prove more expensive than with a targeted 'hostile' group.

NOTE: You would probably conclude by recommending a combination of approaches with behaviour-from-attitude strategies being followed by attitude-from-behaviour reinforcement using Cognitive Dissonance Theory. The conversion of previously 'hostile' customers might also convert other hostile individuals according to attribution theory (attribution towards others), especially if initially targeted hostile customers were opinion-formers.

Answer 1(c)

You are asked how market research techniques might be used to choose between two alternative general strategies.

NOTE: Refer to Unit 6.

Of course, exact research details would depend on the nature of the product/service in question and whether the immediate aim is simply to have fewer hostile potential customers or have more sales. That is, whether your dependent variable is a number of hostile customers (measured as attitudes) or sales. The former is outlined first.

The two alternatives could most easily be compared using an experimental approach. I would recommend a classical experimental design with one experimental group and one control group both consisting of hostile potential customers. You might also, more correctly, consider the use of a second control group of non-hostile (potential) customers to control more fully for external variables.

Dependent variable would be attitudes towards the product or service. Independent variable would be the change strategy. The hypothesis might be that attitude-from-behaviour techniques are less effective at changing attitudes than behaviour-from-attitude techniques.

The sample would be selected on the basis of an attitude questionnaire. If samples were small it would be prudent to match individuals, for age, gender etc., across groups.

Half the members of the experimental group would be exposed to behaviour-from-attitude change techniques, half would be exposed to attitude-from-behaviour change techniques.

Following exposure the attitudes of all the sample would again be measured. This would determine whether, or not, attitudes had been changed. Comparison with the control group(s) would determine whether any outside influences had had any effect on the dependent variable which could confound the results.

I would favour use of the Semantic Differential technique for attitude measurement which would make comparisons of attitudes between groups easier through the use of profiling.

Of course, identifying a change in attitude might not convert into a long-term change in behaviour. For this a follow-up survey would need to be undertaken (a time series design, perhaps) where purchasing behaviour (perhaps sales) was used as the dependent variable.

Answer 2

To:
From:
Title:
Date:

Terms of reference
This report explains the main framework of TQM, shows how the organization can benefit from taking on the practices involved in setting up a Total Quality Management system and provides the organization with recommendations that will lead towards us maintaining a competitive advantage.

Introduction
The central factor in Japanese business success has been their ability to produce high quality goods that are closely tuned to the requirements of the market. In a study carried out by the Profit Impact of Market Strategy (PIMS) programme the single most important factor affecting the performance of a business was the quality of its goods and services.

The importance of quality has been reflected in the growth of TQM.

Summary
The core of TQM is the customer–supplier relationship, where the process must be managed. The 'soft' outcomes of TQM – the culture, communications and commitment – provide the foundations of the TQM model. The process core must be surrounded by the 'hard' management necessities of systems, tools and teams.

In order to achieve this, attitudes to work and skills have to be changed so that the culture of the organization becomes one of preventing failure – doing the right things, right first time, every time.

Total Quality Management means achieving total quality through management's ability in gaining everyone's commitment and involvement and a continual effort is made towards improvement. This will result in a reduction of total costs as waste is avoided by eliminating errors, and value is added to what is being produced because actions are carried out which add value to the production process.

TQM involves training people to understand customer–supplier relationships, not buying on price alone, managing systems improvement, modern supervision and training, managing processes through teamwork and improved communication, elimination of barriers and fear, constant education and expert development and a systematic approach to TQM implementation.

It is the opinion of the writer that an overall approach to TQM can help an organization maintain a competitive advantage but the main difficulties would lie in creating a fundamental change in the way the people within the organization carry out their work.

Description of TQM

The main pillars of TQM are:

1 The foundation framework
    1.1 a customer focus
    1.2 quality chains
    1.3 quality design and conformance to design
    1.4 process understanding
    1.5 working together with suppliers and customers
    1.6 leadership and commitment to TQM
    1.7 empowerment
    1.8 marketing
2 A quality system
3 The tools and the improvement cycle
4 The organisation and team work
5 The implementation

The foundation framework

The foundation framework consists of:

1.1 A customer focus – an emphasis on customer requirements

The concept of TQM is very simple. Each part of the organization has its customers, whether internal or external to the organization. The need to identify what customer requirements are and then set about meeting them reliably on an ongoing basis forms the core of a total quality approach. TQM offers the organization an opportunity to change itself and modify its work practices accordingly and make them customer focused.

In TQM standards are set from the customer's point of view. The emphasis on what customers' expect, want and/or need in relation to what competitors offer helps to ensure that the focus is put on to the customer, not the producer of the product/service. The external focus ensures that quality is related to the requirements of each market segment which may or may not be the same.

Recommendations

That we set our standards from the customer's point of view and the emphasis is on what customers' expect, want and/or need in relation to what competitors offer. The external focus will ensure that quality is related to the requirements of each market segment which may or may not be the same.

This practice will ensure that the focus is put on to the customer, not what our design and production department think they should have.

1.2 Quality chains

The identification of supply chains or so-called quality chains is a key process in establishing TQM. Each department and person should be able to tell where they are in the chain. This is important because people have to agree with the other person what their requirements are. These requirements are often formalized into a customer service agreement.

Suppliers → inputs → process → output → customers

Recommendations

That we create customer service agreements that take into account both the tangible and intangible aspects of the service. These are:

- tangible task elements – quantity, reliability, on-time delivery, quality, presentation, cleanliness, etc.
- intangible behavioural aspects – attitude, professionalism, willingness, promptness, flexibility, courtesy, honesty, reliability, etc.

The identification of the supply chains is the beginning of the whole process of looking at inputs and outputs, mapping processes that improve work-flow and response times and should improve the working relationships both internally and externally.

1.3   Quality design and conformance to design

There are two distinct and interrelated aspects of quality-design and conformance to design:

- Quality of design is a measure of how well the product or service is designed to meet the agreed requirements.
- Quality of conformance to design is the extent to which the product or service achieves the design.

Recommendations

That we investigate these two aspects to ensure that what we intend to achieve is actually achieved and that more importantly our customers think so as well.

1.4   Process understanding

This requires an understanding, design and control of the process by which goods and services are produced and delivered to customers. Processes should be managed through a strategy of prevention, rather than detection of error.

Recommendation

That we investigate all our own processes, a strategy of prevention rather than detection will lower our costs and ensure customer satisfaction.

1.5   Working with suppliers and customers

Involving people and understanding that all employees of an organization have a role to play and this includes employees working for suppliers and distributors.

The way in which business is carried out with suppliers and customers is changed. Suppliers should be treated as part of the organization's supply chain. This means becoming more open with them about our business planning.

Recommendations

That we no longer treat suppliers as adversaries that we have to beat down on price – there are other ways of measuring a satisfactory relationship. This should enable us to develop better relationships in the long term.

Similarly, involving our employees more in the overall strategic objectives of the organization and showing them that the roles they take directly helps us in achieving greater customer satisfaction, should also additionally lead to greater job satisfaction.

1.6   Leadership and commitment to TQM

TQM must start at the top where a serious commitment to quality must be shown. Middle management have also a key role in communicating the message so that each individual at each level is involved. The culture of an organization is formed by the beliefs, behaviours, norms, values, rules and the climate of the organization. Leadership style is an influencing factor.

Recommendations

That managers develop an appropriate vision which will consist of the organization's guiding philosophy, core values and beliefs, a purpose and mission.

1.7   Empowerment

TQM is concerned with moving the focus of control from outside the individual to within. It is based on the understanding that quality cannot be imposed from the outside, as perhaps can a standard or statistical process control, but needs to come from the individual's control over the standards over their own work.

Recommendations

That the organization changes its culture and enables employees to modify the ways in which they take up their roles and move towards common goals and objectives. Individuals need to move the focus of control from outside to within themselves, so that everyone is accountable for their own performance and adopt a right-first-time philosophy.

1.8 The role of marketing

The TQM process starts with marketing and forms part of the foundation framework. Marketing must take the true lead in establishing the true requirements of a product or service.

Recommendation

This must be communicated properly throughout the organization in the form of a specification. It also calls for market research and the ongoing assessment of customer satisfaction.

2 The role of the quality system

To the foundation framework of the customer–supplier chain, processes and 'soft' outcomes of TQM, must be added the first hard management necessity – a quality system based on a good international standard. The International Standards Organisation (ISO) 9000 series sets out methods by which a system can be implemented to ensure that specific requirements are met.

Recommendation

That we attain this standard.

3 The tools and the improvement cycle

- Measurement
  Measures, typically non-financial, are used in process control and performance improvement.
- Bench-marking
  Bench-marking measures an organization's operations, products and services against those of its competitors.

Recommendations

That we look at bench-marking and other assessment methods to ensure our effectiveness in all areas.

4 The organization and team work

Recommendations

We need to organize for quality. The only point at which true responsibility can lie is with the person or group actually doing the job. There must be a clear allocation of responsibilities within the management structure, particularly at the levels of senior executive and first-line supervision.

We need to tackle process improvements and complex problems through teamwork.

5 Implementation

Recommendations

We need to communicate the quality message through training, people must know when and how they will be involved in the TQM process, what the process is, and the success and benefits achieved

We need to look at open methods of communication and participation must take place at all levels. Barriers need to be broken down by concentrating on process rather than departmental issues. Training needs to be looked at as one of the most important factors in improving quality.

Answer 3

Note: Read Unit 3 on Segmentation, the answer is there.

Answer 4

NOTE: Refer to Unit 13. In addition to the answer given for this question it would be helpful to include an example based on a simple model to illustrate some of the benefits. You would not be expected to reproduce any of the complex models in detail.

Answer 5

Introduction

Culture is dynamic and as it changes marketers must be aware of changes in society. If and when people change their ideas of who they are, the social and political culture will change as well and there will be a demand for different goods/services and the marketing techniques across a whole range of dimensions will have to change as well. This presentation covers a few of the major issues, namely, excessive materialism, environmentalism and new technology, that are likely to impact on us in the next ten years.

1 Excessive Materialism

Materialism in general (also referred to as consumerism), and American materialism has been criticized for a number of years. It has also been linked to the excessive use of energy and the pollution resulting from it.

The desire to manage world resources is becoming increasingly integrated and improving the human condition is a common link among all people. Consumerism in the more developed countries is likely to become even more of an issue, especially when Third World countries in order to improve their own living standards and mimic western lifestyles pollute the world environment even more. Asking them to change without changing our own lifestyles is not a possibility. Organizations all over the world will need to confront the crisis in culture and consciousness and break the hypnosis of consumerism.

Reasons why consumers may move to an anti materialistic position:

- They are concerned enough with the polluting effects of industry to take on a less visible and affluent lifestyle.
- They become educated enough to understand the symbolic nature of goods – there is already evidence that goods are judged more on their functional value when income drops.
- The expression and search for meaning is no longer focused on consumer goods but expresses itself through religion, art and creative expression, music, literature theatre and in relationships with people and the natural environment.
- It is felt that some types of advertising cause us to live in ways that are unsuited to our individual natures and creates a psychic imbalance encouraging us to live in ways unsuited to our individual natures.
- People eventually understand that increased consumption does not create happiness.

The lifestyle analyses outlined by VALS and Kotler point to different groups of people who have different concerns.

2 Technology

Kotler (1988) says that products are produced and marketed to meet some underlying need of an individual; the way in which this need is met will depend on the current level of technology. However, new technology will come along and meet the needs in a superior way. He uses demand-technology life cycle to illustrate his point. Each demand-technology life cycle will have a history of emergence, rapid growth, slower growth, maturity and decline but over a shorter period than the more sustainable demand cycle.

Changes in technology have an impact on:

- the environment
- the types of product that are marketed
- methods of production
- the type of work that is done
- the way in which that work is carried out
- the way in which human resources are deployed
- techniques used for marketing
- consumers and society in general

A simple example:

The contraceptive pill has led to smaller families, an increase in the number of working wives, less time, higher levels of discretionary income, convenience foods, time-saving durables and so on. It could also be linked to the higher divorce rate as women with fewer children are less likely to be dependent on men for their support.

3 Environmental consciousness

Many opinion surveys show a clear growth of environmental consciousness among the public. In the UK this has been substantiated by research carried out by Market and Opinion Research International (MORI).

Environmental consciousness is an element of the individual's belief system and is part of the social consciousness which is in itself a complex system of values and attitudes. Environmental consciousness would therefore have cognitive, affective and conative components.

However, the results of surveys only show a change of values on a global level but these are not always reflected in consumer purchase behaviour. It is believed by Dembowski and Hanmer-Lloyd (*Journal of Marketing Management,* Oct. 1994) that at the moment consumers do not translate their conviction into actual purchase behaviour but the increased awareness may be causing people to re-evaluate values within their belief system. New judgements, for example, about environmental compatibility occur only after the consumer has developed an awareness of the inconsistency between values and product choice criteria.

Change is being driven by law makers in Brussels and our own Parliament, by environmental standards, by pressure groups and consumer demand. Protection of the environment requires a corporate response that will affect all areas of a firm's activities.

Examples

These following examples will give you some ideas on how these moves in customer behaviour and expectations are being acted upon by some organizations:

(a) Changes in the marketing for existing products and services:

- Hoover have been awarded the European Commission ecolabel. The award is for three of its New Wave washing machines. They use 31% less water, 40% less energy, 36% less detergent.
- 3M Co. devoted 15% of its $1 billion R&D budget to environmental research and their product developers are considering certain environmental standards as part of a broader green marketing strategy.

(b) The appearance of new products and services:

- Several athletic shoe manufacturers have been touting the use of recycled material in their shoes.
- Changes in office technology will make the truly personal mobile office feasible.
- The family car will still exist but new materials and new manufacturing techniques will mean that every car can be different, with the driver effectively able to design a customized car.

(c) The disappearance of some products and services currently on offer:

- Echikson writing in *Fortune* (January 1995) said that luxury items were beginning to experience a rebound. Ostentation is out but understated quality has replaced designer exhibitionism. He claims that family-owned boutiques, like Gucci, are out and that status now resides in enduring value and utility. 'In' products include microwave-safe porcelain, manual or sports watches and classic suits.

NOTE: It is imperative that students keep a file on up-to-date examples that they can use to illustrate answers to questions like the above.

Answer 6

NOTE: Structure your answer along the following lines and refer to Unit 8. Choose two of the topics listed on p. 275 and use them as examples.

- The economist's view of human behaviour
- The price system
- Factors affecting pricing decisions
- Opportunity cost
- How consumers think about price and value and how they go about maximizing utility
- Consumer perceptions of price and value
- Marginal utility
- The law of diminishing marginal utility
- Equi-marginal utility
- Consumer behaviour and rises in income
- Economic factors that influence behaviour
- Demand and the price of the good
- The price of other goods
- The household income
- The income distribution of households
- Other factors that would influence demand

Answer 7

NOTE: There is obviously quite a lot of personal opinion that could go into the answer of this question. Your answer would certainly benefit from being well illustrated with examples, case studies etc. from your own personal experience or based on success stories you have read about (perhaps from *Marketing Week* and other such news sources). The answer asks for 'points' and it would be legitimate to list bullet points much as might be used for OHP overheads. Remember your target audience.

Outline the scope of market research by way of an introduction to the various techniques available
Market research is a process by which information is gathered from either secondary sources (secondary research) or by direct investigation (primary research). A range of secondary sources are available:

- Government statistics
- Popular media
- Technical or specialist publications
- On-line and electronic databases
- Third party data
- Causal research

The main primary research techniques can be divided in qualitative and quantitative methods. These can be further categorized into:

- Qualitative: depth interviews, focus groups and projective techniques
- Quantitative techniques: observation, experimentation and surveys

Main theme:

A good main theme would be the idea that market research is not magic. It is merely a process and set of tools for collecting, analysing and interpreting data. The quality of any decisions ultimately rests on the quality of the data. At this point you could outline the primary and secondary market research process (Unit 4).

What can market research do?

First focus on the sort of information that market research can provide and then how that information can be used to inform business decisions.

Information that market research can provide:

- Qualitative data about customer motivations, ideas, perceptions, culture, reactions and so on.
- Quantitative data concerning just about anything about the market place and customers that can be measured: sales, attitudes, satisfaction, economic indicators and so on.

This can be used to inform a range of business decisions. Examples of questions that research could answer would include:

Strategic decisions:
- Should we enter a market?
- Should we withdraw from a market?
- Which distribution channels are appropriate?

Provision of information about the market
- Where do our products/services stand in the market?
- Identifying target market segments and appropriate appeals
- What packaging/pack design to use?
- What price to charge for my product?
- Competitive intelligence (pricing, market share)
- What different market segments exist and how do they differ?

Information for new or variant product development:
- What differing needs, motives, satisfactions would a new product need to satisfy?
- Generation of ideas for new product development
- Which of a range of product ideas should I develop further?
- Developing product attributes, design and formulation
- What name to choose for a new product?

Information about effectiveness of advertising/promotions:
- Who should advertising be aimed at?
- What should the message of the advertising be?
- How much should be spent on advertising?
- Which media should be used?
- Has our advertising/promotion worked?

Market research is also able to provide information about the internal workings of the organization in question (i.e. sales, distribution etc.)

What can't market research do?

Most importantly, stress that market research cannot give the right answers to wrong questions. A certain amount of understanding of the problem is therefore required before quality research is initiated. If the research objectives are not given proper thought then the research will not address your questions.

The quality of the data can also be a limiting factor. Data that is not valid or reliable cannot form the basis for accurate decision-making. The quality of data depends on using the correct research methodology and the correct data collection tools.

Market Research is not infallible for several reasons:

- Bias can creep into the research process at a number of points: sampling, data collection, and interpretation. This can be intentional or unintentional.
- The skill of the market researcher may limit interpretation of the data.
- The market place can change, rendering any previously collected data worthless.
- It cannot be expected to predict performance where the market has no prior experience (e.g. no data is available).

Conclusion

A good conclusion would be to say that market research is not a panacea to solving all business problems but that, correctly used, it will lead to better quality decisions being made and leave less to chance.

Answer 8

NOTE: This material is covered in Unit 12.

To: Marketing Director
From:
Title: Are customers selfish people motivated only by self-interest?
Date:

At a basic level I would certainly agree with your view that customers are selfish people motivated, at least partly, by self-interest. Indeed no-one could disagree that if a customer is thirsty their thoughts would turn to obtaining a drink. However, this an over-simplification of what actually happens and not an entirely useful one at that (from a marketing point of view).

What we want to know is why, when a customer is thirsty, do they seek out a Pepsi and not a Coca-Cola, or why a coffee and not a glass of orange juice. Also, what premium would they put on promptly satisfying this need (how much extra would they be willing to pay) and how do they trade-off different motivations (say, for example, the need to drink against the need to be seen to be drinking the 'right sort' of drink).

Motivation theory is useful because it provides a framework within which we can discuss, understand and address these issues (and more).

Motivation theories talk about:

- needs – basic human requirements
- drives – how these needs translate into behaviours
- goals – what these behaviour aim to achieve

At the root of all motivation theories is, indeed, a cycle of need, action and satisfaction. But this is quite discriminatory. According to Hull, the act of reducing a drive reinforces the reducing behaviour making it more likely that behaviour will be used again. So this perhaps partly explains why a customer will return to a favoured thirst-quenching drink. This can help us locate outlets for products and services.

Similarly, behaviours can act as negative motivators. We learn once that salty things make us thirsty so we avoid them at times of thirst.

Needs fall into three broad categories:

- Physiological (or primary) needs – these are the needs that sustain life. They include the need for food, air, sex and self-preservation. These are the needs that we are born with and are generally activated by deprivation of the need concerned, i.e. we drink when we are thirsty.
- Psychological needs – these are the needs that relate to our competence to deal effectively with the outside environment, often termed personal competence. It is said to be intrinsically rewarding and relates to our need to understand, predict and control our

world using mechanisms such as exploration and curiosity. It is generally accepted that we are also born with these needs and that they are less easy to satisfy than the physiological needs in that they tend to persist. For example, there is no easy way to totally satisfy a desire for knowledge.

- Learned (secondary or cultural) needs – we have already seen the influence that culture can have on an individual's behaviour. Learned needs are those needs which arise as a result of our socialization. As the name suggests, they are learned and are dependent on the culture we grow up in. Some cultures value power and status, others humility and a structured life. These are all learned needs.

These different categories of needs are related in complex ways. For example, the food a consumer purchases (a primary need) will depend on secondary needs. If you are hungry at breakfast time in the UK, you are most likely to eat cereal and toast. In the US you may well satisfy your hunger by eating pancakes or even sweet cake – the culturally acceptable breakfast foods in that country. In addition, psychological needs may play a part – does the food look palatable, pleasant and well presented?

Similarly goals can vary in their specificity. As marketers this can help us decide how our products should be branded to take advantage of goal specificity, or lack of it. Milk, for example, has no strong brand image. It is unlikely that a thirsty customer will hold out for a specific brand of milk to quench their thirst. Yet this is what can, and does, occur with branded colas and with many other product types.

As you can see from these examples, the choice of goal to satisfy a particular need is not solely made as a result of pure self-interest but can arise as a result of a number of factors, which may all interact in complex ways. These are:

- Personal experience. If a particular goal has satisfied a need in the past then it is more likely to be selected again. As we have seen with Hull's Drive Reduction Model, the success of a goal in satisfying a need actually reinforces its use again. For example, if a particular washing powder has been successful in cleaning our clothes we are more likely to buy that same washing powder in the future.
- Cultural norms and values. We have seen in the previous unit how cultural norms and values affect behaviour. To give an example, it may be that we shun the purchase of a new washing machine liquid (as opposed to powder) because using such a product is not the 'done thing' in our culture. Of course, as we have seen, culture does change and adapt but usually on an extended timescale.
- Personal norms and values. Our own personal norms and values, possibly religious or ethical, can also affect the goals we select for the achievement of a particular need. For example, if we are 'green minded' we might choose to select an environmentally friendly washing powder or hold out for a vegetarian meal.
- Physical and/or intellectual capacity. It might be some goals are unachievable due to our own personal limitations. Suppose we want to own a cat but are allergic to fur. Our need for companionship must find an alternative goal. Perhaps we will select a parrot instead!
- Accessibility of goal. It may be that the goal we select is determined on the basis of accessibility. We may wish, for example, to go to a particular play but the distance of the theatre precludes us going. We may, instead, select a more local venue.

In marketing a product or service we would need to be aware of all these factors as well as any underlying self-interest.

Maslow's theory

It is worth looking at the applications in marketing of one of the more popular motivation theories; Maslow's hierarchy of needs which categorizes human needs in to five groups: physiological, safety, social, esteem, self-actualization. These are arranged in a pyramid-shaped hierarchy with physiological needs at the base and self-actualization needs at the apex.

Maslow's theory implies that motivation is cyclical in nature. As soon as one group of needs is fulfilled, other drives predominate. The most basic needs are those at the bottom of the pyramid. For example, a person that has fulfilled the need for shelter (by finding somewhere to live), will only then start to think about satisfying the higher order social and esteem needs.

As a theory, Maslow's hierarchy of needs has proved useful in applying a more behaviour-orientated structure to the market. As such, it has found use in market segmentation and brand/product positioning.

Each product/service has a 'natural' needs category which it addresses. Most products only actually address the very basic physiological and safety needs. For example, all the foodstuffs sold actually only address our physiological need for sustenance. However, it is possible to position products to appeal to just about any needs category which broadens the appeal and can be used to create a brand image. As an example, BT adverts appeal to a social need by encouraging you to keep in touch with absent friends and relatives.

Maslow's needs categories can also be used to segment a market. For example, safety needs might appeal to several groups such as families worried about the safety of their young children or wealthy people concerned about house security.

In summary, I hope I have outlined my concerns about your view that customers are merely selfish people motivated by self-interest. Human behaviour is, in fact, a lot more complex that this. By understanding more about the way in which consumers are motivated we can undoubtedly create more effective marketing strategies.

Answer 9

NOTE: Material to answer this question is contained in Units 1 and 13.

For publication

Dear Editor,

I write with respect to an article which appeared in yesterday's edition of your newspaper ('*Buyers are too passive*' date) and wish to comment on its content which criticized many industrial/organizational buyers for their passivity.

I would first, though, like to welcome your coverage of industrial/organizational buying behaviour. This subject is often overlooked in favour of 'end user' buying behaviour forgetting than many companies sell their products, not direct to consumers, but to other companies.

Now I will turn to commenting on the contents of your piece.

I am of the opinion that your vision of the role of an industrial/organizational buyer is perhaps that of an outsider or at least someone with more experience of consumer buying situations. A buyer (or buying department, more accurately) in a large organization must juggle many balls in the air and has many masters. Whilst this may, from the outside, be viewed as a certain passivity to external influences, this is far from the truth.

Buying in a large organization requires the involvement of several departments; purchasing agents, production management and quality control staff. Each of these may have different expectations of the product being purchased depending on the their role within the organizational decision-making unit (DMU). Some might be more interested in delivery, another performance, the third price and quality.

Typically, an organizational DMU consists of a number of roles: gatekeeper, initiators, influencers, deciders, users and financiers as well as buyers. In fact, it is rarely the buyer that makes the purchasing decision. They only make the actual purchase.

Each may be working with different information sources (verbal information from the supplier, specifications, literature, trade magazine reviews). They may also have very different backgrounds, past experiences of a range of products and may well, because of this, interpret any product information in very different ways.

These are just some of the differences between consumer and industrial/organizational buyer relationships with suppliers which make comparisons difficult:

- Many buyers prefer to deal with suppliers who can offer complete systems.
- Large organizations have enormous buying power which naturally means they enjoy more attention from suppliers.
- The buying process is more formal, requiring that buyer and supplier spend more time together reporting, completing contracts and so on.
- There is more likely to be a buyer–supplier dependency link.
- There are several types of buying situations, each requiring different levels of involvement between buyer and supplier.

Of course, I have not even covered the influence on both buyer and supplier of the macro-environment (the so-called PEST factors) which requires the on-going relationship to be reviewed on a regular basis.

There are several well-known organization buying models that show how each of these elements I have mentioned integrate together to determine the buying process. I am reminded of the Sheth model and that of the American Marketing Association. The former focuses more on the buying process, the latter on the influences and main players which affect this process.

In summary, I believe that you have misinterpreted the role of the organizational/industrial buyer in the buying process and in so doing took their role, in relation to suppliers, to be a passive one. Nothing could be further from the truth.

Answer 10(a)   Segments of the population that would be targeted

NOTE: Refer to Unit 14.

I would consider targeting the marketing campaign at several segments of the population. My reasoning is as follows.

1   Innovators and early adopters
The novel nature of the music-and-video system would suggest that it might appeal to innovators and early adopters. These two groups are the first to adopt any new innovation. Together these comprise about 16% of the population. The area of research into how novel products are accepted into the market place is known as the diffusion of innovation.

Innovators (2.5%) are characterized as being risk-takers, more adventurous, having a high spending power, and subscribing to a wide range of publications.

Early adopters (13.5%) are characterized as being a group with a high proportion of opinion leaders, of above average education, they tend to be younger than later adopters, are well-respected and have the greatest contact with sales people.

The problem with segmenting by these groups is that their definition is often circular. That is, who will be an 'innovator' for a particular product only becomes obvious once they have bought it! Having said that, they have been found to share certain personality traits, consumption characteristics, media habits, social and demographic characteristics which would make segmentation possible. For example, innovators tend to be younger, more open-minded, of a higher income and social class, less brand loyal, and more magazine than TV oriented than non-innovators.

Of course, given that a large proportion of innovators/early adopters are opinion leaders then this would assist in the diffusion of innovation throughout the market place. Many more cautious customers are known to take their advice from, and be led in their purchasing decisions by, opinion leaders.

2   Previous purchasers of audio-visual technology (especially quality products)
Research shows that people who have already innovated within a particular product category are likely to do so again. Thus I would include in the target segment(s) those members of the population that were the first to purchase other audio-visual innovations.

As noted, this group may include many general market place innovators but might also include individuals with a very specific interest in audio-visual technology, particularly products with high performance standards.

To narrow down this group I would focus on those individuals that had previously purchased an innovation in a related product group. I would not consider the development of a music-and-video reproduction system as a discontinuous innovation but more one product in a line of dynamically continuous innovations arising from the colour television and video cassette recorder. It would thus make sense to target individuals would had previously bought products such as:

- CD players
- Digital audio tape
- Pocket TVs
- Interactive video

3 Other segments

Casting the net more widely, if this was required, I would start to look at the more general segmentation bases:

- Geographic techniques
- Geodemographic
- Demographic
- Behaviour in the product field
- Psychographic

4 Geographic segmentation

This question doesn't specify whether the product is to be marketed in the UK only. If not, geographic techniques may be important in determining which overseas markets are likely to be suitable. The marketing mix would certainly have to change to take into account the different markets.

I would anticipate that some cultures would be more accepting of new technologies than others. For example, the Japanese are known for their rapid adoption of new innovations.

5 Geodemographic techniques

I would consider using one of the geodemographic classifications to assist in identifying potential target segments. For example, the ACORN profiling system. I would anticipate that some of the types within category C (rising) might be interested in an audio-visual product given that this group contains prosperous academics, affluent city areas, and many young wealthy individuals.

6 Demographic

Given the comments made earlier on the demographic characteristics of innovators, I would expect to target young, wealthy individuals in professional positions. This would put them in social classes A B or C1.

In terms of family life style, I would tend to target the younger and older 'empty nests'.

7 Behaviour in the product field

Segmentation would most likely be based on innovation adoption as explained earlier, although one could look at attitudes to new technology, benefit segmentation and purchase occasion.

One might also decide to look at people with a specific interest in certain sectors of the audio-visual market where high performance standards are paramount (perhaps thirty-something rock fans and classical music lovers)

8 Psychographic

Further work would have to be done to segment to audio-visual market place. It would certainly be useful to categorize buyers in this field, as has been done with motorists.

I would certainly consider the possibility of using lifestyle analysis or adopt one of the classification systems that already exist (Young and Rubicam 4C's, Monitor (Taylor Nelson AGB), Stanford Research Institute's Life Ways).

Answer 10(b) Methods of influence and persuasion

NOTE: Refer to Unit 14.

1 Persuasive communication

A basic communication model is set out below.

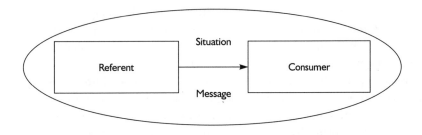

The persuasiveness of the communication can be affected by the characteristics of all those elements:

- Referent – known as the source of the communication, usually a person or written word that is trying to persuade.
- Message – the content of the communication (i.e. advert).
- Consumer – known as the recipient of the communication, the person who is being persuaded.
- Situation – the immediate context within which the communication is taking place.

Once the consumers have been targeted, only the referent, message and situation are under the control of the marketer, although knowledge of consumer characteristics can help with development of the message.

There are a number of standard persuasion techniques that are used. These are briefly described below. Obviously, their applicability depends on the media used to convey the marketing message.

2 Referent

The following characteristics of the source affect its persuasiveness:

- **Status and credibility** – if the source is perceived as an expert then it is more persuasive. Thus reviews of the audio-visual system in a 'reputable' magazine are more likely to be believed, as are endorsements from professionals in the topic being communicated (once might consider using mature rock stars, classical musicians etc. for this purpose). As we have already seen, certain sources are perceived as opinion leaders. By definition, they are more likely to be persuasive. The characteristics already attributed to opinion leader apply equally well to all sources.
- **Attractiveness** – the more attractive, charming, humorous, the source the more persuasive (generally) they are likely to be. Of course, these characteristics are as perceived by the recipient.
- **Trustworthiness** – the more trustworthy the source is perceived to be the more persuasive that source is. The trustworthiness is assessed on the basis of the perceived intentions and motives of the source. For instance, recipients are more likely to be persuaded if the message was overheard (no intent is thus assumed), or to be contrary to the source's best interests.
- **Non-verbal behaviour** – Non-verbal behaviour relates to trust. A 'shifty' disposition, for instance, does not instil trust. One aspect of non-verbal communication which has been extensively covered is that of social distance – the distance of the source from the recipient. This is important in direct selling.
- **Similarity with recipient** – if the source is perceived as being of a similar culture and social status as the recipient, then this can increase the persuasive power of the message.

3 The message

The following characteristics of the message affect its persuasiveness:

- **Non-verbal aspects**   Face-to-face communication is more effective than mass media. In this situation the source can react to the recipient (via eye contact, body posture etc.) and is thus able to anticipate and modify the message accordingly. The confidence with which the message is presented is also important.
- **Implicit or explicit**   This is concerned with whether the recipient is left to draw their own conclusion from the information provided (implicit) or presented with a conclusion by the source (explicit). Implicit messages would probably be most effective for the segments being considered for the audio-visual system.
- **Emotional appeal**   It seems that emotions, such as fear, humour, sympathy and, of course, sex can be used to increase the persuasiveness of a communication. One might consider using these elements to increase appeal.
- **One-sided versus two-sided arguments**   Whether a communication should make any reference to the competition (two-sided communication) seems to depend on the recipient. Putting both sides of the argument is more effective when dealing with educated people (such as our target group) although mass media advertising which mentions the competition is not generally acceptable to UK consumers (but might prove more effective in the US, for instance).
- **Primacy – Recency**   The order in which information is presented can affect its persuasiveness. The most obvious example of this effect is in television advertising. The first and last slots in an advert break are the most sought after as research has shown that they are more likely to be remembered. If our advertising budget stretched to booking these slots we might wish to consider this. There is an interaction between the use of two-sided arguments and the primacy–recency effect which we would need to be aware of.
- **Repetition**   Surprisingly little research has been done in the area of message repetition but it is a matter of common experience that a message repeated many times is more likely to be remembered and thus could lead to a change in buying behaviour. Of course, excess repetition can lead to habituation and this can be avoided by variations in the timing and methods of message presentation.

4 Situations

The following aspects of the situation affect the effectiveness of the persuasive communication. When advertising through the mass media, these aspects of the communication process are not likely to be amenable.

- **Informal situations**   It is easier to persuade in informal settings.
- **Small groups**   People are more likely to be persuaded if they are part of a small group that already shares these norms and values – certain small, primary groups (see below).

5 Other methods

I would also consider the use of 'persuasion' techniques based on Cognitive Dissonance Theory:

- Try and buy schemes.
- Anticipating and addressing dissonance in the advertising message.
- Anticipating and addressing dissonance in the product branding.

6 Group Influence

Groups exert a strong influence on consumer behaviour which is worth considering separately. In particular, it would be important to consider the role that reference groups might play in increasing the likelihood of successfully marketing the product.

The main consumer reference groups are:

- Family
- Peer groups

- Consumer or lobbying groups
- Work groups

The influence that these groups can exert on an individual is used in a variety of ways to market products. Three general approaches are:

- Aspirational appeal – present the product in a situation, or using a celebrity or type of person to whom the consumer aspires.
- Peer appeal – present the product by a person to whom the consumer can relate.
- Expert appeal – have the product endorsed by an expert in the audio-visual field.

Specimen exam paper 2   June 1997

Certificate in Marketing

Certificate in Sales Management

Understanding Customers   3 Hours' Duration

This examination is in two sections.

Part A is compulsory and worth 40 per cent of the total marks.

Part B has six questions, select three. Each answer will be worth 20 per cent of the total marks.

DO NOT repeat the question in your answer but show clearly the number of the question attempted on appropriate pages of the answer book.

Rough workings should be included in the answer book and ruled through after use.

PART A

You should read the following material and answer the questions. The extracts are taken from Colin Egan, *Creating Organisational Advantage* (Butterworth-Heinemann, 1995), p. 29.

The strategic management literature leaves a yawning gap in its discussion of markets by virtue of the lip service it pays to the role of consumer preference. . . . The consumer role is a powerful one, a power base greatly enhanced in an environment characterized by unfettered international trade and its consequences: globalization and excess supply. A point which must be grasped is that, given choice, customers will exercise it.

Industrial buyers are becoming far more sophisticated, radically reducing their supply base and demanding 'partnership sourcing' arrangements, a sharp contrast to the transaction-based relationships of the past. . . .

In the service sector, consumers – enjoying a broader and deeper choice than at any time in the past – are becoming more demanding, punishing those suppliers who fail to meet consistent and ever-higher standards by taking their custom elsewhere. As customer satisfaction has been raised so have their expectations. As Vandermerwe (1993) notes:

> On the threshold of the third millennium, despite earlier fears that standardisation and globalisation would 'massify' the human race still further, the individual has triumphed to become more significant.

In consumer goods, too, expectations of quality – functional and aesthetic – are at an all-time high, a demand which is being met and reinforced by the ever-increasing power of the retail groups who serve them. Customers are choosy and their time has come.

PART A

Question 1

(a) In your own words, produce a handout for a group of student colleagues, covering the key points being made in this passage. **(10 marks)**

(b) You have been invited to take part in a debate about Vandermerwe's observation that globalization and standardization have given way to the triumph of the individual consumer/customer. Choose whether you agree or disagree with Vandermerwe's view and, using examples to support your argument, outline briefly the points you would make. **(15 marks)**

(c) Imagine yourself to be a Marketing Adviser to a major car manufacturer like Toyota, Nissan or Ford. Write a brief report to your Chief Executive in which you explore the action implications, for your company, of the trends which Egan describes. **(15 marks)**

(40 marks in total)

PART B – Answer THREE questions only

Question 2

Write a memo to the Marketing Director of a major toy manufacturer in which you outline your views on each of the following:

(a) The market segmentation systems which would be especially relevant for a toy manufacturer.

(b) The relevance to your business of the distinction between 'customers' (people who pay for the product) and 'users' (people who use the product but who are not the purchasers as such).

(c) The importance of understanding the other roles in the Decision-making Unit, and how your marketing activities might be influenced by them. **(20 marks)**

Question 3

You are preparing to give a lecture to marketing students about 'Primary and Secondary Methods of Data Collection in Marketing Research'. Outline the structure of your talk and summarize the main points you would want to get across to your audience in the 60 minutes allotted to you. **(20 marks)**

Question 4

What are the connections between 'attitudes' and 'behaviour' so far as customers are concerned? Amplify your arguments with references to relevant examples including, in particular, the possible impact on purchasing behaviour of customer attitudes towards environmental issues. **(20 marks)**

Question 5

You have been asked to write an article for *Marketing Success* about the ways in which the economic environment influences customer actions.

Indicate the things you would say about each of the following, giving appropriate product/ service examples to illustrate your arguments.

(a)   The concepts of utility and marginal utility.
(b)   The business cycle.
(c)   The 'feelgood' factor (i.e. people's perceptions about economic trends).
(d)   Disposable income.
(e)   Price sensitivity of demand and supply.   **(20 marks)**

Question 6

You are the Marketing Manager for a product which has reached the 'Maturity' phase in its life-cycle. What methods of influence and persuasion could you use in order to generate higher sales, and how could consumer modelling help you when choosing suitable customer focused initiatives?   **(20 marks)**

Question 7

Set out a plan for a research programme to measure customer satisfaction for an organization which has never systematically investigated such matters before. Illustrate your plan with reference to a named organization of your choice and show how the results yielded by the study could be beneficial for your organization.   **(20 marks)**

Specimen answers   June 1997

Answer – Question I

Senior Examiner's introduction

A total of 40 marks is available for this question: 10 marks for section (a), 15 marks for section (b) and 15 marks for section (c). The major thrust of the question, therefore, concerns the degree to which candidates can amplify on Egan's views rather than simply reproduce them. Credit is given for practical examples which supplement the arguments being advanced, especially for section (c), where some car manufacturers are already seeking to introduce 'customized' products, against design and delivery schedules which appear almost unbelievable when contrasted against the typical practices of the recent past.

(a)

1   Discussions about strategic management have largely ignored the requirements of individual consumers.
2   The consumer has increasingly articulated preferences and is increasingly conscious of the right to choose.
3   Why, then, has unchecked international trade led to globalization, mass marketing, standardization, and excess supply?
4   Globalization has worked for McDonald's (though, as we shall see later, McDonald's allows more local variations than many imagine), and excess supply, such as surplus agricultural production across Europe, may somehow be viewed as acceptable. However, for the customer there are downside implications:

   (i)   Ironically, excess supply eventually leads to reductions in choice.
   (ii)   Globalization rides roughshod over local customs, local culture and the idiosyncrasies of particular tastes in food, language, etc.
   (iii)   Excess supply inevitably means that resources are not optimized.

5   Yet consumers want choice, they want value for money, they want quality; above all, they want to be able to buy what they *individually* want, rather than being simply offered whatever a company happens to be producing and selling. Far too many organizations, in effect, display orientations in which marketing (and concern for customer aspirations) suffers a relatively low priority:

(i)   Some are product and production orientated, driven by Research & Development and/or the need to fill established factory capacity loadings.

(ii)   Some are sales orientated, activated by the desire to persuade people to buy whatever is currently available.

6   So far as industrial buyers are concerned, they too are moving from a fragmented supplier scenario towards a more coherent approach founded on relationship marketing and the partnership process.

7   In essence, consumers are individuals. They have individual needs. The successful organizations of tomorrow will be capable of combining economies of scale with what is now known as 'mass customization': products and services which meet the *precise* and *specific* expectations of each individual customer.

8   It will gradually become apparent that customers don't want choice if the choice does not include their exact preference. What they want is what they want: and increasingly they will not put up with anything else.

(b)

Agreement with Vandermerwe's view

1   A truly marketing-orientated organization will try to anticipate and satisfy the needs, wants, expectations and requirements of each customer. This approach yields a much higher level of profitability potential in the long run, as customers become more aware of their power and their freedom to choose.

2   By contrast, organizations which are focused on sales, production, or even on the priorities of their own employees, will behave in ways which are anti-competitive and contrary to customer aspirations.

3   We live in a global village and many environmental issues affect consumers both physically and psychologically. Suppliers, manufacturers, service providers and retailers are very aware of the inter-relationship between their products and the environment: as a result they must constantly ensure that their activities match the aspirations of customers in the arena of environmental concern.

4   Globalization – if this means the worldwide marketing of a uniform product – will eventually succumb to the desire for individuality and higher-order self-actualization increasingly finding expression in the purchasing process. As trade barriers come down, so consumers have greater and deeper choices; they can enjoy the benefits of trade agreements and technological change. Although at present it is still necessary to endure wide price variations for some products – especially cars – across international boundaries, we can eventually visualize the emergence of a 'world price' for most products as a result of the facility for global marketing through the Internet. Indeed, the impact of the Internet deserves special mention:

(i)   As an Internet site can be accessed by any Internet surfer from any corner of the globe, competitive retail prices can be sought. Consumers will become far more cost-conscious and less inclined to support their domestic producers if the price is not right. Provided that supply problems can be resolved, the lowest price will win.

(ii)   Currently, the Internet offers distinct commercial advantages for companies in financial services, entertainment, communications, and computing, where profits can be made by selling information which can be downloaded on to home computers.

5   In an increasing cut-throat competitive world, manufacturers have to find ways of distinguishing their products in order to secure and retain any advantage – otherwise they will finish by functioning as commodity suppliers, forced to operate with squeezed margins, intensive price rivalry, and rigorous cost controls. As Joseph Pine has pointed out, in his 1993 book *Mass Customisation*, there are at least six ways of creating individually-designed products and services, tailored to the precise requirements of the individual

customer, whilst minimizing the cost implications so that, by and large, the economies of (mass-production) scale can be sustained:

(i) *Component-sharing modularity* – when the same product is used across multiple products, to enable a considerable variety of products to be offered. Black & Decker completely redesigned its power tool product lines – twice – to take advantage of this opportunity, whilst providing more variety and speedier product development.

(ii) *Component-swapping modularity* – where differing components are paired with the same basic product, creating as many different products as there are components to swap. Examples include Swatch and some self-service buffet-type restaurants.

(iii) *Cut-to-fit modularity* – where variables in the product or service can be modified in an almost infinite number of ways. The National Bicycle Industrial Co, a subsidiary of Matsushita, can supply 11,231,862 variations on 18 modules of customized bicycles, in 199 colour patterns and about as many sizes as there are people.

(iv) *Mix modularity* – where components are mixed together in ways which make the outcome totally unlike the elements themselves. When particular colours of paint are mixed together, for example, the constituents are no longer visible in the end product.

(v) *Bus modularity* – where different components are attached to a standard structure. Examples include track lighting or bus services whose routes can be modified in accordance with passenger preferences.

(vi) *Sectional modularity* – where components can be attached together in arbitrary ways, so long as standard interfaces are available. The classic example is the Lego building process.

6 Vandermerwe is right. Even companies which have traditionally been viewed as offering standardized global products – like McDonald's – are in truth being forced to introduce local variations in response to rising customer expectations. Even if products and services themselves continue to be offered globally without any local adaptation, advertising messages and media are always tailored to the requirements of the national or regional market place. It can only be a matter of time before all products and services become similarly adaptable.

(c)

Creating organizational advantage for Carco

Introduction

1 This report outlines the action implications for Carco if it is to secure a sustainable competitive advantage in the long-term.

2 The report has been compiled with the assistance of Colin Egan, author of *Creating Organisational Advantage* (1995).

The nature of the problem: two examples

1 *The Nissan 'Manufacturing 21' Programme.* It is Nissan's explicit intention to introduce the full mass customization of automobiles in the first year of the 21st century, utilizing all forms of modularity but also time-compression, point-of-sale manufacturing, and customizability. As their 1990 document states, 'The most important objective is to create a system to produce low-volume, special-niche vehicles at reasonable cost. The great number of such models makes it obvious that very fast, inexpensive new model development is necessary. . ... Reducing the time and cost of new model development and start-up is the number one priority of the Japanese auto industry.' The success of the Nissan vision depends on cultivating what they call the 'automotive prosumer' who can participate in the design of his vehicle at a work station in the car dealership; it is expected eventually to reduce the lead time from ordering to delivery to a maximum of three days.

2 *The Range Rover Launch, 1995.* Ten days before it launched the 1995 Range Rover, Rover let 10,000 of its most privileged customers into its secret. Each one of them received an

invitation to a champagne breakfast or candle-lit dinner to see the new car – privately – before the rest of the world got to hear about it. Those who came along were not expected to enter into any firm commitments; instead, the aim of the exercise was to turn these 10,000 people into 'brand ambassadors' for Rover. The company, to use its own words, was trying to 'achieve a breakthrough in the quality of our customer relationships'. What is more important, however, is that the new model had been developed, from inception to launch, in three years – a massive reduction on the conventional experience of the past.

Action Implications

1 Cars increasingly need to be designed, manufactured and marketed in order to satisfy individual preferences. The creation of a predetermined model 'range' is no longer enough or acceptable.

2 Customer preferences are not static. They are affected by demographic factors, by movement along the family life-cycle, by socio-economic position, by lifestyle preferences, and by fashion. To keep our fingers on the pulse we must constantly monitor the aspirations of our (actual, potential and past) customers through, say, focus groups and other forms of qualitative investigation. We must understand the significance of social change so far as our business is concerned.

3 Since we purchase large quantities of components and materials from our suppliers, it is essential that they too adapt in response to our changing needs.

4 We must actively promote, stimulate and encourage customer loyalty. Some ways of achieving this are summarized below:

   (i)   The launch of specific initiatives aimed at engaging the customer, e.g. through Air Miles and in-house loyalty or frequent-purchase privilege cards.

   (ii)   Creating a customer proposition offering something which customers feel they cannot refuse, e.g. the ability to select 'free' options from a very wide range of choices.

   (iii) Engaging the customer in a dialogue, thus ensuring that the customer feels an affinity with the product or service on offer – as Rover did in 1995 with the Range Rover launch.

5 Customer loyalty operates on a 'push and pull' basis. In some markets, the push factors tend to be more significant (e.g. banks and building societies, where customers tend to remove their accounts and leave because of mistakes and mishandling). In markets like ours, the pull factors – luring the customer in via attractive offers, stronger identification or corporate image – tend to count for more: and it is these pull factors to which we must give more serious attention as the competitive context becomes more ruthless.

6 Finally, we must be much more subtle and sensitive in our market segmentation system. As customers become idiosyncratic, so old-fashioned segments tend to break down. We must, as in all things, move with the times.

Answer – Question 2

Senior Examiner's introduction

As with many other questions in the examination, the Senior Examiner expects the response to be produced in a businesslike fashion, especially as a memo layout is specified. The question has three clear parts, and in order to achieve a pass mark it is essential to respond to each.

MEMORANDUM

To: Marketing Director, Alpha Toys
From: Marketing Manager
Date: June 1997
Re: 1 Useful segmentation systems for our business – a fresh look
        2 The customer/user distinction and its relevance for us
        3 Key roles in the DMU: how we can exploit them to our advantage

Segmentation in the toy business

1 From our point of view, there are six main recognized ways for segmenting markets and customers: geographic, socio-economic, psycho-graphic, demographic, segmentation by benefit, and segmentation by buyer behaviour. All of these have some relevance for our company: the significance of each is discussed below.

2 *Geographic segmentation* is applicable in the sense that some regions in our market place show greater interest in educational toys, whereas in others the principal driver appears to be play value or even (more prosaically) cost. If we consider our markets beyond the UK and into Europe, we also find geographical variations, many of them partially linked to climate and the ability to promote outdoor toys.

3 *Socio-economic segmentation* divides customers according to social class, status, and occupational classifications. Generally speaking, it may appear that people with higher incomes have more disposable earnings, but this in itself does not imply that toy purchasing is a high priority for expenditure patterns. On the contrary, an attitude of indulgence towards children's requirements is more often to be found among working-class parents, grandparents and other family members.

4 *Psychographic segmentation* concerns itself with lifestyles and, in particular, the values entertained by parents and those in a position to influence (a) whether toys are purchased, and (b) which particular toys are purchased. In many households where football is a major leisure pursuit (whether as spectator or participant), preference is given to toys and other items which enable this activity to be enhanced (and which inculcate 'appropriate' values in impressionable children); in some middle-class households, by contrast, toys which appear to encourage violence and aggression will be actively discouraged.

5 *Demographic segmentation* is particularly relevant to us because of the declining numbers of children in our society – and the need, therefore, to consider new product/market extensions such as 'toys' aimed at adults.

6 *Benefits segmentation* addresses the expectations of either the purchaser or the 'user', or both. Purchasers may be much more interested in the degree to which any given toy has educational value, whether it is safe, its durability and its cost; 'users' (i.e. children themselves) are much less activated by cost, but will be heavily influenced by peer pressure and the requirement for sustained interest through repeated playings.

7 *Buyer behaviour segmentation* addresses such matters as style and frequency of purchasing patterns. Visits to toy shops may occur infrequently (at times of peak relevance to the family, namely, Christmas and birthdays), or may become a regular feature of the domestic routine; alternatively, toys may be purchased through mail order catalogues and even through the Internet (apart from the fact that the Internet can be viewed as a toy in itself).

8 *Conclusion.* In my view, we should concentrate particularly on a *benefits segmentation* approach, since this will also enable us to contemplate the addition of 'adult' toys to our catalogue. If we can develop toys which combine educational/informative appeal, significant play/entertainment value, limited durability but scope for repeat purchase, and the capacity to satisfy 'adult' concerns about, say, stress reduction and control, then we will have some winning products on our hands.

The customer/user distinction

The distinction between 'customers' (who pay) and 'users' (who consume) has been developed by Ted Johns in his 1994 book, *Perfect Customer Care*, and is discussed at length by Chris Rice (*Understanding Customers*, 2nd edition, 1997). Indeed, Rice makes some points directly related to our business when he points out that 'Children do not buy toys; parents, relatives and friends of the family do. . . . Where this is the case, we have to realize that the people we are trying to satisfy and delight are the parents, relatives and friends who part with their money. Thus it may be valuable to focus our attention on the interests, motivations and emotional values attached to toys by these groups.' Rice goes on to argue that the purchase of some toys may indirectly reflect a search for love or peace: 'Granny buying a teddy bear for a grandchild is wanting the child to fall in love with the bear and to express delight and love in return. This is likely to be a major motivation for many 'givers'.'

Alternatively, we can visualize circumstances in which the child pesters the parent mercilessly – perhaps to get a skateboard. The parent, driven to distraction, eventually gives in. In this case the payoff is peace and an absence (admittedly short-lived) of demands. The child will be satisfied – as I have said, temporarily, until some other urgent desire replaces the search for the skateboard – but the child's satisfaction is but a means to an end, the end being the satisfaction of the real, paying customer.

Other possibilities relevant to our company include the scenario in which the toy is purchased by the customer who never had an equivalent item in their own childhood but who now wishes to fulfil that dream. The train set enjoyed by the father, the ballet lessons purchased by the mother, may all be illustrations of this process, despite the incessant protestations of the purchasers concerning the desire to supply stimulation and pleasure to the child in whose name the money is being spent.

It is clear that until quite recently children were toy users but not toy customers. Parents not only did the paying, but also did the choosing. Firms like the Early Learning Centre have thrived very well on this principle, where toys have been designed, packaged, marketed and purchased because parents (predominantly in the middle-class socio-economic categories, one has to say) believe their children need to develop 'acceptable' patterns of motivation. Nowadays, the situation has changed radically. Parents still pay, but they no longer do so much of the choosing. Television advertising, skilful marketing (not least by our company!), video technology and parental permissiveness have combined to place most of the toy purchasing decisions in the hands of children – and many traditional toy manufacturers have gone out of business because they failed to notice this evolution in the customer/user relationship. It is worth noting, however, that some parents are both customers and users if they buy video games (for example) for their offspring but actually monopolize these 'toys' for themselves.

In the context of the toy industry the distinction between customer and user makes a good deal of sense. So far as our company is concerned, the child must remain a significant target for marketing messages, especially as he/she is now a key influencer in the social DMU – so our advertising can continue to be directed towards children. On the other hand, we have to ensure that all our products continue to be viewed as acceptable by our paying 'customers': it may therefore be even more necessary for us to undertake market research to explore, in greater depth, the motivation and emotional values which underpin the behaviour of adults when buying toys for their children (or for themselves). This insight, as Rice says, could give us a significant competitive edge over the organization which thinks, more narrowly, that its customer is the child.

Other roles in the decision-making unit

The decision type and DMU concepts are critical to our purposes in the Alpha Toy Company: understanding how these work will make an enormous difference to our competitive position and ultimately to our growth.

So far as *decision type* is concerned, we are looking at three options: (1) the straight re-buy, (2) the modified re-buy, and (3) the entirely new purchase. Some of our current products fit one or other of these categories, but we need to investigate the possibility of developing new ideas in all three. We can do this, for example, by product extensions, by the gradual introduction of accessories, by a deliberate process of periodic obsolescence, and through the creation of enduring brand names which stimulate long-term loyalty and commitment. These latter phenomena may also be promoted through our equivalent of the Tesco Club Card, in which discounts for future purchases may be offered as an encouragement to sustained customer commitment in the short-term.

The Decision-making Unit (DMU) concept stems from the proposition that relatively few purchasing decisions are driven entirely by individual choice. In practice several 'roles' may contribute to the buyer's 'moment of truth', though not all of these 'roles' are necessarily performed by different individuals. One approach to classifying the DMU 'roles' is to differentiate them as follows:

- The *Starter/Initiator* of the buying process.
- The *Purchaser* of the product/service.
- The *Adviser* who supplies technical and/or professional assistance – perhaps within the toy-shop itself.

- The *Decider* who actually takes the purchase decision.
- The *User* who is likely to operate the product or service being bought.
- The *Financier* who supplies the necessary resources, or who reports on their availability and, if necessary, on the mechanisms by which the necessary resources can be acquired.
- The *Gatekeeper* between the purchaser and the product/service source.

We need to explore more thoroughly the dynamics of the interaction between these 'roles' and, specifically, the extent to which power is concentrated within some roles at the expense of others. Sometimes, for example, the Starter/Initiator and the User are very energized at the prospect of a particular toy purchase, but the Financier will argue that the cost is excessive (especially in relation to the product's life expectancy) or that funds should be more profitably directed elsewhere.

The outcome in such instances of conflict is by no means easily predictable, but if we can plot the probable dynamics then we will be in a much better position to direct our marketing strategies in appropriate ways to the 'significant players' in the decision-making sequence. As Rice points out, 'children are likely to be the key influencers, with the added factor of the emotional influence that a child can wield over the significant adults (our customers).'

Answer – Question 3

Senior Examiner's introduction

The marking scheme for this question provides for a balance between coverage of the subject-matter and adherence to the format requested within the question design. Candidates are expected to organize their material as a combination of 'lecture notes' and 'visual aids' rather than as a straightforward essay. Moreover, substantial credit is given for answers which include one or two examples of marketing research in action, since lectures which consist exclusively of 'theory' and broad generalizations are invariably tedious, especially if the students being addressed have no direct experience of the topic.

1 *Outline plan for the lecture*
- Determine the objective(s).
- Consider the audience: size, current levels of knowledge, motivation for paying attention.
- Select appropriate methods and material.
- Organize visual aids.
- Schedule time for questions and group participation.

2 *Introduction: The reasons why the systematic collection of data is so important to organizations*
- Nowadays many organizations have come to realize that customer satisfaction and customer 'delight' are the only routes to long-term competitive advantage.
- Equally, customers have begun to flex their muscles: they are much less inclined to remain servile and silent in the face of indifferent attention, and are much more willing to take their business elsewhere.
- Thus attracting and retaining customer loyalty is a major issue in boardrooms everywhere.

3 *In practice many organizations do not know how good they are at delivering customer service*
As a result, they tend to become complacent, inhabiting a self-enacted reality which embodies these characteristics:

- The use of vague, generalized statements like 'quite good', 'getting better', 'world-class' (without any comprehension about what being 'world-class' actually means).
- The counting of customer complaints in the belief that the incidence of complaints is a direct measure of customer satisfaction – without realizing that, in most cases, only between 10 and 20 per cent of customers actually complain.
- Reliance on infrequent survey data about customer perceptions and the selective application of the data, plus some wishful thinking.

- So-called 'improvements' which only address front-line 'customer-care' features like answering the telephone within three rings – when what really matters is how customers are handled once the telephone is picked up.

4 *Principal categories of data collection: Primary and secondary methods*
- Primary research consists of studies undertaken for a specific client, or with a specified purpose, generally a problem requiring focused attention.
- Secondary research involves the organizational application of information and/or data originally secured for other reasons (e.g. sales figures, government statistics).

5 *Types of primary research*
- Qualitative
  - Depth interviews.
  - Focus groups.
  - Projective techniques such as role plays, word association, the Thematic Apperception Test, and sentence completion processes.
- Quantitative
  - Experimentation.
  - Observation (which may be covert/secretive, non-participatory, or participatory).
  - Survey methods (including personal one-to-one studies, computer-assisted interviewing, telephone surveys, or direct mail).

6 *Benefits and disadvantages of primary research*
- Benefits
  - Specific.
  - Relevant to the client organization.
  - Up-to-date.
  - Control over reliability and validity.
- Disadvantages
  - Time-consuming.
  - Costly (especially if external research agencies are involved).
  - Requirement for specialized knowledge of research design, implementation and analysis skills.

7 *Primary research in action: Birmingham Midshires Building Society*
- The Society sends out some 200,000 questionnaires every year: 'Where we can ask, we ask – the questionnaire process is the absolute bedrock of our business', says the Society's Chief Executive.
- All customers returning questionnaires are thanked for their co-operation.
- In 1991, 10 per cent of customer complaints came from individuals who thought that their money could be earning a better return. The Society responded in 1994 by automatically upgrading customers to the most appropriate available account, at a cost of £13 million. Over the years between 1992 and 1995, the number of customers seeking more competitive interest rates fell from 949 to 327.

8 *Primary research in action: TNT Express*
- The company issues 14,000 questionnaires annually.
- Based on the information thus provided, it has identified 16 areas of operational excellence, such as call handling, and the speed/reliability of delivery.
- In the words of the Sales and Marketing Director, 'It's not measurement but what you do with it that counts. We use these performance measures continually to improve the service we provide.'

9 *Sources of secondary research*
- Government: Central Statistical Office, Office of Population Census and Surveys, and the Office of National Statistics.
- The European Parliament and Union: e.g. Eurostat.

- Magazines and journals such as *The Economist, The Times, Marketing Week,* and *Management Today.*
- On-line databases.
- Trade fairs, exhibitions and conferences.
- Professional bodies and pressure groups, such as the CBI and the Institute of Personnel & Development.
- Private research publications and reports.

10   *Benefits and disadvantages of secondary research*
- Benefits
  - Cost-effectiveness.
  - Immediate availability through publications and/or Internet.
  - Opportunity to cross-check multiple sources in order to assess reliability and validity of figures.
- Disadvantages
  - Data produced for one purpose or by one single organization may be misleading when applied in a different context, especially if the research questions have been 'loaded' in a particular way.
  - Some secondary information can date very quickly.
  - Validity and reliability cannot be ascertained with absolute confidence.

11   *The systematic approach to research design – and the relevance of data collection techniques*
- *Stage 1:*   Outline the research 'problem' and the aims/objectives of the study.
- *Stage 2:*   Acquire secondary data and evaluate the extent to which it is acceptable on its own.
- *Stage 3:*   If the secondary data is insufficient, it is then necessary to select an appropriate primary research methodology, including the sample to be investigated, the need for 'control' and 'experimental' groups, the investigative methods to be used, and so forth.
- *Stage 4:*   Implement the research plan, and modify as necessary through the execution process.
- *Stage 5:*   Collection, analysis and interpretation of the data.
- *Stage 6:*   Report findings and recommendations.
- *Stage 7:*   Initiate action programme.

12   *Some general caveats about conducting and interpreting research in the field of customer behaviour*
- It is difficult in itself to persuade customers to complete questionnaires and to take part in interview studies.
- The samples of customers in such surveys may be self-selecting, i.e. largely composed of people who have been treated exceptionally well, or handled very badly.
- Many customers unconsciously give misleading responses based, for instance, on one unfortunate experience many years ago which has coloured their attitude rather more thoroughly than many other positive scenarios.

13   *Conclusion: how marketing research can yield better results*
- In 1993, the Brent Revenues and Benefits Service (BRBS) in the London Borough of Brent had the dubious honour of coming bottom in a league table of customer service, when the Council Tax was introduced.
- Yet in October 1994, BRBS received a Charter Mark for excellent service to customers.
- This change was achieved by finding out what customers wanted, and then delivering it.
- Customer focus groups, customer surveys and suggestion cards were some of the ways in which the reactions of customers were assessed: these mechanisms continue, since BRBS is never satisfied with its current level of achievement.

14   *End*
- Reiteration of key points.
- Questions.

Answer – Question 4

Senior Examiner's introduction

Very few marks in the marking scheme are allocated to an extended discussion defining 'attitude' and 'behaviour'; much more important is a full investigation of the degree to which attitudes may cause behaviour, and the other way round. The question's reference to environmental issues stems from the fact that support for what is loosely termed 'the environment' is always much greater than any actual purchase decisions would suggest – a discrepancy which reinforces the view that 'attitudes' may reflect political correctness rather more than a series of deeply-held convictions.

Whereas *behaviour* is about action, *attitudes* are about intention. This admittedly crude and simplistic distinction indicates immediately that attitudes and behaviour do not have to operate in unison. According to Allport, however, an attitude is 'a mental and neural state of readiness, organized through experience, exerting a directive or dynamic influence upon the individual's response to all objects and situations with which it is related'. In essence, therefore, an attitude has four typical ingredients:

1 It is *relatively consistent* over time. Attitudes are not permanent and can be changed; however, they are reasonably well established, and will often be linked to consistent behaviour patterns.
2 It is *learned*. An attitude is the product of earlier conditioning, formulated through experience as a result of factors such as motivation, association and reinforcement.
3 It involves a *predisposition* to act. Attitudes are a predisposition to behaviour, which means that the appropriate behaviour pattern will not necessarily follow or occur.
4 It is associated with an *object*. Attitudes relate to some aspect of the individual's environment: things, persons, concepts, ideas or, indeed, the actions of others.

There is no automatic, direct relationship between attitudes and behaviour. Peter and Olson (1990) have identified seven factors which may reduce or weaken the predictive power of an attitude so far as behaviour is concerned:

1 *Intervening time.* The longer the time interval between the acquisition of the attitude and the possibility of linked behaviour, the greater is the likelihood that other factors may have modified or changed the original intention. Thus, in the field of environmental concerns, an individual may express a strong positive orientation towards 'the environment', but by the time an opportunity to translate this attitude into action presents itself, other priorities may have come into focus.
2 *Different levels of specificity.* When measuring intention, any questions designed to elicit attitude need to be specific and at the same level as the observed behaviour, otherwise the relationship may be damaged. If a survey shows (as one did in 1993) that over 80 per cent of consumers would buy organic fruit and vegetables, then the question must also specify that such products are much more expensive than their non-organic counterparts: if respondents are not equipped with this information, their answers (and thus their attitudes) may be misleading and/or inaccurate.
3 *Unforeseen environmental events.* We may intend to purchase environmentally-friendly products, but perhaps the shelves are empty, or the cost is more than expected, and so substitutes are acquired instead.
4 *Unforeseen situational context.* It is possible that the situation the respondents envisaged when expressing their behavioural intention was not the same as the situation at the time of the behaviour. If we are purchasing a basket of fruit as a present for someone else – a routine present, moreover, rather than one fully prompted by interpersonal affection – then we may find our preference for the organic option is undermined, especially if the organically-grown fruit are more expensive.
5 *Degree of voluntary control.* Sometimes our attitudes are suppressed by a 'force majeure', such as the non-availability of environmentally-acceptable investment opportunities at the time when we have some money.
6 *Stability of intentions.* Some intentions are founded on beliefs and attitudes that are both strongly held and stable over long periods of time (e.g. opposition to smoking). These

give rise to stable intentions and, generally, more predictable behaviour. Other behaviour may stem from much less strongly held attitudes and less important beliefs which are, in effect, transient in character. Thus attitudes about 'the environment' may reflect nothing more than a temporary fashion which in turn will be supplanted by other priorities.

7 *New information.* We may receive information which alters our behavioural intentions and which, in turn, challenges our beliefs and attitudes. Examples could include AIDS education regarding safe sex, or the disclosure that so-called environmentally-friendly products are just as damaging to the ozone layer as those which are now regarded as less respectable.

Rice (*Understanding Customers*) adds some further reasons for the failure of attitudes and behaviour to coincide in certain circumstances:

1 Although we have an attitude which is favourable towards a particular object, in fact we may have little need for the object (or little opportunity to acquire it), and so the attitude remains in the realm of fantasy – at least so far as positive, targeted behaviour is concerned.

2 Taking someone else's wishes into account may mean that we act individually in a way which is entirely inconsistent with our personal attitudes.

3 Inaccurate or incomplete measures of cognition or affect may mean that behaviour, even when linked to attitude, may yield paradoxical outcomes. In these circumstances such behaviour will appear to be unrelated to currently-held attitudes, beliefs and values, when in fact all that has happened is that the selected behaviour has been chosen without proper evaluation of its consequences.

In essence, therefore, attitudes and behaviour may be related in four ways.

Attitudes cause behaviour

A positive attitude towards football 'causes' the individual to attend football matches, watch football on TV, and buy the appropriate artefacts. In the field of environmental concerns, gradual assimilation of ecological sensitivity may prompt a conscious search for, say, suitable soap powders and other household products. Purchase decisions will be made and implemented, thus generating a high level of cognitive consistency. Such decisions will not be impeded or undermined by other (potentially intervening) factors like cost, functionality or performance.

Behaviour causes attitudes

Many training programmes in organizations nowadays work on the assumption that it is much easier to change behaviour than to change attitudes. Thus a shop assistant, normally 'hostile' to customers, may be forced to behave politely towards them, and learns that this behaviour can be very rewarding. An opportunity to try some environmentally-friendly cleaning product, free of charge, may supply evidence which undermines previously sceptical attitudes about the effectiveness of such products.

Attitudes and behaviour are not related

A positive attitude to owning a Rolls-Royce may not influence behaviour at all (apart from prompting the weekly purchase of Lottery tickets), so the attitude remains nothing more than a wish-list. This is why market research (for new products and services) is so suspect, because of the operation of factors which Nishikawa categorized in his 1989 article for the *Journal of Long Range Planning*:

1 *Indifference* – customers often provide negative responses to ideas for new products and services simply because they are indifferent to something they have not thought about or tried before – and, in truth, they cannot easily visualize whether they would welcome the new idea or not if it were physically put in front of them.

2 *Absence of responsibility* – people will say more or less anything when responding to market research surveys, often out of a desire to please the researcher. As Nishikawa says, 'customers are most sincere when spending rather than talking'.

3   *Conservative attitudes* – most customers choose the conventional and the familiar; only about three to five per cent of customers are 'Innovators'.

4   *Vanity* – customers will put on a good appearance, for example, by acting as if they are politically correct when actually selecting their purchases against completely different criteria, giving price a much higher priority than concern for, say, the ozone layer.

5   *Insufficient information* – researchers and organizations often approach customers with information and ideas seen from the seller's rather than from the customer's point of view. In these circumstances it is not surprising if customers fail to understand the issues.

Attitudes and behaviour do influence each other, but in ways far more complicated than a straightforward cause-and-effect fashion

In reality this is the most plausible perspective. Behaviour is seldom the consequence of a single-minded predisposition, but must take account of, say, reference group affiliations, monetary needs, and the acceptability of some attitudes over others. Moreover, some attitudes are inconsistent with others: people may believe in healthy eating, but they also believe in self-indulgence (or 'spoiling themselves').

Conclusion

In this answer we have shown that attitudes and behaviour may be linked in many ways. Identifying and measuring the precise nature of the relationship, in any particular instance, is a task of considerable magnitude – especially when it is borne in mind that individuals may go to some lengths to conceal certain attitudes and project others.

Answer – Question 5

Senior Examiner's introduction

Given the range of subject-matter to be covered, the amount of depth in each part of the response must inevitably be problematic. However, an acceptable treatment would address the basics and seek to include some relevant illustrations. If the answer can be written in a style which could commend itself to readers of *Marketing Success*, then so much the better.

Introduction

It has been argued that there are four broad approaches to customer behaviour: economic, passive, cognitive and emotional. *Economic Man* is rational and logical, analysing all the options before making a considered choice; *Passive Man* is irrational and impulsive, easily swayed by marketing promotions; *Cognitive Man* is relatively risk-averse and will consider all significant purchase decisions very carefully in the light of both personal preferences and environmental change; and *Emotional Man* will act on the desire for immediate gratification. In practice, the issue is perhaps one of emphasis rather than one of neat, tidy classification, especially given the fact that economic factors – involving the allocation of scarce resources – will play a significant part, whatever the passive, cognitive and emotional preferences of the individual.

This article, therefore, sets out to discuss and explore some of the everyday economic concepts which underpin our daily lives as both consumers and marketers.

Utility and marginal utility

Utility theory concerns itself with the feelings which consumers experience when they buy a product or service. If the purchase has been 'successful', it should provide satisfaction, and this in turn should lead to further repeat purchases. *Marginal utility* is the satisfaction gained from purchase of one additional unit of the product or service in question; the law of diminishing marginal utility suggests that each incremental 'amount' of satisfaction is less than the amount of satisfaction gained from purchases undertaken in the past.

The law of diminishing marginal utility works quite well when applied to food and drink, but may be less applicable so far as the purchase of Old Masters is concerned. Further, the law applies only if income and tastes remain unaltered. If income changes, then the utility the customer obtains from a commodity will be affected by the changing consumption of other commodities. Someone previously compelled to drink instant coffee may now afford to switch to fresh-ground coffee: in these circumstances, the utility of instant coffee has fallen to zero. Equally, a change in taste, fashion or attitude may occur as more of a commodity if consumed, and marginal utility may increase where such a change is taking place. For example, a particular customer may become addicted to alcohol, or may progress from being an occasional buyer of pictures into an obsessive art collector.

Whatever the problems with utility theory, it has one important message for the marketer. Seldom are decisions founded on price alone; much more commonly, they take account of marginal utility as well. If the price of a product or service is reduced, this may improve the ratio between marginal utility and price, so that sales will rise; but this is not the only strategy available to the marketer. Another option is to persuade the customer that there are more 'units' of utility to be derived from a particular product or service than previously thought possible. Branding, and in particular a sense of exclusivity, may achieve the desired end in such respects – a relevant example would be the 'designer water', Aqua Libra. Yet another possibility, at the other end of the spectrum, is to make the product or service more conveniently available: if this is done, the customer will derive more net utility from consuming it.

The business (or trade) cycle

The business cycle operates with considerable regularity in all major national economies and, to some degree, within the world or global economy seen as an entity in its own right. It is an important concept for many marketers because the operation of the business cycle influences the amount of money available for spending on goods and services; in turn, it affects consumer confidence and the so-called 'feelgood' factor. Generally, the business cycle follows a four-phase sequence.

The *first phase* is *DEPRESSION*, characterized by low levels of activity in the economy at large. The numbers of unemployed rise, so there are less earnings to be spent, less income for the government and, overall, low consumer demand. Many factories are compelled to operate well below their capacity; thus costs are high, relative to turnover and business profitability. Companies cannot afford to raise their prices, and indeed in many instances they may be forced to reduce them in an effort, at least, to cover their fixed costs. Business confidence is low. However, as the economy is not doing well, the value of the currency on the international market falls: this increases the cost of imported goods and makes domestically-produced items appear significantly cheaper.

During the depression phase, individuals with money to spend are nonetheless reluctant to do so. The savings ratio rises, a fact which benefits some (though not all) financial services institutions. Moreover, well-known brands may be able to sustain their competitive position if consumers decide to make sacrifices elsewhere.

The *second phase* of the business cycle is known as *RECOVERY*. This will occur when companies begin to look under-priced on the stock market. As investment picks up, so new factories are built, new equipment is purchased, more jobs are created and, as a result, consumer spending begins to rise. Business confidence begins to grow and the overall climate turns from despair to opportunity.

In the *third phase*, known colloquially as *BOOM*, consumer spending rises with increasing speed, businesses increase production, full employment is attained, and the economy is operating at full capacity. Labour shortages begin to be noticed; output can only be pushed up by investment in new machinery and equipment, so investment is high; at the same time, because the economy is doing well, the value of the currency on the international exchange markets goes up. The pound looks 'strong' and, from the viewpoint of other countries, British goods begin to appear more expensive; conversely, a strong pound means that goods made in other countries are relatively cheap, or certainly better value. This, together with high levels of demand and limited output, tends to increase imports from abroad, causes problems with the balance of payments, and pushes up prices generally. It is a situation which cannot last.

The *fourth phase*, *RECESSION*, involves reduced consumption, investment and production. Once again unemployment rises and the cycle is complete.

Some organizations experience levels of activity which move more or less in harmony with the business cycle – the car industry is a notable example. Others are counter-cyclical – in addition to the cases already mentioned, it is possible to think about down-market food and clothing retailers. Still others either function independently of the business cycle – because of their long lead-times (as in aircraft manufacturing) – or have deliberately pursued strategies which supply some protection against business-cycle fluctuations. In this way, periodic cyclical 'threats' can be offset by counter-cyclical 'opportunities.'

The 'feelgood' factor

At first sight there may appear to be little connection between the 'macro' concept of the business cycle and the 'micro' behaviour of individual consumers. But in practice the linkage is very close. The individual actions of consumers – which tend to be remarkably homogeneous, despite the fact that they are all acting as individuals – are the ingredients which make up the economy; and consumers' perceptions of the overall economy will have an enormous significance for consumer confidence (or lack of it).

As Rice points out, confidence 'permeates all of life'. If there are redundancies at work, individuals still employed become nervous: they may cancel a holiday, postpone the purchase of a new car, decide to remain living where they are rather than move to a bigger house. In particular, this last 'decision' has powerful secondary effects, because if sufficient numbers of people elect not to move house, then fewer kitchens get fitted, fewer gas cookers are sold, less furniture, curtains, wallpaper and paint are purchased; fewer housewarming parties are held; some removal firms and estate agencies go to the wall.

When the 'feelgood' factor is in place, however, the risks are perceived to be less. Curiously enough, if a 'feelgood' perspective is in place, then the consequent actions of individuals help to justify the perspective in the first place – at least for a while, until the economy becomes over-heated and the more negative dimensions of the business cycle begin to assert themselves.

Disposable income

Whether a consumer will buy, and what he buys, depends to a very large extent on whether he has the disposable income available to make the purchase. Disposable income is considerably less than total income since a large proportion is already committed elsewhere (to rent and/or mortgages, basic food bills, utilities, and so forth). Generally speaking, as income rises, so too does disposable income, thus adding to the total funds available for discretionary purchases. On the other hand, if mortgage interest rates increase, then disposable income falls. Disposable income is also affected by price rises for goods or services defined as discretionary but for which demand is (relatively) inelastic, such as cigarettes, motoring costs, and petrol. Thus one way in which the government may seek to slow down the pace of the economy, during the Boom phase, is to increase the taxation levels on these inelastic demand items, thus taking some disposable income out of the economy altogether.

It is worth noting Rice's admirably succinct account of the connections between the business cycle and the levels of disposable income available, typically, to individuals:

1 *Recession* means a cutback in jobs and overtime – hence a reduction of disposable income.
2 *Depression* takes this even further, with less disposable income reducing the market.
3 *Recovery* sees higher employment and increases in disposable income.
4 *Boom* raises the prospect of very high levels of disposable income – often with people wanting to invest their money while they have it and before the good times come to an end.

Price sensitivity of demand and supply

From a marketing point of view, it is preferable to be promoting goods and services for which demand is inelastic or price-insensitive, since this means that people will continue to purchase them even if they have reduced levels of disposable income. Goods and services normally viewed as inelastic or price-insensitive will include:

1 *Basic needs* – water, electricity, gas, and fundamental foodstuffs.
2 *Addictive substances* – such as alcohol and tobacco.

3   *Goods for which there are no substitutes* – such as the motor-car. In theory the car could be replaced by public transport, but in practice the comparison is untenable once factors like 'freedom of choice' and flexibility are taken into consideration.

As has already been stated, governments will always try to impose taxation on goods whose demand is inelastic. Causing the price of petrol and diesel fuel to rise, through taxation, will not significantly reduce the amounts purchased: in this way the government can increase its total 'take' from the taxation system. If price-sensitive goods were to be taxed, the reduction in demand would more than wipe out the income from the higher taxes.

Clearly many marketers will seek to make their goods and services more price-inelastic. This can be done (or attempted) in several ways:

1   By stimulating brand loyalty as a form of 'addiction' so that people cannot do without the item in question.
2   By developing the perception that a luxury product is in fact a necessity.
3   By emphasizing the brand's unique characteristics, and thus seeking to eradicate the idea that acceptable substitutes can be found.

In 1996, Heinz was able to take advantage of the fact that it had assiduously pursued these strategies over many years in the baked beans sector. Faced with ruthless price competition (some supermarkets had reduced the price of their own-label tins of baked beans to 3p), Heinz actually *increased* their prices. True, they lost some market share from those purchasers who were tempted away, but customers faithful to Heinz – and who believed that the Heinz baked bean was a genuinely superior product – were unaffected by the higher prices and helped to ensure that although Heinz lost some market share, its cash flow was virtually unaffected.

Answer – Question 6

Senior Examiner's introduction
A competent treatment for Question 6 could well begin with a brief outline of the product life-cycle concept, though the majority of the marks are allocated for the two principal issues raised: how to stimulate increased sales in the 'maturity' phase, and how to use consumer modelling in the process of identifying market opportunities. The question does not specify any precise format for the layout of the answer, but credit is given for candidates who clearly subdivide their material into two or three segments.

Introduction
The basic idea of the product life-cycle is that a product will follow a life-cycle from development and introduction, through to growth, maturity and finally decline. The concept itself can be applied to broad product categories (e.g. beer), to product forms (e.g. lager) and to specific brands (e.g. Carling Black Label). In general, as Ennew (*The Marketing Blueprint*) points out, life-cycles tend to be longer for product categories and product forms than for individual brands, though of course the brand name may have a longer life than the specific products to which the brand name is attached.

In the *Development* phase of the life-cycle, the product has not yet reached the market, though it will absorb resources. Once the product is launched, the life-cycle reaches the *Introduction* phase: this is a period of slow growth, with sales being primarily to the more innovative customers. Cash flow and profit in this phase are likely to be negative; from a marketing perspective, the priority is to raise awareness of the product and, as a result, the marketing mix will emphasize informative promotion.

Assuming the product attains the *Growth* phase, this period is characterized by steady sales growth, broad acceptance, and significant profitability. The product itself may generate additional features in order to maintain sales; equally, the distribution network may be extended, with more segments brought into the target population, and price competitiveness may be increased. During the Growth phase, assuming the product has attracted notoriety because of its success, competitors are likely to enter the market place, though in most cases they have yet to establish themselves.

When a product reaches *Maturity*, sales start to stabilize. For many consumer and industrial goods, replacement purchases tend to be more common than new purchases. Prices are likely to be closely linked to those specified by competitors; promotion will be orientated towards attracting consumers from competing brands, since the majority of players are anxious to increase their market share.

During the *Decline* phase, sales begin to drop away noticeably, leaving management with a number of strategic options. First, the product can be retained and cash flow maximized by price cutting and/or reduced marketing support. Second, if it is considered that the product does have a long-term future, then it may be rejuvenated through the addition of new features, through repackaging, or through quality upgrades. Third, the product may be withdrawn entirely or sold off.

Generating higher sales in the 'Maturity' phase

Listed below are several possible routes for maximizing sales and achieving growth at the 'Maturity' point in the product life-cycle.

1 *Advertising.* Extensive advertising is not essential, since the product is already well established; however, occasional and regular reminder advertising can help sustain continued interest and awareness. In addition, it may be worthwhile to present some new advertising approaches as part of a rejuvenation philosophy.
2 *Promotion.* These can include temporary price reductions, extra percentage amounts in a given pack size, 'three for the price of two' offers, special gifts, and so forth. These keep consumers alerted to the product; they create additional loyalty and repeat purchases; further, they may tempt some customers away from the similar products offered by our competitors.
3 *Product enhancements.* Throughout the life-cycle, the product's performance is continually evaluated. Where improvement potential has been identified, stage-by-stage enhancements can be introduced in order to prolong the 'Maturity' phase overall and achieve a competitive advantage over our 'imitators'.
4 *Product extension.* Given that we now have an established brand, we may add some related products in order to capitalize on the brand name and reputation. Clairol, which originally specialized in hair dyes, has extended its line to all kinds of hair care products, from hair dryers to shampoos: the wisdom of this approach is founded on the fact that it is far cheaper for us to associate a new product with a known and trusted brand name than to try to develop a totally new brand. Moreover, if our product extensions can be linked synergistically with the original product, then the sales of the original product can also be expected to rise in parallel. The possible themes for product extension are as follows:

    (a) Product line extensions into different sizes, colours and/or flavours.
    (b) Product form extensions, e.g. from soap to liquid soap.
    (c) Product category extensions, e.g. from disposable Bic pens to disposable Bic razors.

5 *Strategy considerations.* During the 'Maturity' phase we can expect that one or two of our weakest competitors will withdraw from the market place, or be forced out. We should be proactively prepared to capitalize on such scenarios. Moreover, in order to anticipate the 'Decline' stage, we must defend our market share vigorously, seize profit opportunities, focus our attention on efficiency and scale economies (relatively easy at this point in the life-cycle, because of the learning curve), and begin to develop the next generation of worthwhile innovations.

The relevance of consumer modelling

In helping us to determine the optimum strategy for coping with product 'Maturity', consumer modelling is an invaluable tool. Of course, we understand that models must inevitably simplify our portrayal of customer behaviour but, as Keith Williams says, 'it has . . . been found that . . . in practice, a relatively small number of variables account for the vast bulk of consumer behaviour.' In any event, we can always cope with the apparent difficulties of any particular modelling approach by ensuring that we cross-check our predictions against those generated through other models, in order to produce an acceptable consensus.

Modelling should enable us to predict consumer reactions to alternative marketing strategies. Especially valuable to us will be the *personal variable* models which explore the internal decision processes characteristic of the typical customer – his beliefs, intentions, motives, perceptions, etc. Among the *personal variable* approaches of relevance to us, two appear to have potentially the greatest value:

1 *The compensatory or trade-off model* shows that when a customer is faced with a choice between products composed of certain attributes or benefits in varying proportions, he will compromise on his image of the 'ideal' product and may be prepared to accept less of one attribute in return for more of another. This is a judgement about which combination of attributes offers the highest overall utility, or value. In our case we may measure this by asking consumers to rank different attribute combinations in order of preference, in order to structure more sensibly the product variations and 'special price' offers likely to be successful at the point of 'Maturity'.

2 *The threshold model* suggests that for each perceived attribute of a product, there is a perceived threshold of acceptability, below which the product will be rejected. Skilful operation of this model should enable us to specify those attributes which are viewed as critical, and those which are (in varying degrees) 'optional' and which may therefore be tweaked.

In order to produce a more comprehensive and systematic understanding of our market place, I also recommend we use the 1990 version of the Engel, Blackwell and Miniard 'grand' model of consumer decision-making. This model is highly appropriate because it includes an 'alternative evaluation' stage in which the consumer compares alternative brands against evaluative criteria, which are 'product judging standards that have been stored in the permanent memory' (Loudon and Della Bitta). This evaluation process may lead to changes in beliefs regarding each brand in a given market: at the very least, we need to guard ourselves against such changes adversely affecting our sales and our market share. More positively, the evaluation process leads, typically, to an intention to make a purchase of the most favourably evaluated brand. If the product does not meet expectations (either at first purchase or on subsequent occasions), then the search is renewed. We should be able to exploit this sequence in order to wean customers away from competing products, by offering them free trials.

Answer – Question 7

Senior Examiner's introduction

Credit is given within answers for the level of detail supplied about the organization in which the customer research is assumed to be taking place, but overall the content should concentrate on the initial statement of the 'problem' (usually the absence of any definitive data on customer opinions, perhaps coupled with complacent assumptions founded on the absence of complaints), the identification of a credible research design, some guidance on sampling (if appropriate), and an outline of the benefits. It is expected that candidates would specify both proactive and defensive outcomes: the opportunity to prevent customers from taking their business elsewhere, and the need to generate either new or repeat business from the existing customer base.

Two alternative specimen answers are provided here, in order to illustrate the options which the Senior Examiner would regard as acceptable.

Specimen Answer (A): Torring Rovers Football & Athletic PLC

Introduction

As with most Premier League football clubs, Torring Rovers has recently begun to realize the potential of what it can offer, not only to its existing customers, but also to a whole new network of potential clients – many of whom may not actually be interested in soccer at all. Normally, for example, the stadium is used once a fortnight on a Saturday afternoon; but it is increasingly recognized that much higher levels of utilization can be achieved, and that other marketing opportunities can be exploited.

Previously, the major income streams in football were season ticket sales and match day ticket sales, but for now and in the foreseeable future, there are significant chances for new products, new services, and product/service extensions, all aimed at enhancing cash flow and profitability:

- Mail order and 'Roverstore' sales for football artefacts, clothing, memorabilia, souvenirs, and so forth.
- Corporate match day hospitality packages.
- Advertising and sponsorship.
- Non-match day conference and banqueting facilities.
- Alliances with compatible product/service suppliers.

Because these initiatives are all fairly new, and because there are doubtless many other ideas yet to be investigated, we must carry out research in order to evaluate (a) customer reactions to our 'traditional' core products and services, since these must not be forgotten in our enthusiasm for innovation, (b) customer satisfaction so far as our non-core activities are concerned, and (c) customer attitudes towards as yet unimplemented possibilities.

Research methods

A combination of techniques will help us secure the information, feedback and guidance we seek in order to reinforce our marketing strategies.

1 *Season tickets.* All season ticket holders are now captured on a computerized central database and their unique 'Patron Code' tells us in what season they purchased their first season ticket and for how many consecutive years after this they have renewed. We can already identify, therefore, the numbers of supporters who renew each season, and the average number of season tickets purchased in a consumer's lifetime. A direct mailing to all individuals on our database – whether they have renewed their season tickets or not – will take the form of an incentivized questionnaire, seeking its completion and return within a specified period of time. The questionnaires will be personally addressed to each potential respondent and will offer entry into an exclusive prize draw if we receive their response, in the pre-paid envelope supplied, by the required date. The results from the survey may be analysed in order to find out what are the major factors which prompt people to purchase season tickets in the first place, the key influences over the decision to re-purchase, and the services which we might offer in order to enhance the value of the season ticket to its owner. We should make a particular effort to contact those season ticket holders who have decided not to renew, or who are dilatory in doing so: on the assumption that it is much more cost-effective to keep our existing customers than to find replacements, we must investigate reasons for non-renewal and/or delay. In my opinion the initial mailing to these people should be supplemented by direct (telephone) contact.

2 *Mail Order and 'Roverstore'.* Again, as a matter of course, all customer details are recorded on the central database, including each individual's full sales history. From this information we can already determine who is buying what products, how frequently, and which products are generating most sales. Equally we can identify the products which yield the greatest profitability: they are not necessarily those with the highest sales. A small incentivized questionnaire card placed in each customer's bag on purchasing, or in the parcel prior to mail-order despatch, should generate worthwhile data about buying behaviour and reactions to our customer service. We should segment the database into regular and 'impulse' purchasers (the latter being those who buy goods from us on no more than one or two occasions each year). Each group can be approached with direct mail literature, asking about purchase patterns, perceptions of our service levels, and possibilities for new products. It is our intention shortly to introduce a loyalty card and affinity Mastercard, offering discounts and 'club' benefits; the resultant extension to our database will help us to design customized products for individual customers.

3   *Corporate hospitality, conference and banqueting.* Progress, sources of customer satisfaction and customer delight can be monitored by follow-up with trained telesales and front-line customer service staff after each event. Set scripts would be used and loyalty discounts offered for repeat bookings. This can then enable us to tailor packages to the individual requirements of each customer, and thus generate sales, bookings and reservations well in advance.

4   *New product/service development.* Within the marketing function we should not rely on customer evaluations as our principal source of ideas for new products, additional services, or product/service extensions and improvements. If we do this, we shall never be higher than Number Two in our competitive market place. It is essential that we use brainstorming and other creativity techniques within the marketing group in order to suggest imaginative possibilities; equally, we must set up a rolling programme of studies into other organizations (not necessarily direct competitors) which have acquired exceptional reputations for service quality. Such 'benchmarking' should enable us to adapt 'best practice' from global sources.

Specimen Answer (B): The Grosvenor Clinical Research Unit

Background

The Grosvenor Clinical Research Unit is a contract research house which conducts clinical trials on new drugs on behalf of the (ethical and over-the-counter) pharmaceutical industry. Grosvenor's 'customers' consist of some major pharmaceutical companies across the world.

Research design

1   *Define the hypothesis to be tested.* In overall terms, we need to assess whether our customers are satisfied with the services we supply, in terms of quality, price, response times, technical excellence, professionalism of face-to-face relationships, and any other relevant or appropriate parameters. Clearly we must also study the impact of some specific features in our service offering, since until now the feedback from customers has been confined to anecdotal evidence, the occasional letter of complaint and (even more occasionally) the decision of a particular customer to go elsewhere in future.

2   *Determine the sample to be investigated.* We have two options, both of which could be pursued simultaneously or in rapid succession. One choice is to take a random sample of our clients and seek to engage their co-operation through completion of a questionnaire; the other is simply to concentrate our attention on the multinational pharmaceutical companies which supply us with 80 per cent of our business (given that our company, like most others, is subject to Pareto's 80:20 rule), and visit them for face-to-face interviews, perhaps as a supplement to a questionnaire.

3   *Set a budget for the research programme.* It is likely that we will use primary research methods as well as some desk studies. The available secondary sources do not supply us with information which is adequately targeted to our requirements, so our preference for primary research is, in a sense, unavoidable. The financial implications are significant, especially if we propose to carry out face-to-face discussions with major customers across the globe.

4   *Develop the questionnaire.* On the whole, despite the problems associated with achieving adequate response rates, a questionnaire-based enquiry is preferable because of the geographically scattered nature of our clientele. In putting together the questionnaire, however, we need to ensure that:

- The wording of each question is grammatically correct.
- No question should be capable of misinterpretation or ambiguity.
- Related questions should be grouped together in sections.
- Simpler, less intrusive questions should be located at the beginning of the questionnaire.
- The majority of the questions should offer predetermined answers, but these should be complemented by a few 'open' questions inviting longer, more considered and reflective comments.

- The rubric accompanying the questionnaire should be clear and concise.
- In order to stimulate response rates, suitable incentives should be supplied.
- Where questions are accompanied by predetermined forced-choice options, these must be comprehensive and must in any event be accompanied by an 'other (please specify)' choice.

5   *Pilot-test the questionnaire.* This will be undertaken initially within the company, and then with a small number of clients (including some from countries where familiarity with English is more uncertain). Pilot-testing is essential in order to iron out problems with ambiguity, question interpretation, duplication/omission of vital topics, and so forth. Once the pilot-testing is complete, the final version can be despatched.

6   *Analysis and presentation of the results.* If necessary, this phase can be preceded by focused efforts to stimulate additional responses in order to bring the overall replies to a level from which useful conclusions can be drawn. Once the returned questionnaires have been analysed, however, the lessons will be communicated to top management with a view to creating an implementation plan.

Potential benefits to Grosvenor

As a result of this research, Grosvenor Clinical Research should be able to identify a number of important factors:

1   Which clients are using our services the most, and the least, and why.
2   Why clients sometimes prefer our competitors, and what we need to do in order to make it more likely that our clients will remain with us.
3   What it is about Grosvenor which enables us to be viewed as 'different' from our competitors.
4   Our principal sources of, and opportunities for, competitive advantage in the future.
5   The parts of our service which should be expanded.
6   The parts of our service which could be reduced, or closed, or outsourced.

Moreover, the research process itself will communicate to our customers the fact that we value their business and want to develop a more mutually supportive relationship with them.

Specimen exam paper 3   December 1997

Certificate in Marketing

Certificate in Sales Management

Understanding Customers   **3 Hours' Duration**

This examination is in two sections.

Part A is compulsory and worth 40 per cent of the total marks.

Part B has six questions, select three. Each answer will be worth 20 per cent of the total marks.

DO NOT repeat the question in your answer but show clearly the number of the question attempted on appropriate pages of the answer book.

Rough workings should be included in the answer book and ruled through after use.

PART A

Chapter One of a recent book (*Inspired Customer Service*, by David Clutterbuck, Graham Clark and Colin Armistead, published by Kogan Page in 1993) lists five fundamental assumptions which, according to the authors, 'cut across conventional wisdom'. Of these five assumptions, four are particularly relevant to the syllabus for *Understanding Customers*, so it is these which are repeated below, plus some explanatory comments adapted from the authors' text.

1 *Customer care usually doesn't work.* Most of the billions invested in customer care training have been wholly or partially wasted.

2 *The effectiveness of service quality approaches depends on where you are in the quality spectrum.* Companies tackling service quality issues tend to fall into one of four categories:

   (i)   *Naturals* – companies which have institutionalized service quality from their earliest days and have so inculcated service values that employees would not consider operating in any other way.

   (ii)   *Aspirants* – companies which have strong ambitions towards achieving an in-built customer orientation and are determined to become service quality leaders within their own market niches.

   (iii) *Followers* – companies which have been forced into service quality largely against their inclination.

   (iv)   *Laggards* – companies which have developed such poor reputations for service quality that they have to work twice as hard as Aspirants.

3 *Total quality management and service quality management only rarely deliver genuine competitive advantage.* The reality is that quality is a survival tool.

4 *There are no such things as customer or suppliers – only business partners* (i.e. long-term customers) and transients (i.e. customers whom the organization does not expect to see more than once).

PART A

Question 1
(a) What do organizations have to do in order to ensure that money spent on customer care training is not wasted? **(10 marks)**

(b) What do the authors mean when they claim that quality is a 'survival tool'? How far do you agree with their judgement that service quality management rarely generates competitive advantage. **(10 marks)**

(c) What advice would you give, about the significance of customer service, for organizations whose customers are principally 'transients'? **(10 marks)**

(d) Write an Action Plan for your Marketing Director, identifying the steps needed to transform the organization from a 'Laggard' or a 'Follower' into an 'Aspirant' so far as customer service quality is concerned. Place your ideas into the context of your own organization or any other organization with which you are sufficiently familiar, and make sure that your answer includes a brief paragraph outlining your chosen organization's activities and current customer profile. **(10 marks)**

Part B – Answer THREE questions only

Question 2
Your Marketing Director has been distressed by recent instances where your colleagues, and even a market research agency acting on behalf of your organization, have misrepresented or misinterpreted statistics relating to current sales, marketing plans, sales forecasts, and

research results. Produce a document to provide guidance for the marketing department and researchers carrying out commissions on behalf of your organization, in an effort to ensure that such mistakes do not occur again. Use the headings below to structure your guidance:

(a) The circumstances in which it may be tempting to manipulate statistics in order to mislead.
(b) The ways in which statistics can be abused (with examples).
(c) The principles which should govern the proper use, presentation and interpretation of statistics. **(20 marks)**

Question 3

What is the business/trade cycle? Why is it critical to some organizations but largely irrelevant for others? If a company sought your views on ways of offsetting or minimizing the impact of business/trade cycle fluctuations, what suggestions would you offer? **(20 marks)**

Question 4

Imagine that you have overheard a colleague talking dismissively and scornfully about what she believes to be the purely 'academic' and 'theoretical' concepts of 'Cognitive Reinforcement' and 'Cognitive Dissonance'. She evidently believes that such notions have no place in the 'real' world of practical marketing. How would you respond in an effort to change her views? **(20 marks)**

Question 5

You work in the marketing department of a USA company which is contemplating expansion overseas. The company is currently in the data collection phase and the Marketing Director has asked you to identify relevant sources of information about some of the markets that your organization may enter. Write a memo in response to your Marketing Director's request, discussing the types of data typically available and their value. **(20 marks)**

Question 6

'Customers are most sincere when spending rather than talking', says Nishikawa. What is the significance of his view for:

(a) The supposed links between attitudes and behaviour; and
(b) The design of research aimed at assessing the potential for new products or services? **(20 marks)**

Question 7

A marketing lecturer has shown you an article she's written, entitled 'The Death of Segmentation'. The central argument in the article is that because customers increasingly expect to be treated as individuals, then grouping them together into 'segments' will be increasingly inappropriate for tomorrow's organizations. Invited to comment on the article, how would you respond. **(20 marks)**

Specimen answers   December 1997

Answer – Question 1

(a)

Organizations view customer care differently and will place varying emphasis on its importance, but whatever their view, if they wish to employ this tactic to gain competitive advantage, it will be costly.

The measure of this cost will often be closely scrutinized by sceptics and this is why money should be accounted for at every step.

Customer care is now another area which companies use to gain competitive advantage in their particular market. Many companies have seen the light and realize that this added feature will further complement their product/service and often distinguish their company as the best provider or supplier in that particular field.

To enable customer care to be carried out effectively, all staff in the company must be aware of the company values, objectives and goals. They must be committed to supporting their firm in achieving these goals and may have personal targets in their roles within the business that reflect this.

But to arrive at the situation where all staff are signed on and truly committed to this aim is quite lengthy. Some of the issues to be tackled in this process would be:

- To train staff to do their jobs quickly and efficiently
- To communicate effectively with each other internally and with customers outside of the organization
- To maintain, at all times, a top-down approach where all senior management and directors remained committed and supportive
- To eliminate, wherever possible, errors in working practice (i.e. on the production line)
- To ensure that any training undertaken by staff is necessary to the role
- To, wherever possible, allow staff to filter training down through the hierarchy (to save costs) but to ensure that the message is consistent and complete
- To have written procedures and processes for tasks.

Though this may seem over thorough, a process such as this will create a sound base for customer care and total quality management.

It is also important to identify exactly who the customer is. There are several levels in the decision making unit (DMU) in both consumer and industrial circumstances.

For example, it is usually older friends or relatives that purchase toys for younger children. If staff are trained specifically to be nice to the children, who can have a very heavy emotional influence on the purchaser, but are impolite to adults, the money spent on customer care has been wasted.

The same can be true in industrial scenarios, e.g. the purchase of photocopiers. Salesmen will usually demonstrate photocopiers to the management that will be responsible for the decision to buy. These salespeople may show great customer care to the managers, e.g. arranging corporate golf days. However, if the photocopier breaks down and the service engineers from the photocopier company are rude to the *users* of the photocopier, then the whole system will break down. Therefore it is vital that customer care training is directed at all aspects of the decision-making unit.

As well as directing care towards these different levels, it is equally important to train people within all levels of the organization. It is a waste of money to spend money training the frontline staff (e.g. receptionists) in customer care, if they have no empowerment. Upset customers will want problems dealt with quickly and effectively. Therefore if problems have to be handled higher up the organization, then *everyone* needs to be professionally competent in customer care.

Therefore it is clear that in order to avoid wasting money on customer care, organizations must understand exactly who the customer is (e.g. industrial v individual consumers) and everyone within the organization must be trained in the philosophy of customer care.

Companies must also not stop customer care at the purchase stage, particularly if they want customers to come back. An example concerns after sales service for a washing machine. It is equally important that the engineer should be educated in the merits of customer care, in order to ensure that any previous training is not wasted.

(b)

When the authors refer to quality as a 'survival tool', they mean that quality is absolutely essential and without it consumers would not buy particular products or services.

I agree with their judgement that service quality management rarely generates competitive advantage in certain circumstances. Total quality management (TQM) and service quality management (SQM), underpin the customer as king. The theory is that the whole organization is orientated towards the need of the customer, both internal and external. Service quality management is taking this theory of TQM and applying it to the service industry.

Services contrast with physical products as they are intangible. This means that they are often more difficult to market than physical products, which is why many organizations seek to use SQM as a source of differential advantage.

The circumstances under which I agree with the authors' judgement are the following:

1   No other organizations are offering a standards of customer care. However, this is an obvious way to be distinguished from the competition.
2   Organizations are competing on price, e.g. if consumers find cheap petrol, they will often be prepared to sacrifice customer care.
3   If an organization has a monopoly. In these circumstances, customer care will not be a distinguisher.
4   If an organization has an exceptional product for which there are no competitors, with a lack of competition, then customer care cannot easily act as a 'competitive advantage'. Thus ferries used to be the only way of transporting cars and passengers across the Channel. However, the Channel Tunnel has now created more diversified competition.

The problem with all these situations is that today we work and live in an extremely competitive market. It is highly unlikely that a service or product will be in a market without competitors for very long. Therefore, there is a need to look for ways to compete.

As mentioned before, services are intangibles. Therefore, one of the best ways to try and distinguish oneselves in this field is by customer care, so there are instances where customer care generates competitive advantage.

(c)

Transients have been described as customers whom the organization does not expect to see more than once. If an organization is taking up TQM then it is essential that all customers are treated in the same way regardless of whether they are considered long-term customers or transients.

The essence of TQM is all about building relationships with suppliers and customers. One of the critical issues here is that transients are customers whom the organization does not *expect* to see more than once. This is a very difficult aspect to predict because it is very hard to say whether custom is on a one-off basis or not. In certain circumstances it is more likely, e.g. the purchase of an engagement ring in Saudi Arabia whilst on holiday. However, it is possible that the consumer might return on another holiday to buy a different item of jewellery. Therefore, customer service is equally as important.

Customers are much more likely to remember bad service than they are good. In a recent survey a person who had a bad experience with British Airways (BA), on average told ten others. These ten went on to tell another seven. Contrastingly, good experiences with BA were only relayed on average to five others.

This is particularly relevant when discussing the significance of customer service for 'transients'. Even if the 'transient' is unlikely to use the product or service again, they are likely to communicate their experiences to people they know. Therefore, I would advise that equal input is given to such 'transients'.

As mentioned already, customer care does not stop at the purchase stage. For example, if a hospital were to purchase an expensive piece of equipment such as an MRI (magnetic resonance imager), staff would need to be trained in usage of the product. If the supplier were to introduce staff training as part of a customer care package, staff would remember this. Expensive pieces of equipment are often one-off purchases. However, staff can move and may recommend the excellent training to their new employers. Therefore 'word of mouth' about customer service is critical.

In some circumstances, it probably does make more economic sense, particularly where resources are limited, to attend to longer-term customers. However, 'transients' should certainly be given the respect they deserve. They may indeed become a customer for another type of the organization's products.

(d)

Plan to transform Campsons Publishing into a leader of Customer Service

To: Marketing Director, Campsons Publishing plc
From: Marketing Officer

Introduction to Campsons Publishing plc

Campsons Publishing is the biggest educational publisher in the UK and has been established for thirty years. Recently it has begun to expand internationally, into the USA, South East Asia and Central and Eastern Europe.

The majority of Campsons revenue is generated by advertising sales of which my specific expertise lies in the UK graduate recruitment market.

Current and potential customers are any recruiters of UK graduates.

Plan of action

1   Currently we have gained a subjective view that we are 'laggards' in the field of customer care. There is no doubt about the quality of our product, we need to find out why we are perceived as poor so far as customer service is concerned.

2   In order to find out why our customer care is poor is seen as inadequate, we need to conduct some marketing research. Although secondary research would be cheaper, we need to discount this as no data of this type exists.

3   We are looking to target the entire UK, so I would suggest that we conduct our research by either telephone, or postal questionnaires. These questionnaires should identify what we are doing wrong currently, and ways that we could improve.

4   We are operating in an extremely competitive market so I suggest we investigate what the competition are up to. This can be done by conducting 'spoof' calls in which we pretend to be interested in their services. Alternatively, we can seek competitor evaluations from our existing customers with whom we have good relationships.

5   It is likely that a key complaint that we have too many contacts at Campsons per client. We can collate our survey results in such a way as to identify key problem areas. These should be addressed immediately.

6   After a suitable time span, e.g. a year, we should do a follow up survey and it will then be clear that we are progressing from 'laggard' to 'follower' to 'aspirant' over time.

(d) – Alternative answer

Introduction

This document outlines an Action Plan for Laggard Ltd to become an Aspirant in customer service quality.

About our business

Laggard Ltd is a family business which was founded in the late nineteenth century. It specializes in the sale of vending machines and currently has three major contracts with organizations which rent these machines on their office premises. Laggard's range of machines is quite varied and there are approximately 50 machines to be serviced and/or renewed at any one time.

What we want from the future

Clearly, industries are becoming more efficient and cost effective as they grow, they expect a certain level of service from their suppliers which Laggard Ltd wishes to provide. In order to do this a tighter rein must be put on costs and simultaneously customer service must be improved.

How are we going to achieve this?

1   Laggard Ltd must define its company aims, objectives and values.

2   These must be communicated to all 15 staff in the firm through Senior Management.

3   All staff must be firmly committed to, and supportive of the firm's goals.

4   Management must ensure that all staff are trained adequately to do their jobs efficiently.

5 All staff should be customer focused and believe that their individual efforts contribute, in their own way, to the company's success.

6 All staff should be justly rewarded for their time, effort and commitment to the success.

7 There must be standards and written procedures to be adhered to.

8 Constant monitoring of output and service must be done.

9 Continuous improvement approach should be adopted and the 'Get it right first time' saying should apply to all.

10 Customers should always be viewed as the core of the business, essential to success and every endeavour should be made to ensure their satisfaction is always foremost.

The next steps

Inform and obtain agreement of all senior staff onto this Action Plan and begin the process by planning and assigning deadlines to each point.

Answer – Question 2

To: The Marketing Department
From: Market Research Executive
Subject: Guidance notes on presenting Market Research Data and Statistics

I   The circumstances in which it may be tempting to manipulate statistics in order to mislead

It is often tempting to manipulate statistics when presenting to potential customers, as well as internal colleagues, to try and achieve a healthier sales picture. However, this action in fact, has a very serious implication and is not acceptable.

Therefore under no circumstances must you manipulate statistics in the following scenarios:

(a)   When presenting sales figures to potential external clients
(b)   When outlining the sales forecast in each region by individual members of the sales team
(c)   When speaking with the media
(d)   When referring to the competition and attempting to gain a more favourable picture.

2   The ways in which statistics can be abused

Statistics can be abused in various ways. The key mechanisms are outlined below:

(a)   Data can be presented in an inappropriate format, e.g. by using a pie chart to depict sales figures
(b)   If sales figures are not compared with previous years and months, they therefore show an incomplete picture.
(c)   If there is no clearly defined objective when carrying out a research exercise, then it is only too easy to produce misleading results. For example: only asking existing customers if the washing powder they are using is cleaning the whites well, and not asking potential customers to try and then ask them the results.
(d)   Miscalculation and incorrect use of data analysis, distorted figures(s) can be achieved adding up the number of respondents incorrectly and/or choosing the incorrect data analysis method, i.e. calculating percentages rather than averages.

3   The principles which should govern the proper use, presentation and interpretation of statistics

(A)   Presentation of statistical information

- When presenting percentages such as market share or customer satisfaction it is advisable to use a pie chart.
- When presenting sales forecasts for the coming year, it is most suitable to depict the figures using a line graph. It is also important to include a comparable sales figure such as the previous year's sales.

- When presenting comparable data such as £s of sales of the various brands of washing up liquid, year on year, a bar chart is the most applicable.
- If presenting raw data, it is useful to put the data into a table or tally chart first.

(B)   When to use the right presentation method
1   If presenting to a large audience, it is advisable to use visual methods. Not only does this make the presentation more interesting, but also more interactive for the receiver.
2   You should reveal your sources – e.g. *Marketing Magazine*, September 1997 issue.
3   Always label your charts etc.
4   If in doubt, check with the marketing team.

I hope these guidelines prove of use. If you have any questions or indeed would like to have your figures checked, please ask – we in the Marketing Team will be more than happy to help.

Answer – Question 3

The business cycle
It is believed, through research and experience, that economies run in cycles. These cycles follow four phases and in general the phases directly impact on business activity. It is commonly believed that businesses follow an 8 to 10 year cycle.
   The four stages are:

1   Boom
The boom phase of the cycle has these characteristics:

- high employment
- high level of investment
- low interest rates and inflation
- high/increasing prices and profits

The economy has met its maximum. All production meets full capacity, the workforce is employed to its maximum and demand is still increasing. Consumer confidence is high, investments are increasing and prices are rising to try and counteract the demand.

2   Recession (downturn)
After a boom period, an overheated economy can enter into a recession, characterized by:

- decreasing investment
- rising unemployment
- rising interest rates and inflation
- decreasing prices and profits

When the economy is entering recession, consumer confidence is low, investments are starting to fall and businesses finding it difficult to remain afloat. Demand is down, due to this, production is decreasing, due to this less people are being employed and, therefore, this leads to even less demand as people find it difficult to afford goods. Prices as a result start to fall.

3   Slump
Recession is followed by a slump, exhibiting these characteristics:

- high unemployment
- high interest rates
- high inflation
- low confidence/'feel bad factor'
- low investment

The economy is in recession, the future looks bleak, there is not a lot of investment business taking place, demand is low, companies that were struggling have failed in their battles and gone out of business. Production is low and employment is also.

4 Recovery (upturn)

As the cycle comes out of the slump, it can be seen that there is:

- rising employment
- rising confidence
- rising investment
- lowering inflation and interest rates

The recovery. The economy starts to pick up, demand starts to rise and production rises to meet this demand. More people are employed to meet the increase in production. Investments start to happen again and consumer confidence is building in strength. Prices start to rise with this movement.

Some businesses find this cycle critical as the products/services they offer rely on consumers having enough discretionary income (the income left after necessities such as mortgage, loans, food, clothes and energy bills have been paid), as well as a feel good factor.

Some examples of organizations that the Trade Cycle is critical to are:

The construction industry – largely a profitable industry in the recovery and boom phases of the trade cycle. Due to the fact that consumer confidence is high, many people are employed and looking to invest in property. Though when the cycle is entering (and in) the recession, the construction industry suffers as a result of individuals pulling on their purse strings and spending less.

The financial industry – quite the opposite to the construction industry. This seems to do well in recession as people tend to put away their money into savings. Statistics in the past have shown that people's savings went from 8% to 11% in one recession period. The one exception to this rule, of course, is the need for mortgages which go hand in hand with the construction industry pattern.

The UK housing market, which was slow to recover after the last economic slump. Although lower inflation and interest rates meant in real terms consumers had more discretionary income, they were wary of investing this money long term. Consumer spending has increased and more 'luxury' goods (holidays/care/jewellery) are being bought in preference to long term investments.

Other businesses – such as debt collectors, administrators and, to a lesser extent, food retailers – are more protected against the business cycle.

In the case of debt collectors, administration and other businesses like undertakers, the recession/slump will not affect business and may even increase.

Food retailers, though affected perhaps in profit margins/turnover to some extent, in fact offer products that people will always need – we cannot live without food, whatever the cost.

Businesses who want to offset the impact of recessions could:

1 look for products/services that are cycle-proof, such as food, petrol, accountancy etc.
2 Be prepared for the cycle. There are many economic indicators that can offer an idea of increasing likelihood of recession. The Government publishes data on Gross Domestic Product, money supply, inflation, interest rates etc., that could offer a guide.

Companies could then ensure that they are reducing their investments, reducing stock holding, looking for short term labour contracts or planning to maximize profits before a recession starts.

Answer – Question 4

Cognitive dissonance and cognitive reinforcement show that the human animal is not always rational. They are academic theories, but they are academic in the pure sense of the word, i.e. learned men or women basing their conclusions on the basis of controlled experiments.

Cognitive dissonance occurs when a consumer's experience forces him/her to re-evaluate a previously held belief. An extreme example is shown by fervent religious revolutionaries. At first they believe killing is wrong, then they kill an unbeliever. They then believe some killing is OK. A customer will constantly question in his mind, especially with larger purchases, over whether the decision was reached.

The process by which a business executive buys a BMW is illustrative. The executive is aware of the glamour and image of the BMW. He/she buys one. After a while, the executive realizes that, after all, it is just another lump of metal in a traffic jam, which also costs a lot of money. BMW, therefore, target some of their advertising to help persuade people that their 7 Series range is worth the extra money. When this succeeds, cognitive reinforcement has been accomplished; when it fails, cognitive dissonance is painfully experienced.

The marketer in the real world must deal with these problems, as the marketer is trying to ensure that the customer's needs are met, and that also the customer will return to buy the product.

For those working in small-scale retail operations, the problem is smaller. Less commitment has been made to the purchase, and the price is less. Therefore, the rebound question – was I right? – will be less.

For those dealing in durables and specialist goods, the dangers, but also the opportunities are much greater. Hand made curtains, for example, may look fine in the brochure, but will the home builder still believe so when they are in the house? If yes, then an enthusiastic customer will result. If no, the customer will blame the firm for selling the wrong product.

The cognitive theories also have practical implications as we market our products. People like everything to be in balance, with their beliefs and attitudes consistent with their actions.

If, for example, people believe David Bellamy to be a leading 'green' spokesman, and later saw him advertising Shell, who have image problems regarding Nigeria and dumping in the North Sea, they would have to revise their views, as both are incompatible. Either Shell's image would improve or David Bellamy's would suffer.

As far as examples of reinforcement go, if a friend recommends a film, it poses a cognitive dilemma. If the film is good, then your friend's opinion and judgement is reinforced and increased. If the reverse is the case, well . . .

Because marketers recognize that people will punish a firm in their mind if they don't like a product, or reward it with extra vigour if they do, we must be careful to ensure that our strategy incorporates this as a real problem.

This problem can be addressed in several ways. Firstly, the customer can be reassured. Secondly, if there is a problem our customer care programme can try to restore the customer's faith in us. Thirdly, we must make sure we're delivering the right product, at the right price, at the right time, and these problems won't arise so much.

Answer – Question 5

MEMORANDUM

To: Marketing Director
From: Marketing Assistant
Subject: Data collection for informing overseas expansion.

Further to our recent meeting, I am writing to outline some relevant sources of information for our possible overseas expansion. As we discussed, this is a very big step for our company and it is therefore important that we research our potential markets carefully. The decision not to expand UK markets should not be taken without full consideration of available data. I therefore outline my recommendations below for research into the UK market for 'Sam's Supermarket'.

I Types of market research

Market Research is the systematic gathering of data, enabling a company to assemble relevant information on potential and existing customers. There are two main types:

(a) *Secondary data* – or desk research, which uses existing data
and
(b) *Primary data* – Market Research undertaken for a specific problem.

I recommend that, in the initial stages of data collection, we concentrate on Secondary Data sources, which I outline below.

2 Sources of secondary data

(a) *Government statistics*

The UK Government holds a variety of information which will enable us to find out more about the UK market.

The Office for National Statistics is a good source of information on demographics, market trends and financial background.

(b) *Demographic data*

Data sources such as the Electoral Register give information on age, housing, occupation.

(c) *Geodemographic data*

Residential Neighbourhood Classification indexes, such as ACORN, will be helpful in deciding where to locate our supermarkets. These reports presume that people who congregate in certain types of neighbourhood have similar lifestyle characteristics according to occupation, income, education and age. As we intend to aim for the middle market, we can locate our supermarkets in the right areas. We can also use this information later when we want to undertake primary research.

(d) *Retail Prices Index*

RPI is a monthly report which looks at trends in retail pricing. This would help us identify whether our approach to retail is appropriate for the UK.

(e) *Market intelligence*

MINTEL (monthly), and Retail Intelligence Reports (quarterly), provide data on current trends in certain areas of manufacture and retail. They include information on customers and companies.

(f) *Third party data*

Many companies in the UK undertake ongoing market research on a variety of subjects. I suggest that we contact the Market Research Society for information on where we can get hold of these sources

(g) *Homescan*

Companies such as Taylor Nelson and Neilson undertake 'Homescan' research which involves consumers using bar code readers to record weekly purchases. This will enable us to find out what people are buying in the UK, when and how often.

(h) *Published sources*

UK newspapers, such as the *Financial Times*, are a good way to find out up to date market information. I also suggest that we look at trade journals, such as *The Grocer*. In order to find out about consumers' attitudes, we could also investigate consumer magazines, such as *Which*, which will give us information on consumer issues.

(i) *On line data*

In particular, we should use the Internet, and CD Rom data to research our potential UK market. The advantage of this is that it is up to date, global and readily available.

(j) *Competitor research*

Where possible we should get hold of sales reports and annual accounts from our potential competitors.

(k) *Casual*

I suggest that you use some of your contacts in the UK to obtain information on the UK market. I recommend a visit to the Retail Intelligence Conference on Supermarkets, in London in January, to make further contacts, get information and exploit your current network.

(l) *Primary research*

Finally, I recommend that if we decide it makes good business sense to enter the UK market, we undertake primary data collection. This should take the form of both quantitative (statistical) and qualitative (motivation and attitudes) investigations, in order to establish more detailed consumer responses to our company and products.

Answer – Question 6

The links between behaviour and attitudes

Marketers are particularly interested in the link between attitudes and behaviour because if positive and measurable links can be established, then behaviour could be predicted. Unfortunately, as Nishikawa observes, peoples' verbal opinions and subsequent actions don't always coincide.

Richard LaPiere proved this in an experiment where he brought a Chinese couple on a journey across America, visiting roughly a hundred accommodation locations on the way. While each proprietor insisted on paper that they would refuse entry/admission to Chinese people (anti Asian sentiment was high), in practice only a minority did.

The marketer has three main interests in attitudes:

1   Finding out what a consumer's attitudes are to the product or service
2   Trying to turn a negative attitude into a positive one
3   Trying to turn a positive attitude into a physical *purchase* of the product.

Research has also indicated that there are certain factors which can encourage an attitude to materialize in behaviour. These include:

1   The *time elapsed* between the attitude intention and the actual behaviour
2   The *strength* of the attitude
3   The *situation* one is in
4   *Unexpected circumstances* – for example you may be pro or anti abortion until you find yourself or your daughter pregnant
5   *The conflict of interest* – again with the above example and in light of the current media attention given to the abortion cases – opinions and behaviour keep changing.

Suppose that a Mr Smith is interviewed about what he would do if he won £10,000. He replies he would buy a new car. His attitude is positive towards buying an Audi due to (a) the cognitive element comprising what he knows about the model and (b) the affective element, i.e. what he feels about the car (i.e. he believes it is good value for money).

However, when he does win £10,000, he does not buy the car. This may be due to insincerity on his part, or due to a number of intervening variables, e.g.:

(a)   Unforeseen events – he may have lost his job and now needs to pay the mortgage.
(b)   Situational variables – Toyota bring out a better, preferable model.
(c)   The dynamic nature of attitudes – Mr Smith's attitude has changed.

What this example illustrates is that whilst attitudes do influence behaviour, intervening factors can manipulate how they relate to one another. With regard to Nishikawa's comment, we may ask an individual about their attitudes (e.g. on their spending preferences), but these attitudes may not manifest themselves in their shopping behaviour.

It is also important to remember that a person only has a finite amount of money. In other words, while a person may have a very positive attitude towards taking a holiday or buying a new car, they may well need the money to pay their mortgage, i.e. the opportunity cost of the mortgage payment is the holiday. As marketers we must remember that disposable income is being competed for by a whole range of products and services, not just our own particular product or that of other competitors in our industry.

Investigating the attitude/behaviour link

Nishikawa has underlined that people don't always do what they say they do or will. In the context of research for new products or services this is particularly important because we need then to uncover peoples' 'actual' attitudes towards our potential product. To some degree this may mean catching them unaware of being observed or trying to elicit information that betrays their 'hidden' feelings.

Appropriate methods of research for this are primary methods, using qualitative techniques.

These include focus groups, in depth discussions and projective techniques. I think the most valid techniques here are projective techniques. They are based on clinical studies and designed to uncover 'hidden' attitudes. The main types are:

- Role playing
- TAT – Thematic Apperception Testing
- Repertory Grids
- 3rd person technique
- Sentence completion
- Word association

The benefit of these techniques is that they draw on a person's gut or innate feelings towards a product without the 'leading question' bias of other techniques.

Another useful type of research is qualitative research which uses observation, experimentation and surveys. Of particular note is observation. This can be either secretive which, although it does have certain ethical implications, can show the consumer acting in a 'natural' way, participating and non-participating.

In light of Nishikawa's comment, I would be more disposed towards using a secretive technique, such as a hidden camera or video tape, because an interviewee or customer often unintentionally will give an interviewer a biased answer.

Nishikawa himself emphasizes the significance of *consumer sampling* as a mechanism for establishing the degree to which attitudes and behaviour coincide. When Japanese electronics companies develop a new product concept, they manufacture a few hundred and display them in Tokyo shops: the ultimate test of their acceptability is whether or not people buy these new products *with their own money*. Similarly, if promoting new products or services ourselves – especially if the products/services are radically different from anything which our customers have previously experienced – our chances of success will be much greater if we can create sampling opportunities through, for example, trial (no charge) periods and interactive product displays in appropriate retail outlets.

Answer – Question 7

To: Lecturer in Marketing
From: Marketing Colleague
Subject: The Death of Segmentation

I would like to thank you for showing me your article on 'The Death of Segmentation'. I found it an impressive read, and admire your point of view on the future of segmentation.

However, I felt it appropriate to respond to your argument, as I do not completely agree. You argued that because customers increasingly expect to be treated as individuals, then grouping them together into 'segments' will be increasingly inappropriate for tomorrow's organizations.

As consumer society evolves, customers do seem to demand more and more from the companies that serve them. Indeed, today's consumerism is driven by consumer societies and watchdog organizations – all acting as a forum for increasing consumer demands.

As we both know, segmentation is a way of grouping customers together into collectivities of buyers who are broadly similar in personality, age, lifestyle and background. The use of segmentation allows companies to be more customer and marketing oriented and respond more closely to customers' needs.

In contradiction to your article, I think that segmentation is a useful marketing tool. Segmentation can be undertaken in a variety of ways, and for it to be effective, it is important that marketers use the right segmentation base.

Segmentation bases include:

1 Geographic – segmentation based on different towns, cities, countries.
2 *Geodemographic segmentation* – Residential neighbourhood classifications.
3 *Demographic* – Age, sex, family life cycle.
4 *Behaviour* – Lifestyle, attitudes and motivational patterns.

Let's use the 'family life cycle' as an example of segmentation to illustrate my argument. The family life cycle assumes that as people move through life, different stages identify different customer roles, needs and behaviours. For example:

Bachelor stage – Young, still living at home, purchases clothes, music, magazines, cars.
Full nest – Married, 1 child under 3, interested in household goods, such as white goods, furniture, childrens goods. (See appendixes for full family life cycle model)

The family life cycle approach, therefore, groups people into manageable sections for the marketer to tailor marketing programmes.

Segmentation is only the first stage in the Target Marketing Process:

1 Segmentation – select bases
              – develop segment profiles
2 Target   – select which segments to enter
              – target produce re segments
3 Positioning – position produce in relation to competitor.

So while segmentation approaches are largely generalized, and make assumptions about customer characteristics, we have to accept these limitations.

Segmentation approaches are better than nothing, and provide general guidelines to consumer behaviour.

As marketers, as long as we are aware of these issues, we can continue to use segmentation effectively.

In terms of the future of marketing, there are other issues which we need to be aware of, but which relate closely to segmentation. Rather than the 'death of segmentation' as suggested in your article, there is room for the modification of the process. It should take in factors such as:

Stereotyping – while many 70 year olds require products relating to a sedentary lifestyle, many others can be found in a sports centre.
Changing demographics – Women's roles are changing as they return to work. The population is also ageing dramatically, and there are fewer young consumers.

In conclusion, I would like to stress the importance of segmentation techniques, especially as there are practical alternatives.

Please get in touch should you require to discuss this further.

Glossary

Ad hoc research Research that has been tailor-made to meet market research needs that cannot be met by standardized surveys.

Adoption The decision an individual takes to become a regular user of a product.

Adoption process The mental process an individual goes through from first hearing about an innovation before deciding to adopt a product.

Advertising Any paid form of non-personal presentation or promotion of ideas, goods or services through the media.

Advertising elasticity The measure of the extent to which changes in advertising spending affect demand. If a small increase in the amount of advertising spent causes a considerable increase in the demand for a product or service, then the product/service would be called advertising elastic.

$$\text{Formula} = \frac{\%\ \text{change in demand}}{\%\ \text{change in advertising spending}}$$

Advertising ethics Ethics covers the moral issues that are raised by the influence advertising has on people's minds.

Advertising objective The specific outcome that the advertising is intended to accomplish with a specific target audience in a defined period of time.

Advertising strategy The plan that is used for meeting the advertising objectives. It will cover the target market, the preferred media and frequency, costs, method of evaluation and the overall style of advertising.

After-sales service The action a firm takes to cover any needs a customer may have once a sale has been made.

Alternative evaluation A stage in the DMP in which the customer will use information to evaluate other brands in the choice set.

Attention, interest, desire, action (AIDA) A method of explaining the stages through which advertising should work.

Attitude The favourable or unfavourable evaluation, feelings or tendencies a person consistently shows towards an object or idea.

Available market A group of customers who have the money, an interest in and access to a particular product or service.

Baby boom Refers to the increase in birth rate following the Second World War and lasting until the 1960s. The 'baby boomers', many of whom are already middle aged, represent a considerable target-market.

Barriers to communication Attitudinal or physical reasons as to why messages fail to be communicated.

Behaviour segmentation The division of the market into groups of people based on their knowledge, attitude, response to, or use of, a product or service.

Belief A thought that a person holds about something.

Bench-marking Standards that are based on the achievements of the most efficient producers within a market place. They are used by companies to set standards by which progress can be measured.

Bias An opinion or influence that favours one line of thought rather than another. For example, the presentation of market research data may be biased to favour a particular viewpoint which is not necessarily borne out by the data.

Blind product test A test in which consumers are asked to evaluate two or more rival products where the brand name is not revealed.

Body language The way in which humans use their bodies either consciously or unconsciously to convey non-verbal messages.

Brainstorming A creative activity in which a group of people are encouraged to express their ideas however bizarre they may appear to be. Once the ideas have all been expressed each idea is considered and evaluated.

Brand A name, sign, symbol, design, colour or combination of these used to identify and differentiate goods and services from their competitors.

Brand image The beliefs that consumers have about particular products or services.

Brand loyalty The consistent loyalty that consumers show in their purchasing habits towards a particular product or service. Brand loyalty can be active in that consumers prefer a particular brand, or passive in that they are used to a pattern of purchasing and cannot be bothered to change.

Brand mapping The selection of key variables that distinguish and differentiate brands within a market and the plotting of the position of each one against the other in order to establish gaps and niches in the market place.

Brand mark The non-verbal elements of a brand name, such as colour, typeface, design, sign or symbol.

Brand name The verbal element of a product or service name.

British Standard 5750 A certification system for ensuring that a firm sets quality targets and then monitors their performance in relation to those targets.

British Standard 7750 A certification system for ensuring acceptable environmental management standards.

Brown goods The term used for goods such as televisions and hi-fis that were traditionally made with wood casings.

Business cycle Periodic fluctuations in economic activity. *See* Unit 9.

Business environment Includes factors outside an individual firm's control such as economic circumstances, changing technology, government legislation and policy, the social environment – commonly referred to as PEST factors.

Business ethics Moral principles that should underpin decision making.

Buyer readiness states Refer to the stages consumers pass through in the decision making process – awareness, knowledge, liking, preference, conviction and purchase.

Buyers Refers to an aspect of the decision making unit (DMU) – the people who make the actual purchase and have formal authority within the DMU to select suppliers, negotiate and contract.

Casual research Research carried out on an informal basis such as might occur from contacting friends, special interest groups, and meeting people at conferences and fairs.

Causal research Marketing research that tests ideas about cause-and-effect relationships.

Cluster samples Respondents taken from a relatively small area and chosen to represent a particular aspect of a product or services target market.

Company culture The shared values and beliefs the people in an organization have about itself and its environment.

Company marketing opportunity The marketing area in which a company would have a competitive advantage.

Competitive market intelligence Data collected about your competitiors.

Concentrated marketing A marketing strategy in which a company goes after one or a few sub-markets.

Concept testing The testing of new ideas for a product or service with target consumers to establish their appeal.

Consumer durables Goods owned by households but not consumed by them, examples would include washing machines, cars etc.

Consumer goods Goods bought by the final consumer for their own personal consumption.

Consumer market Goods and services acquired by individuals and households for personal consumption.

Consumer panel A group of consumers chosen from the target market that are regularly consulted for market research purposes.

Consumer profile A quantified demographic description of an organization's customers.

Consumer resistance A term given to the reasons why potential customers may decide not to purchase a product or service.

Consumerism A movement organized by consumers and government to regulate and improve the relationship and rights between purchasers and sellers.

Content analysis A historical analysis of the contents of one or more sources (usually printed publications) which is used to map changes in culture.

Continuous research Surveys carried out on a regular basis.

Convenience goods Goods bought frequently with the minimum of effort and comparison.

Copy testing The measurement of the effect of a communication before and after it is printed or broadcast.

Corporate identity The company image that is created for an organization by the use for example of a logo, name, stationery, uniform etc.

Corporate image The view held of an organization by its stakeholders.

CSO The Central Statistical Office – now part of the ONS.

Cultural environment Values, preferences, perceptions and behaviours that exist within different societies.

Culture Values, preferences, perceptions and behaviours that exist within different societies and are learned by members of that society from the family and other institutions.

Customer value analysis The analysis an organization carries out to find out the benefits its customers value in relation to offers made by competitors.

Database Collection of data usually available via computer. This might be in the form of supplied computer disks, CD-ROM or via other means such as over the telephone line.

Delphi technique Subjective long-range forecasting using expert panels.

Demand curve A curve indicating the number of units a market will buy at different prices in a given period of time.

Demands Human wants that are backed by buying power.

Deming, W.E. (b. 1900) Worked on product quality at Hawthorne lighting plant and asked by the Japanese to help rebuild their industries after the Second World War. Known for his work on statistical process control and is regarded as a founder of total quality management (TQM).

Demographic segmentation The division of groups of people based on demographic variables such as age, sex, occupation, income, education, religion, race, nationality, family size and family life cycle.

Depth interview An unstructured, lengthy interview aimed at gaining detailed information from the interviewee about a particular product or service.

Descriptive research Marketing research that is carried out in order to find out better ways to describe marketing problems, situations or markets.

Desk research The process of collecting secondary data. Also known as secondary research.

Differentiated marketing A marketing strategy in which an organization decides to target different segments and to use a different marketing mix for each one.

Duopoly A situation where there are only two producers in the market.

Economic environment Factors such as taxes, consumer spending, investment and inflation which influence or reflect the state of the economy.

Economic man The assumption about human behaviour based on the idea that s/he is influenced by rational motives such as the desire for financial gain and the fear of financial pain.

Environmental audit A check carried out by firms on their environmental impact e.g. pollution levels, wastage levels and recycling practices.

Experimental research A scientific method of research designed to determine the specific relationship between, usually two, factors. For example, the relationship between price and packaging design.

Focus group technique   A group of, usually, seven to ten persons brought together to discuss a particular product or service.

Forecasting   The estimation of future demand in the market by anticipating how buyers are likely to behave under given conditions.

Frequency   The number of times an average person in a target market in a given period is likely to be exposed to an advertising message. Also a statistical term that refers to the number of observations made of a particular value.

Gatekeeper   The role a person within the decision making unit plays in controlling the flow of information from the outside environment.

Generation X   The 18- to 29-year-old post-baby boom generation.

Generic brands   Products that are unbranded, for example, aspirin, paracetamol, potatoes, milk.

Geographic segmentation   The division of a market into different geographical units based on nation, state, regions, counties, cities or neighbourhoods.

Group dynamics   The interactions between members of a group such as might occur in a focus or work group.

GSS   The UK Government Statistical Service, replaced in 1996 by the Office for National Statistics (ONS).

Hierarchy of needs   Categorization of human needs into a 'pyramid' with the basic, survival needs at the base. Theory first proposed by Abraham Maslow in 1954.

HMSO   Her Majesty's Stationery Office – publishers of government documents such as those from the ONS.

Human need   The state of a felt deprivation.

Human want   The form a human needs takes when it is shaped by personality and culture.

Hypothesis   A prediction about what a particular piece of research will find.

Idea screening   A process of sifting through a number of new ideas in order to drop bad ideas and take advantage of good new ideas.

Impulse purchase   An unplanned decision to buy a product or service.

Income elasticity   This measures the way in which demand changes when consumers real incomes change.

$$\text{Formula: income elasticity} = \frac{\text{percentage change in demand}}{\text{percentage change in real income}}$$

Index-linked   Linking a value specifically to the changes in the retail price index (RPI), which is used as the standard measure of inflation in the UK.

Industrial goods   Goods bought by businesses for further processing or used in the process of carrying out a business.

Inelastic demand   This is where, for a given percentage change in price, there is a proportionately lower change in demand. For example, if the price of a product rises by 10% and demand only falls by 5%.

Inferior goods   A product for which demand rises when real incomes fall. For example, own-label supermarket goods.

Influencers   The role carried out within the decision making unit by people whose advice carries some weight within the decision making process.

Information search   The stage in the buyer decision process in which the consumer looks for additional information.

Initiator   The role carried out within the decision making unit by people who first suggest buying a particular product or service.

Intangibility   Services cannot be seen, felt, heard or experienced before they are bought.

Just in time (JIT)   The planned flow of resources used in the production process that is designed to minimize the costs of holding stocks of raw materials, components, work-in-progress and finished goods.

Just noticeable difference (JND)   The change to a particular stimulus (picture, sound, texture) which is just detectable by our senses.

Kaizen   A Japanese term meaning continual improvement.

Kanban   The Japanese system of order cards that pull component supplies through a factory.

Learning   The process by which people acquire experience and knowledge.

Lifestyle   The pattern of living expressed by a person's activities, interests and opinions.

Market   The set of actual and potential buyers for a product or service.

Market positioning   Ensuring a product or service occupies a clear place in the minds of the target consumer relative to competitor products.

Market saturation   This occurs when all the people who want a product already have one.

Market segment   A group of consumers who respond in a similar way to a set of marketing stimuli.

Market segmentation   The process of classifying customers into groups with different needs, characteristics, behaviour and responsiveness to the marketing mix or groups of products/ services with like attributes.

Market share   The percentage of all the sales within a market that are held by one brand or company.

Market size   The total sales of all producers within a market measured by value or volume.

Market structure   A description of all the competitive forces within a market.

Market targeting   The evaluation of the attractiveness of each market segment and the selection of one or more segments to target.

Marketing   Marketing is the management process which identifies, anticipates and satisfies customer requirements efficiently and profitably.

Marketing control   The measurement and evaluation of the results of marketing plans in order to ensure that the objectives are being met.

Marketing information system (MIS)   Is a system by which accurate information is gathered, sorted, analysed and distributed on time to people involved in making marketing decisions.

Marketing mix   The main variables through which an organization carries out its marketing strategy, often known as the 4Ps – product, price, place and promotion. Three additional Ps are added to cover the service elements – people, place and process.

Mean   A measure of location calculated by adding together all raw data values and dividing by the number of values collected. More correctly called the arithmetic mean.

$$\text{Formula: mean} = \frac{\text{sum of values}}{\text{number of values}}$$

Measures of dispersion   Statistics which indicate the 'spread' of values in a distribution. The most common measures of dispersion are the range, the interquartile range, the quartile deviation, the mean deviation and the standard deviation.

Measures of location   Statistics which provide an indication of the 'average' response. The most common measures of location are the arithmetic mean, the mode and the median. Sometimes called measures of central tendency.

Median   A measure of location defined as the 'middle' value in an ordered set of observations. When an even number of observations have been collected then the median is calculated by taking the mean of the two 'middle' observations.

Mode   A measure of location defined as the most frequently occurring data value in a frequency table or frequency distribution.

Model   A simplified representation of 'real world' processes.

Monopolistic competition   A market where many buyers and sellers trade using a range of prices rather than one single price.

Moral appeals   An appeal that is used to the sense of what is considered correct.

Motivation   Underlying driving force within a person.

Motivational research   Qualitative research aimed at uncovering a person's motivations.

Non-durable goods   Tangible goods that are usually consumed in one or a few uses.

Observational research   A quantitative research technique where data is collected by observation of buying and/or using behaviour, usually in a natural context.

Oligopolistic competition   A market in which there are a few large sellers who are sensitive to each other's marketing strategies.

ONS   The Office for National Statistics – the main source of government data.

OPCS   The Office of Population Censuses and Surveys, now part of the ONS.

Opinion leader   A person whose opinions are an important influence on others.

Organization image   The way in which people perceive an organization.

Own-label   Products branded with the retailer's own name or a name developed by them.

Penetrated market   Consumers within a market who have already bought the product or service.

Perception   The process by which people create a meaningful picture of the world by selecting, organizing and interpreting information.

Personality   The psychological characteristics that distinguish one person from another and lead to consistent responses to their environment.

Political environment   Government, the law, political parties influence society and create a particular culture that can either encourage or limit the business interests of certain organizations.

Post-purchase behaviour   The stage within the buyer decision process in which the consumer will behave either positively or negatively based on their satisfaction or dissatisfaction with the product or service.

Potential market   The group of consumers who say they have an interest in a particular product or service.

Price elastic   Where the proportionate increase or decrease in price leads to a proportionately greater increase or decrease in the quantity sold.

Price elasticity   A measure of the way the demand for a good responds to a change in its price.

$$\text{formula: } \frac{\text{percentage change in quantity demanded}}{\text{percentage change in price}}$$

Price inelastic   Where the proportionate change in a product's price leads to a proportionately smaller change in the quantity sold. These goods tend to have high product differentiation and consumers perceive them as having no acceptable substitutes.

Primary data   Data collected by means of primary research.

Primary demand   The total demand for all brands of a given product or service.

Primary research   Original research carried out to fulfil specific objectives.

Product concept   The idea for a new idea for a product expressed in terms that the consumer would understand.

Product position   The place in the consumer's mind that the product occupies relative to that of competing products.

Projective techniques   A range of Qualitative research techniques designed to provide an insight into consumer psychology (motivation, perception etc.). Examples include sentence completion, Thematic Apperception Tests, and more exotic techniques such as the Repertory Grid.

Promotion mix   The mix of promotional methods a company uses to achieve its marketing and communication objectives.

Psychographic segmentation   The technique of measuring lifestyle. It is commonly known as AIO analysis – activities, interests and opinions.

Purchase decision   The stage within the buying decision making process where the consumer makes the purchase.

Pure competition   A market in which many buyers and sellers trade in the same commodity so that no one buyer or seller has much effect on the going market price.

Pure monopoly   A market in which there is only one supplier.

Qualified available market   The group of consumers who have money, access, and interest in a product or service.

Qualitative research   Research which produces data which is primarily non-numerical in nature. Usually the spoken or written word. The three main categories of qualitative research are depth interviews, focus groups and projective techniques.

Quality assurance   The attempt to make sure that standards of quality are agreed upon and met within the organization and that customer satisfaction is ensured.

Quality circles   A group of people that meets regularly to identify and discuss quality problems, consider different solutions and make recommendations to management.

Quality control   The process in which work that is either bought in or newly completed is checked.

Quantitative research   Research which produces data which is primarily numerical in nature. Usually the result of answering multiple choice or other coded questions or the classification of behaviours. The three main categories of quantitative research are experimentation, observation and surveys.

Quartile   Dividing an ordered distribution of data into four equal parts creates what are known as quartiles. The lower quartile (Q_1) separates out the lowest 25% of observations, the upper quartile (known as Q_3) separates out the top 25% of the observations. The middle quartile (known as Q_2) is equivalent to the median. Interquartile range and quartile deviation are two measures of dispersion calculated using quartiles.

Random sample   A sampling method where individuals are randomly selected from a sampling frame.

Range   A measure of dispersion defined as the difference between the highest and lowest value observations.

Raw data   Unprocessed data; data which is in the same form as when it was collected.

Reference group   A group which is used as a reference point by a person in the formation of their attitudes, values or behaviours.

Repeat purchase   Occurs when a first-time buyer purchases a product again.

Research   'The collection and analysis of data from a sample of individuals or organizations relating to their characteristics, behaviour, attitudes, opinions or possessions. It includes all forms of marketing and social research such as consumer and industrial surveys, psychological investigations, observational and panel studies' (The Market Research Society).

Response rate   The rate of reply to a survey.

Retail Price Index (RPI)   A single figure economic indicator which measures the change in prices of a 'basket' of products and services over a period of time compared with a 'base' or reference year.

Sample   A group of individuals selected from the target population

Secondary data   Data originally collected for any purpose other than the current research objectives, usually by a third party.

Selective demand   The demand for a specific brand.

Shopping goods   Consumer goods that the consumer will shop around for and compare.

Skewness   A frequency distribtion which is assymetrical is said to be skewed. That is, it has a 'tail' on one side rather than being 'bell-shaped'. If distribution has a longer 'tail' to the right it is said to be positively skewed. A distribution with a longer 'tail' to the left is said to be negatively skewed.

Social grade   The occupational category that shows to which social class each household belongs.

Social marketing   Marketing programmes designed to increase the acceptability of social ideas, causes or practice within target markets.

Speciality goods   Goods which consumers are willing to make a special effort to acquire because of their unique branding or characteristics.

Status   The respect people in society give to a role.

Subculture   Value systems that are shared by a group of people based on their common experiences in life.

Subliminal advertising Advertising below the level of perception.

Survey research A quantitative research method, usually using a questionnaire to collect data.

Target market The segments of the market that the organization decides to concentrate on.

Technological environment Developments in technology that can effect existing products, create new products and market opportunities.

Test marketing The stage in the development of a new product in which the product and marketing mix are tested in realistic market conditions.

Third party data Data collected by an organization other than your own – such as a market research company. Such data may have originated from consumer panels or other regular surveys performed by the organization in question.

Total market demand The total volume of a product or service that would be bought in a specific geographical area, under specific marketing conditions, in a defined time period.

Total quality management (TQM) The establishment of a culture of quality within organizations.

Undifferentiated marketing A marketing strategy in which the organization goes after the whole market with the same marketing mix.

Unique selling point (USP) The product feature that can be concentrated on in order to differentiate it from the competition.

Users The role carried out within the decision making unit by the people who actually use or consume the product.

Index